Rochester
on the Genesee

THE GROWTH OF A CITY

New York Classics
Frank Bergmann, Series Editor

Rochester on the Genesee

THE GROWTH OF A CITY

SECOND EDITION

BLAKE McKELVEY

SYRACUSE UNIVERSITY PRESS

Second Edition 1993
93 94 95 96 97 98 99   6 5 4 3 2 1

This book is published with the assistance of a grant from the John Ben Snow Foundation.

The paper used in this publication meets the minimum requirements of American National Standard for Printed Library Materials, ANSI Z39. 48-1984. ∞™

Library of Congress Cataloging-in-Publication Data

McKelvey, Blake, 1903–
    Rochester on the Genesee : the growth of a city / Blake McKelvey.
    —2nd ed.
        p.   cm.—(New York classics)
    Includes index.
    ISBN 0-8156-2596-0
    1. Rochester (N.Y.)—History.   I. Title.   II. Series.
F129.R757M33   1993   93-12303
974.7'89—dc20

Manufactured in the United States of America

Contents

ILLUSTRATIONS   vii

PREFACE TO THE SECOND EDITION   xiii

ACKNOWLEDGMENTS   xvii

1. Historic Origins   1
   Selecting the Site   1
   Colonel Rochester's Settlement   8
   Incorporation   12

2. The First Boom Town, 1817–1834   19
   Struggle for Autonomy   20
   Boom Town Character   24
   Becoming a City   35

3. The Flour City, 1834–1854   43
   Prosperity and Adversity   43
   Organizing the City   49
   Social and Cultural Expression   56
   The City at Full Tide   62

4. The Flower City, 1855–1875   70
   Flower City Prospects   70
   The Civil War   79
   Flower City Responses   86

5. The Cosmopolitan City, 1876–1890   95
   Economic Diversity   95
   Technical and Specialized Industries   102
   New Civic and Political Functions   110
   A Cosmopolitan Society   116

6. The People's City, 1890–1910   124
   Depression and Recovery   124
   Civic and Political Reforms   130
   Social and Cultural Expression   138
   "Rochester Made Means Quality"   147

7. George Eastman's Town, 1910–1929   155
   Declining Power of the Boss   156
   Interlude of War   162
   Civic and Economic Renewal   168
   New Dimensions of Urban Life   180

8. The Great Depression and
   World War II, 1929–1946   190
   Onset of the Depression   190
   The New Deal   195
   World War II   201
   The Urban Response   204

9. Metropolitan Emergence, 1946–1960   209
   An Interdependent Economy   209
   Civic and Political Responsibilities   215
   Cultural and Institutional Accomplishments   221
   Metropolitan Attainments   231

10. Rochester—A Grass-Roots Metropolis, 1960–1980   240
    A Mobile and Changing Population   240
    A Resurgent Economy   243
    Antecedents of the Riots   247
    Riots and Repercussions   252
    Civic Repercussions   267
    Social and Cultural Responses   274

11. The Sesquicentennial Generation   289
    The Community of Monroe   289
    Rochester at 150   291
    Rejuvenating Downtown   293
    Housing and Educating a Changing Population   296
    A Resilient Economy   300
    Public Health and Welfare   303
    Cosmopolitan Trends   306
    Governmental Responsibilities   307
    The Future   313

INDEX   317

Illustrations

Following page 42

View of the main falls by Jacques G. Milbert, French naturalist and painter, made on a visit to the Genesee in 1818. From an original sepia drawing. Courtesy of the Rochester Historical Society, its present owner.

Map of Rochesterville, 1814, by Edwin Scrantom and Phederus Carter for the catalogue of the Pioneer Gallery, 1854. Courtesy of the Rochester Historical Society, which reproduced it in volume XII.304 06.

Basil Hall's "camera lucida" sketch of Rochester's Court House Square, made in 1827 and reproduced from Hall's *Forty Etchings* (Edinburgh, 1829).

View of the first aqueduct from the northeast, reproduced from Cadwallader D. Colden, *Memoir . . . of the New York Canals* (New York, 1825).

Main falls of the Genesee, reproduced from a woodcut appearing in *Atkinson's Casket* (Philadelphia, 1831). On the island at the right is a representation of the platform from which Sam Patch made his last jump, Friday, November 13, 1829.

View of Athenaeum and Corinthian Hall, erected in 1849, reproduced from an advertisement of it in the *Monroe County Directory* of 1864.

First New York Central station at Rochester, 1853–1883, reproduced from a photograph of 1865. Courtesy of the Rochester Historical Society.

View of the Rochester House, erected at Exchange Street, south of the Erie Canal, in 1827, reproduced from an engraving that appeared in Henry O'Reilly's *Sketches of Rochester* (Rochester, N.Y., 1838).

Map of Rochester, 1859, drawn by Silas Cornell and published by Curtis, Butts & Co., 1859.

Rochester from the west, 1853, reproduced from a lithograph made by D. M. Moody from a drawing by J. W. Hill. Courtesy of the University of Rochester.

Interior view of the Reynolds Arcade, reproduced from "The Agricultural Society Fair," *Illustrated American News, Supplement* (1851). Courtesy of the Rochester Public Library.

Jonathan Child: canal merchant, first mayor of Rochester, Courtesy of the Rochester Historical Society.

Colonel Nathaniel Rochester: founder of the village; portrait at age seventy by Horace Harding, 1822. Courtesy of the Rochester Historical Society.

Daniel W. Powers: banker, owner of Powers block and art gallery.

Hiram Sibley: founder and president of Western Union.

William Pitkin's mansion on East Avenue, built in 1838–1839, reproduced from a painting, ca. 1855, showing young elm trees planted by East Avenue Trade Tree Association in early fifties. Courtesy of Edward T. Dickinson.

Victory Arch at Four Corners, 1865. Courtesy of the Rochester Historical Society.

Banquet scene in Corinthian Hall, reproduced from *Illustrated American News, Supplement* (1851).

Semicentennial parade, 1884. Courtesy of the Rochester Historical Society.

Flight of the *Hyperion*, October 19, 1869, attracted a crowd to see S. A. King take off. Stereogram, courtesy of Dr. G. S. Howe.

Sailboat at Charlotte pier, ca. 1880. Stereogram, courtesy of Dr. G. S. Howe.

Powers block as headquarters for McKinley campaign in 1896. Courtesy of the Rochester Historical Society.

Main Street, view to the west, 1880s.

View of the second aqueduct from the east, late 1880s.

Otis Arch, Main Street and East Avenue, 1900. Courtesy of George Eastman House.

Sibley fire, February 26–27, 1904. Courtesy of George Eastman House.

Following page 94

Rattlesnake Pete's Saloon, Mill Street. Courtesy of the Gannett Press.

Dedication of Civil War Memorial in Washington Square, May 30, 1892. Courtesy of the Rochester Public Library.

Flying Circus at Crittenden Park Field, 1910. Courtesy of the Gannett Press.

Ontario Beach Park, 1890s. Courtesy of the Rochester Public Library.

Solio printing at the Kodak plant, 1905. Courtesy of the Eastman Kodak Company.

Professor Ward in his museum, University of Rochester, 1896. Courtesy of the University of Rochester.

Voting machine demonstration, 1896. Courtesy of the Rochester Museum and Science Center.

Dossenbach's Rochester Orchestra, 1912. Courtesy of Mrs. Paul Smith.

James G. Cutler: architect, industrialist, mayor of Rochester. Courtesy of the Rochester Public Library.

Frederick Douglass: editor, author, statesman. Courtesy of the Rochester Public Library.

Susan B. Anthony: leading advocate of woman's suffrage. Courtesy of the Rochester Public Library.

Bishop Bernard J. McQuaid. Courtesy of the Rochester Catholic Diocese.

George Eastman's mansion on East Avenue, opened in 1905. Courtesy of George Eastman House.

Colonel Henry A. Strong in his Kodak office. Courtesy of the Eastman Kodak Company.

Monroe Community College, 1971. Courtesy of Monroe Community College.

University of Rochester, River Campus, 1945. Courtesy of the University of Rochester.

New Citizens Banquet, 1959. Courtesy of the Chamber of Commerce.

View of old Front Street, 1960s. Courtesy of the Gannett Press.

Aerial view of Downtown Rochester, 1971. Courtesy of the Gannett Press.

Eastman Kodak office building and tower, 1946. Courtesy of the Eastman Kodak Company.

Rochester War Memorial building, dedicated on Memorial Day, 1957. Courtesy of the Gannett Press.

Bragdon's New York Central station, 1914. Courtesy of the Gannett Press.

Aerial view of Rochester's business district, 1940. Courtesy of the Gannett Press.

Dr. Rush Rhees: president of the University of Rochester.

George Eastman: founder of the Eastman Kodak Company.

Joseph C. Wilson: president of the Xerox Company.

Frank E. Gannett: founder and publisher of the Gannett Press.

Rochester Institute of Technology, new campus, 1971. Courtesy of John Massey, photographer.

Aerial view of Rochester and Monroe County Civic Center Plaza, 1972. Courtesy of the Rochester city photographer.

Midtown Tower, 1962. Courtesy of Midtown Holdings Corporation.

Midtown Plaza, 1962. Courtesy of Midtown Holdings Corporation.

Following page 208

Minister Franklin D. R. Florence, left, and Deleon McEwen, first and second presidents of FIGHT. Courtesy of the Gannett Press.

Mrs. Harper Sibley and Professor Dexter Perkins, cofounders of RAUN, commemorating its 25th anniversary, July 1969. Courtesy of the Rochester Public Library.

Dedication of the Rochester Sister-City Bridge. Photo by Richard Goldstein. Courtesy of the City of Rochester.

Mayor Thomas P. Ryan, Jr., and County Executive Lucien Morin leading the march into the Masonic Temple Auditorium for the Sesqui Gala Ball, April 28, 1984. Photo by Ira Srole. Courtesy of the City of Rochester.

Town of Wheatland float in the Sesquicentennial Parade, June 9, 1984. The float symbolized the mill Ebenezer Allan, Wheatland pioneer, erected at the upper falls of the Genesee in 1789. Photo by Ira Srole. Courtesy of the City of Rochester.

Official inauguration of the Sesquicentennial Year in the atrium of the new City Hall, January 1, 1984. Photo by Richard Goldstein. Courtesy of the City of Rochester.

Rochester's Sesquicentennial Finale, Main Street Bridge, packed with citizens awaiting the spectacular fireworks display that ended the Sesquicentennial Year, December 31, 1984. Courtesy of the Gannett Press.

Ice storm, March 4, 1991. View on South Goodman Street and typical of other residential streets. Photo by Dennis Floss. Courtesy of the Gannett Press.

New entrance wing of the Rochester Museum and Science Center. Courtesy of the architects, Frank Grosso & Associates.

Interior sculpture garden of the Memorial Art Gallery. Courtesy of the architects, Frank Grosso & Associates.

BLAKE MCKELVEY, for many years City Historian of Rochester and now retired, is a pioneer in the field of urban history. He is the author of the widely known and distinguished four-volume history of Rochester and of many articles and reviews. In 1938 he launched the quarterly *Rochester History*. Two of his twelve books are *The Urbanization of America: 1860–1915* (1963) and *The Emergence of Metropolitan America 1915–1966* (1968). Dr. McKelvey received his A.B. from Syracuse University and Ph.D. from Harvard University.

Preface to the Second Edition

"ROCHESTER is the best place we have yet seen for giving strangers an idea of the newness of this country," wrote Mrs. Basil Hall to her sister Jane in England on visiting the Genesee mill town in 1827. While her husband was making his oft-reproduced "camera lucida" sketch of the Court House Square, she "visited the lions" and marveled at the number of "small houses and large handsome ones standing in the mist of stumps" of forest trees, one of which she saw two axmen fell, despite its four-foot girth, "in three minutes all but ten seconds."

Most visitors in the mid-years, too, were enthusiastic. In 1860 a Presbyterian clergyman, after viewing the town from the court house cupola, driving to the falls, visiting Mount Hope nurseries, and enjoying a hospitable reception at Freeman Clarke's Alexander Street mansion, wrote to assure his friends in Philadelphia that "Rochester is a *city*. A beautiful city. Beautiful in its situation; beautiful in its plan; beautiful in its improvements, . . . and the people seem as pleasant as the place."

Thirty-five years later, Samuel R. Hole, Dean of the cathedral in Rochester, England, was similarly impressed. "Arriving at Rochester in America . . . I received the heartiest and happiest of many welcomes which it was my privilege to enjoy in the States," he reported. "Rochester is known as the 'City of Flowers,' " he added, "chiefly because the most famous nurseries of America are in its suburbs . . . Rochester has another pleasant title, 'The City of Homes,' and it is so called because it is said to have more houses occupied by those who own them than any other city in the States."

"Rochester is America, proof of its basic character," declared Garson Kanin when recalling its ready acceptance of his immigrant

mother in the early 1900s. A beautiful young Russian Jew, she had
found a job making buttonholes to support herself, but she had joined
a dramatic society to express herself. There she had played the hero-
ine's part in a Yiddish play written by an immigrant carpenter, who
soon won her hand, and together they gave birth to Rochester's 1972
Literacy Award winner.

"Rochester is one of the brightest, busiest and most attractive
cities in this country," wrote Ray Stannard Baker in an *American
Magazine* article in September 1910. But what interested him most
was its spirit of self-criticism. "If Rochester to-day possesses any preeminence over other cities of its class, it is due not to any material
prosperity, but rather to the extent and earnestness with which this
spiritual dissatisfaction has been expressed." Baker, a perceptive
critic of America's urban development, correctly identified one of
Rochester's persistent characteristics. While most of its articulate visitors were agreeably surprised by its laudable features, many residents
in successive generations have been outspoken critics, sometimes
with historical relevance. Thus a disgruntled miller, who in 1855
bemoaned his failure to move west when still young, was unwittingly
marking the town's transition from Flour City to Flower city specialization. Similarly, Walter Rauschenbusch's critical appraisal of the
city's neglect of its swelling immigrant population in 1904 awakened
the community for a surge of new efforts in assimilation. And, more
recently, the clarion protests of the leaders of FIGHT have alerted
Rochester to the need for renewed efforts to develop the full potential
of its increasingly numerous black inhabitants.

Rochester, characterized from the start as an open city, has derived
a major portion of its growth from the influx of newcomers. The successive and variegated waves of immigrants, mingling with an increasing body of older residents, produced a sequence of at least
eleven fairly distinct generations of Rochesterians. Some members of
each generation have overstepped its borders but seldom without
experiencing a change in character, as George Eastman vividly demonstrated. Rochester, an integral part of New York State and of the
larger federal union, has shared in their remarkable development, but
the city's relationship with these larger entities has not been constant.
Each generation has had its distinctive historic experience on these
broader horizons, influencing developments on the local level and
tying Rochester's history with that of the nation at large.

Thus it is interesting to see how the pioneers finally settled on the Genesee falls as the proper site for a mill town; how the villagers there readjusted to the fact that it was becoming a city; how the Flour City gave way to the Flower City, and that, in turn, to a cosmopolitan city; how the emphasis on good government evolved; how George Eastman's interests and leadership developed; how Rochesterians responded to two world wars and the Great Depression, as well as to new metropolitan problems; and, finally, how the present generation is handling its new diversity and its expanding regional and international horizons.

Of course, Rochester's history reflects the presence of more variables than this emphasis on generations suggests. The successive waves of ethnic newcomers, of varied origin, density and duration, constituted a challenging diversity to the generation of their arrival and contributed more significantly as they found an acceptable and accepted place in succeeding generations. The strategy of their adjustments and the nature of their contributions differed, but both benefited from the restless mobility that characterized Rochester's inhabitants both native and foreign-born as they moved in and out in search of fresh opportunities. The city's economic and technological shifts contributed to this mobility and fostered appropriate social and cultural institutions. The city's consciousness of itself as a community, developing as a continuum over the decades, experienced changes at a slower pace and with more gradual transitions. Yet if Rochester's character as a city had a protean quality, its history as a societal unit and identity commands our attention.

November 1992   BLAKE MCKELVEY

Acknowledgments

ACKNOWLEDGMENTS for this book's first edition, an abridgment of my four-volume *History of Rochester,* were inadvertently omitted before publication. They had been excerpted from the *History* and are now included for the first time. My indebtedness was noted to the following people: Miss Emma Swift, for many years the able librarian in charge of the local history division in the Public Library, and to her associates and successors for assistance in my efforts to probe the rich documentary resources of that repository; the librarians in charge of the local history collections at the University of Rochester; the editors and journalists of the weeklies and dailies, those community diaries, I had followed day by day throughout the 140 years of Rochester's growth. Also noted was the assistance I had received from the incomparable newspaper index compiled by the National Youth Administration during the depression. I also attempted to justify the absence of footnotes and other documentation by referring interested scholars to the profuse notes in the first two printed volumes of my four-volume set and to the similar documentation provided in typed copies of the third and fourth volumes on file in the local history division.

In this updated edition I have relied heavily on the profuse collection of newspaper clippings and related documents from the local history division, and on the numerous reports of the varied institutions involved in Rochester's current developments. I owe a special note of thanks to City Historian Ruth Rosenberg-Naparsteck for her aid in the selection of appropriate illustrations for this edition.

Rochester
on the Genesee

THE GROWTH OF A CITY

1

Historic Origins

A PRODUCT of the westward movement in the early years of the Republic, Rochester began under circumstances that differed strikingly from those of several other regional cities of the period. Although its site had many geographic advantages, these did not hold the attention of the first promoters of the Genesee country as did the forks of the Ohio River at Pittsburgh, its bluffs at Cincinnati, and its falls at Louisville, each of which initially attracted the land promoters of the Ohio Valley. The proprietors and settlers of Rochester had an uphill struggle to attain a position of leadership in the Genesee country, but their rivalry with older pioneer settlements in western New York, together with the geographic circumstances and historical developments that influenced the outcome, helped to determine the character of the city that ultimately arose at the falls of the Genesee River and linked it firmly to the history of the nation.

SELECTING THE SITE

The forces of nature, operating slowly during the last million years of the Cenozoic, or fifth, era of geologic time, not only created a fertile valley but also carved out an ideal urban site near the Genesee's northern outlet. After the melting of the vast glacier, which had brought a rich accumulation of sediment from the north for distribution over the Genesee country, the north-flowing river that reappeared, on finding its old route through the Irondequoit Bay area clogged by deep deposits in the vicinity of the Mendon ponds, cut a new course farther west to form the lower Genesee gorge.

Named by the Indians for the pleasant loveliness of its broad val-

1

ley, the Genesee had a modest volume compared with that of the Niagara to the west, which also cut a gorge in its drop from Lake Erie to Lake Ontario. The mighty Niagara, after breaking through the thick layer of limestone known as the Lockport dolomite outcrop, had crashed through several less resistant strata to reach the Ontario level. In contrast, the Genesee, after gradually (in the course of a half-mile or more) breaking through the same layer of dolomite, paused on reaching another limestone stratum some ninety feet below; it broke through that and a third resistant stratum, but only after another two miles and an additional half-mile of rapids. Thus, the Genesee carved a gorge with three major cataracts, the top one conveniently divided into a small upper falls and a spectacular main falls, which together provided an ideal site for a mill town (as several early visitors declared). But the falls had to await the arrival of men equipped and impelled to use them.

The Indians, whose chief villages were located in the hilly lands some twenty miles to the southeast, paddled birch-bark canoes along the numerous waterways of western New York but found the Genesee falls an effective barrier and portaged from the upper river into the Irondequoit Bay when they sought access to Lake Ontario. The French and the British explorers and fur traders, who for a century contended for dominance over the Ontario basin, established their principal posts at Oswego and Niagara. Other points along the southern shore of the lake, including Irondequoit Bay, attracted their attention briefly, but only a few ventured to take a curious glance at the Genesee falls. One such visitor, Captain Thomas Davies of the English Royal Regiment of Artillery, made the earliest known sketches of the Genesee falls during a journey along the lake sometime between the years 1755 and 1763. The situation would have changed in another century if either France or Britain had acquired full sway over the development of the Ontario basin, but their focus on the lake trade would probably have given Oswego or Sodus the advantage over any port at Irondequoit or the Genesee. Rochester's primacy depended on the establishment of an independent nation south of the lake.

The potential of the falls as a source of power first won practical recognition from Oliver Phelps during his negotiations with the Indians at Buffalo Creek in July 1788. He was endeavoring to purchase most of the Seneca lands in western New York, and the reluctance of the

Indians to part with any territory west of the Genesee River prompted Phelps to offer to construct mills for their use at the small upper falls in return for the grant of a mill lot west of the river at that location. The proposal was scarcely ingenuous for the tract they were persuaded to cede comprised the western half of present Monroe County and excluded the Indians from any effective use of the mills at the same time that it supplied an inducement to white settlement. Ebenezer Allan, who served as interpreter at the Buffalo Creek council fire and who already had a sizeable squatter's clearing at Scottsville, up the river, may have proposed the stratagem; in any event, he agreed to build and operate the mills, a job for which he received a more modest allotment of one hundred acres.

While Allan was building his crude mills at the falls of the Genesee in 1789, Phelps was busy promoting the settlement of Canandaigua and other sites that he considered more important. A New Englander, his approach to the Genesee country was from the east, along the old Indian trails heading west from the Mohawk Valley, and he and his associates chose townships easily reached by that route. When, because of the competition of other frontiers, land sales in western New York were slow, Phelps and Gorham sold the unassigned portions of their vast estate to Robert Morris. But Morris, more interested in land schemes farther west, sold it again quickly to a group of Scottish investors headed by Sir William Pulteney, who designated Charles Williamson, another Scotchman, as agent in charge of its development. Williamson established his headquarters in populous Philadelphia and, making his approach to the Genesee country by way of the Susquehanna Valley from the south, gave his chief attention to the promotion of the lands that drained southward. A correction in the original survey gave Williamson the site of Geneva, which he promoted as a rival to Canandaigua; he also established settlements at Sodus on the lake, and at Williamsburg above Geneseo on the river, but he gave scant heed to the potential of the lower Genesee.

Allan, more of an adventurer than a promoter, had the qualities essential to the pioneer, but lacked the endurance required for permanent settlement. To raise the heavy frame for his gristmill, he assembled thirteen white men from up the valley and from a lake schooner that made a timely stop at the mouth of the Genesee. The raising, which required two days, was properly celebrated with the aid of a keg of rum brought from the schooner. The excitement soon abated as the men departed, and Allan, who that summer had cleared half an acre on the west bank, overlooking the small upper falls, returned to his farm at Scottsville for the winter. Allan completed his sawmill and enclosed his gristmill before moving his family to the falls the next spring. But trade was slack, for his nearest neighbors, other than the Shaeffers who had bought his improvements at Scottsville, were the first settlers at the site of Pittsford and the Irondequoit landing, both several miles through the forest to the east. After spending two fruitless years at the falls, the restless Allan delegated the care of the mills to Christopher Dugan, his brother-in-law, and turned again to trading expeditions up the Genesee and down the Susquehanna, where he soon found a purchaser for the mill lot.

Dugan, an Irishman who had met and married Allan's sister in New Jersey before the Revolution, had joined Allan's venture at the falls in 1790. He expanded the clearing and erected a log shed to house the cook stove and to provide extra bunks when the mills were in operation. Although such occasions were rare, Dugan and his wife remained in charge at the mills until early in 1796, when they joined the pioneer settlers in Wheatland, where Mrs. Dugan taught school for a season. While at the mills, the Dugans entertained occasional visitors, including Thomas Cooper, who on this his first visit found the Genesee, because of its greater distance from available markets, less inviting for settlers than the Susquehanna, where he soon located. Dugan continued to operate the mills under two successive owners, but he abandoned them when Charles Williamson, the third speculative purchaser, failed to respond to his request for some recompense for their operation.

After a brief lapse, during which settlers who brought grain to the mill sometimes did their own grinding, Williamson, late in 1796, placed Josiah Fish, a recent arrival from Vermont, in charge at the falls. A new era was dawning in western New York state, for the British, who had held onto their posts at Oswego and Niagara after the Revolution, finally relinquished them in August that year and abandoned their efforts to exclude American boats from trading on the lake. Among the new settlers who now hastened to acquire tracts along the lower Genesee were the Kings and the Grangers from Connecticut who established a settlement on the high banks on the west side below the lower falls. On their arrival in the spring of 1797 they found Fish and his family already established in the mills at the upper falls. While the Kings and the Grangers built their log houses at Fall Town and constructed a landing and a schooner in the river below, Fish tended the mill and opened a road to the landing. Together they assembled one hundred men and boys from neighboring settlements to build a bridge over the Deep Hollow gully in order to complete that road in 1798. However, Mrs. Fish and several of the Kings died of the Genesee fever; when John Maude, a British traveler, visited the Genesee in 1800, he found both settlements practically deserted. "The Grist Mill," he noted in his journal, "is not at present able to grind more than ten bushels a day; were it in good order, it would grind sixty." Finding no accommodations there, "not even a stable" for his horse, he pushed on to the landing three miles beyond. There he had "a good breakfast on wild pidgeons," but found the docks in poor repair for want of boards.

Several other western New York settlements likewise stagnated, especially Williamsburg, up the river; Canandaigua and Geneva, to the east, and Bath, to the south, prospered. As the seat of Ontario County, organized in 1789 with jurisdiction over all settlements west of Seneca Lake, Canandaigua was also the principal land office until 1796, when it was forced to share both functions with Bath, the seat of newly created Steuben County and Williamson's frontier headquarters. The Baron of the Backwoods, as Williamson was sometimes characterized because of his imaginative and flamboyant promotions (notably, the Williamsburg Fair of 1793), was even more successful in the development of Geneva, where he located his northern land office. Williamson established the first weekly newspaper at Bath in October 1796 and the second at Geneva a month later, seven years before the *Western Repository* made a more permanent appearance at Canandaigua.

Both Phelps and Williamson recognized the primary importance of improving the interior trade arteries. The Phelps and Gorham associates had promoted the opening and improvement of the Genesee road west from Utica through Geneva and Canandaigua to Avon on the Genesee and beyond, and they backed the efforts of the Western Inland Lock Navigation Company to open channels around the rapids and other obstructions to boating on the Mohawk and its western tributaries. Williamson's first great project was to open a road north from Williamsport, on the Susquehanna, through the Tioga Valley to Painted Post and Bath. He also supported improvements in the river trade to the south as well as that east of Geneva. Both groups supported the efforts of the Cayuga Bridge Company, incorporated in 1797 to construct a bridge or causeway across the Cayuga marshes, and both supported the move by the legislature to establish turnpike companies, such as the Seneca Road Company, chartered in 1801 to build an improved road into the western part of the state. Progress on these trade arteries enabled the settlers to ship out their excess produce in order to meet the installments due on their lands, and this trade greatly stimulated the rival land offices.

All three settlements were thriving villages by 1800, with bustling inns and provisioning shops, ready to accommodate migrating settlers and speculators while they negotiated for suitable plots. It was to these towns that Rochester, Fitzhugh, and Carroll, three gentlemen from Maryland, resorted in 1800 and again in 1803, when they journeyed north to seek promising investments. Like many others, they were on prospecting visits, and each made deposits on sizeable tracts up the valley, but before their return to Maryland from their second journey, a Williamson agent in Geneva persuaded them to examine the mill site at the upper falls of the Genesee. After riding horseback through the forest, they forded the river below the small falls and found the gristmill idle and the sawmill in ruins. Nevertheless, the situation appeared ideal for a mill town, and they agreed to purchase the 100-acre tract at $17.50 an acre.

Unfortunately, however, 1803 was not the year for a mill town on the lower Genesee, as Fish could have told them had he not been off somewhere, probably fishing below the lower falls where the catch was often rewarding. The Marylanders, prepared to wait until the prospects brightened, returned to their homes, while other and less affluent settlers moved in to open clearings on every side. Silt at the mouth of Irondequoit Bay was hampering the development of Tryon Town on the old Indian landing site, but when Samuel Latta joined William Hincher and a few others at the mouth of the Genesee in 1805, its promoter, Robert Troup, successor to Williamson as the agent of the Pultney estate, laid out fifty town lots priced at ten dollars each and named the prospective village Charlotte in honor of the new proprietor's wife. Several schooners visited Latta's dock shortly after its construction a year later, and the shipments mounted in each succeeding year.

The Genesee port received an added incentive as a result of the advance of settlement west of the river. Not only were pioneers taking up lands in Riga, Parma, and Ogden within the bounds of the mill plot ceded in 1788, but new negotiations with the Indians had opened the way for settlements in the Morris tract to the south and in the vaster regions acquired by the Holland Land Company to the west. Batavia, located on an extension of the turnpike west of Avon, was the land-office headquarters for that region and became in 1805 the seat of newly formed Genesee County, which encompassed all towns west of the river. Many of the supplies required for these settlements were brought by schooner to Charlotte for transhipment up the river and its tributaries, and over new roads to the interior.

This renewed activity was evident at several other points on the lower river. Fall Town, long blighted by the Genesee fever, experienced a rebirth with the arrival of seven Hanford brothers from Rome. Frederick, the oldest, soon advertised a "well chosen assortment of Dry Goods, Groceries, Hardware and Crockery" as available at his store, as well as "ash kettles, window glass, sole leather, shoes, etc." Another brother opened a tavern, and the others repaired the road to the landing and the dock, which thus made the site a serious rival to Charlotte. In *A Guide to the Wilderness*, published in 1810 by Judge William Cooper of Cooperstown, Fall Town and the harbor below were described as "one of the most favorable town sites left undeveloped in the State." Three miles up the river, Charles Harford, an Englishman of considerable means, had cleared a plot near the main falls in 1807 and built a mill that supplied the needs of local residents. He filled the role formerly performed by Allan's mills, which were now in ruins, but the half-mile portage from the landing place at the small upper falls inhibited commercial operations and proved so discouraging to Harford that he sold his mill and 200-acre site two years later to Matthew and Francis Brown from Rome. It was significant that both the Hanfords and the Browns, in contrast with most of their predecessors, had had previous experience in a growing town, for the pioneer makeshifts familiar to Allan, Dugan, and Fish no longer sufficed.

Distant events were exerting an unexpected impact on the lower Genesee in these years. The old rivalries between England and France had brought new hostilities on the high seas, and President Jefferson, in an effort to prevent American entanglement in that struggle, had declared an embargo against trade with either party. The embargo and the Non-Intercourse Acts that followed checked the export trade and so glutted the Atlantic ports that the flow of produce from the interior was halted. Settlers, pressed for payments on their lands, had to find other outlets, and because the embargo was not rigidly enforced against trade with Canada, shipments down the Genesee replaced those previously carried down the Susquehanna or the Mohawk. New facilities were required to accommodate this trade, especially at the small upper falls where the rafts were unloaded for the difficult portage around the falls or to Tryon Town on the bay.

COLONEL ROCHESTER'S SETTLEMENT

It was at this point that Colonel Nathaniel Rochester determined to move his large family to the Genesee country. Possibly the dull times in Hagerstown, Maryland, blighted by the embargo, spurred his migration in 1810, but most of his eleven sons and daughters were now grown and ready to strike out on their own, and the aged colonel, already in his fifty-ninth year, determined to move to a new country where opportunities for all abounded. Because his family was accustomed to urban ways, Rochester chose to locate in the thriving hamlet of Dansville, up the valley, rather than in the backwoods at the falls. With two of his sons he soon became so absorbed in the village life that he considered withdrawing from the venture at the falls, but the interests of his partners, still resident in Maryland, and the increased flow of produce down the Genesee prompted him to ride down in 1811 to survey the one hundred acres into town lots. A move for the opening of a road from Pittsford to the falls had already commenced, and Rochester helped fix the location of the bridge to carry it across the river at the midpoint in his tract.

Because of his familiarity with Philadelphia and Baltimore, Rochester gave his town a southern rather than a New England design. He made a generous provision for streets on a gridiron pattern, with one broad highway, named Buffalo Street, leading west from the bridge. A second highway crossed it at right angles a block from the bridge and connected the mill lots to the south with the road to the north, past the main falls to the docks at Fall Town. Quarter-acre lots on these two business streets were offered at $50 each, except for the choice northwest lot at the Four Corners, which was priced at $200. Lots on the adjoining streets were $30, and prospective buyers were asked to make $5 down payments and were required to erect a house or shop twenty-by-sixteen feet in size within a year to secure each claim. He reserved a large lot on the south side of Buffalo Street for public buildings but made no provision for a village common such as that provided at the center of Francis Brown's town plot, which was laid out a few months later on the adjoining 200-acre tract at the main falls. Before returning to Dansville for the winter, Rochester engaged Enos Stone, a settler who had already built a modest frame house east of the river, as his local agent in charge of sales.

Rochester and his partners were boldly promoting a mill town, not a regional market center. Their success depended on the development of a thriving village, not on the sale and improvement of adjoining farmlands. For outward shipments they had to rely on the harbor facilities at Fall Town or Charlotte, but they were conveniently situated to receive the discharge of rafts and barges from the upper river, and they had a dozen lots for mills to process their products. Unfortunately, the outbreak of the War of 1812 checked urban developments at the falls for a time by halting shipments to Canada. However, Rochester's confidence was unshaken, and he therefore placed an advertisement in the *Ontario Messenger* offering his mill, two shops, and two houses at Dansville for sale and declaring his desire "to remove to the Village of Rochester at the Falls of the Genesee River."

The upper falls offered a safer location than many others on the New York frontier in these troubled times. Numerous settlers were moving in to build homes and shops on modestly priced town lots. The Scrantom family was the first to arrive on May 1, 1812, and found shelter with Enos Stone on the east bank until their cabin at the Four Corners was ready in July. Hamlet Scrantom soon secured the job of miller for Francis Brown, who had taken over the Harford mill at the main falls. First, however, he helped Stone finish a sawmill on the east bank to cut planks for the bridge and to supply boards for the frame structures that other settlers were erecting. Abelard Reynolds arrived from Pittsfield, Massachusetts, and established a pioneer saddlery and the village post office on the site later occupied by the Reynolds Arcade. Silas O. Smith, who had opened a store at Fall Town the year before, now moved it to the village at the upper falls, where he acquired the southwest property at the Four Corners. Elisha and Hervey Ely and Josiah Bissel, Jr., newly arrived from Massachusetts, not only built a second store but also secured permission from Fitzhugh and Carroll (on their long-deferred second visit to the falls) to make temporary improvements in the raceway and to erect a gristmill there. Rochester reluctantly confirmed the lease and deferred his own plans to build a mill; instead, after negotiating the sale of his Dansville properties, he acquired a farm on the turnpike through Bloomfield, some twenty miles south of the falls, from which vantage point he could more easily supervise the town's development.

Despite the interruption in its growth occasioned by the hostilities on the lake, the Rochester settlement received several decided benefits from the War of 1812. Because the British fleet frequently threatened Charlotte and other points along the shore, most shore settlers fled inland, some to the upper falls. Furthermore, although the Canadian market was shut to the Rochester settlement, the task of supplying the troops stationed along the Niagara frontier kept its mills, saddlery, and other shops fully occupied. The mill erected by the Elys' on the old Allan race and painted red was equipped with four run of stones, two more than the Harford-Brown mill at the main falls. Neither operated at capacity, however, because of the limited supply of grain. Too many settlers up the valley were diverted from farming to military activities. Indeed, most of the men in the village were enrolled in one or another of the militia units that rallied to the defense of Charlotte when a British fleet approached the mouth of the river in May 1814. The settlers, who acquired a new sense of community in the process, joined in a boisterous celebration when news of peace arrived in February 1815.

The chief benefit to Rochester from the war came after its conclusion, when the state resumed its efforts to open a new commercial artery into the west. Despite the service rendered by the Western Inland Lock Navigation Company, after the completion of improvements in 1803, its inability to maintain repairs combined with other drawbacks to exert pressure on the legislature to build a canal across the state. The first plan to link Lake Ontario at Oswego with the Hudson at Albany seemed the most feasible, but many western settlements urged instead a route tapping the Finger Lakes and reaching west to Lake Erie. The legislature, although it authorized surveys of both routes in 1808, clearly preferred the shorter and less costly one. The outbreak of the war, however, not only deferred action but also demonstrated the futility of basing the western end of the canal on Lake Ontario, which the British could control. Perry's early victory on Lake Erie had established the lake as American, and all agreed that it should be the western terminal for the canal. Rochester and most of the Genesee country would surely benefit from such a canal.

The extent of Rochester's benefits were scarcely dreamed of. Few, if any, of the early settlers at Rochester were aware of the fact that the surveyor, in his search late in 1808 for a possible western route, had tentatively chosen the river crossing between the main and the small upper falls as the most feasible, for the report, when published in 1811, still stressed the Oswego route. When the discussion revived in 1816 and the preferred course of the western end of the canal became known, numerous communities along the turnpike through Geneva, Canandaigua, Avon, and Batavia, petitioned for a new survey to determine the feasibility of building the canal through these established communities. Colonel Rochester, now resident in Bloomfield, served as secretary of a convention that gathered at Canandaigua to endorse such action. A second survey, however, confirmed the impossibility of carrying the canal over the rolling hills (surmounted today by Route 20) and, instead, fixed the river crossing at the old fording place, just below the small upper falls. When the Canal Act was passed on April 15, 1817, the economic future of the Rochester settlement was assured.

The year 1817 was a crucial one for Rochester in several respects. It saw the construction of the Mansion House, Rochester's first tavern of any size, on the east side of Carroll (State) Street, a few doors from the Four Corners. Daniel Mack, its first proprietor, soon sold to John G. Christopher, whose talents made his house a focal center of village life. An equally significant event was the arrival in April that year of the *Ontario*, the first steamboat on the lake, at the Fall Town docks, three miles to the north. A boat 110-by-24-by-8.5 feet, it carried two masts to spread sails when the wind was favorable. It also had a steam-driven paddle wheel, built on the pattern supplied by Robert Fulton, to provide locomotion during periods of calm. The steamboat made more rapid progress through the lower Genesee gorge than the numerous schooners, which had to be towed upstream by a team of oxen that plodded slowly up and back along the east shore of the river. Speed, however, had scarcely been the object in the pioneer days, which lasted from sunup to sundown and permitted each man to take his own pace. Now the community's growth required some organization, and the most important event of 1817 was the grant of a village charter.

INCORPORATION

The move for the creation of a village had commenced in 1815 as a part of the drive for the establishment of a new county, with Rochester as its seat. But the need for a new county was more urgently felt because of the inconvenience of journeying to Batavia, on the west, or to Canandaigua, on the east, to register deeds and transact other legal matters. Colonel Rochester and Francis Brown had successfully meshed the street patterns of their adjoining settlements, and these, with Fall Town and Charlotte, were in the township of Gates in Genesee County, a long day's journey from Batavia, the county seat. Across the river the towns of Brighton and adjoining Pittsford, still parts of old Ontario County, were similarly inconvenienced by the length of the journey to the court house in Canandaigua. Representatives of the three towns began circulating a subscription in 1816 and secured pledges of $6,722 for the construction of court buildings for a new county on the lower Genesee. Most of the pioneers in the neighboring settlements to the east and the west supported the cause, and nine towns formally endorsed the petition carried by Colonel Rochester to Albany in February 1817. Neither Canandaigua nor Batavia wished to see its sphere of influence reduced, however, and their combined strength was sufficient to block action on the colonel's motion. His second petition, for a village charter, was more favorably received, and the incorporation of Rochesterville, comprising 655 acres on the west bank of the river and numbering about 700 inhabitants, passed the legislature on March 21.

Unexpectedly, Rochester's incorporation was marred by an unhappy but spirited village quarrel. The general rejoicing that greeted the news of the bill's passage stopped suddenly when the leading merchants prepared a slate of candidates excluding all mechanics. Some of the latter angrily rallied their fellows behind a ticket dominated by their own candidates, and in the election at the school house on May 5, the slate of the mechanics, as workmen were then called, carried the day. It was the merchants' turn to feel indignant, and rumors soon spread that they were discharging mechanics responsible for the opposition. News of the untoward development soon reached Colonel Rochester at his Bloomfield estate and prompted a letter full of sound advice to Dr. Matthew Brown:

> I would rather have sacrificed $500 than that such an event should have happened. . . . I have constantly endeavored to impress it on the inhabitants to harmonize among themselves as well as with the inhabitants of the neighboring village of Carthage in order to make it all one place. . . . It will be pleasing to the enemies of Rochester, and you know she has a great number who envy her growing consequence. I would entreat that you and Esquire Mastick will endeavor to heal the wound before it becomes an ulcer.

Dr. Brown, leader of the group that was promoting the development at the main falls, was equally concerned by this early sign of friction within the community. After "expostulating and reasoning" with both sides and warning "they were making themselves and the Village ridiculous," he wrote to assure Colonel Rochester that "after cooling and reflection they are on all sides willing to drop the whole business."

Fortunately, the successful slate of trustees was fairly representative. It included Daniel Mack, proprietor of the Mansion House; William Cobb, a blacksmith who soon established an ax and scythe factory; Jehiel Barnard, Rochester's first tailor; Everard Peck, a book dealer; and Francis Brown, Dr. Brown's younger brother and business partner.

The trustees held the first meeting on May 7 and elected Francis Brown as their president. They held the second meeting at the president's office, overlooking Brown Square, on May 20 and chose a clerk, a treasurer, and a pound master. They met for a third time on June 2 to consider a list of proposed bylaws. Some of these regulations graphically reflected the more urgent village problems. They prescribed fines against those who permitted hogs and cows to run at large, and against those who threw dead animals into the streets. They ordered each householder to equip himself with a fire bucket and to keep his chimneys and stovepipes clean. They banned hunting and the firing of guns within the village limits, and bathing in the river except after dark. They required licenses for those wishing to sell liquor or to slaughter animals within the limits.

Several of these matters soon demanded further action. Under the first village charter the trustees had no power to raise money except as authorized by a vote of the inhabitants. When the pound master reported the need for a suitable pound in which to confine stray animals, and the clerk requested authorization to purchase a proper book for the village records, the trustees decided to call a second town meeting in July, at which a budget of $350 was adopted to cover the expenditures for the first year. These funds permitted the lease and fencing of a lot on the outskirts for a pound and the lease of another lot near the bridge for a hay scales. The trustees met in October to choose a list of men to serve as a volunteer fire company, but it was not until May of the second year that they felt compelled to appoint a village watch to maintain a night patrol during the spring months when many newcomers were arriving.

Eager as most settlers were to see the community grow, they often examined newcomers with a critical eye. Although the falls settlement contrasted with many that were founded and developed by migrants from one town or, at most, a single region, the very diversity of Rochester's origins gave added significance to each newcomer. Aside from the families of the three Maryland proprietors, few southerners found their way to Rochester. Colonel Rochester, as an Episcopalian, and Charles Carroll, as a Catholic, each took the lead in organizing a congenial religious group; the more numerous migrants from New England were Presbyterians, Baptists, and Methodists; the Presbyterians, who built the first meeting house in 1817 on forest stumps to avoid the more expensive task of laying a foundation, welcomed the other Yankee denominations to share their facilities. When Colonel Rochester persuaded A. G. Dauby, an editor in Utica, to move his weekly paper to the falls in 1816, many Yankees found the Jeffersonian tone of the *Gazette* objectionable and backed Everard Peck, the newly arrived book dealer, in establishing the rival Rochester *Telegraph*, which made its appearance in July 1818.

Further evidence of local factionalism appeared with the development of new settlements east of the river. Colonel Rochester had maintained cordial relations with the Stones on the eastern bank, as well with the Browns and the Hanfords to the north on the west bank, but an element of dissension appeared as new promoters arrived to develop a rival port on the high eastern banks below the lower falls. The fact that its leaders hailed from Canandaigua, where the colonel had experienced difficulty in securing a bank loan, which forced him to resort to Utica instead, may have accentuated the rivalry. Elisha B. Strong and his associates frankly announced their intentions of establishing the leading metropolis; the town plot that Elisha B. Johnson, also of Canandaigua, drew in 1817 for Carthage, overlooking the lower falls, clearly suggested its ambitious character. Ontario Street, ending in a centrally located public square, connected with a new highway to be opened to Canandaigua. A road leading down to mill lots at the middle falls and plans for a trestle reaching down to docks to be constructed below the lower falls were shown, but the most ambitious feature was Bridge Street, affording a broad approach to a bridge to be constructed across the gorge to connect with the ridge road to the west.

The plan clearly was to bypass Rochester and to plant a combined milling and trading town at the lower falls, with direct access to the lake trade and direct connections with the principal settlements, both east and west. To succeed, the project also required access to the commerce of the upper river, and Johnson hastened to purchase the main portion of Enos Stone's farm on the east bank at the upper falls. There he laid out another, somewhat more modest subdivision that featured a landing above the falls, an east-side raceway, and a public square adjoining a suggestively named Court Street. His East Rochester subdivision terminated on the north at Main Street, which connected the old road to Pittsford with the Rochester bridge, but he also laid out a new road to Pittsford from his public square.

Johnson's upper-falls project had potential links with both Rochester and Carthage. A practicing engineer, he secured Colonel Rochester's consent for the construction of a dam to serve both his east-side raceway and the new race that Rochester, Fitzhugh, and Carroll were digging on the west side. Plans for a horse railroad from the Johnson landing to Carthage were only faint rumors in 1817, like those for the bridge over the gorge, which seemed incredible. But these rumors made some of Colonel Rochester's associates suspicious of Johnson, and their fears mounted in November that year as a result of a threatened river flood. Heavy rains up the valley had sent rushing waters down to Rochester, where the partly completed Johnson dam turned part of the stream onto the low west bank. The Red Mill was partly damaged, and the western end of the bridge was threatened. Apparently the injury to the village was not excessive, but Carroll, now residing on his estate at old Williamsburg, up the valley, wrote to Colonel Rochester in great alarm:

> My Daughter H. informs me, that you are of opinion that if any injury had arisen to the Village of Rochester, that we & Johnston should have borne the brunt, if so, ought any consideration to induce us to suffer the Dam to remain higher than it originally was when we sold our village Lots. I think not, & under my now Impression I never would consent to their raising it an Inch higher even were we not responsible for inundations. We have water enough for our purposes & we owe it to our families to run no risk, therefore let us without hesitation say at once, take down the Dam to the original height & run no possible risk, we will do nothing to incur damage to ourselves or to the Village. This is my decided opinion, & one from which I will not depart. We have already in public estimation sustained irreparable injury by the report of the destruction of the mills & the inundation of the Village, this abroad operates to our Injury & purchasers will look out for Scites not liable to those casualties. It is all important to us, & the more we suffer in the eyes of the Public, the better for Brighton. I have learnt enough of Yankees to dread & fear their wiles & offers. You are too honest & unsuspicious—take heed my frd or they will be yr ruin.

Much more would be heard about that and other river floods in the years ahead, but meanwhile both Johnson and the Browns were rushing the completion in 1817 of their races and promoting the sale of mill lots. William Atkinson from New York built the first mill at the north end of the Johnson race near Main Street that fall and painted it yellow. The first attempt to take advantage of the newly opened Brown race was made by a group of enterprising residents who organized the Genesee Cotton Manufacturing Company and erected a building overlooking the main falls at the foot of Factory Street. Machinery for 1,400 spindles was brought in and installed, ready for operation by the members of three large families that had migrated from a similar factory in the Black River country. Their timely arrival and the completion of the race enabled the factory to commence operations late in 1817, and the hanging of a bell high above the factory entrance supplied the first public timepiece west of the Genesee.

Despite its recent establishment, Rochester was acquiring other aspects of a settled community. The first stagecoach line had made its appearance in 1815 and announced a regular schedule of trips to and from Canandaigua twice a week. A visit by a traveling musician prompted the organization of a village band in the fall of 1816, and a group of young men formed a debating society that winter. The arrival at this time of the first resident minister, the Reverend Comfort Williams, a graduate of Yale, gave promise of more regular religious services and called attention to the presence of other college graduates: four in the village, as well as E. B. Strong at Carthage, from Yale, and Elisha Johnson, east of the river, from Williams College. With other vigorous residents, they supplied an abundance of leadership; it was time that Colonel Rochester made his long-deferred removal to the falls.

The contrasting trends in land values must have impressed the colonel, for the Bloomfield farm he had bought in 1814 for $12,000 was assuming the character of a frozen asset, whereas the number-one lot in the village, sold in 1811 for $200, had risen to $11,200 in value when acquired in January 1817 by Azel and Russel Ensworth. The Ensworths proceeded to erect a tavern on their choice lot at the Four Corners, thus providing rival accommodations to those offered at Christopher's tavern across the street. The Canandaigua stage, which now extended its route to Lewiston on the Niagara, made three regular stops each week and, with a variety of other wagons and carts, increased the flow of newcomers to the bustling village. In order to maintain more adequate ties with its affairs, the aging colonel determined late in 1817 to establish his residence at the falls. Accordingly, he purchased a large house recently completed by Dr. Levi Ward, Jr., and began to set out a number of young pear trees in the garden overlooking the river and bordering the route of the projected canal a block south of the Four Corners.

2

The First Boom Town, 1817–1834

BEFORE Colonel Rochester's pear trees could produce first fruit, the prospects of the village were radically transformed, and the orchard had soon to be uprooted. The modest developments anticipated by local boosters in 1820 fell far short of what actually occurred when the Erie Canal channeled the increasing flood of westward migrants through Rochester. The town's growth during the twenties would prove as great a surprise to the villagers themselves as to everybody else, for never before had America witnessed the phenomenon of such a town springing up almost overnight in the midst of a forest.* The boom town was soon to become a standard feature of the westward movement, as the great migration poured through successive focal points in its rush across the continent; many a louder and more protracted boom would be heard, but meanwhile the experience left its mark on Rochester.

There was a disjointed, not yet urban quality about the village during the decade of its most rapid growth. Rival factions, with conflicting standards and divergent interests, quickly acquired a foothold, and the settlement was distracted for several years by internal quarrels. Its unprecedented expansion prompted an early assertion of local aspirations for autonomy, which gave the town something of the character of an aggressive upstart among older communities. "Froth and puffing is the order of the day," declared one recent arrival who, in 1818, regretted to find that "Connecticut maxims and habits are reversed." Yet the "mushroom," as it was frequently described, continued

---

* Rochester's growth in the first five years to approximately 800 by the time of incorporation in 1817 was not unique on the frontier. However, its tenfold increase to 8,000 in the next ten years was unprecedented, although Lowell (a "company town"), St. Louis, and Chicago would later experience greater booms.

to grow. Almost giddy from the stimulus of the canal, Rochester preened itself as a representative of the New West. Two more decades would pass before this strain in its early character was largely outgrown.

STRUGGLE FOR AUTONOMY

Although the settlers at Rochesterville, the aged colonel included, failed in 1820 to anticipate the remarkable growth that lay ahead,* they were nonetheless determined to free themselves from dependence on neighboring rivals. Canandaigua, in particular, seemed to obstruct Rochester's path, for its leaders resented the mill town's rising influence. The issue was first joined in the struggle for a separate county, but it appeared in other fields as well, notably in the protracted effort to establish the Bank of Rochester. Inevitably, the close harmony that characterized the drive for the county disappeared in the more complex battle for the bank, and the power struggle that developed there soon became enmeshed in the emerging political contest for control of the village.

Even the campaign for a separate county aroused political and regional jealousies. Several old Federalists in Canandaigua, recognizing the need for a division of the two vast counties of Ontario and Genesee, encouraged the aspirations of the Yankee settlers at Avon to make it the seat of a long county straddling the river from the lake southward to Steuben. A Clintonian faction in Canandaigua stimulated residents of Palmyra to entertain a similar dream of providing the seat for a long county bordering the lake between Sodus and Irondequoit bays. But these moves suggested a comparable strategy to Colonel Rochester. The incorporation of his village had given it an advantage over both Avon and Palmyra, and its thriving growth drew the support of twelve lower Genesee towns behind a renewed plea in the 1819–20 session for a separate county. When that application was again blocked, Colonel Rochester agreed to head a new delegation to Albany the next winter as soon as sufficient snow arrived for good sleighing.

---

* The Rochester *Telegraph*, October 3, 1820, after noting with pleasure Rochester's growth to 1,502, as tabulated by the census that year, boldly forecast that the population might be expected to double in the next ten years.

Before departing, however, he alerted friends in Geneseo, up the valley, to apply for a new county straddling the river from Avon south, and other friends in Lyons to bid for a lake-shore county from Palmyra east into the giant-sized Cayuga County. This realignment of settlements proved effective at Albany, and the bill creating Monroe County passed the legislature and received the governor's signature on February 23, 1821.

Named after the nation's fifth President, who had recently sailed westward on Lake Ontario and had passed the Genesee on his ceremonial journey around the country, Monroe County acquired an area of 607 square miles, which made it slightly larger than any other new county of the period. Despite the tardy settlement of the lower Genesee region, it already contained 27,288 residents, and by 1825 the population exceeded that of much-reduced Ontario County. Its mounting numbers had contributed to the success of its drive for autonomy, but only because of the harmony maintained among its diverse residents. It therefore seemed proper that all factions should share in the first appointments, and the state Council of Appointments named a former Federalist, Elisha B. Strong of Carthage, as first judge; a Clintonian, Elisha Ely of East Rochester, as surrogate; a Bucktail Jeffersonian, Colonel Rochester, as county clerk; and Timothy Childs of Canandaigua, who planned to move to Rochester, as district attorney. When the supervisors of the now fourteen towns met at Christopher's Mansion House on May 8, they chose Matthew Brown of Gates, which included Rochester, as their chairman.

The designation of Rochester as the seat of the new county had met no opposition, but the location of the court buildings remained undetermined. Colonel Rochester and his partners had reserved a site at the center of the 100-acre tract for a court house, but so had the Brown brothers on their 200-acre tract at the main falls, and so also had Johnson, proprietor of the East Rochester subdivision across the river. Because of its more central location, Colonel Rochester's Court House Square won the favor of the commission named in the act to locate and plan the new buildings. When the supervisors met in June to receive the commission's announcements, they authorized construction of a modest court house. Built of stone at a cost of $7,000, it was ready for use in September 1822.

The bright prospects of new court business at Rochester attracted a group of enterprising lawyers, whose presence quickened the political, social, and intellectual life of the bustling mill town. Vincent Mathews, the first lawyer admitted to the bar of Ontario County in 1790 and already a veteran jurist and legislator from western New York, was among those prompted in 1821 to locate at Rochester, where he soon became a respected leader of the profession. James K. Livingston hastened west from Dutchess County, and Addison Gardiner from Manlius. Shortly after young Gardiner had hung his shingle on Buffalo Street, he persuaded his friend Thurlow Weed, a struggling Manlius printer, to locate in Rochester. There quickly gathered not only a distinguished bar but also a plentitude of aspiring politicians, as events soon demonstrated.

The most heated aspect of the struggle for autonomy erupted in the financial field and spilled over into politics. Albany again provided the scene for the conflict, and the prevailing sentiment there, which favored a drastic limitation in the number of banks, accentuated the contest. Rochester's rapid growth intensified its need for credit, and representative villagers petitioned each successive legislature for a bank charter. Frustrated in these efforts, local merchants had to resort to Canandaigua, Geneva, or Utica banks, which gave the town's rivals an undue influence over its affairs. The simulated good feelings that had marked the campaign for a separate county disappeared early the next year when both the Ontario Bank in Canandaigua and the Bank of Utica applied for the privilege of establishing a branch in Rochester. The rival petitions split the village into hostile camps. Rebuffed on one or two occasions in Canandaigua, Colonel Rochester had turned to eastern sources for credit and had become a director of the Bank of Utica. He naturally favored its application and branded the supporters of the Canandaigua branch as Yankee Federalists. From the viewpoint of the opposition, the Rochester clan itself appeared the major grievance, for it was becoming difficult, many felt, to turn about in the bustling village without stumbling over a member of the proprietor's family.

The fate of the proposed branches soon became entangled in state politics, and both met defeat. That outcome, however, cleared the way for a renewed campaign for an independent bank for Rochester. Nine separate groups, including one headed by the aging colonel, petitioned the next legislature, and several joined in dispatching young Thurlow

Weed to Albany as a "legislative solicitor" to coordinate the drive. Weed, an assistant of Everard Peck on the *Telegraph*, had Clintonian ties, but in his eagerness to secure the authorization of a Rochester bank, he endorsed the bill drafted by Colonel Rochester, which entrusted its organization to a commission headed by himself. Confident that their greater numbers in Rochester assured control, the local Clintonians honored Weed for his legislative accomplishment by electing him to the assembly that fall.

Rivalry over the bank's control increased in intensity with each step in its organization. When the commissioners opened the subscription books in May 1824, the $250,000 capital stock was oversubscribed fivefold. The oft-expressed desire to bring eastern capital into the village had prompted Dr. Brown as well as Colonel Rochester and several others to collect applications from Albany and New York investors, and Judge E.B. Strong had several from Canandaigua. All had to be scaled down, but when the apportionment revealed that Colonel Rochester's Bucktail friends had been assured of control, twenty-one villagers, in a spirited remonstrance, declared "their intention to withdraw their business from the institution while it remained under the control of Nathaniel Rochester." Concerned for the safety of his investments, one of the eastern subscribers hastened to Rochester to vote his stock in person and endeavored to conciliate the opposition. The mixed board of directors that resulted included Dr. Brown, Dr. Ward, and Enos Stone, among other moderate Clintonians, and Charles H. Carroll, Abelard Reynolds, and Jonathan Child as supporters of Colonel Rochester, who was elected president with the understanding that he retire at the end of the year. When the time came to choose his successor, Dr. Levi Ward won preference over the colonel's son-in-law, Jonathan Child. A year later the "black-spirited rascal," Judge Strong, was elected to the presidency, but by that date his ties with Canandaigua had been severed, and Colonel Rochester's attitude towards the older village mellowed as fear of its dominance was outgrown.

Rochester's confidence was enhanced by two dramatic events in the early twenties. The challenge posed by Carthage, the projected lake port and mill town at the lower falls, was suddenly removed by the collapse of its bridge in July 1820. Built of logs, fastened end-to-end in a great arch soaring 190 feet above the water, it had successfully spanned the 718-foot width of the gorge and supplied a marvel that won the admiration of many visitors. The great bridge, the longest single-arch structure in the world in its day, withstood the ravages of two winters but finally, almost without warning, gave way under the pressure of its heavy framework and tumbled the visionary hopes of Carthage with it into the gorge. The settlement on the high east bank would survive and serve for at least two decades as the lake port of Rochester chiefly because of a second pair of dramatic developments—the completion of the Rochester aqueduct in September 1823 and the opening of canal traffic east of Rochester to the Hudson a month later.

Rochester had likewise spanned the river that year by annexing the east-side subdivision of Elisha Johnson. It had thus increased its acreage to 1,012 and its population to an estimated 3,700 by that June, when Horatio Spafford made a last-minute check before sending his second *Gazetteer for New York State* to the printer. No town in the state west of Albany and Troy could rival it in either size or growth rate. Colonel Rochester, who had extended Mill (soon to be renamed Exchange) Street through his ill-fated pear orchard, was hastily completing a new three-story brick house on nearby Spring Street in order to escape the noise and confusion of the canal that adjoined his former homestead. Yet, it was difficult to escape the sound of construction in a town in which, as Spafford reported, one church, nine three-story brick buildings, and 150 houses of lesser size had been built during the preceding twelve months, not to mention two additional mills and an aqueduct that was the longest stone bridge in America. The shipment of 130,000 bbl. of flour to Canada that year had helped to defray the cost of Rochester's expansion, even before the opening of the canal assured its stability.

BOOM TOWN CHARACTER

The construction and opening of the Erie Canal inevitably quickened the town's economic activities and brought a flood of newcomers to swell its population. Their divergent origins and interests added new dimensions to Rochester's social and cultural scene and created new problems for its civic and political leaders. The very rapidity of these developments created tensions that often interrupted the progressive organization of the growing town. Some of the pioneers became disheartened and moved on to new frontiers, but many held their ground, and a host of newcomers arrived, eager to share in the fortunes of America's first boom town.

The building of the aqueduct at a cost of $83,000 brought new energies into the village. William Brittin, the first contractor, made a false start with a gang of convicts from Auburn prison, a plan that had to be displaced when several convicts escaped. Brittin's untimely death and the discovery that the sandstone quarried at Carthage was unsuitable for use in construction and would have to be replaced by a more durable stone brought from Cayuga enforced delays, but the 802-foot structure spanning the river on eleven Roman arches was completed in good time and provided Rochester with a notable landmark that attracted many visitors. More to the point, it supplied convenient access to the heart of town and enabled the *Monroe Republican* to report on November 4, 1824, almost a year before the official opening of the canal, the arrival during the previous week of "75 tons of Merchandise, 9 do Castings . . . 1572 bbl. Salt . . . and many passengers" as well as the departure of "56 Boats with 2000 bbl. Flour, 210 bbl. Ashes . . . 0000 ft. lumber and many passengers."

Rochester's preparations for the canal trade centered around the construction of a series of slips or basins for docking purposes and the establishment of a number of boat yards to supply the needs of merchant shippers. At the west end of the aqueduct, Child's Basin, extending to the north between present Exchange and Aqueduct streets, quickly became the most active harbor in town; however, a half-dozen others appeared to facilitate loading and unloading near the principal mills and warehouses. Abundant supplies of lumber from up the valley made Rochester the favored boat-building center, and by the late twenties, six well-organized boat yards were producing packet and freight boats, valued at from $800 to $1,200, by the score every year. Freight and packet companies, several of them owned and operated by Rochester men, soon acquired a major portion of the shipping trade; one of these, the Pilot Line, organized by Johnathan Child in 1827, scheduled trips by 34 freight boats drawn by 180 horses, with regular stops between New York and Buffalo.

The first effect of the canal was to stimulate Rochester's commercial activity and to enhance its status as a market center. Transport costs to and from Albany dropped from between $60 and $100 a ton by wagon to a maximum of $10 a ton by boat, thus increasing the volume and variety of both landings and shipments. This trade, which mounted by 1827 to $1,200,000 in value of shipments from Rochester and $1,020,000 in imported merchandise, gave a new spurt to commerce on the upper Genesee, where a flat-bottomed steamboat made its appearance in 1824. Yet although some thirty-five boats drew up daily at the Rochester docks in the late 1820s, several of them packets carrying numerous passengers, the flood of migrants and other travelers now kept six daily stages operating to and from Rochester by four well-established routes, as reported in the village *Directory* of 1827, when the town's thriving activity first justified such a publication.

The canal likewise gave a new impetus to local industry. Its major contribution was to the processors of area products who now acquired easy access to eastern markets. Chief among these were the seven flour mills, nine lumber mills, two distilleries, and numerous asheries already listed in the 1827 *Directory*. In addition, the canal helped promote a number of processing industries by its imports of raw materials and machinery. Several woodworking and ironworking shops appeared to make and repair the tools and implements needed in adjoining shops or on the expanding frontier. Among other metal products were scythes, axes, plows, and nails; the coopers and other woodworkers made barrels, handles, furniture, and building materials to supply local and regional needs.

No local demands rivaled those of the building industry, which was frantically endeavoring to keep pace with the town's population increases. A census of houses late in 1827 found a total of 1,474, of which 352 had been built in that season, when the families numbered 1,664. In addition, the town boasted "five extensive and excellent hotels, each . . . capable of accommodating between fifty and seventy persons," and had two more under construction. Two recently completed stone churches vied for preference, but no structure except the aqueduct rivaled the new four-and-one-half-story Arcade, which Abelard Reynolds was erecting at his old site on Buffalo Street. Completed at a cost of $30,000 in 1828, it supplied an interior arcade extending up through its successive stories to a skylight and provided a sheltered concourse for citizens calling for their mail at the post office on the ground floor or visiting one or another of the numerous craftsmen housed in the upper stories. If any traveler doubted the town's growing consequence, he could do nothing better than visit the Arcade, mount its successive stairs to the turret over the roof, and there enjoy a pleasant view of the thriving settlement.

The bellfry atop the graceful three-story stone court house provided a similar outlook, as well as a mount for a bell acquired in 1828. A log house surrounded by a stockade served as the county jail until a stone structure could be built overlooking the river south of the aqueduct in the early thirties. The county sheriff and his occasional deputies assisted three judges in the suppression of crime, but the county's major function was to record deeds and supervise other legal transactions. Its responsibility for roads and bridges was cautiously assumed, but when a series of floods weakened the Rochester bridge, the county billed the village for half the cost of replacing the original frame bridge with a more substantial wooden superstructure erected on stone piers. A group of private investors built a second bridge over the river at Court Street shortly after the completion of the Canal.

The official opening of the Erie Canal, marked at Rochester by the visit of Governor Clinton and his party on a ceremonial boat excursion from Buffalo east to New York in October 1825, inspired numerous demands for a city charter. Dr. Brown, whose long service on the village board had convinced him of the need for full municipal status, was an active proponent, but those who were reluctant to grant large taxing powers to a group of aldermen dominated a public meeting convened that December to consider the question. The majority favored a revised charter, which, when passed, divided the village into five wards, raised the tax limit to $2,000 a year, and extended some of the powers of the trustees. The editor of a recently established new weekly, the *Album*, derived some amusement from the situation:

> Although Rochester is in point of business the first village in the state, we are too young to ape the fashions or merit the name of a city. Our streets are neither paved nor lighted, we have no markets, no shipping, no theatres, or public gardens, no promenades for exquisites, and our aldermen would experience a great scarcity of turtle. Besides, as was remarked by one of the speakers at the meeting, "while Buffalo, & Brooklyn, & Utica are striving for city charters, to become a city can be considered NO GREAT TRICK.

Apparently, however, the need for greater authority was genuine, for when the revised charter passed the legislature, the same editor commented, "Heretofore, disorder has bid defiance to wholesome law, but the presumption now is that a new state of things will take place." The newly elected trustees, all inexperienced except Dr. Brown, who was chosen president, soon found themselves burdened with pressing problems. In place of the leisurely meetings, held once every two or three months during previous years, the trustees gathered for busy sessions every week or so, sometimes twice a week. For this service they received the modest reward of fifteen dollars a year, yet the dignities of the office attracted leading citizens, such as Vincent Mathews, a former assemblyman.

The first task of the new board was to formulate a policy for the regulation of groceries and theatrical performances. With a theater under construction and a traveling showman requesting permission to exhibit a caravan of strange animals, the prospect that other performers would soon visit the most thriving town west of Albany forced a decision. Unfortunately, the trustees were sharply divided over these questions. An attempt to ban all theater licenses was voted down, three to two, but the compromise ordinance fixing the annual license fee at $150 proved unenforceable, and a new charge of $30 a week had to be substituted to meet the convenience of visiting showmen. Although some residents opposed these questionable influences, pleasure was expressed over the fact that the fees assured that "nonresidents among us may contribute to the improvement of our Village." Rochester had in fact grown to the point where the number of travelers and other strangers thronging the taverns and eager to relax around billiard tables or to purchase whiskey even on the Sabbath, made it difficult for respectable villagers to maintain strict regulations. Although groceries appeared at every turn, and almost one hundred persons procured licenses to sell liquor in 1827, efforts to enforce the Sabbath-closing rule or to check the exuberance of canal boatmen passing through Rochester on Sunday proved futile.

Other civic problems also pressed for attention. The first fire engine—a hand pump attached to a tank fed by the bucket brigade—had been purchased following the burning of Francis Brown's mill early in 1818, and a second fire engine five years later. The outbreak of numerous fires in the mid-twenties prompted the inhabitants in 1827 to vote $1,000 for a third engine and 300 feet of leather hose, which was procured from Philadelphia. An excess of applicants sought appointment to the three volunteer fire companies, but because service on the night watch was more taxing, modest payments had become necessary in 1819. Mounting disorders following the opening of the canal prompted the trustees to increase the number of night watchmen to ten in 1827, each to patrol a specified ward half the night, at ten dollars a month. An appalling number of deaths, particularly of young children (seventeen of the proprietor's sixty-three grandchildren died before age five, though not all in these years) prompted the purchase in 1821 of a larger cemetery on Buffalo Road with the proceeds from the sale of the smaller lot on Spring Street that had been set aside for that purpose a few years before by Colonel Rochester. The trustees subsidized the digging of several private wells, which thus made them available for public use, and directed the construction of vaults under the "necessaries" required on all occupied properties. They prescribed other sanitary regulations and in 1828 named two doctors to serve with three of their members as a board of health.

Their most dramatic action was the creation of a public market. The need had become apparent as numerous teamsters crowded the streets of the thriving market town with loads of hay, grain, and other produce. Every attempt to prescribe the points at which such wagons should stand while awaiting buyers brought protests from lot owners, and the only acceptable stand for market wagons appeared to be near the west end of the bridge. When Elisha Johnson, who had recently completed the reconstruction of that bridge for the county, proposed that a market be constructed at its northwest corner, extending out over the river to the first pier, the trustees hastily endorsed the plan and convened a meeting of the inhabitants who gave their approval and authorized an expenditure of $1,000 on the project. The building of the market, which trebled that cost and induced the trustees to negotiate the first sizeable loan, set another significant precedent by its encroachment on the river. A half-century would pass before the river was blotted from view on Main Street, but the process of joining the two parts of town was initiated by the construction of the market building.

Less striking perhaps, but more extensive and necessary, were the street and sewer improvements launched under the second charter. The Buffalo Street sewer, started by private agreement in 1824, was pressed forward with vigor under the direction of the trustees in the summer of 1826. Though little more than a shallow ditch with flagstone sides and capping, the sewer diverted surface water from the backyard cesspools and helped to drain the adjoining wetlands into the river below the bridge. The expense, as in the case of sidewalks ordered constructed on the central streets, fell on adjacent property owners, though not without protest from those who favored the simple ways of the pioneers. Authority to proceed with further street improvements was finally secured in an amendment to the charter in 1828, and rock broken in the yard of the county jail was spread over the more troublesome mud holes to smooth the surface of the principal streets. The labor on such repairs still came from male residents, each required, as in rural areas, to serve two days a year on the roads and an extra day for every $300 in real property within the limits. As the limits expanded with the town's growth, the promoters of outlying subdivisions opened new streets or extended old ones; fortunately, the urge to attract buyers assured the provision of generous rights-of-way.

A reliance on private initiative also characterized the development of the town's cultural facilities. Even the district schools, established under state authority by the decentralized townships, depended on the leadership and support of interested residents. The rapid increase in the number of children of school age in the village by 1821 overtaxed the school buildings supplied by Gates Districts 2 and 10 and Brighton Districts 4 and 8. When the 480 children enrolled in these four schools that year increased to 2,000 in eight schools by 1827, only the brief terms attended by most pupils saved the system from collapse. An effort by Colonel Rochester to form the Lancastrian Society, to operate the schools of Gates and Brighton as a union school, met defeat at Albany in 1821. Fortunately, a number of enterprising young men and women were settling in the village during these years and establishing private academies for boys and seminaries for girls. Although most of these efforts were short lived, several private seminaries persisted and supplied accommodations for those able to pay the modest charges. To meet the needs of the less fortunate, a group of ladies organized a weekday charity school in 1821; moreover, the Sabbath School Union, formed that year to give direction to the varied

Sunday school programs of the separate denominations, concentrated these efforts for a season or two on four nonsectarian schools.

Still unsolved was the problem of providing more advanced instruction. One of the few shortcomings lamented by the *Directory* of 1827 was the absence of an "institution of learning . . . an edifice built for science." Favored youngsters could enroll in neighboring academies at Canandaigua and Geneva, even Henrietta, and a move soon developed to establish a "retreat for the muses" in Rochester. The assistance offered by the newly formed state regents provided encouragement, and Brighton Districts 4 and 14 secured permission to form a union school. The High School, as it was proudly named, opened in a new three-story brick structure in August 1828 and attracted a combined enrollment of 300 in the elementary and secondary divisions. Unfortunately, the cost proved too great after three years for the combined districts, and only the offer of its principal to lease and operate it as a private seminary saved the struggling institution from collapse.

If some Rochesterians in the 1820s urged the establishment of an "academic grove" for the village youth, others desired facilities for the intellectual life of adults. Two book stores maintained by local printers already provided circulating libraries in 1822, when Dr. Levi Ward invited interested citizens to join him in establishing the Rochester Library Company, which located its collections at the E. F. Marshall book store and maintained a forum for a season or two. Dr. Ward took an active part in the organization of the Franklin Institute in 1826, which two years later absorbed a newly formed apprentice's library. Before its demise during the anti-Masonic controversy, the institute sponsored a chemical class that featured lectures by Professor Amos Eaton of Troy and held an exhibit of a painting by George Catlin of New York, which it had commissioned of the great patron of the canal, DeWitt Clinton. Several other visiting artists were permitted to exhibit their works at the local taverns, and J. S. D. Mathies, who operated a soda fountain and sold musical instruments at the Mansion House, maintained a working gallery for a time and completed a portrait of the aging chieftain Red Jacket for display in the parlor of his refurbished tavern on Exchange Street.

Rochesterians acted promptly and energetically in the development of religious institutions, and the stress many experienced as the village became a boom town appeared most dramatically in this field. The

Presbyterians achieved an early lead under the Reverend Comfort Williams, the first resident pastor. Their temporary structure on Carroll Street accommodated other denominational groups as well as the first Sabbath school. Colonel Rochester hastened to organize an Episcopal society and pressed forward with the construction in 1820 of a frame church on Fitzhugh Street, facing the public square reserved for the court house. The Reverend Francis H. Cuming became its first settled pastor and developed a thriving congregation that enrolled, in addition to the proprietor's numerous family, such leading residents as Elisha Johnson, Silas O. Smith, Enos Stone, John Mastick, and Samuel J. Andrews. The members of the Presbyterian church, including the Elys, the Bissells, the Chapins, and the Wards, were equally distinguished and more numerous; they soon acquired a lot behind the court house and began to erect a new edifice practically across the street from St. Luke's, as the Episcopal church was named. When the Episcopalians discovered that the Presbyterians were building a stone church, they moved their frame structure to the rear of the lot and launched the construction of their own stone church.

The rivalry produced a number of spirited exchanges, for each group aspired to provide the leading church in the village. Fortunately, hostilities subsided shortly after completion of the churches, when the town's rapid growth overcrowded both structures and brought the establishment not only of the second and third Presbyterian churches but also of a second Episcopal church, and presented so many unexpected challenges to religious folk that the assistance of almost any denomination was eagerly welcomed. The Quakers and the Catholics had built modest chapels in the early twenties, and although the local Methodist and Baptist societies were content for a time to hold their meetings in the temporary structure on Carroll Street, they also were actively developing congregations that would soon erect churches of their own. Lively disputes raged among the several denominations and between the high and low branches of the Episcopal church and the conservative and evangelical factions among the Presbyterians. These differences tended to disappear as the town's booming growth attracted a few disciples of Tom Paine and other agnostics, and as the turbulent life of the canalers presented a serious challenge to local traditions.

The traditional ways of the pioneer village were not as sober and stiff as some wished to depict them. Local taverns had provided dining and drinking rooms, billiard tables, and dancing parties from the start, and Colonel Rochester's annual family picnics had engendered enough merriment to prompt residents who failed to receive invitations to organize a rival community picnic on the same day in 1825. The reception staged for General Lafayette on his visit to Rochester on June 7, 1825, was boisterous as well as ceremonial, and it apparently delighted all participants. The visit of Governor Clinton, heralding the opening of the canal several months later, was full of pomp, though somewhat marred by a steady rain. The annual Fourth of July celebrations—featuring parades by local militia units and the village band, community picnics on Brown's Island or Falls Field, patriotic addresses and successive gun salutes, and generally ending with military balls at the rival taverns—gave vent to the community's mounting spirits.

The event destined to serve as a climax to the increasingly reckless pageantry of the boom town was Sam Patch's leap over the main falls. Patch had earned a reputation for daring jumps in the East and at Niagara before his visit to Rochester in the late fall of 1829. Sam's laconic remark that "some things can be done as well as others" was passed along as a fit motto by his admirers as he announced a last jump of the season over the main falls of the Genesee. A platform erected on Brown's Island overlooking the falls increased the height above the pool to 120 feet, and on Friday, November 13, a great throng gathered from the town and the country around, and lined the natural amphitheater of the gorge to see the widely advertised spectacle. Whether or not Sam had relaxed his self-control at a tavern beforehand, the bold jumper lost his customary poise in the descent. With arms whirling he struck the water with a great splash and failed to reappear in its swirling eddies. Rochester gained wide fame from Sam's last jump; Patch became the subject of much doggerel verse and won a place in the folklore of the young Republic. Nevertheless, it was a chastened and more thoughtful populace that quietly dispersed from the falls that day.

The need for sober reflection had become evident in still another field—the boom town's fourth estate. A. G. Dauby had sold his pioneer weekly *Gazette* in 1821 to Derrick and Levi Sibley, who renamed it the *Monroe Republican* and chose young Edwin Scrantom as editor.

Scrantom's moderation offered little opposition to the vigorous editorial policy that Thurlow Weed, Everard Peck's new assistant, brought to the *Telegraph*, which in 1824 became a semiweekly. The *Album* was professedly nonpartisan, but a new paper, the *Advertiser*, established in 1826, not only was the first daily west of Albany but also, under the dynamic editorship of young Henry O'Reilly, a newcomer from Ireland and New York, vigorously espoused all democratic causes. Weed, who acquired part ownership of the *Telegraph*, absorbed the *Republican* in 1827 and also launched a daily edition. Two new weeklies made their appearance: the *Observer*, dedicated to moral reform, and the *Craftsman*, which often opposed the alleged self-righteousness of the *Observer*.

These journalistic rivalries acquired a new intensity with the outbreak of anti-Masonry in 1827. It was perhaps not surprising that the Genesee boom town became the focal center of this movement, for the building of the aqueduct and other stone structures had attracted a number of working masons to Rochester, and together with other enterprising men drawn to the village, many aspired to membership in the popular Masonic lodges. Some, but not all, were admitted, and William Morgan, who became a member shortly before completing his job assignment in Rochester, but who found himself excluded when he moved to Batavia, determined to cash in on the secrets he had learned by publishing a full account of the mysterious rituals. Reports of that plan prompted a few Masons to attempt to abduct Morgan and transport him to Canada, but the scheme apparently miscarried, and rumors began to circulate late in 1826 of his forced drowning in the Niagara River. When Thurlow Weed quickly took the lead in pressing for an investigation of the Masonic order, O'Reilly protested the effort to hold an entire society responsible for the possible actions of a few members. When Weed's Clintonian partner on the *Telegraph* also urged moderation, Weed sold his interests and early in 1828 established the *Anti-Masonic Enquirer*, which championed a separate anti-Masonic slate in the elections that year.

The contest became more bitter as the election approached. Colonel Rochester, who distrusted Jackson because of his reliance on "military renown," found himself working again with Elisha Ely and even with Elisha B. Strong in support of Timothy Childs, their candidate for Congress. Weed charged Jacob Gould and Addison Gardiner

with an attempt to bribe the electorate because of the aid they gave
to O'Reilly, labeled the "foreign" editor of the *Advertiser,* which vigorously supported Jackson. The timely discovery of a man's body in the
lower Niagara provided a "good enough Morgan until after the election," as Weed was quoted as saying, and the anti-Masonic slate won
in the three-cornered local election, which enabled Weed to move into
a broader political world at Albany, where he took up permanent residence. O'Reilly, who had completed his naturalization that spring,
could rejoice in a Democratic victory at Albany and Washington, but
Weed and his associates won sufficient strength locally to prompt the
ten Masonic lodges in Monroe County to surrender their charters in a
dramatic "Address . . . to the Public" in which William B. Rochester,
Vincent Mathews, and other prominent citizens declared that because,
under the "baleful influence" of the controversy, "Reason seems to
have lost her empire and Charity to have resigned her seat . . . the
responsibility will not rest upon us." Yet despite the aggrieved tone
of their address, they must have recognized that in renouncing the
glories of a make-believe world, they were losing something of limited
value only in a village setting and were freeing themselves for more
effective participation in the business and political life of the emerging
city.

Becoming a City

Several of the tensions confronting the town in the late twenties
and early thirties were aspects of the urbanizing process that was
transforming it into a city. As the surging growth that characterized its
boom days tapered off, Rochester acquired new and more stable economic functions and secured an opportunity to face and catch up with
some of its turbulent civic problems. The experience stimulated the
development of new and sometimes conflicting purposes, which resulted in an outburst of social and religious ferment. Several old leaders passed from the scene, but new ones arose and played a role in
the assumption of new community responsibilities that marked the
attainment of urban status.

The distinctions between the boom town and the Flour City were
clearly evident in the changing character of Rochester's population.

The procession of westward migrants along the canal accelerated as newcomers from abroad joined its ranks. However, more persons now continued their journey into the West and carried many from Rochester with them. A sufficient number of newcomers, both from the East and from abroad, notably Ireland, took up residence at the falls to give it a growth of 50 percent in five years. But because approximately 70 percent of a sampling of those listed in the 1827 *Directory* had died or moved on before the next and much longer list appeared in 1834, even a conservative estimate, heavily weighting the size of the families of those who remained, would have classed approximately nine out of ten of the Rochesterians of 1834 as newcomers within the previous seven years.

The emigrants from Rochester, as well as the new arrivals, reflected the changing character of the town. Some able but restless men of means moved on to take the lead in the development of new towns in the West, but the migrants were most numerous among the boarders; only 22 percent of that group, as identified in the 1827 *Directory*, remained, in comparison with 36 percent of the householders. The call of the expanding West and of its new boom towns was more enticing to those who had not achieved a secure place in Rochester or who had been disillusioned by the collapse of its boom. Some who had become victims of the earlier speculative mania and who were unable to meet their obligations sought to escape their creditors by migrating to new states. An attempt to devise a more effective means of collecting small loans prompted the publication of a list of such debtors, which spurred the formation of a mutual association to combat the Shylock association and to campaign for the abolition of imprisonment for debt. When a tabulation of the obligations of the 628 committed to jail in Monroe County in 1830 produced a total of only $6,399, popular indignation mounted and helped to speed the passage of a bill at Albany that curtailed imprisonment for sums under fifty dollars.

No reforms could relax the pressure to find new economic functions to replace those of the boom town. The restricted limits of Rochester's geographic position had become apparent as the boundless opportunities of the Mississippi Valley and the upper Great Lakes developed in the early thirties. The multiplication of steam vessels on these greater water routes quickly overshadowed the canal and river facilities of Rochester. Attempts to improve the Genesee lake port resulted, but the opening of the Welland and Oswego canals in 1829 provided an alternate route to and from the West that threatened to bypass Rochester. The boom town of the Erie Canal was becoming a way station; its days as the leading western market town had passed, and its best hope for continued growth was to develop the industrial potential of its falls and to transform it into a fabricating and pro-visioning center for the western country.

That strategy called for the improvement of its transport facilities and the promotion of its industries; for a time, the former took prece-dence. If Rochester was to secure a share in the Canadian trade, and that from the West by way of the Welland Canal, it needed a more accessible lake port. After several appeals the federal government, which had constructed a stone lighthouse at Charlotte in 1825, was persuaded to build two log piers cutting through the sandbar at the mouth of the river to provide a safe entrance for lake shipping. Steam-boats could then proceed up the gorge to the landing below the lower falls. Here local investors were finally building the inclined trestle to haul shipments up and down the steep banks of the gorge to con-nect with the horse railroad that had been constructed in 1832 from the east end of the aqueduct to the site of old Carthage. The comple-tion of these improvements the next year assured Rochester convenient access to the lake and prompted the city, on the receipt of its charter in 1834, to extend its boundaries north to include the Carthage landing.

These commercial improvements facilitated the importation of Canadian wheat and helped to promote the development of Roch-ester's mills, which increased to eighteen by the mid-thirties when the town acquired its position as the leading Flour City. Elisha Beach, who had built the large Aqueduct Mill on the west side in 1826, had brought Robert M. Dalzell, a leading millwright, to Rochester to supervise construction. Its location adjoining the Child Basin had prompted Dalzell to improvise and install a bucket elevator to lift grain out of boats or wagons at its base to the sixth, or top, floor of the mill, whence it passed by gravity and belts through successive sepa-rators and grinders until it reached the barrels on the loading platform. The efficiency of the mill won Dalzell contracts to build a dozen more, including the great mill erected by Hervey Ely at the eastern end of the aqueduct.

As the output of Rochester's mills mounted to an early high of

300,000 barrels in 1833, its transport in Rochester boats to eastern markets assured a large cash return. A major share went, of course, to area and more distant farmers for the wheat, but much of it was spent in Rochester stores, and an increasing number of local craftsmen and mechanics helped to produce the articles most in demand. Although a second attempt to operate a cotton factory failed because of the difficulty of importing its bulky raw material, a small carpet factory expanded to meet the demands of an active market, and three sawmills became furniture factories to supply the chairs, tables, and cabinets in constant demand throughout the area. Other skilled wood and metal craftsmen joined to establish the first local carriage factory and the first shop to produce grain cutters and other farm machinery. To coordinate the development of these varied enterprises, Dr. Brown took the lead in 1829 in organizing the Rochester Board of Manufacturers, which undertook, among other services, to answer inquiries from any quarter concerning Rochester's productive facilities.

The enterprise and the markets were abundant, but many in Rochester complained of the shortage of credit and of the excessive hazards that faced Rochester industries. So great were the demands on the Bank of Rochester that its leaders finally withdrew their opposition to a second bank, and Abraham Schermerhorn, the cashier of the first bank, became the principal organizer and president of the Bank of Monroe. Outside investors supplied most of the funds for the second bank, opened in 1829, and subscribed to other local enterprises as the depression lifted. The Monroe Fire Insurance Company, organized in 1827 by Everard Peck and other villagers, likewise secured most of its working capital from Manhattan investors, and competed with other New York insurance men for the local business. The hazards that they, along with the millers and other promoters of large enterprises faced, increased their concern for improved fire protection and other civic services.

Most of the responsible community leaders had, in fact, become advocates of full municipal status in the late twenties. After petitions for a city charter had been tabled by the state legislature in 1826 and 1828, a public meeting at Rochester strongly endorsed a renewed application the next year, but the legislature, noting a persistant fear of higher taxes, again deferred action. As a result, the trustees had to limit themselves to makeshift programs. They issued frequent orders for the construction of sidewalks and flagstone sewers by the property owners along the central streets, and nearly two miles of such sewers and three miles of sidewalks were completed by 1834. The emergence of a central urban core was enhanced by the erection of fifteen street lamps at the two major intersections and the approaches to the town's two bridges. When pleas for similar oil lamps at additional corners prompted a doubling of their number a year later, the cost of their maintenance exhausted the funds available in the early spring and forced residents to rely again on the moon and the stars in the summer of 1833.

The need for a community water supply was similarly postponed, yet fire precautions could not safely be suspended. A new volunteer company was organized to operate the fourth fire engine acquired in 1829, but the outbreak of seven fires in 1831 and of sixteen the next year prompted the hasty purchase of two more engines and the organization of two additional companies. Fines against church sextons who failed to ring their bells on the outbreak of a fire were replaced in 1833 by a more effective scheme of awarding those who were first to sound the alarm. Many doubted that the fire hazard could be brought under control without the provision of an adequate supply of water, and Elisha Johnson was persuaded to draft a plan for a waterworks. The outbreak late in January 1834 of a fire in the wooden buildings that had crept out along the north side of the principal bridge not only consumed these structures, including the public market, at an estimated loss of $100,000 in property, but also speeded the dispatch of a petition to Albany for authority to build a waterworks. Apparently, the appeal hastened the adoption of a city charter that granted a waterworks and other more adequate powers. An earlier charter, drafted for Rochester in 1832 by John C. Spencer of Canandaigua, had become entangled in legislative rivalries and again failed to pass. A new draft that assured Rochester full control over the election of its aldermen and the appointment of local justices finally secured legislative approval in April 1834.

The organization of the first city government brought a new political struggle to the foreground. With popular interest in the anti-Masonic controversy flagging, the National Republicans, or Clay supporters, adopted the temperance issue as their principal plank. "Whiskey," their editorial spokesman declared, "runs like water in

Dublin [the Irish quarter]. We intend to be ready for them." When the temperance, or anti-Jackson, forces, soon to be named the Whig party, triumphed and named Jonathan Child as first mayor, the editor of the recently established *Liberal Advocate* soon found occasion to report, with some asperity, that "the work of regeneration has commenced—a war of extermination against *Barber poles and tavern signs.*"

The temperance issue was but one aspect of the highly charged religious movement that gripped the community in the early thirties. Curiously enough, it was the foolhardy leap of Sam Patch that touched off the emotional powder keg in Rochester. News of revivals in the East and up the valley had stirred enthusiasm for Bible distribution, temperance pledges, and Sabbath reform at Rochester in the late twenties, and several clergymen had conducted annual "concerts of prayer" in the Court House Square. But it was on the Sunday following Patch's fatal leap that Josiah Bissell rose in the Third Presbyterian Sabbath School and warned that "any who had by their presence encouraged that soul to leap into eternity would be held accountable on the Judgement Day." To save Rochester from its many shortcomings, Bissell, who was the chief backer of the six-day stage and packet lines, pledged to a strict observance of the Sabbath and, as a patron of the zealously pious *Observer*, brought Charles G. Finney, the noted evangelist, to his church for a protracted revival in the winter of 1830–31.

Finney's dynamic spirit and logical arguments commanded the respect of sober church folk and drew many nonbelievers to the three services every Sunday and the numerous weekday prayer meetings. A holy band of assistants, under the direction of his young disciple Theodore Weld, pressed the campaign for converts into the homes and workshops of those who showed signs of repenting. Among the approximately four hundred families drawn into the fold of the several participating churches were several who assumed positions of leadership in the emerging Flour City, notably Alvah Strong who became a pillar in the Baptist church and, later, a leader in the establishment of the university. Indeed, several of the men brought to the fore by Finney's earnest preaching eventually gave a new urban direction to the charity and temperance movements, as well as to the religious and educational developments of the community. The unexpected death of Josiah Bissell, patron of the *Observer*, and of "Obediah Dogberry" (as the editor of the *Liberal Advocate* styled himself), which brought the demise of their contentious journals, cleared the way for the rise of more stable men.

Rochester's increased heterogeneity afforded opportunities for many newcomers. The passing of Colonel Rochester in his eightieth year on May 17, 1831, and the migration of three of his five sons with their large families to Buffalo and other cities dispelled the apprehension that the town would remain the preserve of a proprietory clan. Although Colonel Rochester performed his last public service as first president of the Rochester Athenaeum, founded in June 1829, William A. Reynolds, who made a hall on the second floor of his father's Arcade available for the meetings and library of the Rochester Athenaeum, Dr. Ward, and Henry O'Reilly, who arranged for the Rochester Athenaeum's absorption of the old Franklin Institute and of the newly formed Young Men's Association, emerged as its true leaders. Animosities springing from the anti-Masonic controversy had disrupted the Franklin Institute, and a new altercation between Josiah Bissel and Father Michael McNamara, the priest in charge of St. Patrick's Church, which prompted a debate over the dangers of popery at the Young Men's Association in 1831, threatened its existence. However, the moderation of O'Reilly and young Levi A. Ward assured its future.

There were many other signs of the town's increased urbanization. Hamlet Scrantom, the first permanent resident, still set his hens and took an interest in the arrival of a new calf in the barn behind his homestead on State Street. Nevertheless, his third son, Edwin, who had established the Rochester *Gem* in 1829, was attentively observing the changing manners of the bustling town where, as he reported on one afternoon, "Ladies, dandies, gentlemen, children, dogs, horses, carts, wagons, trucks, stages . . . kept alive the streets."

Few of Scrantom's contemporaries were able to match his lighthearted touch, and some local events, notably the cholera epidemic of 1832, merited more sober coverage. Yet although nobody in Rochester or elsewhere knew much concerning its cause or treatment, both the *Observer* and the *Liberal Advocate,* which, respectively, blamed it on excessive drinking and on an overabundance of cholera sermons, seemed to miss the point. The most courageous as well as the most useful response was that made by Colonel Ashbel W. Riley, who was appointed to fill a vacancy on the Board of Health that had been occasioned by the hasty departure of a less intrepid member. The fearless colonel personally assumed the task of burying most of the town's 118 victims and assisted Constable Simmons in caring for other sufferers in an improvised hospital in an old cooper shop. After the last fatality was safely buried, Rochesterians, rallying quickly from the affliction, determined to prepare for more effective municipal action in future emergencies.

Milbert's view of the main falls, 1818

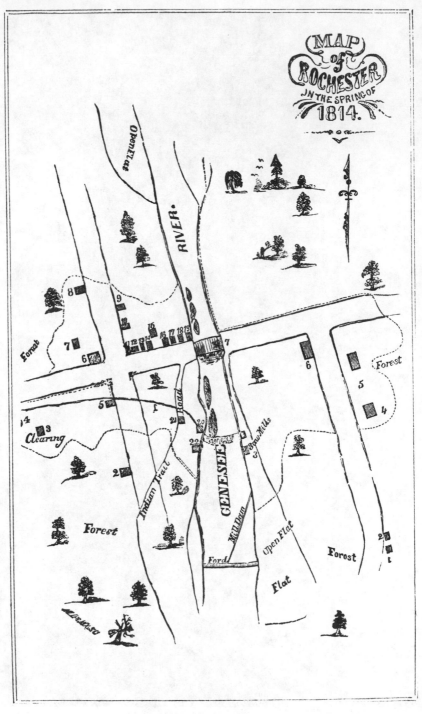

Map of Rochesterville, 1814

Hall's sketch of Court House Square, 1827

First aqueduct, from the northeast, 1825

Main falls, 1831

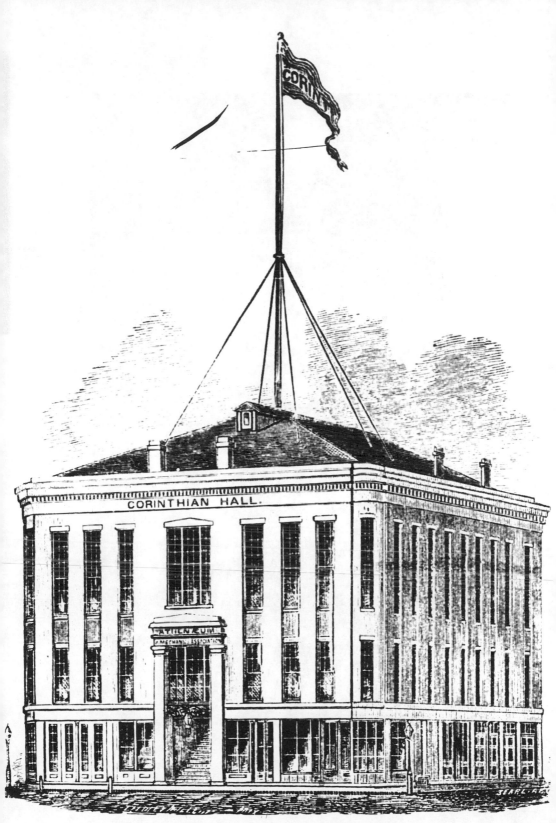

Athenaeum and Corinthian Hall, 1864

First New York Central station, 1865

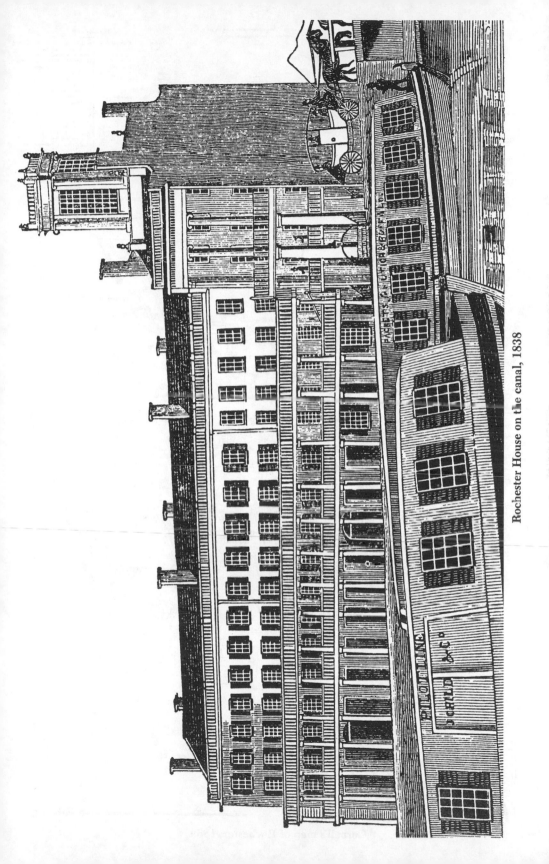

Rochester House on the canal, 1838

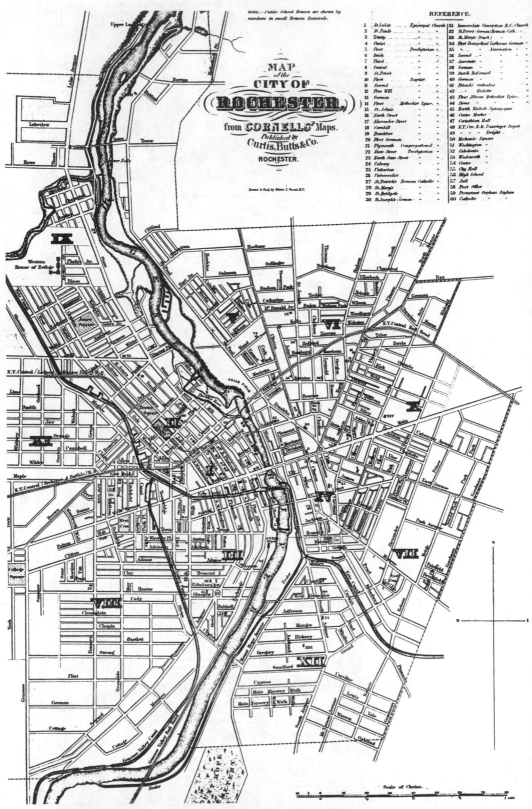

Cornell's map of Rochester, 1859

Rochester from the west, 1853

Interior of Reynolds Arcade, 1851

Jonathan Child: canal merchant,
first mayor of Rochester

Colonel Nathaniel Rochester:
founder of the village

Daniel Powers: banker,
owner of the Powers
block and art gallery

Hiram Sibley: founder and
president of Western Union

William Pitkin's mansion, ca. 1855

Victory Arch at Four Corners, 1865

Banquet scene in Corinthian Hall, 1851

Semicentennial parade, 1884

Flight of the *Hyperion*, October 19, 1869

Sailboat at Charlotte pier, ca. 1880

Powers block as headquarters for McKinley campaign, 1896

Main Street, view to the west, 1880s

Second aqueduct, from the east, 1885

Otis Arch, 1900

Sibley fire, February 26–27, 1904

3

The Flour City, 1834–1854

THE FLOUR CITY enjoyed several years of surging optimism before the nationwide depression of the late thirties brought renewed hardships. Its growth no longer matched the rate of the boom town's advance, but with a twofold population increase in two decades, from 12,252 in 1834 to 36,403 in 1855, Rochester acquired greater stability and achieved proportions sufficient to sustain the functions of a bustling city. Among the new leaders who undertook to perform its enlarged economic, civic, and cultural functions, Jonathan Child as the first mayor and Levi A. Ward as the fifteenth were transitional figures, and Henry O'Reilly and Chester Dewey were representative of the many vigorous newcomers who contributed to the life and growth of the Flour City.

PROSPERITY AND ADVERSITY

Rochester's economy was no longer assured by outside forces. Formerly a natural beneficiary of the Erie Canal and of the progressive settlement of the Genesee Valley, by the mid-thirties it had exhausted these advantages and faced the task of opening new trade arteries and developing new industries and services to maintain the regional leadership it had acquired. Having emerged for a time as the world's leading producer of flour, it could not have escaped the hardships brought by a nationwide depression, but in the course of its varied efforts to surmont these difficulties, Rochester developed a broader economic base and acqured a new, urban vitality.

Leaders of the Flour City were early concerned over the deficiencies of the Erie Canal. The seventeen-foot channel of the original aqueduct was too narrow for the passing of boats, and the right-angle turn at its eastern end proved especially difficult. When, in addition, the sandstone of the oft-admired aqueduct began to crumble under exposure to water and air, causing serious leaks that threatened the safety of the structure, cries for its replacement began to mount. The owners of the principal boat lines, led by Jonathan Child, dispatched Henry O'Reilly, editor of the *Advertiser*, to Albany with petitions for a new aqueduct. Some advocates of economy urged the construction of a wooden trough (as in several Mohawk aqueducts farther east) on the old piers, but after a long debate the state, prodded by a convention at Rochester, finally determined in 1837 to build a second and larger stone aqueduct a few yards south of the crumbling original in order to assure the continuation of its lucrative canal trade.

Rochester merchants were similarly involved in efforts to speed the flow of commerce up and down the Genesee Valley. Recent improvements at the mouth of the river and at the Carthage docks attracted numerous lake boats, which made 400 landings in 1836. Horsedrawn cars transported their cargoes to and from the central city. However, although steamboats were able to reach the Rochester port from the lake, repeated efforts to operate such boats on the upper river had been abandoned because of its many obstructions. Instead, a campaign for a new canal up the valley had developed, even though the cost seemed prohibitive. When, however, Pennsylvania completed its joint canal and railway between Philadelphia and Pittsburgh in 1835, New York merchants rallied to the support of the Genesee Valley legislators and in 1837 voted for the construction of a canal from Rochester to Olean to connect the trade of the Erie Canal with that of the Allegheny River and thus open a rival route to Pittsburgh.

While these improvements awaited state action, Rochester capital boldly pressed forward with the construction of a railroad to Batavia. Jonathan Child was among its backers, and Elisha Johnson became its construction engineer, completing the 32-mile road at a cost of $10,000 a mile by May 1837. Powered by small wood-burning engines brought by canal boat from the east, its two six-car daily trains expedited travel to and from the west and stimulated the hasty construction of a similar railroad from Rochester to Canandaigua, Geneva, and Auburn on the east. By the time of its completion to Auburn in November 1841,

other short roads linking the upstate towns and cities were in operation, and Rochester acquired connections by steam with Albany on
the east and Buffalo on the west.

Lightly constructed as replacements for the pioneer stage lines,
these early railroads offered no competition to the freight carriers on
the canal, and Rochester followed with interest the slow progress of
the Genesee Valley Canal up the valley and the painstaking construction of the second Genesee aqueduct. Officially opened in April 1842,
a few months before the final collapse of its predecessor, the second
aqueduct escaped the paralyzing effect of the Stop Law of that year,
which halted construction on the valley canal after it had reached
Mount Morris (and Dansville) and stalled work on the enlargement of
the Erie.

Limited as they were, these commercial improvements helped to
sustain a remarkable development in Rochester's productive enterprise
in the late thirties. Its flour mills increased to twenty-four, including
three that boasted nine and ten millstones each; with a total output of
500,000 bbl. in 1840, Rochester's output exceeded that of any other
city. However, Henry O'Reilly, Rochester's leading publicist, was quick
to declare that "the flouring business, although . . . most celebrated,
is by no means of such importance . . . as the other branches of manufacture." He proceeded to list twenty-five industrial categories, including cooper shops, lumber mills, boat yards, furniture and carriage
factories, tanneries, and a paper mill, as well as many handicraft shops,
such as those of the shoemakers, the tailors, and the printers, among
others. None of these was as impressive in size or equipment as the
principal flour mills, but because of their ingenious mechanisms, all
driven by waterpower, the mills required few workmen, and the newly
remolded carpet factory, employing forty hands, was in 1835 the
largest local employer.

Because of the close ties between the production and the sale of
handicraft products, the census of 1840 reported 2,916 persons working in manufacturing and trade as against 759 engaged in commerce.
Both activities relied heavily on credit, prompting the organization of
a third bank in 1836 and justifying the activity in Rochester of agents
of several New York investors, including John Jacob Astor. The New
York Life Insurance Company extended loans as well as policies to

Rochester men, and Levi A. Ward took the lead in organizing the Monroe County Mutual Insurance Company in 1836 to help meet the need for insurance against fire and other hazards.

The complexities of an urban economy prompted repeated efforts to establish cooperative agencies, but few survived for long. Jonathan Child's Board of Manufacturers of 1828 had succumbed within a year, and most associational efforts among business leaders in subsequent years focused on specific objectives, such as the enlargement of the canal, the building of a railroad, or the establishment of a bank, and expired upon their accomplishment. The constant stream of new-comers, many seeking jobs, prompted varied groups of craftsmen to band together to secure adequate working conditions. But when the journeymen carpenters and the journeymen masons joined in a demand for a ten-hour day in 1835, a hastily organized builders' association successfully resisted the move. A coopers' union endeavored a year later to safeguard the jobs of its members by inserting announcements in upstate village papers warning of the surplus already produced by barrel factories in Rochester. The onset of the depression quickly extinguished these societies.

The panic of 1837 and the depression that followed were national in scope, yet Rochester, despite its dependence on distant markets, escaped some of its early hardships. Rochester's banks proved sound, and although all joined in the general suspension of specie payments, they were among the first to resume normal business after many elsewhere had closed. Mounting flour prices in New York returned handsome profits to local millers and shippers and spurred efforts to organize three new banks at Rochester in the late thirties. Work on the second aqueduct and on the new canal up the valley supplied numerous jobs and created such a demand for dry goods that Edwin Scrantom, who had become a storekeeper the year before, felt encouraged in 1838 to tear down his modest shop and erect a four-story exchange. He gathered fifteen guests around his Thanksgiving table that November and subscribed for $1,000 of the new Commercial Bank's stock. Unfortunately, the January inventory caused alarm, but his creditors proved reluctant to foreclose. Faced with the necessity to carry on in a hazardous situation, the former editor borrowed from Shakespeare for a diary entry: "That either makes us or foredooms us quite."

Scrantom survived, but many others were less fortunate. The booming flour prices had produced an oversupply of wheat and a flood of shipments that tumbled flour from $11 to $4.50 a barrel in 1839 and imposed serious losses on several leading merchants and millers, including Jonathan Child. Before the crisis ended, both Hervey Ely and Benjamin Campbell had lost their Greek Revival mansions, and Abraham Schermerhorn, the banker who had extended generous credit to the builder of the Eagle Tavern, found himself its principal proprietor as a result of foreclosure action. One of the new banks closed its doors and a second avoided that fate by replacing its president and cashier with abler men. Business failures produced losses that exceeded $150,000 in 1841, and the legislative enactment of the Stop Law a few months later, which halted work on the Genesee Valley Canal, proved discouraging to Elisha Johnson, its construction engineer. Blocked in his effort to carry the canal over the highlands south of Mount Morris, Johnson left Rochester to undertake large projects farther west.

Although Rochester had escaped some of the hardships of the early phases of the depression, it experienced many later blows that retarded its recovery. The state's failure to enlarge the western portion of the canal prompted several boat yards to move east to Syracuse in order to supply large barges for the eastern section. The railroads, though successful as passenger carriers, were slow to develop freight facilities and carried only 4,500 tons out of Rochester in 1846, when local canal boats loaded 100,800 tons. Buffalo's shipments and tolls more than doubled those of the Flour City, and Oswego's trade was also bounding ahead. Although these gains represented transshipments from lake steamers to canal boats, rather than local manufactures as at Rochester, these interior ports and others farther west—Cleveland, Detroit, Milwaukee, and Chicago—enjoyed a more rapid growth throughout the forties. In addition to Elisha Johnson, Benjamin Campbell and Henry O'Reilly were among the many drawn away by brighter prospects elsewhere. Out of a sampling of 400 names in the 1838 *Directory*, only 166 reappeared in the 1844 list—a loss of 60 percent, which dropped to 55 percent for the next five-year period.

Fortunately for the city's future, the stream of newcomers more than filled all vacancies. A few were still arriving from New England, but Germany was now almost as well represented; Great Britain and her possessions (especially Ireland) accounted for more than one-fifth of Rochester's total population by 1845. According to the state census of that year, approximately one-third of the city's residents were foreign born, many of them, as well as many natives, recent new-comers. This continued mobility, although unsettling in political and cultural fields, added to the bustling character of the Flour City and strengthened its capacity to withstand the decline that set in during the early fifties in the grain trade by introducing new specialties.

Several of the new specialties were promoted by pioneer craftsmen whose enterprise and perseverance enabled them to win the status of industrialists. Lewis Selye, listed as a blacksmith in the 1827 *Directory*, began to manufacture fire engines and other machines within a dec-ade; Seth C. Jones, starting as a carpenter, became, successively, a boat builder, a construction contractor, and the builder and principal owner of a cotton factory. Jacob Gould and Jesse W. Hatch, who ar-rived as shoemakers in the early village days, became shoe merchant-manufacturers by the forties and thus provided employment for numer-ous shoemakers drawn to Rochester by the opportunity to supply footware to the steady stream of migrants through the city. By the midcentury Rochester had ten well-established shoe firms that em-ployed an average of fifty workers each and that produced approxi-mately 175,000 pairs of shoes annually.

Enterprising newcomers from abroad were establishing other in-dustrial specialties. Myer Greentree from Germany became the city's first merchant tailor and gave employment to a number of his fellow Jews in the manufacture of clothing. By the mid-century he had more than a dozen competitors whose cutting shops, clustered in the build-ings that had crept out along the north side of Main Street bridge, made that central location the focus for the employment of more than a thousand workers, most of whom took bundles of partially made gar-ments out for sewing and finishing at home. Two other newcomers, Patrick Barry from Ireland and George Ellwanger from Germany, be-came leaders in the forties in the development of still another specialty —the nursery business. Their discovery of the fact that the vast ex-panse of Lake Ontario's seldom-frozen waters, a few miles to the north, provided a temperature stabilizer that safeguarded young seedlings from the deep freezes that threatened growers in less-favored localities encouraged them to develop nurseries that soon became the principal suppliers of the demands of western settlers for fruit trees and bulbs.

While Ellwanger journeyed back and forth to Europe and imported fresh plantings, his partner, Barry, became the leader in organizing the Genesee valley horticultural fair and other agricultural fairs that drew thousands of valley farmers into the city on repeated occasions and promoted the development of fruit culture in lake-shore towns east and west of the Genesee. These developments foreshadowed the transformation of Rochester from a milling to a horticultural center in the years ahead.

ORGANIZING THE CITY

The continued growth and mobility of the city's population, although promoting economic expansion, also presented new challenges to its civic and institutional structure. Increasing size created additional pressure for a solution of the town's service needs, but other concerns commanded first attention and delayed attempts to provide some basic municipal functions. Private and voluntary associations endeavored to fill the gap in some instances, and Rochester developed the mixed public and voluntary community pattern that was to become characteristic of most American cities by the mid-nineteenth century.

Although the drive for a city charter had been sparked by the need for improved services, the Whigs who captured control of the first city council included several staunch temperance men who gave priority to that issue. Elected by narrow majorities, they chose Jonathan Child, one of their number, as first mayor and hastened to move against the liquor traffic. Unable to ban it entirely, they raised the license fees to forty and fifty dollars a year, which reduced the number of dealers from more than a hundred to a favored few and stirred such opposition that the Democrats won all but one seat in the next council and promptly enacted a more liberal license program. Mayor Child, whose term overlapped, on having found himself obliged to sign numerous licenses granted by the second council, tendered his resignation. To replace him the council chose Jacob Gould, a prominent Democrat and prosperous shoe merchant, who was more actively interested in the provision of municipal services.

Street and sewer improvements were the most urgent, and within a year the city had macadamized Buffalo Street and partially improved several others. Assessments on the adjacent property and loans based on the anticipated payments met these charges. However, as the cost of the flagstone sewer built under Buffalo Street exceeded $4,000, which raised the total expenditures on these improvements to almost $60,000, the issue of economy became dominant and enabled the Whigs to capture six seats in the third council. Other improvements launched by the second council had included the acquisition of a fifty-acre tract south of the city for Mount Hope Cemetery and the rebuilding of the public market after its destruction by fire. Abraham Schermerhorn, the banker chosen as the third mayor, soon resigned to take a state job; Thomas Kempshall, a prominent miller, was named by the Whigs early in 1837 to succeed him. The optimism of the millers in that first year of the depression encouraged Kempshall and Elisha Johnson, who became the fifth mayor a year later, to press ahead with additional street and sewer improvements and to undertake the construction of Andrews Street bridge above the main falls and the repair of flood damages on Main Street bridge.

These outlays compelled successive councils to boost their tax levies and to increase the bonded indebtedness. To supply jobs to the unemployed, the council issued over $50,000 in "shinplasters" to pay for labor on the public works and to be secured by the local assessments. Unfortunately, many of the latter obligations were hard to collect, and as the city's scrip declined in value, the opposition of many workmen mounted and turned the council against further outlays. Mayor Johnson, one of the city's ablest and most enterprising men, instituted the practice of issuing licenses to garbage collectors. He also prepared a plan for a public waterworks, but the council refused to authorize its construction. That reversal, followed shortly by the state's action stopping work on the Genesee Valley Canal, prompted Johnson, as mentioned previously, to leave for Tenessee in 1839. Thomas H. Rochester, the sixth child of the town's proprietor, became the city's sixth mayor, but the deepening gloom of the depression darkened his term and hastened the withdrawal of the Rochester clan from local politics.

Samuel G. Andrews, the east-side miller who became the next mayor was the last to be named by his fellow councilmen. A state law in 1840 called for the popular election of mayors and other municipal officials. Later amendments to the charter increased the mayor's status by giving him veto and appointive powers, but the gradual provision for 129 separate elective positions limited his authority as well as that of the council. Because of their absorption in private affairs, only two of the next fifteen mayors stood for reelection after the completion of their first one-year term, and only one secured reelection. Only two aldermen served three two-year terms on the council, where a similar turnover occurred, although seven later won election as mayor. Party control shifted back and forth every two years or so, which served as a further obstacle to long-term improvements. A few able men managed, however, to make important contributions, notably Joseph Field who, as Rochester's fourteenth mayor, drew the various drainage sewers into an integrated system and recorded their routes, and Levi A. Ward his successor as mayor who reorganized the night watch, reappointed the Board of Health, and made health board members useful agents in the city's effort to meet the crisis presented by a second cholera epidemic in 1849.

The council devoted considerable attention in the forties to the development of the volunteer fire companies. Lewis Selye, who served three terms as alderman, built fire engines at his foundry for each of the ten companies organized in this decade, but their service was hampered by the lack of a water system. The city paid dearly in annual fire losses for the economy its inaction in this field assured, and owners of several large buildings, such as the Reynolds Arcade, installed private pumps to be ready to battle the flames in case a fire should occur. A prospect of lucrative fees prompted the council to expend $10,000 for the acquisition of a hay market equipped with scales where, in March 1848, the weigher reported processing 349 loads of this essential commodity.

Because of the popular opposition to taxes, the officials left many costly services to private groups. Efforts by successive men to form a water company faltered because of uncertainty over its ability to meet expenses, but in 1848 when the legislature passed a law authorizing the creation of private companies to supply gas for street lights and other purposes, the prospects for profit seemed good. "Troy is about to emerge from darkness," reported the *Republican* on March 28, which urged Rochester to do the same. Mayor Field took the lead by calling a number of business leaders together to launch the new venture. Three former mayors and Levi A. Ward, who would succeed

Field in that office, joined in the application for a charter to establish the Rochester Gas Light Company. Eager to press ahead, the company engaged the aid of a Philadelphia contractor experienced in the construction of the gasworks there and proceeded to erect its retort house on Mumford Street and to lay its pipes through several of the central streets. On December 6, 1848, the company began to manufacture gas for distribution to both private and public users, and on December 13 the first lights were turned on in the twelve open-flame gas lamps installed at downtown street corners. Five years later the number of gas lamps had increased to two hundred in the central district, where many private establishments were likewise lit by gas, and oil lamps served the remainder of the city until the mains could be extended.

Rochester continued to rely on the county for several services. The sheriff and his deputies were chiefly responsible for maintaining law and order and for keeping the jail. Convictions for criminal offenses in the county, which occurred chiefly within the city, increased to one hundred annually by mid-century. At the start the most frequent charge was assault and battery, but keeping a bawdy house and selling liquor without a license accounted for an increasing number of convictions. A grand jury in 1839 recommended the provision of special cells in the jail for the separate confinement of women, most of them arrested as inmates of disorderly houses. A decade passed before a group of charitable citizens opened the Home for the Friendless to provide a more humanitarian approach to the problem.

A more serious problem was that of the numerous children left stranded by families migrating through Rochester or by the death of their parents. In 1837 a group of charitable women took the initiative in organizing the Rochester Orphan Society. Its first modest quarters soon proved inadequate, and after outgrowing a larger house, the society undertook to build an asylum on Hubble Park, where it opened its doors in 1844. The Catholics had opened a similar asylum near St. Patrick's Church two years before. Despite these efforts many children found lodgment in jail, and in 1849 the state, in response to the new humanitarian spirit, established the Western House of Refuge, the fourth institution of its kind in the country, at Rochester to provide correctional care for delinquent youngsters.

Rochester made its most creditable civic advances during this period in education. The county gradually surrendered full control to the city, which, spurred by emerging democratic forces, achieved real progress in the development of a public school system during the forties. Several private academies served the need for advanced studies, and some of the abler teachers, backed by interested citizens, helped to supply facilities for the edification of adults who wished to continue their education.

Yet these achievements must have appeared far in the future to the small group of citizens who advocated educational improvements in the thirties. Dissatisfaction with the old district school system had been one of the arguments for a city charter, and that document gave a measure of control over the districts to the common council. That body, preoccupied with other matters, had little time for its educational duties, though it named five school inspectors to oversee the districts. The trustees of the separate districts held the administrative responsibility, and the county supervisors, dominated by representatives from the towns, retained control over the funds for school maintenance. However, the council now had authority to grant a district's request for an extra tax for building purposes.

In 1835 old Gates District No. 2, renamed Rochester No. 1 and responsible for the most densely populated area of the city, voted to undertake the construction of a new stone schoolhouse at a cost of $3,000 on its old site facing the court house. Within a year the two-story structure, with four spacious rooms, was ready for use, but a rapid increase in the number of pupils soon crowded its facilities, which prompted the district trustees to request an additional assessment of $2,500 to build an annex in the rear to house separate classes for girls. When the alderman rejected this application and tabled the pleas of other districts for permission to raise funds for building improvements, a movement for the creation of an independent board of education developed. A succession of public meetings at the court house late in 1838, with the public-spirited physician Dr. Maltby Strong presiding, disclosed the mounting sentiment for free schools under the administration of a superintendent to be appointed by an independent board of education. To press for the adoption of these measures, the public meeting authorized the creation of a citizens committee comprised of three representatives from each ward. Among others active in the movement were Dr. Strong, Levi A. Ward, Selah Mathews, and Henry O'Reilly, who dispatched earnest pleas to the state legislature. Finally, in May 1841 that body passed an amendment to the Rochester charter that provided for an elective board of education to control a system of free, tax-supported, common schools.

The first board, which included men such as O'Reilly and Ward active in the campaign, promptly chose the latter as its president and endeavored to integrate the work of the various districts. It soon organized two new districts in populous sections and undertook the construction of nine new school buildings during the first three years. By 1844 Rochester had fifteen district schools enrolling over 4,200 pupils in classes directed by forty-four teachers. Isaac Mack, the first superintendent, formerly a custom miller, recommended the establishment of a high school to serve "the talented and ambitious youth of our city," but mounting demands for economy forced the postponement of such action for another decade.

Most of the private school principals were relieved to hear of this decision. The ill-fated High School of 1827 had severed its ties with the east-side districts a decade later and under the direction of its new principal, Dr. Chester Dewey, had reorganized as the Rochester Collegiate Institute. One of the country's pioneers in physical and natural science, Dr. Dewey assumed the lead in providing instruction in geology and biology as well as in chemistry, which was his specialty. The enthusiasm displayed by the 150 lads who annually paid from $20 to $25 for enrollment in his classes prompted the heads of several seminaries for girls to introduce more serious studies. Both the Rochester Female Academy on Fitzhugh Street and the Seward Seminary on Alexander Street offered instruction in botany and physics as well as in moral philosophy, history, and rhetoric during the forties.

The free school program of the forties, which eliminated the fees previously charged by the district schools, considerably reduced the field of activity of charity and select schools alike. Not only did the improved common schools with enlarged enrollments find it possible to classify their pupils into departments, but in many cases they separated the girls from the boys, thus depriving the small select schools for girls of their chief appeal. By mid-decade the thirty-three private schools of 1840 were reduced to sixteen, and their 1,226 pupils had dwindled to 622, most of them attending the seminaries that gave advanced instruction. The state census of 1845 gave Monroe County a high rating in school attendance and credited it with thirty young men enrolled in distant colleges. Nine older counties in the East had more sons in college, but Monroe's delegation almost equalled the known graduates resident in Rochester.

The city's growth and increasing heterogeneity prompted the establishment of new types of private schools. Partly because of the language difficulty, St. Joseph's Catholic Church opened a school for the children of its German-speaking members in 1836, and the German Lutheran and Second German Catholic churches provided schools shortly after their establishment. The Irish at St. Patrick's followed suit in 1839, and the Sisters of Charity who assumed charge of the Catholic Orphan Asylum in 1845 offered advanced instruction as well, but the attempt three years later to establish a College of the Sacred Heart at Rochester met failure. Several special schools appeared that offered part-time courses to meet the needs of the more complex urban society. "Writing professors" frequently advertised a series of lessons guaranteed to provide young ladies and gentlemen with an elegant handwriting or a knowledge of bookkeeping. Music and dancing instructors engaged rooms at the Mansion House and other hotels where they taught aspiring youths the rhythms of the waltz and the more graceful Spanish dances to prepare them for appearance at the popular gatherings in their ballrooms.

The intellectual needs of adult citizens likewise received the attention of varied societies. When the activities of the Athenaeum and the Young Men's Society of the early thirties declined as their leaders advanced in years or became absorbed in other matters, young William A. Reynolds took the lead in 1836 in the establishment of the Mechanics Association, which soon acquired rooms on an upper story of his father's Arcade for its debates and a library where some 1,500 books were gradually accumulated. A startling report a year later of the community's first murder prompted editor O'Reilly to deplore the lack of an institution that would supply "intellectual and moral attractions to counteract the vicious allurements to which the young men of the city are largely exposed." Determined to remedy the situation, O'Reilly established the Young Men's Association to maintain a library and conduct a program of public lectures for adults. It was an opportune development, because the lyceum movement was just then spreading into the West, and the enterprising editor was able to schedule lectures by traveling Britishers and other Europeans, as well as by a number of literary figures from New England such as Elihu Burritt, the learned blacksmith, who made repeated visits. The moribund Athenaeum soon merged with the new association and quickly enrolled 500 dues-paying members; their consolidated libraries totaled nearly 4,000 books, which were housed in a reading room decorated by busts of such notables as Franklin, Washington, Cicero, and Demosthenes and ambitiously designated the City Library. When O'Reilly, its first president, removed to Albany in 1842, Dr. Chester Dewey assumed the tasks of arranging the lecture programs and supervising the care of the library. In the late forties a further consolidation with the Mechanics Association brought the election of William A. Reynolds as president, with plans to hold its annual lecture series in the elegant new Corinthian Hall, which he would open at the rear of the Arcade in 1849. The Athenaeum and Mechanics Association, as it was now named, looked forward to a prosperous era during which the proceeds from its popularly attended lectures maintained an increasingly serviceable library located in newly refurbished quarters in the central Arcade.

SOCIAL AND CULTURAL EXPRESSION

In many respects the city's social and cultural developments proved more gratifying than its attainments in civic and economic fields. The increased urban heterogeneity appeared most dramatically in the diversity of its religious organizations, which engendered and gave dynamic force to numerous reform movements that responded in varying ways to the new urban environment. Rival group and institutional aspirations created a tension that found vent in political, journalistic, and popular struggles and that contributed a dramatic intensity to the community's urban growth. Among the host of newcomers were many with professional training and talents who filled the places of some of the aging or departing pioneers, which enabled Rochester to share in the cultural flowering of the East. Although many older settlers moved on, others remained, and the late forties saw them basking for the first time in reminiscences of the town they had helped to build.

The fifteen churches of the mid-thirties, which represented the major group activity in the newly established city, increased to thirty-five by 1850, but more important than their number and membership was the wide choice they offered to interested residents. Some retained the customs of village churches—Sabbath morning and evening sermons, mid-week prayer meetings and Bible classes, and frequent pastoral visitations. Others, quickened by the revivals of the early thirties, displayed an evangelistic spirit that found expression in testimonial meetings and zealous drives for temperance and other moral reforms. Still others supplied the ritualistic services cherished by particular denominational or ethnic groups. The city's continued growth brought such an influx of newcomers that representatives of almost every sect and persuasion known to America could find fellow believers in Rochester. But so intense were some of their doctrinal positions and defenses that the freedom of choice often acquired a traumatic character quite unknown in the more homogeneous village or rural setting from which most had sprung.

These differences created sharp divisions within some of the principal denominations, even within several churches, and deepened the fissures between them. Thus, the Presbyterians, whose Third and Free churches had experienced a greater impact from the Finney revival than either First or Brick churches, were torn between the rival influences of Lane Seminary and Oberlin College after their split in the mid-thirties. After a few years, however, when both Third and Brick churches acquired new pastors, their positions were reversed; George Beecher at Brick expounded a moderate version of "entire sanctification," and Albert D. Hall turned Third, despite some internal strife, towards a more orthodox Calvinism. A few dissidents in First Church withdrew to found Bethel Chapel and then withdrew again to found First Congregational, which endorsed not only the evangelism but also the antislavery sentiments emanating from Oberlin. The Baptists escaped doctrinal controversy, but whereas First Baptist emphasized its Sabbath school and other educational programs, Second Baptist espoused reforms and was the first church in Rochester to admit Negroes to the main body of its pews.

The Episcopal churches, now three in number, struggled to distinguish their rituals from those of the more numerous Methodists and Catholics. St. Luke's Episcopal, surviving the internal tensions of the anti-Masonic controversy, maintained its traditional low-church forms, but St. Paul's, reorganized after a fire and a scandal at Grace Church, introduced some high-church customs and on one occasion startled one of its original founders who mistook the sound of passing sleigh bells for that of an altar bell hidden under the clergyman's robe. The Methodists, warmly responsive to frequent evangelistic visitations, escaped most doctrinal disputes and shunned ritual, but they made no move to draw the newly founded African Methodist Episcopal Zion church into their fellowship. The Catholics, whose number was increasing most rapidly of all, also experienced ethnic divisions but managed to diffuse them by organizing separate Irish and German parishes. Any internal doctrinal or ritualistic differences were submerged in face of the mounting hostility all encountered in the predominantly Protestant environment.

Several small denominational groups found a place in the growing city, and four additional sects arrived, further extending its diversity. The Quakers split into two small societies of Orthodox and Hicksite Friends, and the latter, with the still more dissident Unitarians, became leading advocates of the antislavery cause. The Universalists finally mustered sufficient support to erect a church in 1847, and the newly arriving German Jews organized B'rith Kodesh Synagogue a year later. German Protestants were becoming numerous enough to prompt the withdrawal of some members of their original Zion Lutheran church of 1832 to found Trinity Evangelical Lutheran in 1847; a group of German Methodists also opened a chapel a year later. Two free-thought weeklies quickly expired in the late thirties, and all organized groups of agnostics dissolved, but two challenging new doctrines made their appearance. The predictions of the followers of William Miller concerning the Second Coming of Christ, expected in March 1844, created a flurry of excitement in many homes and attracted a throng of converts to Talman Hall on the twenty-first who were prepared to greet their Lord with song and prayer. Enough survived that disillusioning experience to form a permanent group of Second Adventists. Fewer Rochesterians took the Fox sisters seriously when, in 1848, they revealed the strange knockings they had first heard in nearby Hydesville and claimed an ability to communicate with the spirits of departed friends and other deceased persons. But as the years passed a number of local residents and increasing numbers elsewhere became devoted Spiritualists, respecting the Fox sisters for their pioneer revelations.

The tensions created by the diversity in fundamental religious beliefs on issues that could not be resolved found vent in numerous reform efforts that promised a practical application of the challenged doctrines. In addition to the Sabbath schools and the temperance and Bible societies of the earlier village days, Rochester in the mid-thirties supported the Moral Reform Society and the Sabbath Observance movement. Concern over the plight of the slaves received more active expression in the late thirties as members of varied religious groups took up the cause and transformed the small Rochester Anti-Slavery Society into the Monroe County Anti-Slavery Society. Soon the national split between the advocates of moral or political approaches to the question divided and weakened the movement locally, until the arrival of Frederick Douglass to establish the *North Star* at Rochester in 1847 supplied a new and persuasive leadership. Douglass, by embodying rather than defining the issue, transformed it from a doctrinal to a humanitarian cause and made Rochester a focal center of the movement.

An increasing participation of zealous women in these reform efforts gave birth to still another agitation, that for women's rights. When the formation of the Ladies Temperance Society in 1841 and of the Young Ladies Temperance Hope Society and the Female Moral Reform Society in the next two years brought rebuffs from many who declared that a woman's place was in the home, a feeling of resentment spread and involved many not concerned by the other issues. Indignation mounted as ladies who gave support to temperance, anti-slavery, and other moral reforms were made the butt of editorial humor and welcomed to be seen but not heard at numerous conventions of reformers. A few weeks after the first Woman's Rights Convention met at Seneca Falls in July 1848, a second convened at the Unitarian church in Rochester. The theoretical arguments expressed in the former village setting acquired a more substantive character in the urban environment of Rochester where one lady, Mrs. Abigail Bush, was ready and able to serve as chairman, relegating even friendly males almost completely to the sidelines, and where another woman, Mrs. Roberts, was moved to voice the grievances of seamstresses against the prevailing working conditions that greedy men had applied in their shops and factories. One editor derived amusement from the resolution that the word "obey" should be stricken from the marriage vow, but the reaction to the formation two weeks later of the Woman's Protection Union among the seamstresses was more sober.

To maintain their position in the expanding city, the leading churches eagerly sought the services of learned clergymen. Two early pastors of First Church later became college presidents, and both Dr. Henry J. Whitehouse of St. Luke's and Father Bernard O'Reilly of St. Patrick's became bishops. Most of their successors were D.D.'s, and the emphasis on education promoted each of the five leading denominations to plan the establishment of a local college. When the Presbyterians, who endeavored to consolidate these efforts behind their move in 1845 to establish a University of Western New York, faltered chiefly because of dissension within their own ranks, the Baptists seized the lead. Ably backed by Dr. Chester Dewey, the head of the Collegiate Institute who had received three D.D.'s during the decade, the Baptists successfully established the University of Rochester and the Rochester Theological Seminary. A move to transfer Madison College from Hamilton, New York, to Rochester failed, but five of its professors and three of its trustees moved to the Flour City where, with Dr. Dewey as professor of Science and E. Peshine Smith, Rochester's first Harvard graduate, as professor of political economy, they launched both institutions in the old United States Hotel on Buffalo Street in November 1850.

Formal organizations contributed less to the emerging city than did its informal social and cultural developments. A marked improvement in domestic comforts occurred as the city's more moderate growth permitted builders to catch up with the demand for houses. Modest frame cottages were most numerous, but scores of substantial dwellings, including a number of mansions, made their appearance. Large or small, most houses were overflowing with residents as large families predominated, held in check only by the high mortality rate, particularly among infants. Numerous infectious and contagious diseases wrought havoc in the crowded neighborhoods in 1844 and provided employment for thirty-one practicing physicians and fourteen dentists. Several of these doctors developed specialties and acquired reputations, and all enjoyed the stimulus of working in an expanding profession. At the same time, residents who occasionally saw "nine funerals in one day," as one editor recorded, developed a sentimental interest in Mount Hope Cemetery, which became a gathering place for subdued family outings on warm Sunday afternoons.

Warm Saturday evenings brought thousands of citizens down town to stroll in endless streams up and down Main and Buffalo, State and Exchange streets. Some paused to pay a visit to the museum on Exchange Street or to borrow a book from the Athenaeum library. Many patronized the bars in nearby taverns or joined the throng of dancers in their ballrooms. Sidewalk strollers dwindled in number in the late fall and winter when citizens seeking relaxation patronized an increasing variety of indoor amusements. The midwinter balls of the several local militia units and of the more numerous volunteer fire companies provided festive occasions open to all, whereas the more exclusive mansion parties were limited to invited guests, who arrived in carriages or sleighs. Visiting theatrical troups had practically disappeared during the hard times of the late thirties, but in 1840 Edwin Dean, a theater manager in Buffalo, opened a theater in Rochester, too, and presented alternating weekly performances for several seasons. By mid-century Rochester had two theaters to accommodate thespian and other entertainers. Occasional band concerts and other musical programs attracted numerous listeners to the City Gardens, the Court House Square, or to one or another of the leading churches. When Mason and Webb of the Boston Academy of Music chose Rochester in 1843 for their first two-week course in vocal music held outside Boston, local music lovers flocked to First Church for the first of a dozen annual music festivals that proved a boon to the community as well as to several church choirs.

Traveling circuses paid over forty visits to Rochester during these years and made it the hub for one-day stops at regional villages. Local militia units and fraternal and ethnic societies made occasional excursions to nearby picnic grounds and staged events that made Rochester the focal point for their fellows in neighboring towns. The opening of Turner Hall by the German Society and of Corinthian Hall behind the Arcade at mid-century supplied Rochester, already equipped with two theaters and three hotels that had spacious ballrooms, with ample facilities for its varied social and cultural activities. Despite the lack of a suitable gallery, visiting artists readily found opportunities to exhibit their paintings in hotel lobbies or in the session room at the court house. Several of the daguerreotypists who had had studios in Rochester since the early forties developed impressive galleries such as Kelsey's Emporium of Art in the Gaffney block.

The most articulate agents of the new urban society were the editors and publishers of its newspapers. The two dailies, each with its weekly edition, and five other weeklies of the late thirties grew into four dailies and ten weeklies and monthlies during the next decade; although the four-page edition persisted, they managed together to cover a widening range of topics. Their advertisements, though still limited in large part to matter-of-fact announcements in small print, filled most columns and kept readers informed of all new business developments. National politics absorbed the attention of the political journals, but temperance and other moral reforms, agricultural interests, working conditions, and the slavery question each had its specialized journal. The opening of telegraph connections with Albany in June 1846 brought the news of the world more quickly to Rochester; it enabled each of its dailies to feature "by telegraph" columns and prompted an increased use of commercial reports from the metropolis.

Most of the editors and publishers were active in more than one journal, and several contributed to the increasing stream of articles and books that issued from local presses. None was more productive than O'Reilly, whose lively and informative article on Rochester in 1835 attracted so much interest that he wrote a second a year later and then proceeded to write and assemble material for the 480-page *Sketches of Rochester, with Incidental Notices of Western New York,* which was partly printed in Rochester but finally published in 1838 by Harper Brothers in New York, where facilities for the production of its numerous engravings proved more adequate. O'Reilly's success not only prompted an outburst of reminiscences that resulted a decade later in the formation of the Pioneers Society, but also stimulated other historical contributions, notably those of Orsamus Turner and Lewis H. Morgan, respectively, on the pioneers and Indian antecedents of the region.

THE CITY AT FULL TIDE

The early 1850s brought to fruition many of Rochester's early aspirations and opened new vistas. The measure of achievement experienced in several fields matched the fullness of years enjoyed by the scattered pioneers who remained. Fresh ventures interested their sons, some already in the prime of life, who shared with able newcomers the direction of the city's economic, civic, and cultural affairs, while vigorous younger men were rising to positions of influence. The influx of newcomers from abroad who brought new cultural patterns foreshadowed the transformation of the Yankee city into a more cosmopolitan community.

The water power of the Genesee turned more wheels than ever before, and the volume of canal trade reached a new peak, yet more rapid developments occurred in other directions. An increased reliance on steam, the rise of corporate capital and its stride toward monopoly, the efforts of labor to organize, and the expanding national markets were to become the long-range economic features of Rochester's midyears, but their appearance in the fifties marked its transition from a regional milling and commercial center to a more diversified industrial city.

Despite some progress in long-desired transport improvements, Rochester barely held its own as a commercial center. Slow work on the enlargement of the western section of the Erie Canal and the halting of the extension of the valley canal gave advantage to Oswego, which, with other lake ports, quickly moved ahead of Rochester. Even the opening of the Rochester and Lake Ontario Railroad in 1853, which moved the city's port from Carthage to Charlotte at the mouth of the river, failed to bring the expected revival, for Rochester had few goods for outward shipment on that route. The construction of the Rochester and Niagara Falls Railroad to Lockport and of the Rochester and Genesee Valley Railroad to Avon, also in 1853, gave promise of future trade links but, like the Rochester and Syracuse completed the next year, brought little immediate benefit. The consolidation of the nine lines running between Buffalo and Albany, achieved with the formation of the New York Central in 1853, speeded traffic to and through Rochester and also promised great benefits in the years ahead, but it brought few immediate gains.

Rochester's prospects depended on the development of new industries, and here also several fresh starts appeared. A number of metalworking shops clustered in the Novelty Works on the western edge of the business district, with convenient access to both the canal and the railroad, but their products as well as those of a thermometer shop, a paper mill, a refrigerator factory, two stove foundries, and an agricultural implements plant served chiefly the local and regional markets.

A major problem confronting these industries was the short supply of coal. Jonathan Child had imported some soft coal by canal boat from the east in the forties, but it was not until the opening of a new rail route to the south that larger supplies of anthracite became available in the late fifties. Neither the shoe nor the clothing industries required steam power, but enterprising merchant-manufacturers in both fields were experimenting with the use of sewing machines and cutting dies that forecast future industrial achievements. Their chief need, like that of the nurserymen, was to expand their market; the nurserymen were already exploring the way by sending out traveling agents to seek orders for young seedlings and bulbs, and they were so successful that Ellwanger and Barry had to treble their acreage and thus became by 1855 the largest nursery firm in the country.

The instrument that did most to speed the development and integration of national markets was the telegraph, and Rochester enterprise contributed significantly to its organization. When Henry O'Reilly, disappointed in a newspaper venture in Albany, acquired the option to develop telegraph lines between various cities, he returned to Rochester to find backers for several independent lines in the interior. Unfortunately, none of the separate lines paid its expenses, and efforts to consolidate them failed until Hiram Sibley, Samuel L. Selden, Henry A. Ward, and other impatient Rochester stockholders in the O'Reilly-Morse lines organized a new company to build a rival system using the new House patent. The new venture, which soon established an alliance with Ezra Cornell and other telegraph men, pressed a drive under the new name of Western Union for a unified system throughout the interior that was a harbinger of national economic integration.

Although a third attempt to establish a board of trade collapsed after a brief trial in the mid-fifties, Rochester's banks, which had increased to eleven by this date, enjoyed great prosperity. The general incorporation law of 1848 had made possible the formation of limited liability stock companies, sixteen of which appeared in Rochester during the next five years. When Freeman Clarke, who had moved to Rochester in 1845 from nearby Albion and rapidly emerged as a most astute financier, moved from his north-side villa into the classical mansion of Jonathan Child, a few years after Child departed for Buffalo, Clarke brought renewed confidence to the city's business community and a new gaiety to the social life of the Third Ward.

The increasing complexity of its urban environment appeared in the urgent character of Rochester's civic problems. Mounting pressure for local improvements finally broke the economy restraints of the late forties; the tax levy almost doubled, and the city's bonded indebtedness trebled. Yet several important public works were neglected, and institutional efforts to care for the disadvantaged proved insufficient. The limited civic facilities were dramatically revealed during a renewed cholera epidemic in 1852 and again the next year by waves of destructive fires and outbreaks of juvenile delinquency. The task of assimilating thousands of immigrants, many in desperate circumstances, presented problems that, as in many communities, proved too complex for quick solution, with the result that the Flour City's civic achievements lagged far behind those in the economic and cultural fields.

To secure accommodations for its officials, the city persuaded the county to add a third story to the enlarged court house, under construction in 1850, and paid more than half its total cost. A new city charter adopted that year provided for the election of seven assessors who undertook a complete reassessment of all properties and, in 1851, more than doubled the total tax base to ten million dollars. Attorney Nicholas E. Paine, elected mayor that spring, took advantage of the city's improved fiscal situation to press for the paving of the principal downtown streets with Medina sandstone blocks, introduced on Broadway in New York two years before, and ordered an extension of its drainage sewers and an increase in the number of its gas lamps. A renewed attempt to launch a waterworks company collapsed when the projected cost of $575,000 to tap Hemlock Lake, thirty miles south of the city, was announced. Several spectacular fires, one gutting the Blossom Hotel in 1854, with an estimated loss of $155,000, revealed the inadequacy of the volunteer companies, which, despite their inefficiency and poor discipline, repeatedly pumped the city's underground reservoirs dry without checking the flames. The city could do little but increase the number of the night watch to twenty men that year, with the hope of deterring crime and detecting fires more quickly.

It was the cholera epidemic of 1852 that brought Rochester's civic shortcomings into the limelight. Previous experience with the dread plague prompted the authorities to spring into action with the first rumor of its approach, and before the first case was reported in June, most of the principal streets had been cleaned and much refuse had been removed from the canal basins. Many open drains on back streets remained clogged, however, and numerous cesspools and cellars were green with slime, as a member of the board of health reported after visiting the two adjoining rookeries where the first six deaths occurred. The same open sewer ran through the cellars of both structures, one of which, an old factory block, housed fifty-six persons, including twenty-five children. As the plague spread, causing over 400 fatalities during the next four months, the conscientious board members had occasion to visit numerous wretched hovels where in some cases nearly half the occupants died. In desperation the board requisitioned a building on High Street for a pest house and managed to close some of the most unsanitary blocks. In its final report, after the epidemic had subsided, the board declared that the conditions it had found furnished "a potent argument in favor of a law requiring all persons proposing to erect buildings to submit their plans to some competent tribunal for its approval with special reference to light and ventilation."

Several decades would slip by before that advice was heeded; meanwhile the ravages of cholera and other misfortunes had inundated Rochester with gangs of homeless boys and girls who roamed the streets and found shelter in vacant lofts and other obscure places. The city opened the House for Idle and Truant Children in an old tavern to accommodate some of these waifs and committed others to the Western House of Refuge. It pressed a campaign, now backed by state law, to enroll all children in public or private schools for at least part of the year. To accommodate the mounting registration, the city expended $30,000 on new buildings, which increased their number to sixteen, and appointed male teachers or principals to eight that were equipped to instruct the older children. The destruction of the old Collegiate Institute by fire in 1851 had deprived the city even of that semiprivate high school, but pleas for its replacement were deferred for another six years. The board did, however, open an evening school, which quickly enrolled 400 students, mostly youthful immigrants eager to learn English. The University of Rochester established a grammar school to supply improved instruction to seventy or more older boys who aspired for admission to college.

Indeed in the cultural field, despite deficiencies elsewhere, Rochester could boast of numerous accomplishments. The religious diversity that had appeared so unsettling at the start became an attribute of the city's urban fullness. Anti-Catholicism persisted in some quarters; an outburst of nativism occurred, but it failed to reach the stage of violence experienced in many places and soon subsided. Disturbing social issues provided a new sense of purpose to many and kindled a new interest in community well-being. Social diversions acquired a new respectability, and skill in as well as an appreciation of the arts became a mark of distinction, which helped win acceptance for many of foreign or other minority origin and thus to provide a new conception of their identity.

The establishment of a dozen new churches brought the total to fifty by 1855, and this number now appeared an accomplishment rather than a divisive hazard. Despite some friction arising from the formation of a new Old School Synod in the Rochester area, the Presbyterians retained a position of leadership among the Protestants, although the Baptists, strengthened by their association with the university and the theological seminary, enjoyed a new prestige. The dissident sects seemed in this setting an interesting novelty rather than a threat, and Professor John H. Raymond, D.D., of the seminary could discuss his disagreement with the transcendentalism of the Reverend William H. Channing of the Unitarian church without friction over the dining table for an entire season. Simon Tusca, son of the Rabbi at B'rith Kodesh, won a scholarship at the university, where he earned the respect of his professors and wrote a book explaining the Hebrew ritual to strangers. The Second Adventists, with their predictions concerning the end of the world somewhat muted, assumed a more normal denominational role. Even the Spiritualists began to appear mildly eccentric rather than diabolic, as their messages from the spirit world failed to acquire significance.

Only the Catholics, whose growth exceeded even that of the Methodists and who now outnumbered the Presbyterians as well, continued to appear a challenge. When the Reverend Henry W. Lee attacked papal aggression from his pulpit in St. Luke's, Bishop Tinon's reply at St. Patrick's received equal coverage in the *Advertiser*, and when the Monroe County Bible Society pressed a campaign to distribute Bibles to all Catholic families, at least two-thirds refused to accept them. When a conservative faction of the Whig party, seeking to sidestep the antislavery issue, launched a drive to exclude all foreigners from political activity, the American, or Know-Nothing, party they organized captured a slight plurality in three-way contests in local and state elections in 1854 and 1855, but took no distinctive action and soon passed from the scene. Mayor Maltby Strong supplied a police guard to accompany the Angel Gabriel, an itinerant anti-Catholic evangelist, on the occasion of his visit to Rochester, but as a graduate of Yale and now advanced in years, Strong sought to avoid controversy. The much younger and more assertive Charles J. Hayden, who displaced Strong, delivered a bitter attack on Catholics and other immigrants at his inaugural, but he stirred such resentment that little was accomplished in his term.

In contrast, the antislavery issue, the question of women's rights, and the temperance cause were all acquiring new force. Frederick Douglass and his paper were bringing national distinction to Rochester as a focal center of the antislavery movement, and his dramatic oratory attracted capacity crowds to Corinthian Hall for occasional addresses on the subject. His editorial assistant, Julia Griffiths, played a leading role in the Ladies Anti-Slavery Society, which helped to draw Susan B. Anthony to the cause and to awaken her to the struggle for women's rights. Miss Anthony's first cause, however, was temperance, and she accepted the task of organizing the Woman's State Temperance Society at Rochester in 1852. When with other earnest ladies in these societies she met rebuffs at the national conventions of the reformers, Miss Anthony took the lead in calling a series of woman's rights conventions at Syracuse, Rochester, and elsewhere in 1853 and won the local support of Douglass, Channing, and the Posts, the new leaders of these reforms in Rochester.

These and other issues added a new vitality to the lecture program maintained each winter by the Athenaeum and Mechanics Association in Corinthian Hall. Some visiting lecturers, such as Emerson, dealt with lofty topics, notably "Culture" on one occasion; Professor Louis Agassiz focused on the natural sciences; Wendell Phillips and Theodore Parker, among others, tackled contemporary problems. Together these lectures attracted a sufficient following to pay the fees of these famous speakers ("fame," as Emerson is said to have put it, "means fifty and my expenses") and to net a surplus of several hundred dollars each year to maintain the library, which had grown to 8,000 books and attracted adult readers to its rooms on the second floor of the Arcade.

Under the management of William A. Reynolds, who shared responsibility for the Athenaeum programs and library with Professor

Dewey, Corinthian Hall became the focal center of many community activities. Not only were the commencement ceremonies of the university and the theological seminary held there each spring in these years, but its great hall accommodated receptions for visiting statesmen, such as President Fillmore in 1851, and performances by visiting artists, such as Jenny Lind and Ole Bull, on numerous occasions. Local as well as visiting musical groups held concerts there, and varied associations conducted programs in its hall, including formal banquets on occasion. Its facilities were supplemented in the dramatic field by the two theaters, which supplied a fairly continuous schedule of plays thoughout the winter and spring months.

The ballrooms of the hotels accommodated other social events that multiplied in number after each Christmas season, which was, with Thanksgiving, still a family occasion. Some of the ethnic groups supplied special programs open to interested citizens—the German concerts of the Maennerchor, for example, and the gymnastic performances of the Turnverein. Two local cricket teams, formed by young men born in Britain, played occasional matches on one of the five public squares. Aside from these events and the horse races staged infrequently at the Union Course in old Carthage, organized sports were almost unknown. Impromptu contests at numerous picnics in summer, as well as skating and sleighing in winter, provided outdoor amusements. The first mention of adult bathing in the lake appeared in 1853 when a correspondent of the *Democrat*, observing over one hundred men and women in the water near Charlotte during the "melting season," suggested that some enterprising citizen erect tents there on hot days as more convenient than closed carriages for dressing.

Citizen efforts had already supplied gratifying opportunities for urban association in the cultural field. The appointment in 1853 of Dr. Martin B. Anderson, former editor of the Baptist *New York Recorder*, as the university's first president added new dignity to the small but choice society of scholars that was emerging in Rochester. The venerable Professor Dewey and Lewis H. Morgan, whose first book, *The League of the Iroquois*, was receiving wide acclaim, invited ten of these men to join in forming in 1854 what became known as the Pundit Club. Its semimonthly dinner meetings at the homes of its members provided opportunities for scholarly papers and thoughtful discussion on a wide range of topics and marked the attainment of a new urban status.

4

The Flower City, 1855–1875

"ROCHESTER is a *city*. A beautiful city," wrote a visitor from Philadelphia in 1860, who added, as an afterthought, "and the people are as pleasant as the place." Most visitors in the late 1850s, impressed by the acres of blooming tulips and other nursery plantings that practically surrounded the city, and delighted by its animated and colorful social life, were enthusiastic. But numerous residents, including some old timers, were less enchanted. Many uncertainties loomed in the economic field, and the civic services left much to be desired. One aging miller, regretting that he had not moved west while still young enough to make a new start, cited Main Street bridge, severely damaged by a river flood in 1855, as an example. "Many workmen have been hewing and hammering at it in an old fogy way . . . for almost two years," without much progress, he bemoaned.

The bridge, however, was shortly completed and in such substantial form that it helped to dam and aggravate a greater flood a few years later. Many disillusioned residents moved on in search of brighter prospects, but more newcomers arrived, adding to the city's diversity. Rochester's efforts to meet the economic and civic challenges its growth had brought were interrupted by two historic calamities—the Civil War and the nationwide depression of the mid-seventies—which linked the city's development more firmly with that of the country at large.

FLOWER CITY PROSPECTS

Rochester's new nickname, the Flower City, was a happy one and has proved enduring, but it lacked the substantive quality of its prede-

70

cessor, and in the late fifties, groups seeking a local identity still called themselves the Flour City Bank, the Flour City Baseball Club, and the like. After 1853, however, other milling towns had a better claim to that title than did Rochester after 1853. Although Rochester's status as the leading nursery center was already established, the millers continued to hold positions of power in the city's economic and civic fields, where their conservative interests sometimes obstructed action. Yet newcomers abounded; some were launching promising new ventures; many more were adding to the gaiety that now began for the first time to characterize Rochester's social life.

As partially discovered in the late thirties, the key to the city's future was held by its inhabitants whose numbers continued to increase, though at a slower pace than in previous decades. Rochester's population was highly mobile, and a check of its directories revealed that approximately 53 percent of those listed in 1855 had died or moved before the end of the decade. Yet the resulting stability ratio of 46 percent was higher than that of any previous five-year period. The addition of some 4,500 to its total represented little more than the natural surplus of births over deaths, but to replace those who departed, the city had to attract newcomers from its Conesee hinterland and other sections of the Northeast or from abroad.

A major portion of the increment of several of the more rapidly growing inland cities in these years came from the immigrant trains that generally made a stop at Rochester on their route westward. The actual number of foreign born in the city declined slightly, from 19,389 to 18,897 over the five years, bringing the percentage down to 39.2 by 1860, which contrasted with 45 percent in Buffalo and 59 percent in St. Louis. Ten other American cities reported higher percentages, but Rochester's foreign born already boasted large families, and the increased number of their American-born children not only reduced the immigrant ratio but also presented new religious, political, educational, and social issues. The boisterous parades of the Irish, still the largest ethnic group (6,786 residents) in 1860, the diversified customs of the 6,451 from Germany and the 4,335 from Great Britain and Canada, plus slightly more than 1,000 from other lands and 410 Negroes, added to the variety of the social scene. Naturalized voters numbered three to every four natives in 1855 and matched them equally by the close of the decade, but their influence was less effective there than in social and economic fields.

Several of the Yankee pioneers and their sons who had helped to promote Rochester's commercial development in earlier decades had already passed from the scene. Jonathan Child had moved to Buffalo, Josiah W. Bissel to St. Louis. Control of local railroads as well as the canal trade had fallen into outside corporate hands. Local boat yards continued to build most of the boats launched in the canal each season, including two experimental steamers, and Joseph Field, Rochester's fourteenth mayor, became its representative on the New York Central board, where he pressed for an extension of its double track westward from Syracuse to Rochester and Buffalo. Jacob Gould, who succeeded Field on that board, was to see that project completed in the early sixties. However, Rochester's interests seemed so lightly regarded by the Central that Freeman Clarke, the banker who had helped to launch the Lockport and Charlotte lines as well as the direct road to Syracuse, only to see them absorbed by the Central, now vigorously opposed its efforts to gain control of the Genesee Valley Railroad as well. By preserving its independence as a link with the Erie Railroad that crossed the state farther south, he assured Rochester a competitive outlet. But the southern trade was slow to develop, as was that at the lake port, though the latter was somewhat stimulated by the Charlotte line. As a result, the Flower City saw Buffalo and several other ports and rail centers on the upper lakes surge ahead in these years.

Rochester's hope for continued growth depended on the development of industries that would strengthen its hold on the trade of the Genesee Valley and, at the same time, produce a surplus for export. The city's ties with its hinterland were drawn closer by a series of disasters that crippled grain growers up the valley in the mid-fifties and idled millers at Rochester to such an extent that wheat farming and flour milling drifted farther west. Fortunately, Rochester's nurserymen, lead by Ellwanger and Barry, were ready to supply young trees for new fruit orchards and seed for truck gardens, and by 1860 Monroe had won first and second place in these categories among new York State counties. Rochester merchants acquired a lucrative new commerce in foodstuffs to supplement the stagnant grain trade, and area cattle and sheep farmers swelled the output of meat and hides and stimulated the work of local slaughter yards, tanners, and wool merchants. The millers continued to command the largest investments, nearly $1 million in thirty-six mills in the county in 1860 (most of it in the city); their products trebled the nearest rival, clothing, in value and generally netted comfortable profits, but the number of workmen employed, even when the more numerous coopers were included, fell far short of those in either clothing or shoes. It was, however, the millers and nurserymen who, with the printers and publishers of farmers' papers, the lumbermen and sawmill workers, the cattle and wool merchants, maintained Rochester's leadership in the Genesee country despite the slow progress of the valley canal and the threat posed by the Erie Railroad, which had better connections with Buffalo than the Genesee Valley Railroad supplied for the Flower City.

Yet by providing an outlet for valley produce, Rochester maintained a market for its old and new industrial products. Its wagon and carriage makers, headed by James Cunningham from Ireland, increased their output and the number they employed, as did the harness and whip manufacturers, the chair and furniture makers, and the paper-mill workers, all producing for Rochester and regional consumption. Foundries and machine shops, twenty or more in number, employed some 500 men in the manufacture of stoves, steam engines, saws, and safes, as well as car wheels, locks, and a variety of tools and implements for both urban and rural use. Several ingenious craftsmen patented devices that launched new ventures—George Hand Smith's headlamp for railroad engines, for example—and the Novelty Works or one of its competitors acquired the rights to produce such varied items as a "reservoir pen," a carpet sweeper, and the cutting dies in demand among the shoe and clothing firms.

The city's increased reliance on its craftsmen was graphically revealed in the two latter fields. A half-dozen of Rochester's early shoemakers had become merchant-manufacturers and operated busy factories in the central district, where they made ready use of water or steam power to operate their newly introduced sewing machines and cutting dies. Custom shoemakers still abounded, but most of the younger men found employment in the factories that produced ready-made shoes for sale throughout the valley and to migrants stopping at Rochester on their route west. The boot and shoe workers, who numbered approximately one thousand in 1860, were second only to the clothing workers, who multiplied in these years, while enterprising merchant-manufacturers, mostly German Jews, experienced in peddling their products throughout neighboring towns, gave employment to an influx of skilled needle workers, both men and women, from abroad. Their increased output prompted a dispatch of salesmen into the West, a practice that had been initiated by the nurserymen a few years before and that became a standard feature of Rochester's economy.

With six banks reporting a circulation of $1,366,000 in 1855, not including the assets of three savings banks, two insurance companies, and four private bankers, the Flower City seemed adequately equipped in financial respects. Several enterprising Rochesterians were investing in western lands, notably in an iron mining venture in upper Michigan headed by Lewis H. Morgan. The largest and most remunerative investments were in telegraph lines, and Hiram Sibley's success in drawing several of them together into Western Union in 1856 brought handsome profits to these associates. A brief financial panic the next year forced several less fortunate men to the wall, including two private bankers, one of whom had backed the large Ely mill in an unfortunate speculation in wheat. However, Rochester ended the decade with two private and nine chartered banks whose directors included several Yankee metal and shoe men as well as millers and merchants. A renewed attempt to establish a board of trade quickly subsided, but the two leading dry-goods merchants enlarged and improved their stores. The opening of the imposing Osburn House at the corner of Main and St. Paul streets, with a sumptuous banquet in August 1857, assured visitors of elegant accommodations.

Several men built new mansions, and some persons boasted of new conveniences such as bathrooms with hot and cold running water supplied from a tank in the attic. George Ellwanger, who built such a mansion with Gothic trimmings on Mount Hope, also built a number of more modest but comfortable houses for his workmen on nearby Linden Street. Few workmen were so well provided for, because rents were increasing on the four-room cottages that still predominated on the side streets. To conserve fuel, homeowners were installing chunk stoves in place of fireplaces, but the cost of the firewood they consumed was rising because nearby supplies were exhausted. The hopes of numerous craftsmen that organization would assure improved hours and wages faded when six of the nine trade unions of the mid-fifties collapsed during the recession. Renewed prosperity in 1858 brought a revival of the craft unions, ten of which made their appearance, as well as the Laboring Men's Association, which enrolled 600 men in a noisy but ineffective campaign for a ten-hour day. The steady influx of new-comers dissuaded most unions from striking, and when a group of canal laborers, protesting a reduction in wages by the contractor, endeavored to halt work at a canal break, the authorities called in the militia to terminate the dispute.

The civic authorities were not generally so prompt in meeting their problems. Samuel G. Andrews, elected mayor in 1856 by a reform movement that sought a reduction in expenditures, soon recognized the imperative need to press ahead with the rebuilding of Main Street bridge and to undertake street improvements. The city had borne the major burden for the construction of a suspension bridge at Carthage the year before, only to see it collapse nine months later under a heavy fall of snow. But new crossings were needed, and the reformers secured the creation of a bridge commission to complete the Main Street structure and to replace the Court Street and Andrews Street bridges and to repair that at Clarissa Street. Work on these projects helped to relieve unemployment during the recession. On their completion in 1858 the city undertook to rebuild several of the major sewers and to extend the new Medina stone pavement on downtown streets. The council doubled the number of street lamps and authorized other improvements that could be charged against adjoining property owners, but its rejected pleas for the acquisition of a public park at Falls Field and refused to back the efforts of the Rochester Water Works Company to supply the city with water from Hemlock Lake. Instead it subsidized the digging of additional private wells and constructed new underground cisterns to provide the volunteer fire companies with a water supply in districts not served by the river or the canal. Two spectacular murders and an increase in the number of crimes prompted the appointment of additional police, though the turnover that accompanied the annual rotation of mayors limited the efficiency of these officers.

Rochester continued to rely on independent or volunteer agencies for many public services. The Relief Society, organized in 1855 to operate a clothing depot and to supply aid during the hard times, soon dropped from view, but charitable folk maintained the two orphan asylums, the Home for the Friendless, and a new industrial school that opened on Exchange Street in 1857. Efforts to establish both a Protestant and a Catholic hospital made slow progress, but the city did benefit from the new regime developed at the Monroe County Workhouse and Penitentiary, where Zebulon Brockway conducted a work program that not only paid all expenses but also inspired his search for other reformatory techniques. His example stimulated the manager of the Western House of Refuge to assign work tasks to his boys and to provide elementary classes for their instruction.

Despite the resistance of advocates of economy, the Board of Education made considerable progress in meeting the needs of the swollen ranks of children of school age. It not only built a new district school every year, which increased its total to seventeen by the end of the decade, but also remodeled old School No. 1 to serve as a high school, which opened in September 1857 with 165 students selected from the eight schools with grammar departments. The chief difference, one student later recalled, was "the change from mere declamation to original speeches and essays." If some Rochester youths thus received a stimulus to think for themselves and to prepare for college, others studied mathematics and practical sciences in preparation for business. Four private academies for girls continued to supply special refinements to some two hundred who aspired to become young ladies, and two collegiate institutes served young men who needed additional training to enter college or to prepare for a military career. Four Catholic orders opened new special schools, two in German Catholic parishes; these, with five other Catholic parochial schools and two in German Lutheran churches, enrolled well over one thousand pupils in 1860 and outnumbered those in public schools in four predominantly immigrant wards.

Increasing numbers of young men were continuing their studies at college. The 29 local boys among the 163 enrolled at the University of Rochester in 1856 increased to 48 among 168 in 1860, and the 20 or more who graduated annually were matched by a similar number returning with degrees from other colleges. Susan B. Anthony urged the provision of similar opportunities for young women, but the university was preoccupied with plans for its new campus on the eastern outskirts of the city. Approximately one-third of the graduates each year entered the Rochester Theological Seminary, which still shared the university's temporary quarters on Buffalo Street. The white-haired professor of science, Dr. Dewey, continued to supply leadership to the Athenaeum and Mechanics Association and scheduled visiting lecturers and an annual series of science lectures that crowded Corinthian Hall almost weekly in these years. One of Dewey's protégés, Henry A. Ward, grandson of Dr. Levi Ward, returned in 1859 from extended geological excursions abroad with fifty huge crates of fossils and other specimens, widely acclaimed the finest geological collection in America, to become the new professor of natural science at the university.

But the most pervasive and influential institutions in the community were the churches. With the Presbyterians still in the lead, local Protestants established three new societies and built six new churches, three replacing earlier churches on Main Street, which became a business thoroughfare. The new Third Presbyterian Church on Temple Street, built in the Gothic style, achieved architectural excellence. One new Catholic church increased the total number to seven, second only to the Presbyterians. A return visit by Charles G. Finney, the revivalist, launched a series of noontime prayer services in 1856 that won increased attendance during the hard times. The revival spurred the work of the temperance and Bible societies and enlisted many businessmen as leaders of adult departments in the numerous Sabbath schools that enrolled over 16,000 scholars by the end of the decade. Interdenominational rivalry became less intense as Rochesterians grew accustomed to their greater diversity, but friction between Protestants and Catholics persisted and contributed to the activities of the short-lived Know-Nothing party in 1855 and 1856. That controversy, however, was soon pushed aside by the dispute over the slave question. Yet the response was apathetic, and when several dedicated abolitionists staged an antislavery rally at Corinthian Hall in 1859, Frederick Douglass, Rochester's distinguished Negro editor, was provoked to ask, "Why were not the Churches of Rochester more largely represented?"

The churches and many other institutions were responding more actively to the budding interest in leisure-time activities. Sabbath school picnics vied with those of the ethnic and fraternal societies and the volunteer fire and militia companies for the use of nearby groves in summertime and for the staging of annual dinners in winter months.

Newly opened Newport House on Irondequoit Bay and McIntyre's remodeled fish house at Charlotte attracted family and group outings and supplied dressing accommodations for bathers as well as boats and tackle for fishing enthusiasts.

The appearances of organized sports was, however, the unique feature of this period. A cricket club, organized a few years earlier by migrants from Britain, continued to stage occasional games, but the response was minimal compared with that which greeted the Flour City, Live Oaks, and University baseball teams on their sudden arrival in the spring of 1858. Franklin and Jones squares overflowed with hundreds of excited onlookers as these teams engaged in spirited contests with each other or with visiting teams from Buffalo, Syracuse, and Brooklyn. Two boat clubs on the upper river, horse racing at the Union Course, visiting circuses at Falls Field, a balloon ascension, and an acrobat who demonstrated his skill by walking a wire stretched across the river at the main falls supplied additional excitement in the summer months; several bowling alleys, numerous billiard rooms, and a newly introduced gymnasium competed with sleighing and skating for favor among those who sought active amusements in wintertime.

Numerous opportunities for more passive amusement and for the expression of local talent brought an enrichment of the city's cultural life. Several visiting pianists, operatic stars, and troups of minstrels attracted crowds to Corinthian Hall, and local and neighboring bands drew throngs to Washington and Brown's squares on special occasions. A visit by a concert orchestra from New York in 1858 stimulated an abortive effort to organize a local orchestra from the students of several music teachers, but the concerts of the leading church and ethnic choirs proved more gratifying. The increased patronage enjoyed by successive dramatic groups that visited the remodeled Metropolitan Theater on South St. Paul prompted the managers of Corinthian Hall to expand its stage in 1869 to accommodate theatrical performances. Local portrait and landscape artists welcomed opportunities to display their work at Kelsey's Emporium of Art and other exhibit galleries maintained by the daguerreotype photographers who made Rochester a leading center of that popular trade. Several bookstores helped supply the community's increased demand for papers, magazines, and books. D. M. Dewey, one of the busiest, reported the sale in 1856 of 6,000 out-of-town papers and 2,000 periodicals a month from his counters in the Arcade. The publishers of three local dailies and seven weeklies also printed twenty-five books and numerous pamphlets in these five years, including three addresses by Frederick Douglass pressing for a righteous response to the slave question.

Unfortunately, that outstanding moral issue of the period was not destined for a happy solution. The controversy over slavery raged in the Rochester press as throughout the nation, but political leaders, seeking alignments that would assure success, endeavored to steer clear of the question. Most citizens were little inclined to meddle with a problem that could be dismissed as belonging to the South, with which they had few close ties. Western developments, however, brought the issue into sharper focus. Reports from several former Rochesterians who had migrated to Kansas, one of them the younger brother of Miss Anthony, supplied graphic accounts of the struggle there and spurred the local Anti-Slavery Society to action. At least a dozen forthright citizens, inspired by the example of Frederick Douglass, courageously sheltered fugitive slaves and assisted approximately 150 annually in their flight to Canada. When reports of their activity brought John Brown to Rochester in search of support for his plans for direct action, however, Douglass refused to participate in the dramatic assault on Harpers Ferry, though rumors of his complicity forced the Rochester editor to flee to Canada after the collapse of that raid. Seward's famous "Irrepressible Conflict" speech, delivered in Corinthian Hall on October 25, 1858, gave warning of the impending crisis and strengthened local Republican forces, enabling them to carry the city for Lincoln two years later. But apparently nobody in Rochester suspected that a war would shortly erupt and exact the lives of a fearful number of the city's young men.

THE CIVIL WAR

The Civil War had, in many respects, a traumatic effect on the Flower City. Rochesterians, for a long time, had proudly considered themselves citizens of a young republic destined to enjoy a great future. They had participated boisterously in national elections and had displayed much partisan fervor, but the results had not generally affected local developments. The election of 1860 did not appear to differ greatly from previous contests. Most voters, preoccupied with local and private concerns, felt no threat of war and no desire to take up arms to free the slaves. When, however, the issue was joined, challenging the permanence of the national union, the finality of a decision at the polls, and the honor and bravery of the North, the residents of Rochester acquired a new sense of their identity as citizens of a national union and rallied with patriotic zeal for its preservation.

The country's drift toward war in the winter of 1860–61 was reflected in the shift of opinions in Rochester. Lincoln's slim majority of 975 had contrasted with the larger contrary majority of 1,642 by which the community had opposed the grant of state suffrage to Negroes. When a few forthright abolitionists staged a convention at Corinthian Hall in an effort to induce Lincoln to endorse their cause, citizens of opposing views disrupted the proceedings, which prompted the police to adjourn the meeting by dimming the gaslights. Miss Anthony and her associates reopened the convention the next day in the less conspicuous quarters of the African Zion M. E. church but attracted only a modest crowd compared with the turnout of workingmen who assembled two weeks later in support of compromise. Yet a larger throng, estimated by one observer at 15,000, gathered on the morning of February 18, 1861, to greet the train bearing the president-elect towards Washington.

News of the attack on Fort Sumter brought a surge of patriotic unity to Rochester. Mayor John C. Nash, elected only a few weeks before, convened a public meeting on April 18, the first in the city's history, to hear the president's message. Thousands gathered in the streets, unable to gain access to two packed halls where Lincoln's call for troops was read. Dr. Anderson of the university, long an advocate of moderation, declared in a brief speech that "the Rubicon was passed" and the time for action had arrived.

Rochesterians acquired a new sense of membership in a community as the enrollment of volunteers commenced. Several officers of earlier militia units recruited men for the eight companies initially requested from the city. Adolph Nolte, editor of the local German weekly and a veteran of the French army in Algiers, enrolled his fellow countrymen in a German-speaking company. Other volunteers, primarily of Irish or Scottish origin, rallied behind trusted officers, and older Rochesterians who saw their sons enlist were pleased to know that they would be supported by eager and sturdy comrades. A cheering throng of about 20,000 lined State and Exchange streets on May 3 as the eight companies marched to board the train for Elmira where the 13th Regiment of New York State Volunteers was mustered in. Isaac F. Quinby, professor of mathematics at the university and a former graduate of West Point, was chosen colonel; four weeks later he led the "Rochester Regiment" to join others in the defense of Washington.

Back in Rochester local enlistments continued, and the Soldiers Relief Committee raised $36,280 to support the wives and children of needy volunteers. As the number of companies recruited at Rochester increased to fifteen, confidence mounted and cries of "on to Richmond" found vent in both the *Democrat* and the *Express*, the conservative and radical spokesmen for the Republicans. The Democratic *Union* was more critical of Lincoln's preparations and read its rivals a lesson after the disaster at Bull Run. Indeed it was on the evening of July 22, 1861, that Rochesterians first began to grasp the sober implications of the war. Crowds jammed the Arcade and adjoining streets as friends of the boys in the 13th and other units known to be in the fight waited for telegraph messages from the battle zone. Excitement mounted as early confidence in a Northern victory gave way to wild rumors of huge losses. The facts, when they arrived, were bad enough: 12 killed, 26 wounded, and 27 taken prisoner out of 600 from Rochester engaged. Shortcuts to victory were proved illusory, and Rochester, together with other Northern communities, began to prepare for a long and costly struggle.

The impact of the war on the city's economic, civic, and cultural affairs soon became apparent. Rochester escaped the severe economic disturbances that hit some cities but soon encountered other setbacks. Local bankers, having few investments in the South, were in a stable condition and began to expand. All area lines of communication remained open and benefited from the obstruction of lines farther south. The Genesee country, as a producer of wheat, meat, and other foodstuffs, profited from the increased demand for these products, though the more rapid advance in the price of coal quickly erased the advantage for city residents. Perhaps the first industry to experience an upturn in business was the press as the three dailies boosted their circulations to around 3,000 each and sometimes sold as many as

20,000 at critical stages in the conflict. Army contracts spurred the expansion of L. & H. Churchill's shoe factory and Sigmund Stettheimer's clothing operations, winning them high places on the local list of income-tax payers in 1863. Aaron Erickson, the wool merchant, likewise won a place there. But it was Hiram Sibley, president of Western Union, whose vigorous leadership in rushing the construction of telegraph lines across the continent greatly strengthened the Union cause and netted profits that placed him at the top of that list.

The benefits some experienced were offset by hardships in other lines. The enlargement of the Erie Canal, finally completed throughout its length in 1862, enabled local boat yards to build the larger boats, but also speeded shipments through the canal with fewer stops at Rochester. If millers had difficulty in buying sufficient wheat to keep their stones busy, other industrialists and householders alike faced greater shortages as well as higher prices for coal to fire their engines and warm their homes. The Erie Railroad, with its Genesee Valley Railroad link to Rochester, benefited from the new demand for shipments to and from the South, and all branches of the New York Central, including the main line, which was now double-tracked throughout, enjoyed a rapid increase in traffic, both of passengers and freight. But concerted efforts to break the blockade that appeared to obstruct the shipment of coal to Rochester proved futile, and the city suffered a coal famine each winter. The chief sufferers, of course, were the poor, many of them workingmen whose ten local unions, despite occasional strikes that achieved modest increases, failed to hold wages in line with price rises for food as well as wood and coal and other necessities. Increasing numbers of widows and orphans, victims of the war's mounting casualties, added to the ranks of the destitute and spurred new charity efforts.

Appeals in behalf of sick and wounded soldiers stirred a ready response from the more affluent. The Ladies Hospital and Relief Association, formed in January 1862, began within a month to dispatch bales of bedclothes and other supplies to the United States Sanitary Commission for use at emergency stations in the battle zone. It staged a Christmas bazaar in Corinthian Hall, featuring ethnic and church booths among other displays that attracted thousands of visitors and netted over $10,000 for the cause. The friends of the two local hospitals redoubled their efforts. Both St. Mary's Hospital, opened in temporary quarters in 1858, and the City Hospital, sponsored by the Female Charitable Society, completed the construction of permanent buildings in 1862 and welcomed detachments of wounded soldiers to their hastily furnished wards. Each staged bazaars and other appeals for funds to maintain their services.

Several of the earlier civic concerns acquired new priorities during the war years. The former agitation for a public park and for a waterworks subsided, but as the fire hazard increased, the department purchased its first steam fire engine in 1861 at a cost of $3,800, added three more within two years, and substituted horses and a small paid staff for the rowdy volunteers in their operation. Mayor Nash, who initiated that reform after an inspection of municipal procedures in Albany and New York, also directed all police officers to acquire uniforms and to wear them when on duty. The city deferred most street improvements but welcomed the offer of the newly chartered Rochester City and Brighton Railway, capitalized at $200,000, to operate horsecars on the city streets. Encouraged by the grant of a thirty-year franchise, the company, headed by Patrick Barry, rushed construction of its track on State, Exchange, and Mount Hope in the winter of 1862–63 and launched service on that north-south line the next July, extending it east on Main to Alexander Street and west on Buffalo to the two hospitals before the end of the year.

The city hastily curtailed or suspended most cultural efforts during the first years of the war. After the completion of a new No. 9 school early in 1861, the Board of Education undertook no new construction, and the High School, renamed the Free Academy in 1862, suffered, along with the private schools, the loss of several male teachers to the army. The university sustained a 40 percent drop in enrollments, and the Athenaeum experienced a drop in memberships when a dispute erupted over the scheduling of abolitionist speakers. A recently organized Academy of Music and Art installed a collection of "70 fine paintings," brought to Rochester by a New York art dealer, in its rooms on the second floor of the Rochester Savings Bank in 1862, but interest soon flagged and the dealer removed his collection to Buffalo. A reorganized YMCA, the product of a fervent revival in several churches early in 1863, attracted greater support as many Protestants became concerned for the welfare of young men returning from the battle front. Yet its weekly prayer services proved less popular than

the performances of occasional troupes at the Metropolitan Theater, or
in Corinthian Hall or newly opened Washington Hall where many
residents sought an escape from the tragic war news in melodramas,
such as "Ten Nights in a Bar Room," or in the melodious concerts of
Charlotta Patti, who made three visits to Rochester.

It was not possible, however, to escape the effects of the war. Recruiting continued, almost without letup, until its very end, and with
the aid of bounties ranging upward from $100 to $300 and more as the
years advanced, the city mustered approximately 5,000 men for the
army, roughly one-tenth of its population. Most of them served in units
that numbered many local boys, and Rochester followed with keen
interest the fortunes of the 13th, the 108th, the 140th, the Reynolds
Battery, and the several other units in which its recruits predominated.
As one or more of these regiments became engaged in the Seven Days'
battles, the second battle of Bull Run, and those at Fredericksburg,
Chancellorsville, and Antietam, the fearful losses they suffered cast a
somber shadow over the city. The victory at Gettysburg brought a
renewal of confidence, but news of the Rochester casualties, especially
those suffered by the 140th in its successful defense of Little Round
Top, dampened the celebration. Ten days later, crowds of Protestants
and Catholics alike followed the funeral bier of its fallen commander,
Colonel Patrick O'Rorke, to St. Bridget's church.

Rochesterians were acquiring a new sense of community from their
war efforts. Even the vituperative Isaac Butts of the *Union*, long hostile to the abolitionists, accepted the Emancipation Proclamation as a
"Great Fact" and expressed the hope that the country could now "get
on with the war." As Yankee Protestants applauded the heroism of the
Irish Catholic O'Rorke, many whites rejoiced to hear that Lincoln had
received and conferred with Douglass at the White House and had
agreed to accept the blacks he recruited into the armies of the North.
So many from all elements of the population enlisted, encouraged by
the bounties that helped to sustain their families, that when the draft
was applied in the fall of 1863, less than 400 were needed to fill the
quota in Rochester's two-county district. Yet dissension continued
among the successive editors of the local dailies and within the Republican party. As a result, the Democrats elected three mayors in
succession and carried the city by small pluralities for a Democrat for
governor and for McClellan for president, but the criticism thus ex-

pressed was directed at the conduct of the war, not at its objective, which all factions now supported.

As the summer of 1864 brought a series of desperate battles in the wilderness that inflicted many casualties on Rochester units, criticisms of the war mounted. The severe coal famine in the city that winter and the hardships suffered by most workingmen from generally inflated prices produced several abortive strikes that further depressed morale. Lincoln's second inaugural intensified the discussion of possible terms of peace; the *Union* favored compromise, and the *Democrat* and the *Express* urged a speedy adoption of the Thirteenth Amendment by Southern as well as Northern states as a guarantee of democratic equality for all. The Republicans recaptured the city administration the next spring and increased the bounties to $600 in an effort to stave off a second draft.

It was in the midst of that dispiriting struggle, aggravated by news of the appalling casualties in the drive on Richmond, that an unprecedented Genesee flood hit Rochester. A drenching spring rain up the valley had loosened the winter's unusually heavy blanket of snow. Because the city had become accustomed to reports of spring floods on the upper Genesee, its residents did not take alarm until the morning of March 17, when the rushing torrent, having filled the arches of the aqueduct, spilling over its top as over a dam, also filled the arches of Main Street bridge and, blocked by the buildings lining its north side, coursed westward into Buffalo, Front, and State streets. For two days rowboats supplied the only communication around the Four Corners, and the flooding of the gasworks created a blackout at night. After the muddy water receded, citizens worked for several weeks clearing away the debris and making the essential repairs.

Fortunately, Rochester was able to forget its own troubles with the arrival on the evening of May 10 of news of Lee's surrender. The joyous clangor of the big fire bell in the court house and of every church bell in the city brought citizens flocking into the downtown streets, where some lit bonfires and others discharged guns or delivered impromptu speeches to the milling throng that was too excited to listen. The celebration continued until dispersed by a cold rain at two in the morning.

For a brief period it appeared that the great struggle had ended in triumph, vindicating the joint cause of union and democracy. The sense of relief and joy that swept over the North could at least assuage the grief of those whose menfolk would never return. Rochester shared this sacrifice to the extent of 650 men, an honor roll that included representatives from all elements of the community, thus greatly strengthening its bonds. Unfortunately, the prospect of a peaceful reunion of the States was shattered by the assassination of President Lincoln, and the noble sentiments prompted by Lee's surrender gave way to a spirit of vindictiveness. Not only did the *Democrat* hold all leaders of the South accountable, but, with the *Express*, it virtually charged the Rochester editors of the *Union* with complicity in the foul deed. A solemn procession, nearly two miles in length, marched down Main and Buffalo streets in observance of Lincoln's funeral on April 19. Thousands stood with bared heads in a vast throng in front of the court house to hear Congressman Roswell Hart and Dr. Ezekiel Robinson of the theological seminary eulogize the martyred president. However, expressions of genuine sorrow could not still the mounting cries for revenge that would embitter local as well as national political rivalries for years to come.

FLOWER CITY RESPONSES

The Civil War had drawn Rochester out of its regional sanctuary and confronted it, as Frederick Douglass had predicted, with national issues, both moral and political. A nationwide depression in the mid-seventies would compel it to make new social and economic adjustments. But it was the problems of urban growth that, in the long run, presented the basic challenges, inducing responses that would eventually transform the community from a regional center into a cosmopolitan industrial city of national stature.

The Flower City was beginning, even before the Civil War, to outgrow its status as the market town, processing center, and cultural headquarters of the Genesee country. That district was now fully settled and would experience further growth only in its scattered urban centers—all except Rochester still small in size. To expand its markets or tap new resources, the Flower City had to reach out to broader regions. Fortunately, its new leaders, the nurserymen, were fully aware of that need; they had been the first to seek new markets in the West, and in 1872 Ellwanger and Barry filled an order from the Japanese government for several thousand trees in over two hundred varieties.

Other local industrialists were following that lead. James Vick, Charles Briggs, and other seedsmen vied with the nurserymen in scattering thousands of catalogues, many illustrated with hand-colored plates, throughout the states. Although local coopers were declining in number as mechanical devices displaced hand labor, wood- and paper-box makers were taking their place and supplied containers for the marketing of food and dry goods. At the same time, Curtice Brothers and other packers introduced jars and cans to expedite their shipments. Several of the leading clothing firms expanded their workshops, equipped them with sewing machines, adopted trademarks to identify their products, and engaged additional agents to market them. The shoe firms, major beneficiaries of war orders, also dispatched agents into the West and, by an alert utilization of new peg-driving and welting machines, increased their output and maintained local industrial leadership.

Many and diverse merchant craftsmen, some newcomers from abroad, contributed to the Flower City's industrial growth. Several carriage and furniture manufacturers, including Charles J. Hayden, who paid the highest wages in town, acquired a reputation for their products and marketed some in distant cities. Local brewers were likewise gaining a reputation, notably Henry Bartholomay from Germany, and local tobacco men, led by William S. Kimball, achieved advances by introducing new methods of packaging their products. Among other metalworking firms, Sargent & Greenleaf won distinction for their time locks and safes, and D. R. Barton for edge tools. When one small foundry closed its doors, Henry Cribben, head of the molders' union, persuaded his members to form a cooperative, which took over and expanded its operations. But when the newly formed Rochester Iron Manufacturing Company erected a blast furnace at Charlotte, its easy access to iron ore shipments was offset by the area's continued coal shortage, which repeatedly forced its closure.

Rochester had acquired most of its transport lines by the late sixties but still lacked a good coal road. That deficiency, however, reflected the mounting struggle for control of the existing lines. A renewed effort to establish a board of trade, with George J. Whitney in the lead, finally proved successful in 1867. However, Whitney, the leading flour merchant and now Rochester's director on the New York Central, diverted the board's attention from proposals for the regulation of railroad rates to a campaign for the elimination of canal tolls, and interest soon flagged. Protests against discriminatory railroad rates could not be dismissed so easily, however, and several public meetings endorsed the views of the Anti-Monopoly Cheap Freight Railway League organized in New York by Henry O'Reilly. The city's hopes for competitive rates on the Erie were dashed as the manipulation of its stock by Gould, Fisk, and Drew weakened its freight services. Renewed pleas in 1872 by shoe, clothing, and nursery firms for more adequate service prompted both the Central and the Erie to keep a sufficient number of freight cars at their Rochester yards to assure shippers through billing service to the major cities on their lines. Whitney blamed the Erie for Rochester's coal shortages and took the lead in the organization of the State Line Railroad, designed to tap the coal fields of western Pennsylvania. Mounting interests in the recently discovered oil fields there gave added support to the proposed line, and the Common Council voted to invest $600,000 in its stock.

Rival interests also battled for control of the city's banks. Five commercial banks, previously operated under state charters, became national banks in 1865, but three reverted to state banks within a few years because of the less rigid controls. The Flour City National Bank elected both Ellwanger and Barry as trustees in 1869, when the directors of all the other banks were of old Yankee stock. The next year, however, the Stettheimer brothers, the leading wholesale clothiers, also established a private bank, one of several such enterprises, some of which proved too generous with their credit. The Ward brothers, grandsons of Dr. Levi Ward, were forced to close in 1869, but Daniel W. Powers, the private banker who had undertaken the construction of a five-story block at the Four Corners, reassured his depositors by stacking $800,000 in greenbacks in his corner window. His action won support that enabled him to add a sixth floor in a mansard roof extended over both wings of the Powers block, which had a full roster of tenants. Numerous other investors were likewise converting their funds into substantial improvements. When Hiram Sibley sold a major block of stock in Western Union, he took a mortgage on a 40,000-acre farm in Illinois but also erected the Sibley block at Main and St. Paul streets.

Ellwanger and Barry subdivided another portion of their nursery and built additional houses for their workers, and George Nichols laid out a graciously designed subdivision with a row of magnolia trees planted along the central mall of what later became Oxford Street.

The transformation of Rochester's industries from handicraft to factory production had its greatest impact on the workers. Earlier craft societies had become trade unions, but in the post–Civil War years some of these acquired a new character as unions of factory workers. The Knights of St. Crispin, organized by the workers in the new shoe factories, and the clothing workers' and molders' unions, among others, represented workingmen who had accepted their status as wage earners and sought to reduce the number of hours and improve the rates and other working conditions. The Rochester Trades Assembly, formed in 1863, served as host to the second National Industrial Congress, which met at Rochester in 1874. But the mass meeting of workingmen that their leaders addressed in front of the court house was more interested that April in the problems of unemployment than in agitation for the eight-hour day or for the formation of strong national unions as urged by Christopher Kane, leader of Rochester's Knights of St. Crispin.

The post-war years had been troubled times for many businessmen, though only a few had succumbed. Perhaps the most shocking bankruptcy was that of George J. Whitney who was caught in 1871 in the battle between Gould and Vanderbilt and lost his grain elevator and several other investments. Whitney soon recouped his fortune, but the panic that developed when the failure of Jay Cooke in New York was reported in September 1873 carried many in Rochester to ruin with him. One local bank collapsed and several shoe and furniture factories shut down for extended periods. As unemployment increased, union membership declined, and the Workingmen's Association dropped from the news. In its place appeared the Rochester Benevolent Association, organized in 1872 to study the causes of pauperism and now faced with the sober facts of poverty in the midst of an abundant output of nature.

Fortunately, Rochester's civic leaders, though torn by jealous rivalries, managed in the early seventies to launch several projects that relieved some old deficiencies and supplied numerous jobs as well. The Taxpayers Association, headed by Daniel Powers and Isaac Butts, two of the largest property owners, combated efforts in the late sixties to build new bridges, new schools, and a water system, but its opposition was silenced in 1871. News of the Chicago fire, reporting the destruction, in the midst of its vast carnage, of several cast-iron buildings, suddenly shattered the confidence of Daniel Powers in the fireproof character of his new block and prompted him to organize a new committee that demanded the immediate construction of a water system. The need for a city hall likewise came to a head in 1871, when the county bought out the city's share of the court house. Mounting pressures for a new high school and for other public works finally won council support.

The decision to act on such issues precipitated a bitter struggle for power. To assure adequate facilities in each case, a Republican faction headed by Lewis Selye collaborated with George Lord, the city's Democratic assemblyman, in providing for the creation of three special commissions to be appointed by Mayor A. Carter Wilder to manage the construction of these projects. Although heated protests erupted, especially when it developed that Lord had received the contract for the construction of the waterworks, the fact that many jobs became available as these projects moved forward during the depression greatly eased local tensions.

The use of special commissions to circumvent the annual political turnover was widely practiced in these years. A police commission created in 1865 achieved greater stability and, under the administration of Sam M. Sherman as chief of police, saw the development of a detective service as well. The Board of Health launched a new program of garbage collection and hired teamsters for the job, but it resisted pleas for regular food inspections, though it directed its city physicians to make emergency vaccinations in 1872 to ward off a threatened epidemic. Of course, the Board of Education was the oldest of these special commissions, but because its members were elected, the Selye ring assigned the construction of the new Free Academy building and four new district schools to the public works commission, which promptly gave the contracts to the former partner of the new acting Mayor, George W. Aldridge, Sr.

The state of low political morality was frequently deplored. Francis Beckwith, an observant jailer whose diaries supply many valuable insights on this era, placed much of the blame on the "avarice and dishonesty of the leaders," whose sons, in several cases, fell under his charge. A more prevalent view blamed the inrush of foreigners and the upsurge of naturalized voters who outnumbered those of native birth after 1865. Both parties eagerly assisted in the naturalization of aliens, especially on the eve of an election, and both named representatives of the foreign born as aldermanic candidates in the wards of their concentration. Because the Republicans were generally more committed to temperance, the Germans and the Irish, many of them frequent imbibers of beer and ale, were more strongly drawn to the Democrats, and it was that party which nominated and elected John Lutes as the first German-born mayor of Rochester in 1870. His frequent use of the veto obstructed some shady deals but delayed forthright action and helped to bring about the alliance between a few impatient Republicans and the greedy George Lord who turned several vital functions over to appointive commissions. Only the collaboration of Henry L. Fish, a former Democratic reform mayor, and Lewis H. Morgan, Rochester's scholarly senator at Albany, checked the designs of the Selye-Lord ring and assured the election of Fish to the legislature and of British-born George A. Clarkson as mayor.

The most dramatic political event of the decade in Rochester was the unsuccessful attempt of Susan B. Anthony and fourteen of her followers to cast their votes in the 1872 elections. Although their votes were disqualified, the Rochester ladies gave public expression to the surging movement for women's rights, which had one of its most effective centers in the Anthony home at Rochester. Other Rochester ladies were playing active roles in supporting and staffing the hospitals and related welfare institutions. Their work in temperance and other reform groups had buttressed their self-confidence, and their voice in church and family affairs was winning increased recognition. In numbers they exceeded men over age eighteen 22,000 to 21,000 in 1870, and a study of the assessment books of 1873 revealed that they paid taxes on property valued at $1,500,000, or slightly over one-tenth of the city's total. Although political leaders refused to consider their pleas for the vote, merchants were eagerly courting their favor with newly installed window displays of ladies' fashions in hoop skirts, "water falls," and perfumes, among numerous personal items, as well as household furnishings in the new Victorian designs. Dancing masters and music teachers vied with the managers of the expanding retail stores, notably the Boston Store established on Main Street in 1868 by Rufus Sibley, Alexander Lindsay, and John Curr, in catering to feminine needs and tastes.

Despite the uncertain times, living standards were, in fact, rising. The construction of new houses, many of them one-story cottages in subdivisions promoted by cooperative associations, increased the total to 11,644 by 1870, when the families numbered 12,213. Rochester's ratio of 5.36 persons per dwelling was lower than that of other major American cities, and the proportion of homeowners was said to be the highest in the land. Few of these homes had running water or other plumbing fixtures at that date, but many homeowners hastened to install them as the construction of water mains progressed in the mid-seventies. Former residents who had built new homes beyond the city limits now petitioned for the annexation of their tracts in order to secure an extension of the water mains. The Flower City practically doubled its acreage in 1874, adding or reclaiming 8,500 residents to reach a total of 81,722. Despite the onset of the depression, 61 percent of a sampling of 1869 *Directory* names reappeared in the 1874 *Directory*, the highest stability ratio yet achieved.

Its increased stability no doubt reflected the city's greater variety of social and cultural activities. Not only were the baseball teams and boat clubs of the late fifties hastily reorganized after the return of peace, but bathing and other outings at the lake and bay acquired new popularity. Favored residents began to build or rent summer cottages on nearby lakes, and the less affluent participated in group picnics or other excursions by steam train to these resorts. The outings of the various ethnic societies multiplied as their numbers increased and assured a congenial welcome even to those who had lost their jobs. Indeed the ethnic societies continued to supply food and other relief to their unfortunate fellow nationals after the Rochester Benevolent Association, which undertook to supervise the distribution of welfare in 1873, was diverted a year later to a campaign for temperance. Dr. Henry W. Dean was, however, able to revive the Benevolent Association in 1875 and to resume the distribution of relief to needy families; he pressed a year later for the creation of an employment agency. The German beer gardens not only survived but attracted an increased patronage, and the German singing and gymnastic societies acquired new prestige as they competed with similar societies from other cities in annual festivals at Rochester or elsewhere.

The new favor displayed for some foreign customs reflected the broadening perspectives that a few Rochesterians were securing from travel abroad. Hiram Sibley returned from Europe early in 1874 with "54 fine paintings," which served as the nucleus for several exhibits by Rochester's newly organized Academy of Art. Daniel W. Powers was busily acquiring a still larger collection for display on the fifth floor of his new block. Visiting opera and dramatic stars with European credentials enjoyed a ready welcome, and aspiring local artists and performers eagerly journeyed abroad to enrich their experience. Fanny Danforth finished her education in 1866 with a tour through France and Italy, where she visited numerous galleries in the company of several other youthful Rochesterians encountered along the way. In his European tour five years later, Lewis H. Morgan sought and secured opportunities to confer with several of the most learned men of Britain and France.

A number of Protestant clergymen enjoyed extended trips abroad, one to the Holy Land, and thus refreshed their ministry at home, but the establishment of the Roman Catholic Diocese in 1868 and the appointment of Bernard McQuaid as Rochester's first bishop assured that church, now the largest in number, a stronger voice. Anti-Catholic sentiments still found expression on frequent occasions, but the successful completion of St. Patrick's Cathedral in 1873, the largest and most imposing edifice in the city, demonstrated the substantial character of many of its predominantly immigrant members. A more spirited controversy developed within the Protestant fold between a few advanced thinkers who, with the Reverend Newton Mann of the Unitarian church and Professor Ward at the university, were considering the implications of Darwin's evolutionary theories and the great majority who, with the presidents of the university as well as the seminary, took the Scriptures literally. The gorilla that Henry A. Ward mounted in the upper corridor of Anderson Hall was too challenging, and the young professor was encouraged to move it to his Cosmos Hall workshop across the street, where he was preparing exhibits for installation in several other colleges. Yet President Anderson, though always mindful of possible criticism from the more orthodox divines of the theological seminary where Augustus H. Strong, son of one of the university founders, assumed the presidency in 1872, hastened to accept the gift of a new building by Hiram Sibley to be used as a joint library and museum of science.

To most residents, science had a practical and modern connotation that was in no sense disturbing. Many were excited to hear that Lewis Swift, a hardware merchant, had built a telescope with which he was the first to catch sight of a new comet and had received a gold medal from an observatory in Vienna in recognition of that discovery. Crowds gathered early in 1875 to hear "Professor Swift," as the press generously titled him, when he lectured on "The Wonders of the Moon" before the Athenaeum. That association, crippled by the death of Professor Dewey in 1867 and of William A. Reynolds in 1872, had been unable to pay the rent asked by Samuel Wilder, who had remodeled Corinthian Hall into the Academy of Music. The Athenaeum tried to keep afloat by holding its meetings in the council room of the new city hall. Its right to charge admission was under dispute, and the officers suspended further meetings. When the Athenaeum failed to promote the new interests developed by the Swift lectures, young Dr. Samuel A. Lattimore, the new science professor at the university, announced a series of free lectures for workingmen. The science lectures attracted a good response, but the Athenaeum, which still declined to endorse them, quietly faded from the scene, a victim not only of the depression but also of the changing city that would soon develop more specialized institutions.

Rattlesnake Pete's Saloon

Dedication of Civil War Memorial, Washington Square, May 30, 1892

Flying Circus at Crittenden Park Field, 1910

Ontario Beach Park, 1890s

Solio printing at Kodak, 1905

Professor Ward in his museum, 1896

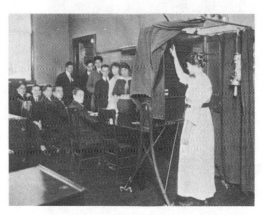

Voting machine demonstration, 1896

Dossenbach's Rochester Orchestra, 1912

James G. Cutler: architect,
industrialist, mayor of Rochester

Frederick Douglass:
editor, author, statesman

Susan B. Anthony: leading
advocate of woman's suffrage

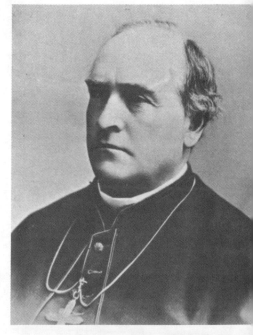

Bishop Bernard J. McQuaid

George Eastman's mansion, opened in 1905

Colonel Henry A. Strong in Kodak office

Monroe Community College, 1971

University of Rochester, River Campus, 1945

New Citizens Banquet, 1959

Old Front Street, 1960s

Aerial view of Downtown Rochester, 1971

Eastman Kodak office building and tower, 1946

Rochester War Memorial, 1972

Bragdon's New York Central station, opened in 1914

Aerial view of Rochester's business district, 1940

Dr. Rush Rhees: president of
the University of Rochester

George Eastman: founder of
the Eastman Kodak Company

Joseph C. Wilson: president
of the Xerox Company

Frank E. Gannett: founder and
publisher of the Gannett Press

Rochester Institute of Technology, new campus, 1971

Aerial view of Civic Center Plaza, 1972

Midtown Tower, 1962

Midtown Plaza, 1962

5

The Cosmopolitan City, 1876–1890

AN ASSORTMENT of newcomers and former residents with new energies and fresh ideas transformed Rochester in the late seventies and eighties into a cosmopolitan and more sophisticated city. One of its most prestigious leaders, Daniel W. Powers was a self-made banker who had grown up in the city, but the elegance of his new block and the sumptuous character of his art gallery reflected outside, principally Victorian, influences and helped to revitalize Rochester's downtown. The city's development, however, was plural in character and no man, not even Cornelius R. Parsons, its long-term mayor, or Mortimer F. Reynolds, son of a pioneer, touched all interests in the increasingly complex community. William S. Kimball, for example, supplied leadership and innovation in industrial production and business organization, and other men such as Bishop McQuaid and Emil Kuichling, both recent newcomers, as well as Lewis H. Morgan, made significant contributions in disparate fields. New ethnic and social as well as political and economic groups contributed to the dynamic quality of the cosmopolitan city.

ECONOMIC DIVERSITY

The depression that gripped Rochester, as it did most of the nation in the mid-seventies, revealed the importance of its major wage-paying industries. Because the city could do little to restore their stagnant markets, however, its business leaders were more pessimistic in October 1876 than those of cities less dependent on industrial employment. A reporter for the *Democrat,* after reviewing several optimistic forecasts from Chicago, St. Louis, and New York, recorded the less sanguine responses received from local merchants and industrialists. At Cunningham's, for example, although orders for carriages were picking up, the demand for wagons was sluggish; at the cooperative foundry the market for chunk stoves had slumped, but a new hot-air furnace was attracting interest. Rufus Sibley was hopeful, but not confident, that couples returning from the Centennial Exposition at Philadelphia would spark new demands for his merchandise.

The formula for recovery, as H. H. Warner the patent-medicine king saw it, was more vigorous sales promotion, but in Rochester it appeared necessary at the start to master several old difficulties. Little could be accomplished until the coal shortage was relieved, monopoly control over commercial outlets was broken, and credit uncertainties were removed. The sudden switch in the early seventies from national to private banking had proved disastrous to several bankers, including Sigmund Stettheimer whose foreclosure in 1879 not only inflicted losses on many modest depositors but also aroused distrust when the efforts of several insiders to safeguard their own interests before the crash were revealed. A similar scandal occurred at the City Bank when its president Charles E. Upton, another respected resident on East Avenue, misappropriated $330,000, for which he was sent to jail and to an early death by his own hand. Fortunately, however, other trusted citizens were ready to assume the presidencies of the faltering institutions and proceeded to convert some into national banks, again, of which Rochester had seven in 1885, plus four savings banks and three well-established private banks.

Financial transactions increased dramatically in the late eighties. Daniel W. Powers, the strongest private banker, finally acquired a national charter in 1890 when he saw his neighbor Frederich Cook, founder of the German-American Bank, increase his deposits threefold in five years. Cook was also president of the Rochester German Insurance Company, the largest of three local companies that competed with the agents of more than a score of outside insurance companies. In addition, a fluctuating list of benefit and building and loan societies, many of them associated with ethnic or church groups, collected small sums from modest but thrifty members and loaned them to other members for home building or emergency expenses. Despite the losses some had suffered during the depression of the mid-seventies, little thought was given to the regulation of these agencies; the leading bankers did, however, follow the example of New York and other cities and establish a clearinghouse to expedite the clearing of checks and to perform other cooperative services.

As Rochester's credit resources increased, the pressure for improved transport facilities mounted, and the need for a good coal road became imperative. The State Line Railroad, projected in the early seventies in response to this need, had been delayed by the depression and when finally completed to Salamanca in 1878, was discovered to have fallen into Vanderbilt's hands. A threatened suit by the city to recover its $600,000 investment sent the road into bankruptcy, but a group of citizens headed by Daniel Powers and Patrick Barry persuaded the city to abandon that claim in order to enhance its chance to secure the sorely needed coal deliveries. It was April 1883 before the reorganized Rochester and Pittsburgh brought its first train of twenty coal cars into the city. The new road increased its service to three trains daily within five months and spurred the development of a new trade with Canada. Oil shipments from western Pennsylvania likewise increased, boosting the output of the Vacuum Oil Company, which now fell under the control of the Standard Oil Company of Cleveland. Rochester viewed the arrival of that monopoly with little concern in 1884, partly because of its success in developing a working arrangement with Vanderbilt and the New York Central.

Mounting casualties at railroad crossings had spurred demands in the mid-seventies for the elevation of the tracks, but disputes over the nature of the embankment and over the division of the costs dragged on for almost a decade. Finally, in October 1882 the elevated tracks were placed in use, though another year slipped by before the new east-side station was opened for business. Despite the construction of two additional regional roads, the Rome, Watertown, and Ogdensburg (the successor of the Lake Shore), which entered Rochester in 1888, and the Genesee Valley Canal Railroad built in that abandoned ditch a few years before, the Central continued to overshadow all other lines combined in both volume and value of trade. Even the Erie Canal, despite the final removal of all tolls in 1883, gradually lost its local trade, except coal and stone shipments, to the Central. Fortunately, the final passage in that year of the Hepburn Bill, for which many Rochester industrialists had petitioned during the previous five years, supplied a measure of state regulation. Local shippers did not get protection from the long-haul differentials and other monopoly abuses until the creation of the Interstate Commerce Commission in 1888.

The elevation of the New York Central and the opening of the new station on North St. Paul Street had a dramatic impact on the city's internal structure. Grade-crossing accidents had inhibited the development of the northeast sector until the mid-eighties when the extension of the horsecar lines through the new underpasses spurred the settlement of new subdivisions beyond the tracks. Because most of the newcomers in these years were immigrants from Eastern and Southern Europe, colonies of Sicilians, Poles, Ukranians, and Eastern Jews, each with its favorite building and loan societies, made their appearance there. The relocation of the station prompted the principal clothing firms, which dispatched numerous salesmen to distant cities every week, to move their headquarters from Mill Street to St. Paul Street in order to maintain easy access to the trains. That migration necessitated the demolition of the homesteads of former Mayor Samuel G. Andrews and his neighbors to make way for the six- and seven-story office and factory buildings that made St. Paul a rival of Main, State, and Exchange streets for commercial priority.

Rochester was not easily pushed about. Even before the new challenge was clearly posed, the leaders at the old Four Corners had launched improvements that would assure their position for decades to come. The erection of the seven-story Elwood building in 1879, with the gargoyles on its tower looking down into the sixth-story office of Daniel Powers, had prompted him to add a seventh story under a second mansard roof in order to maintain the priority of his massive block. Vanderbilt might move east, but Powers and his associates determined in 1881 to erect a sumptuous new hotel facing the court house a block west of the Four Corners. Soon the seven-story Powers Hotel, said to rival in elegance, size, and safety the Palmer House in Chicago, took its place adjoining the Powers block and, with the recently remodeled Rochester Savings Bank, formed an impressive architectural facade for the civic square in front of the court house. When in the late eighties Frederick Cook erected the ten-story German Insurance Company building on the south side of Main Street, and Samuel Wilder constructed the eleven-story block across Exchange

Street, Powers added two more floors and a third mansard roof, plus a tower that retained his claim to top place on the Rochester skyline.

Several vigorous new leaders were, however, turning eastward. H. H. Warner and George W. Archer joined the march to North St. Paul where each erected a seven-story factory building. Archer engaged the services of Harvey Ellis, a young architect who also designed three of the new clothing factories that arose on that street. Ellis gave these buildings a lofty expression that would later be hailed as the creative link between Richardson and Sullivan in American architectural history. A. J. Warner and other local architects soon caught something of Ellis's zeal for tasteful designs. The extension of the high-pressure Holly mains, giving increased fire protection and supplying water power to operate elevators, spurred the construction of fifty-seven new business blocks in 1889. Although the Four Corners and West Main Street retained their hold on banking, the courts, the hotel and office trade, and most civic functions, North St. Paul became the wholesale and clothing district, and East Main attracted new retail and department stores and displaced State Street as the favorite shopping district.

The city's rapid growth in the 1880s intensified its need for new organizational efforts. As the volume of real estate transactions multiplied, a number of prominent dealers gathered in October 1887 to form the Real Estate Exchange to determine the proper fees and commissions and perform useful cooperative functions. The Clearing House established by the bankers focused on a specific function, although the Commercial Travelers Association, organized by some of Rochester's leading salesmen in 1880, had more convivial objectives, but each represented an adjustment to the city's increased complexity. The resurgent struggle of various groups of workers to form trade unions was an old story and involved a more fundamental organizational effort, but the creation in 1883 of the Central Labor Union to coordinate the local affairs of various units of the Knights of Labor, and the establishment five years later of the Central Trades Council were more directly a response to the complexities of the community than to divisions in the economy. In similar fashion the organization, after many attempts, of a successful chamber of commerce in 1888 represented the attainment of a new industrial complexity sufficiently diversified to avoid the domination of any one special faction and sufficiently dynamic to undertake to coordinate the interests of all sections of the business community.

It was perhaps significant that leadership in the establishment of the Chamber of Commerce came from a secondary industry. Some of the prestigious millers, merchants, and bankers who had failed in earlier attempts to organize a board of trade were still around, and the output of Rochester's mills, as well as the size of its shipments, was greater than ever before, but these men, though still jealous of each other, were content to follow other leaders. Representatives of both the shoe and the clothing industries were now included among the directors of the various banks and insurance companies, yet they seldom sat on the same boards, and they were generally absorbed by their own industrial problems. The nurserymen, deeply involved in agricultural and horticultural societies, were busy maintaining the city's regional leadership. Thus, in 1887 when Cornelius R. Parsons, in his eleventh year as mayor and after answering repeated inquiries from organized groups of businessmen in other cities, invited twenty industrial and business leaders to his office to consider the formation of a permanent association, they elected H. H. Warner, the flamboyant head of a minor enterprise, as president. Warner welcomed the opportunity, and his broad interests and promotional talents set the pattern for future chamber presidents.

The city's development depended more directly on the output of its industries, large and small. The 735 industrial establishments tabulated in 1880 more than doubled in number within the decade, boosting Rochester from twenty-third to eighteenth place in net value of products and to sixteenth in numbers employed and wages paid. Most of these enterprises were small ventures, owned and operated individually or in partnership, and the average number employed in 1890 was seventeen; some, however, had already attained a considerable size, and three employed more than one thousand each. Most of the larger enterprises were incorporated, and the 1890 *Directory* listed 165 as chartered and functioning in Rochester. Only four reported a capitalization of $1 million, but several others exceeded $500,000, and some failed to supply such information; some also failed to report or incorporate, for the list included only one of the numerous shoe and clothing firms that supplied fully one-third of Rochester's employment.

Although the men's clothing industry had become one of the two largest in Rochester, rivaled only by the shoe industry, its organizational structure and work patterns reflected earlier practices. The sixteen firms of 1880 were merchant-manufacturers who operated cutting rooms and wholesale departments but who distributed the sewing and finishing tasks under the family system brought from the old country. Several of these firms, endeavoring to build a reputation for quality suits, gathered their workers, both men and women, into new factory buildings during the eighties. They introduced cutting and sewing machines and supervised the performance of specialized tasks in order to speed production and maintain trademark standards. With the influx of Polish and Russian Jews in the late eighties, enterprising men among them organized production teams and open sweatshops where these newcomers could find employment among neighbors who spoke their own tongue. By 1890 the number of clothing firms had multiplied tenfold, but the great majority were sweatshops operating under contracts for the principal wholesalers who had joined in 1883 with the leading manufacturers in organizing the Clothiers Association to standardize the trade.

As the number of workers increased, some of the skilled tailors and cutters made repeated efforts to form unions. The Sons of Adam, a benevolent organization, collapsed in the late seventies when its treasurer absconded with the dues. The newly formed Knights of Labor organized a cutters union in 1881 but expelled it a year later when the officers called an unauthorized strike. A new benevolent society, which organized chapters in the five leading factories, joined the Knights of Labor in 1888 and won a nine-hour day and a modest wage increase from the Clothiers Association. That victory, however, brought a reorganization of the association into the Clothiers Exchange, pledged to conduct the industry independently of the union. Less peaceful times lay ahead.

The shoe industry, which had made an earlier shift to factory production, experienced labor difficulties throughout these years. Hoping to encourage a reopening of the factories early in the depression, the Knights of St. Crispin had accepted a 30 percent reduction in wages, but they bitterly resisted a second cut in 1875. Defeated after a strike of two months on that occasion, they won a restoration of that cut four years later and, after successful tussles with separate firms, joined the newly arrived Knights of Labor in 1881. Suddenly the next January the local assembly of lasters presented new wage demands and withdrew these skilled men from the workbenches. Other shoe workers, including many women who comprised approximately half the work force, joined the strike, and most firms hastened to reach a settlement. When two firms held out and secured more favorable terms, their owners, Patrick Cox and John Kelly, took the lead in forming the Shoe Manufacturers Association, which resisted new demands in 1887 and supported a lockout that proved more damaging to their factories than to the workers who readily secured other jobs.

Part of the problems at the shoe factories was the introduction of new machines. Local firms, producing high-grade women's shoes, had to pay royalties for use of the McKay and Goodyear machines to maintain their competitive position. Each new device permitted a reduction in the number of skilled craftsmen but called for the employ of additional machine tenders, including women and boys who could be engaged at lower rates. Although disputes with the Knights of Labor persisted, the companies increased the total number employed and organized specialized teams of vampers, fitters, pasters, lining makers, buttonhole and eyelet sewers, as well as cutters, lasters, welters, and sewing machine operators. By standardizing their production methods, they increased their output and captured a wide market that brought an increase of local shoe factories to fifty-one by 1890, when the numbers employed and the total wages paid exceeded every other industry in Rochester and gave it fifth place among the nation's shoe producers. That local accomplishment brought the National Retail Shoe Dealers Association to Rochester for a convention at the New Osburn House in 1888, but it also brought seventy-five delegates to the same hotel in Rochester that June for a convention of the Shoemakers National District Assembly of the Knights of Labor. Mayor Parsons welcomed the visiting Knights, and local union groups staged a parade in their honor, a demonstration that provided a trial run for the first Labor Day parade that September.

TECHNICAL AND SPECIALIZED INDUSTRIES

Despite the number of jobs they supplied, the profits they returned to some at the top, and the labor-management experience they brought, neither clothing nor shoes set Rochester's industrial pattern. The city's standard of living and its economic future would have been poor indeed had it depended on the relatively low wages and the limited range of external economies they afforded. Fortunately, the metalworking and woodworking trades were nurturing a number of ingenious inventors and enterprising managers who, together with a multitude of skilled artisans, were developing a variety of specialized industries. Though small in size, the foundries, tool and safe makers, and machine shops gave employment to over 1,000 men in 1888 and nearly doubled that force within a decade. Their average annual wage in 1890 was $626, the highest of any major group in the city. Good wages nurtured a sense of responsibility among the metalworkers, and one union displayed samples of its employer's products in a Labor Day parade. The Co-operative Foundry continued to demonstrate the capacity of union leaders as managers. The most significant developments in this industry were the new inventions it fostered, such as the time locks patented by James Sargent and produced for wide sale by Sargent & Greenleaf, and the gear cutting machine patented by William Gleason and manufactured to order by the Gleason Works for new industrial ventures springing up across the land.

Similar examples of innovation and specialization occurred in the woodworking industry. The furniture factories, hard hit by the depression, made a successful recovery in the late seventies and doubled their output in the next decade. Two chair factories specialized in barber and dental chairs and accessory products. Several cabinetmakers specialized in the building of showcases for Ward's natural science exhibits in scattered museums and for department store displays in cities near and far. The Stein Manufacturing Company employed many skilled cabinetmakers in the manufacture of caskets and, after the completion of its new factory designed by Harvey Ellis on Exchange Street, exceeded all competitors in the volume and style of its products. James Cunningham's carriage factory, the largest in the city for a brief period, never rivaled the major carriage works of several larger cities but nevertheless attained distinction for the ornate hearses it produced and exhibited at regional and national fairs.

With few exceptions Rochester's industrial pioneers were barely holding to their earlier pace while others surged ahead. Most of the older millers had given place to younger men, among them George Motley, a recent arrival from England who had substituted steel rollers for millstones and utilized steam power in periods of water shortage in order to maintain full production in a reduced number of mills. As some old milling families recouped their fortunes by selling excess mill sites to other industries, several nurserymen reaped generous profits by subdividing their original nursery fields to meet the city's expanding need for homes. A few retired in the process, but Ellwanger and Barry developed new lands farther out, sufficient to maintain their national leadership. Among the seedsmen, James Vick and Hiram Sibley, a new entry in this field, pressed ahead with dramatic campaigns for leadership in a nationwide mail-order market. These firms helped to maintain Rochester's hinterland ties and to sustain its numerous printing and publishing enterprises, which together employed the city's sixth largest work force.

But the most glamorous advances in these years occurred in three relatively new industries—tobacco, beer, and patent medicine. William S. Kimball, whose control of a patented bailer for making plug tobacco created a market that called for the construction of a new factory in 1881, quickly emerged as one of the city's most dynamic leaders. The tasteful design of that structure, situated on the island between the aqueduct and Court Street, and the perfection of a cigarette cutting machine by an inventor he had financed, prompted Kimball to convert the new building into a cigarette factory. By March 1883 his 800 workers, mostly female, comprised the largest work force in the city and with other improved machines, soon produced a million cigarettes a day. To counteract the doubts that certain Victorian social leaders held concerning the cigarette, which was still regarded as a decadent French product, Kimball ordered the construction of a 21-foot statue of Mercury, which, when mounted on the top of his massive smokestack in 1885, became Rochester's favorite skyline symbol. He built an impressive mansion on Troup Street that overshadowed all of its more sedate companions in the Third Ward; he added an art gallery that rivaled that of Daniel Powers, in value if not in size, and he joined with H. H. Warner in the establishment of the Chamber of Commerce and became its second president.

Though somewhat less dramatic, the brewers of Rochester experienced an even more substantial expansion than the tobacco men enjoyed, and their impact proved more enduring. Again, success sprang from new patents, in this case a bunging apparatus that facilitated fermentation under conditions of a partial vacuum. While Henry Bartholomay, one of the two contenders for control of that patent, vigorously promoted the development of the largest of four local brewing firms, Casper Pfaudler, his rival for the patent, organized the Pfaudler Vacuum Fermentation Process Company and pressed the search for a means of building a tank that would hold a vacuum without spoiling the brew. Bartholomay, who prided himself on the sleek and robust appearance of the horses that hauled his beer kegs to market, erected an impressive new factory and office building near the new Central station. Embittered by the attacks of the temperance forces, he seized the first opportunity to negotiate a profitable sale of his firm and his two leading competitors to a group of British capitalists for a reported $3.5 million in 1889, after which he was able to return in baronial splendor to his native Germany. Pfaudler, in contrast, secured the aid of James Sargent in perfecting a process for constructing glass-lined tanks, which soon developed promising new uses and assured a bright future for the Pfaudler Company.

It was H. H. Warner who played the most dramatic role on the Rochester scene in these years. Lacking the more dashing character of Asa T. Soule, whose enthusiastic promotion of sporting events, including those of the local baseball team, named the Hop Bitters, made his product a household term, Warner won, by the sheer size of his promotions, an international market for his Safe Liver Cure pills. To give his product a scientific aroma, he built an imposing observatory for Lewis Swift, Rochester's amateur astronomer who had won fame for his comet discoveries, and announced a Warner Safe Liver Cure prize of a gold medal and $100 to be awarded at the Warner observatory to the first discoverer of each new comet. That award brought continuing publicity, but the promotion he announced in 1883, possibly the original puzzle contest, attracted wider attention. His promise of $1,000 for the correct solution of ten enigmas and the largest numbers of words composed from the letters in the sentence "Beware of injurious imitations of Warner's Safe Kidney and Liver Cure, etc." brought thousands of replies to his headquarters on North St. Paul Street. As orders also rolled in, Warner assumed a posture of leadership in the city and, as previously mentioned, was elected first president of the Chamber of Commerce. His inaugural, delivered at a banquet he munificently gave to its 274 members in the new Powers Hotel in January 1888, set a precedent for annual promotional reviews by the city's leading businessmen.

Dramatic as these accomplishments were, it was on another group of industrialists that Rochester's future depended. Although promotion played a part, the chief reliance was on technical and scientific skills and on the development and protection of patents. George H. Smith's headlamp was only one of several local lamp inventions, including the famous Rochester lamp with the round wick that added so much to the efficiency of oil lamps, and successive lamp companies gave employment to several hundred skilled men in these years. The elevators of L. S. Graves, the mail chutes of James G. Cutler, the water meters of Jonathan B. West, and the thermometers and barometers of George Taylor were only a few of the ingenious products of Rochester inventors that would return large profits. George B. Selden's automobile patent, though never put into production, would ultimately produce rich royalties. Meanwhile, Rochester firms were paying royalties to distant inventors for patents useful in local production.

One of the first to make profitable use of both outside and local patents was Bausch & Lomb. Their exclusive license to use hard rubber in the manufacture of spectacle frames and other optical parts had prompted the erection of a four-story factory on North St. Paul Street in 1874. The first four-page price list issued the next year to announce the production of five microscope models was soon replaced by longer lists and, in 1889, by a 112-page booklet listing microscopes, telescopes, and other optical supplies invented and produced in its expanded factories. The one hundred skilled operatives of 1875 had more than doubled in number as the company increased its list of patents to two score and was negotiating an agreement with Karl Zeiss in Germany for the manufacturing rights in America on his patents. Although two of his early assistants, Ernst Gundlach and Philip H. Yawman, were already forming independent optical ventures, John Jacob Bausch was able to increase the capitalization of his firm from $50,000 to $200,000 in 1890.

More surprising, was the announcement that year of an increase in the capitalization of the Eastman Dry Plate and Film Company to $1,000,000. Few were aware in the late 1870s of the experiments conducted by George Eastman in his mother's kitchen, but Rochester, as a center of daguerrotype and other photographic studios, was an ideal base for an amateur interested in improving the techniques of that intriguing hobby. Impatient with the necessity to coat the wet plates in improvised dark rooms, Eastman was eagerly striving to perfect the formula for a dry-plate emulsion that he had found in an English photographic almanac. By 1879 he was ready to undertake the manufacture of dry plates and hastened to secure patents in England and America on an apparatus he devised to coat the plates. He opened the first workshop on the third floor of a State Street music store in 1880, but with the backing of Henry A. Strong, the whip manufacturer who boarded at his mother's lodging house, Eastman soon moved into larger quarters nearby and gave up his clerkship at the Rochester Savings Bank in order to devote full time to the new enterprise.

Eastman quickly began his search for a flexible film to replace glass plates. His first success was in the preparation of a paper-backed film, which was patented in March 1884. With William H. Walker, a camera maker employed in January that year, he soon produced a roll holder to mount the film in a camera. In October he reorganized his firm as the Eastman Dry Plate and Film Company, capitalized at $200,000, half of it represented by patents. By 1888 he was ready to market a small box camera equipped with film for one hundred exposures. Named the Kodak and priced at twenty-five dollars, it was marketed with the understanding that buyers would return the used camera to the company; for ten dollars the company removed and developed the film and delivered the reloaded camera with the finished pictures to the owner. Increasing numbers of amateurs were soon attracted by Eastman's catchy slogan, "You press the button; we do the rest."

Not satisfied with his paper-backed film, Eastman hired a young chemist from the university, Henry M. Reichenbach, to make a transparent film. After a year's search, Reichenbach developed a suitable film and, jointly with Eastman, secured patents on the film and the drying and spreading apparatus for its production. One of the first orders for the new film came from Thomas A. Edison who was experimenting with the development of a motion-picture camera. As the potential of his new product became evident, Eastman hastened to buy useful and possibly conflicting patents in order to maintain a practical control of the industry's development. Thus, in 1889 he acquired from a North Dakota farmer a film-puncturing device that facilitated the use of motion-picture film. After establishing a subsidiary in England, he again reorganized as the Eastman Company, capitalized at $1 million.

Most Rochesterians were more concerned in the 1880s with the development of a number of utility companies whose performance was, at the time, much more crucial. When in 1880 the Mutual Gas Light Company, an eastern concern with the exclusive right to manufacture water gas, entered Rochester, the city welcomed its challenge to the two older companies that had divided the city in order to avoid competition. However, when the council granted a franchise and the municipal company began to lay mains on the west side, the old Rochester Gas Light Company hastened to effect a merger that avoided any major reduction in rates. Disillusioned by that experience, the city refused to grant a franchise to the Natural Gas Fuel Company when it sought entry in 1886, and Rochester lost the competitive advantage that Buffalo and some other cities secured with the introduction of cheap natural gas. When its three gas companies finally effected a consolidation, the city had to look to its new electric companies for a competitive check on the rates for its street lamps. Unfortunately, the competitive utopia that seemed to have arrived in 1887, when the lamp committee announced its contracts with two gas companies and three electric companies, was illusory, because the charges for the various types of street lamps that totaled 1,951 showed an advance of 40 percent over the previous year without a commensurate increase in service. Moreover, the confusion presented by the tangle of overhead wires, like that of duplicating mains in the streets, presented a troublesome new problem.

Rochester's special interest in the telegraph prepared it for quick use of the telephone after its demonstration at the Centennial Exhibition of 1876. The city, in fact, installed telephones in place of the proposed telegraph stations along the line of its water conduit from Hemlock Lake to Rochester on its completion the next year. It granted franchises in 1879 to both the Bell and the Edison telephone companies but soon discovered that two separate systems with a few hundred phones each had limited advantages. Few protested when the two lines merged the next June, but when the combined Bell Telephone Company raised its rates in 1883, and three years later introduced a meter system effecting additional increases, protests mounted.

Most of the one thousand subscribers joined in a users' strike that continued for two full years and silenced the lines until a move by the Common Council to compel the company to remove its unused poles from the streets brought a hasty compromise that enabled the company to extend its services into the more affluent residential areas and to establish a long-distance linkage attractive to subscribers in the business district.

This graphic demonstration of the threat of monopoly control prompted citizens to look more searchingly at other utility franchises. The failure of the Rochester City and Brighton Railway to extend its lines into the northeast and southwest districts prompted the organization of rival companies and the submission of bids for franchises to serve these areas. In the debate that followed it was suddenly discovered that the old company had neglected to pay the annual five dollar license fee due on each car and was liable for large back claims. Moreover, its repeated refusals to deal with the union of its drivers and its use of strikebreakers, aided by a group of Pinkerton detectives imported from the East, stirred popular sympathy for the drivers and gave added support to the applicants for new franchises. George E. Mumford, who held the presidency of both applicants, had the backing of capitalists in Pittsburgh and Philadelphia who were eager not only to build new lines but also to take over and electrify the horsecar lines of the old company. Everybody rejoiced when the old company agreed to sell out, but a new hassle developed when the new company insisted that its franchise, which was due to expire in 1892, had by a vague provision been extended to 1967. After lengthy negotiations the new company agreed to assume the five dollar payments due under the old franchise until 1892 and then to pay one percent on gross receipts for fifteen years and two percent during the balance of its corporate life, or until 1967. The company undertook to speed the electrification of its old lines and to extend them into the new built-up districts; it also agreed to limit all fares to five cents and to grant free transfers for continuous rides. With a capitalization of $4,000,000, the reorganized Rochester Railway Company emerged in 1890 as the largest corporation in the city. Its contributions to the efficiency and flexibility of Rochester's economy would be great, but not as significant as its impact on the spatial distribution and spread of its residents.

NEW CIVIC AND POLITICAL FUNCTIONS

Rochester's economic resurgence, accompanied by and, in large part, powered by a 63 percent growth in population between 1875 and 1890, greatly intensified many old civic problems and introduced new dilemmas. The increased absorption of its industrialists in private affairs enabled other men to develop careers in civic leadership, and the city's continued growth both in size and diversity placed a high premium on their performance. The struggle between old Yankee mores and new Continental standards dominated the political scene and complicated the search for efficient administration. Fortunately, an awakening social consciousness fostered the development of a new conception of public health and a new concern for private welfare.

In spite of its rapid growth, Rochester enjoyed an era of unusual stability in civic affairs. Two closely related administrative developments contributed to this situation. The successful collaboration in 1875 of Republican reformers under Scottish-born Mayor Clarkson and Democratic reformers under Assemblyman Fish secured the creation of a bipartisan executive board and removed many of the more difficult administrative problems from the always turbulent political eddies of the Common Council. It also relieved the mayor of many responsibilities and thus enabled him to give more attention to other tasks, including the increasingly important nominations to various boards and the new ceremonial functions. Cornelius R. Parsons, son of an English-born lumber merchant and alderman, found the mayor's duties so agreeable during his first two years in that office (1876–78) that he stood for repeated reelections and served for an unprecedented succession of seven terms. By his nominations to the Executive Board, he kept it in able bipartisan hands until 1880, when a charter revision reduced the board to three elective officials. His long experience and continued popular support enabled him to preside effectively and graciously over the city's semicentennial observance in June 1884.

Because of its many functions, the Executive Board quickly displaced the mayor and the Common Council as the crucial center of power. Former Mayor Fish served as chairman for the first four years, to be replaced briefly by Byron Holley, another reformer, and then in 1883 by George W. Aldridge who made it the base for his increasing dominance over local Republican forces. However, the Executive

Board's tasks were administrative rather than political, and they grew, in large part, out of the successful completion in its first year of the waterworks. The high-pressure streams available at the Holly hydrants had retired all but two of the steam fire engines in 1875, but as builders took advantage of the wide availability of water for the operation of elevators and erected new five- and six-story blocks, the Executive Board had to reactivate the old steamers and expand the department, with Aldridge as its special patron.

The abundant supply of water raised other new problems. The steady advance of the water mains had stimulated a rapid installation of private water closets, which focused attention on the need for a new sanitary sewer system. When a survey in 1880 revealed that 15 percent of the city's homes had already installed water closets, even the Board of Health demanded action. Fears concerning the probable costs produced delays, but after two abortive starts, Emil Kuichling, an engineer born and educated in Germany who had won election to the Executive Board in 1884, accepted the task of planning and building the east-side trunk sewer to pick up the flow of neighborhood sewers and to discharge it in the river below the lower falls. To speed the restoration of the macadamized street pavements over the sewer ditches, the board ordered a second steamroller similar to the one it had acquired to repair the roads after the laying of the water mains a decade before. It also acquired a sprinkler to lay the dust on the macadam streets and a sweeper to clean the Medina stone pavements. It laid a stretch of "Dude Pavement," as the newly introduced asphalt was called, on West Avenue in 1886, but no other neighborhood was willing to vote the necessary outlays.

Although overshadowed by the Executive Board, several other authorities exercised important civic functions. The Board of Health supervised the collection of garbage by contractors who sold it to nearby piggeries until 1880, when the westward migration of several hog farmers closed that outlet and forced the board to hire drivers to haul the garbage out for burial in nearby nurseries and truck gardens. The board pressed its vaccination program in the schools, but plans for the inspection of milk and meat were blocked by the lack of funds until a group of milk dealers, determined to weed out dealers who watered their product, collected fees to maintain an inspector. To give the inspectors proper authority, the board soon took over the inspection of a sampling of the 12,000 quarts of milk delivered daily in the city and undertook periodic checks of meat and fish markets as well.

Despite the crucial importance of the health and assessment boards among others, none rivaled the prestige quickly acquired by the newly created park commission in the late eighties. Local city neighborhoods had long cherished the six small parks donated by early promoters to enhance their subdivisions, but the Common Council had repeatedly rejected pleas, even offers of land, for a city park. Fortunately, the wide publicity that accompanied the opening of the national park at Niagara Falls in 1885 helped to revive interest in Rochester. A renewed offer by Ellwanger and Barry of the hilltop center of their old nursery grounds finally won a hesitant acceptance by the council, but a group of leading citizens, headed by Dr. Edward Moore and backed by Mayor Parsons, had meanwhile secured legislative provision for a park commission empowered to issue $300,000 in bonds with which to establish a well-rounded park system. Organized in 1888 and headed by Dr. Moore, the twenty-man commission solicited the advice of leading park authorities, including Frederick Law Olmsted, and, in the face of much criticism, proceeded to purchase lands along the river on the city's northern and southern outskirts and to develop these, with the donated highlands, into a park system that would eventually win wide acclaim.

It was the police board that faced the most controversial issues. Baffled by the perplexing task of enforcing a miscellaneous collection of blue laws on a cosmopolitan population that regarded these restraints with scant respect, the police tended to blame the excise commission for its indiscriminate grant of liquor licenses. An investigation in 1879 revealed a lax collection of license fees and prompted a list of indictments of the mayor, which were quickly dropped when Parsons won an increased majority at the polls. A marked improvement in the collection of license fees nevertheless occurred, increasing the total to 1,433 in 1882. Although the police could not legitimately apply that technique to the suppression of gambling and prostitution, their practice of conducting periodic raids and levying moderate fines on offending keepers had somewhat the same effect and proved equally disturbing to the reformers. Their temperance, antigambling, and antivice campaigns helped to deprive Mayor Parsons of Republican support but enabled him to win a sufficient backing from ethnic and labor groups under varied party labels to assure his repeated reelection.

Some champions of middle-class mores chose the humanitarian rather than the legalistic approach. The charitable impulse was, however, firmly ingrained among immigrants as well as Yankees, as the simultaneous development of St. Mary's and the General hospitals and of Catholic and Protestant orphan asylums and industrial schools demonstrated. Wealthy patrons of new medical philosophies took the lead in establishing the Rochester Homeopathic Hospital in 1887 and the Hahnemann Hospital a year later. None of these institutions had commitments to particular moral codes, but difficulties frequently developed when rival clergymen sought to visit patients. However, the controversies were not as intense as at the penal and correctional institutions, where Bishop McQuaid finally secured the appointment of Catholic as well as Protestant chaplains.

A similar zeal marked the early years of the YMCA in its quarters on the south side of Main Street bridge, and of the Women's Christian Association, founded in 1883. Nevertheless, an interest in wholesome recreational activities soon began to overshadow their evangelistic programs. When the Young Men's Catholic Association, established by Bishop McQuaid in the early seventies, succumbed to the depression, German and Irish benevolent societies in the various churches answered the social needs of their young men. Some citizens who deplored the socializing trends and moral complacency of some of these bodies gave their support instead to the Temperance Reform Society in the late seventies, followed by the WCTU and the Salvation Army, which made their appearance locally in the early eighties. Other citizens, more concerned for humanitarian than ideological goals, established and supported the local Humane Society and America's second local Red Cross chapter. Finally, under the leadership of Oscar Craig, Rochester's representative on the State Board of Charities, humanitarians formed the Society for Organized Charity to coordinate these various institutional activities.

Although the enthusiasm evident in its early years had flagged somewhat, the most important integrating agency was the school system. The school board, with a member elected from each ward, had degenerated into a training program for potential aldermen, and neither Sylvannus Ellis, superintendent throughout most of this period, nor Nehemiah Benedict, principal of the Free Academy until 1883, enjoyed its support. When demands for economy cut out funds for a program of evening courses, the protests of numerous Germans who had enrolled in language courses in English and German prompted the board to open several buildings for evening classes conducted by volunteer teachers. Many of the same folk supported the music classes and secured their reinstatement. A new principal at the Free Academy introduced gymnastic exercises and placed a greater emphasis on science and business courses in the mid-eighties. The first free kindergarten, opened in 1887, and the introduction a year later of experiments in science and demonstration work in other academy subjects provided hopeful signs of a more creative approach. The occasional replacement of an able instructor by a political friend of a board member brought repeated pleas for a small and more dedicated board. While the reformers bided their time, Bishop McQuaid pressed ahead with his campaign to open parochial schools in every parish. Despite some dissension over the program, which supported fourteen parochial schools by 1890 (when the public schools numbered thirty-two), the Sisters of St. Joseph, who staffed most of them, contributed to the education of some 7,000 youngsters who could not have found room in the city's public schools, where the attendance averaged 13,063 that year.

Only limited numbers of the graduates of the district and parochial schools secured admittance to the Free Academy, and a still smaller number went on to college. Eight private teachers offered courses in business subjects, but it was the establishment in 1885 of Mechanics Institute, and a year later of the Reynolds Library, that represented the most promising new beginnings. When Captain Henry Lomb, the chief backer of the institute brought Eugene C. Colby to Rochester to organize its program of technical courses, he launched developments that had wide-ranging influences on the public schools as well. Although the Reynolds Library, at the time of its opening in the Reynolds Arcade, represented little more than a reorganization of the collections of the old Athenaeum library, which had closed for lack of support nine years before, its new staff, under the direction of Professor William C. Morey of the university and with the backing of Mortimer

F. Reynolds, quickly improved the selection and arrangement of books and made them more accessible and useful.

Yet important as these institutional efforts were, they did not rival the educational and informational contributions of the daily and weekly papers. Not only did the three dailies of 1875 increase to five during the period, but beginning with the *Democrat & Chronicle* in 1884, they enlarged their size from four to eight, and sometimes twelve, pages and, in the case of the *Union* and the *Democrat,* boosted their circulations to 12,000 and 14,000 a day by the close of the period. Their larger size provided space for columns on sports events, fashion notes, and extended quotes from sermons and lectures, as well as police reports and other local news events. Editorials, boosting the paper's favored political faction, filled two or more columns daily, and although the contention often seemed excessive, the effort to draw readers into a participatory relationship had a democratic effect. Readers had discovered in the 1870s that if the *Democrat* or the *Express* attacked one's cause, the *Union* would defend it, and they learned as the years passed that there were not only two different Republican views on most subjects, but at least three as the *Herald* made its appearance in 1881. The establishment of the *Times* in 1887 supplied a second voice for the Democrats. Germans who could not read English had a choice of two, sometimes three, German dailies and several weeklies, each with distinctive political or ethnic viewpoints. Readers who could not afford the time or the money for a daily paper could peruse one of several Sunday papers in the seventies, and the *Democrat* boldly entered that field with its own Sunday edition in 1879. That action revealed that even the old "Granny" of the Rochester press, as the *Democrat & Chronicle* was described, was becoming more cosmopolitan and was endeavoring to meet and communicate with the newcomers it had formerly castigated. The pious protests of those who did not wish to see the Sabbath desecrated found vent in the *Union,* which could not hope to win permanent support from such folk. It too was becoming less doctrinaire and more urbanized, stressing its news coverage more than its politics; in 1890 it introduced the first rotogravure sheet published in Rochester.

As the editors expanded their coverage and gave more attention to the production of their journals, they lost the dominant position in politics. Neither Charles Fitch of the *Democrat* nor Joseph O'Connor of the *Express* achieved the influence held by Isaac Butts and Lewis Selye before them, and even William Purcell in his long years as editor of the *Union* discovered that politics, like journalism, was becoming a specialized activity and finally chose the newspaper over the party as his responsibility. Yet the division was by no means distinct, and the *Union* continued to champion local Democrats who generally controlled the Common Council in these years; the *Democrat & Chronicle*, the *Express*, and the *Herald* supported separate Republican factions, which frequently merged in national elections and challenged George Aldridge on the Executive Board to distribute patronage more widely in order to win state and local elections as well.

A COSMOPOLITAN SOCIETY

It was in the social and cultural fields that the cosmopolitan influences were most apparent. Few would have predicted at mid-century that within a quarter-century a Catholic bishop, a professor of science, and a dancing master would supply leadership in important Rochester fields. Nor would many have guessed that a leading banker's chief pride would be his art gallery, that other businessmen would seek distinction as sponsors of a baseball club or as patrons of the theater, or that their sons and daughters would be returning from trips to Europe with new talents in art or music and would be competing for local favor with recent newcomers from abroad. Even residents of the Flower City who had taken these developments in stride were somewhat surprised on November 30, 1887, when four trainloads of excursionists from upstate towns inundated its hotels and crowded its streets with villagers and other rural Americans eager to see the marvels of a cosmopolitan city.

Still the most inclusive cultural institutions of the time, the churches provided the simplest gauge of Rochester's increased diversity. Bishop McQuaid's forthright leadership brought the establishment of three new Catholic churches, making fourteen in all, and the final dedication of St. Patrick's Cathedral after its debt was paid off in 1883. The joyous ceremonies that marked the blessing of their bells and the grand procession in memory of Pope Pius IX supplied memorable community events that stilled some of the acrimony that developed when Protestant and Catholic clergymen debated their respective beliefs or when German, Italian, and Polish Catholics demanded and finally received recognition of their own ethnic traditions and clergy from the Irish-dominated diocese. New fissures developed among the Protestants, and also among the Jews, who now formed three distinct bodies. However, most of the dissident groups recognized the need to work together in combating crime and other evils. Dr. James B. Shaw voiced the new cosmopolitan spirit in his thirty-eighth anniversary sermon in December 1878. "There was a time," declared the white-haired dean of Rochester Presbyterians, "when I could not bear the noise of the Methodists, . . . when I could not look into a Baptistry, . . . when I thought my Congregational friends were a bit loose, . . . when I believed many of the bad stories told me about the Pope and the papists. . . ." But after many years of close association with devoted men of all faiths, he had learned, he said, to cooperate with those who were sincere and who recognized his rights in return. And on his retirement, nine years later, Bishop McQuaid joined with Protestants and Jews in expressions of appreciation for Dr. Shaw's moderating influence.

An increased emphasis on social activities may have helped account for the moderation of doctrinal differences. The mutual benefit societies and parish halls of several of the Catholic churches, drawn together by the bishop into a Roman Catholic Union, prompted the local Baptists and Presbyterians also to form social unions and spurred the Methodists to organize Young People's Christian associations, which stimulated the formation of Christian Endeavor societies in a dozen other churches. Adult men's Sabbath school classes in leading Protestant churches and women's missionary and temperance societies developed a lay leadership that drew the churches more extensively into community action in the fields of welfare and education, as well as temperance, although the clergy no longer provided effective leadership.

In the intellectual field the crucial development was the scientific awakening, which resulted from a variety of influences, local and worldwide. The university, led by President Anderson, maintained a restraining attitude throughout most of the period. Anderson's conservatism prompted Professor Ward to resign, but Professor Lattimore continued his lectures on science and in 1881 took the lead in the formation of the Academy of Science. Newton Mann, the Unitarian minister who had been one of the first to discuss the Darwinian thesis in Rochester in the early seventies, became the second president of the academy—an event that gave encouragement not only to those interested in making scientific collections and technical experiments but also to those who raised philosophical questions or battled doctrinaire traditions. The academy drew support from the members of the Spencer Club, a small group of gentlemen who had debated the implications of Spencer's writings in the library of Lewis H. Morgan for several years. Robert Mathews, a hardware merchant who was the most faithful member of the club, became third president of the academy. Lewis Swift, also a former hardware merchant but now director of the Warner Observatory, opened on East Avenue in 1883, delivered occasional lectures on the heavens before the academy or the Rochester Society of Natural Sciences, organized by a group of ladies in 1884. When the liberal sermons of the Reverend Myron Adams of Plymouth Church alarmed a number of influential members of the rural-dominated Ontario Association and prompted them to expell him from its Congregational fellowship in 1880, the members of his church rallied to his support and maintained Plymouth Church as an independent body. The press reproduced extensive portions of his series of lecture-sermons on "The Continuous Creation" in 1889; it also welcomed the election of Dr. David Jayne Hill, author of a book that had objectively discussed the question of evolution, as successor to President Anderson, with the hope that the University of Rochester would now assume a more progressive position in local intellectual circles.

Indeed, in spite of the prestige of the professors at the university and the seminary, most of whom had studied at least a year in Europe, leadership in literature as well as science came from other callings. Although Professor Joseph H. Gilmore surveyed English literature in twenty public lectures that attracted an enthusiastic adult audience in 1879–80, and Professor Albert H. Mixer introduced the Pundits to Racine and other French dramatists, other men were doing the creative work. The essays and other writings of three newspapermen, Joseph O'Connor, Edward S. Martin, and Samuel H. Lowe, and the fictional writings of H. Pomeroy Brewster, Charles W. Balestier, and Mrs. Jane Marsh Parker, as well as the historical writing of Mrs.

Parker and William F. Peck who produced memorial volumes in commemoration of the city's semicentennial, all achieved some distinction. Like George H. Ellwanger, eldest son of the nurseryman, who returned to Rochester after study and travel abroad, most of these writers were Rochesterians of long standing who had, however, spent years in distant cities and now brought the fruits of wider experience to expression in the Flower City. Their contributions added vitality to the meetings of the Pundit Club and of new groups such as the Fortnightly Club, successor to the Spencer Club in 1882, and to the sophisticated but more informal gatherings at the homes of J. Sherloch Andrews in the early eighties on St. Paul Street and, later, the series of "conversations" at the residence of DeLancey Crittenden on Lake Avenue.

Distinguished visitors, such as J. D. Bell of Edinburgh, were favorably impressed by the high level of these activities, but the Rochester public was more aware of and more responsive to current developments in the arts. The sumptuous displays in the Powers art gallery not only stimulated a succession of excursions from upstate towns but also attracted a steady stream of residents to view its increasing list of paintings and sculpture. Local artists welcomed the opportunity to open studios in or near the Powers block and to hold art club exhibits and receptions in its galleries. Several other Rochester business leaders, tutored by Myron G. Peck, a cultivated teacher and art critic, developed art collections—Hiram Sibley, William S. Kimball, and H. H. Warner, among others—but Powers purchased the bulk of the Sibley collection and made his gallery and the adjoining Cobleigh Hall the undisputed center of displays and receptions long after the death of that fashionable dancing master in 1879.

Rochester's accomplishments in the field of music rivaled those in art although the programs were not as spectacular. Several of the players in the volunteer orchestra of the Philharmonic Society had attained such skill under the direction of Henri Appy that they were encouraged to pursue their studies in the East or abroad. A few of these talented men returned to Rochester in the mid-eighties to establish groups of their own, and although the Philharmonic dissolved, a plethora of instrumental and, especially, choral groups supplied a profusion of musical events under the aegis of the Maennerchor, the Apollo Singing Club, the Mendelssohn Society, and the Choral Union, among others. Some of these men collaborated with the local Comedy Club in the production of Gilbert and Sullivan operettas. These performances marked and perhaps helped stimulate the revival of interest in grand opera and the legitimate theater in the middle and late eighties.

Although the depression of the mid-seventies had snuffed out the two stock companies that had supplied dramatic entertainment for a number of years at the Opera House and the Corinthian Academy, Rochester soon enjoyed renewed activity in this field. Several troups of variety players visited for a week or more each winter in the early eighties, and an occasional dramatic company made a one-night stop, as in March 22, 1881, when Sarah Bernhardt played *Camille* at the Opera House. The popularity of burlesque and other amusements at a newly opened Dime Museum and the successful presentation of *Pinafore* and other light operas demonstrated the mounting desire for entertainment and prompted the organization of a company to build a new legitimate theater. The opening of the Lyceum on Clinton Avenue, just off Main Street, with a presentation of Belasco's play *The Wife*, a Broadway hit of the previous year, attracted a full house on October 8, 1888, and launched a dramatic season that extended Rochester's renaissance to the theater as well.

Local sportsmen also developed more diversified interests in these years. The Rochester baseball club, hard hit by the depression, failed to regain its former popularity. The three annual teams Asa Soule maintained as a promotion for his Hop Bitters Manufacturing Company proved disappointing, and it was not until the opening of Culver Field in 1886 that a new Rochester club gained admittance to the newly formed International League and ended in second place. Other competitive sports such as lacrosse, cricket, and the new lawn tennis attracted small numbers of participants and limited crowds of onlookers—nothing to compare with the throngs of 15,000 or more that flocked to Driving Park to witness the races that the Grand Trotting Circuit brought to the city annually during these years.

Driving Park provided a setting for many unusual spectacles. Buffalo Bill's Wild West Show spent a week there in June 1883, and local bicycle clubs and animals shows met there later in the decade. Bicycle racing, which made its appearance in 1879, the same year that saw the introduction of roller-skating, had its start in indoor rinks or on outdoor tracks in summertime; it attracted wider participation with the appearance of the safety bicycle in the late eighties. Local enthusiasts bought seven hundred bicycles in 1889 and opened the first bicycle path to Charlotte that fall. A football team made its first appearance at the university that year and after losing to Cornell, redeemed itself by defeating a visiting team from Syracuse. The crowds attracted to these sports events did not rival those drawn to Charlotte, Summerville, and Sea Breeze on the lake on hot Sundays or to private parks along the river and bay for picnics or boat excursions. The wider adoption of Saturday half-holidays by Rochester stores and factories (it was first introduced by Alfred Wright in his perfume factory in 1881) increased the excitement at local resorts in the late eighties.

The increased interest in public recreation reflected three significant developments. Not only was the foreign-born segment of the population becoming more diversified, but the number of their American-born children was increasing, and their restless desire to get out of their crowded homes brought them into the streets and to the lake and bay resorts. Their increasing numbers also fostered the city's trend towards active recreation, and the increasing proportion of women in the population created a demand for social activities. Each of these developments had wide-ranging effects on the city's growth.

One of the most dramatic developments in the city's social life was the profusion of its clubs and societies. Fraternal lodges, religious and charitable societies, social and sports clubs, and organizations devoted to music and the arts all multiplied in number and expanded their services. Not only did the old fraternal bodies such as the Masons and Odd Fellows establish new lodges, some in immigrant neighborhoods, but some of the ethnic groups founded fraternal societies of their own, such as the Harugari of the Germans and the B'nai B'rith of the Jews. The Jews had their own Phoenix, later the Eureka, Club. The Rochester Club, organized in the loft of the Rochester Savings Bank building in 1874, moved to new quarters on East Avenue a decade later. The new Genesee Valley Club, organized in 1885, opened a clubhouse on Washington Street that was equipped with dining facilities and other accommodations for its business and professional members; four years later it moved to a new clubhouse on East Avenue that boasted, among other facilities, a well-stacked wine cellar. Several other gentle-

men's clubs had regular nights to dine out at the Ocean Oyster House
or in one of the dining rooms of the new Powers Hotel.

The women, who outnumbered the men of Rochester ten to nine in
1890, had few comparable social organizations, but their increased
activity in church and other community affairs was attracting comment. The gentlemen of the press were still a bit amused at the action
of the ladies, led by the Anthony sisters and Mrs. L. C. Smith, in
establishing the Women's Political Equality Club in 1886, yet they
soon became more respectful. An effort by a half-dozen ladies to register to vote in a school election in 1881 had been blocked amidst un-
favorable news accounts, but after Susan B. Anthony returned from a
trip abroad during which she met with many prominent men and
women, the Women's Political Equality Club took the lead in 1890 in
arranging a reception in honor of her seventieth birthday in the rooms
of the Chamber of Commerce over the Rochester Savings Bank. A
second women's group, the Ignorance Club, formed by a number of
professional women, including Mrs. Jane Marsh Parker and Dr. Sarah
A. Dolley, provided an outlet for their intellectual interests, but the
most successful women's organization was the Ethical Club established
by Mrs. Mary T. Gannett, wife of the new Unitarian minister, who
soon filled the largest church auditorium with women of all denominations eager to see and hear the "Lady from Philadelphia" preside at
monthly discussions of current ethical problems.

Even more dramatic than the increased presence of women in
public life was the increased activity of foreign-born persons in city
affairs. Over 7,700 male immigrants secured their naturalization during
these fifteen years, which reduced the number listed as aliens in 1890
to under 4,000. Almost half the 40,000 foreign born of that year were
Germans and Eastern Europeans, outnumbering those from Britain,
including the Irish, who were now declining, and the Canadians. Each
group now had its churches—Protestant, Catholic, or Jewish—and a
variety of social organizations and welfare societies. The Sons of St.
George, the St. Andrew's Society, the St. Patrick's Society, the numerous Turner societies, the Swabian Society, and the Eureka Club maintained a profusion of social and cultural activities.

Several of these organizations made a deliberate effort to propagate
their ethnic traditions among their American-born children who now,
in most groups, outnumbered the foreign born. But other groups such

as the Young Men's Jewish Association and the German-American Society, by conducting courses in English, endeavored to facilitate the adjustment of newcomers to the American scene. Both German and Jewish societies maintained an agent to meet incoming immigrant trains and assist newcomers in finding relatives, jobs, and homes. An Italian benevolent society, the Bersagliere La Narmora, undertook in 1889 to safeguard the welfare of the 516 from that land. The St. Casimir Society, formed two years before in the Polish settlement on the city's northern border, successfully established the St. Stanislaus's Church in 1890. The African Zion Methodist church and the Douglass Union League continued to serve the small colony of Negroes, and some of the old residents of native stock began for the first time to make an effort to preserve their traditions, although the first local chapters of the SAR and DAR were not formed until 1894.

6

The People's City, 1890–1910

THE PERVASIVE OPTIMISM and high spirits that generally characterized Rochester were sharply challenged in the early 1890s in the economic and civic fields, but the city retained its basic vitality and emerged with greater strength. When, among others, H. H. Warner collapsed at the start of the depression and Daniel Powers and William S. Kimball died, younger and abler industrial and business leaders—George Eastman, Joseph T. Alling, and James G. Cutler, among many more—took their places. They successfully dispelled the last traces of hard times before the end of the decade and proceeded to meet the challenge of rapid urban growth by checking the excessive display of boss rule by George Aldridge. With other new leaders in ethnic and institutional circles, such as Walter Rauschenbusch and Mrs. Helen Barrett Montgomery, they would considerably increase popular participation in Rochester's social and cultural life and promote a fuller expression by all factions of the population.

DEPRESSION AND RECOVERY

The depths of the depression in the mid-nineties exceeded that of all earlier depressions in Rochester partly because of the surging height of the boom that preceeded it. With four suburban trolley lines and six steam railroads, plus three branch lines, the city preened itself in the early nineties as a budding rail center. The surging growth of its population in the eighties, exceeding that of Buffalo and all other cities in the state, prompted ambitious forecasts of future gains. With over half its 130,000 residents of 1890 under twenty-five years of age, Rochester had a youthful outlook and confidently expected to reach

200,000 by the turn of the century. Although it would require still another decade to reach that goal, local promoters were already constructing buildings that were transforming the character of the business district. Two in particular, the Granite and Keeler buildings, both of steel-frame construction and rising thirteen stories high on diagonal corners at Main and St. Paul streets, would finally overshadow the Powers block and Wilder building at the old Four Corners. But these accomplishments, even before their final completion in 1894, were marred by the onset of the depression, which brought the foreclosure of the Keeler building a few months after its opening, with the Chamber of Commerce proudly ensconced on its two top floors.

The youthful chamber had survived an earlier crisis before the financial panic erupted, but not without acute internal stress. J. Y. McClintock, the able civil engineer who served as first secretary, and George W. Elliott, city editor of the *Union & Advertiser,* had inaugurated a study of charter reform by a civic committee of the chamber headed by George C. Buell. Its main objective had been to devise civic procedures for improving utility services chiefly by preserving competition. When, however, the consolidation of the several gas and electric companies into the Rochester Gas & Electric and the reorganization of the Rochester Railway Company by outside capitalists brought two powerful monopolies onto the scene, businessmen who hoped for a more effective development of these services rose to their defense and called for the discharge of the civic committee. Buell, one of the original organizers of the Chamber of Commerce, had been slated for election as its fourth president, but critics of his committee's antimonopoly position engineered a shift at the last moment to Eugene T. Curtis, a shoe manufacturer who had become one of the owners of the *Union & Advertiser* and who favored strictly promotional functions for the chamber. Curtis replaced McClintock with a less controversial executive secretary, and his own successor, Max Brickner, the first Jew and first representative of the clothing industry to become president of the chamber, had won distinction as a star salesman and reemphasized the promotional program.

By selecting some presidents in the early nineties from the city's two dominant industries, the chamber identified itself to a degree with their attitudes towards organized labor. Both the shoe and clothing industries were involved in these years in repeated struggles with their employees, but despite their bitter opposition to the unions, both the Shoe Manufacturers Association and the Clothiers Exchange had to seek compromise settlements with their workers. Because of the declining power of the Knights of Labor, whose assemblies had enrolled many men in these industries in the late eighties, the manufacturers were prompted to announce lockouts, which provoked a boycott and two strikes in retaliation and brought the intervention of the State Board of Mediation. Disillusioned by the inability of the loosely structured Knights to support a protracted strike, the shoe and clothing workers were turning to the rival AFL unions but accepted compromise settlements. Unfortunately, the failure of the unions to secure binding contracts prolonged the uncertainty that also troubled several of Rochester's minor industries in these years. Although the Rochester Trades Assembly increased the number of its affiliates to twenty-two trade unions and pressed a drive for the eight-hour day and for the negotiation of binding contracts, none of its members was prepared for the layoffs that followed the panic of 1893.

Despite the chamber's refusal to take a stand against monopoly in the utility field, an attempt by the Rochester Coal Exchange to bind local dealers to a price-fixing pledge in 1892 stirred a popular reaction that brought a hasty dissolution of the combine. The collapse of the coal pool seriously embarrassed Arthur G. Yates, the leading coal dealer, but his major difficulty arose from the endorsements he had exchanged with H. H. Warner in various speculations. Warner, who had sold his Safe Liver Cure enterprise to a group of British capitalists and guaranteed them handsome profits for a period of years, had invested the proceeds in western copper mines and was hard pressed to meet his obligations in early April, just as the tumbling coal prices embarrassed Yates. Each sought to avoid the obligation of redeeming the other's notes, and soon both were plunged into bankruptcy. Yates resigned from the presidency of the Buffalo, Rochester & Pittsburgh Railroad, which escaped serious injury, but Warner lost his East Avenue mansion and, with the outbreak of the financial panic in New York on April 22, their losses mounted to some $5 million. The astonishing collapse of two of the city's most flamboyant business leaders precipitated a dozen other local failures, though none was as extensive as theirs.

Fortunately, the city's ten commercial and six savings banks enjoyed a fairly strong position, and the repeal of the Silver Purchase Act in October restored their confidence. Some of the numerous loan associations were, however, less fortunate. Their practice of treating gross premiums as present profits had spread distrust, and because most of their borrowers were modest homeowners, pressure for prompt payments brought frequent foreclosures, which added to the spreading gloom. Shortages of credit forced a number of firms to close their plants, and many others reduced their schedules or their work forces. Several unions accepted wage reductions in order to forestall a shutdown, and although others protested such action, none ventured a walkout, except the engineers and firemen of the Lehigh Valley Railway, who were soon glad to have their jobs back again on company terms.

Local editors endeavored for a time to dismiss the problem as "the late uncertainty," but by the end of October the volume of unemployment compelled a frank appraisal of the situation. The *Democrat* found half the city's tailors, half the shoemakers, and practically all the carpenters and other building tradesmen idle. Over one hundred additional families applied for relief in the first two weeks of November, which brought the total to 600 and, a month later, to 900, more than double that of any previous year. Unemployed single men willing to chop wood for their meals so crowded the Rescue Mission that it called for the donation of one hundred extra blankets to enable them to sleep on the floor. A cold spell prompted the mayor to launch a drive for old clothes to be distributed to needy families. Although three city wagons made daily collections and gathered some 5,000 garments and shoes during Christmas week, relief applicants who crowded into city hall soon exhausted these supplies.

Mounting cries for relief brought several quick but not very effective responses. The pleas of the Reverend William C. Gannett and other prominent ministers for action to create new jobs prompted the Chamber of Commerce to call a special meeting early in December to consider possible relief measures. When other suggestions failed, George C. Buell launched a drive for a relief fund with a check for $100, which brought in $1,000 that evening and grew to $12,000 within two weeks. The Society for Organized Charity accepted the responsibility of distributing this fund and gave emergency relief to some 1,354 destitute families during the month, but a mass meeting of unemployed members of the building trades assembled in January to protest the inadequacy of such measures. Joseph T. Alling, president of the YMCA, endorsed the appeal of the mass meeting for jobs, not charity, and the city increased the number and size of its work gangs on the streets and at the work camps along the route of the new conduit to Hemlock Lake. Hastily approved plans for the construction of a police headquarters promised additional jobs, and work soon commenced on the four-story structure on Exchange Street.

The hardships were more cheerfully endured the first winter because of the conviction that they could not last. When a survey at the close of the year revealed that only 85 of the city's approximately 2,000 enterprises had made assignments during 1893, many of the survivors took heart. Several new firms appeared and old ones expanded their operations. Joseph T. Alling addressed a mass meeting called by the building trades, and encouraged them to accept all jobs offered, because full employment would bring speedy recovery and increased wages. With the return of spring the mayor closed his old clothes depot, and the chamber raised $2,600 for street decorations and other expenses for the Fourth of July parade, which required half an hour to pass the reviewing stand. As the marchers disappeared down Main Street, the officials, headed by Mayor George Aldridge, turned about and with impressive ceremony laid the cornerstone for a new courthouse whose construction promised many jobs that fall and winter. Several industrialists had discovered that they could not afford to close their plants, but few had the courage of George Eastman who seized the opportunity to expand his operations because of the abundant supply of cheap labor.

The average citizen was pressed as never before. Many had now exhausted their savings and faced the necessity to seek small loans to meet unexpected expenses. A provident loan society, established by the Reverend James H. Dennis in 1893, was unable to supply all the funds needed, and many poor folk became victims of loan sharks, which prompted the hasty passage in 1895 of a bill to curb their activity. As the number of homeless children increased, the overcrowded orphan asylums created placement committees to help find proper homes for some of their charges; the newly established Children's Aid Society undertook to supervise the placement and care of foundlings and other infants. The Humane Society opened a shelter for young children; the Rescue Mission added an additional dormitory; and several forthright members of the Female Charitable Society, after much hesitation, secured backing to establish the Door of Hope to shelter the wayward girls expelled from the stall saloons and other centers of vice by the police in the wake of a series of revivals conducted by Dwight L. Moody, L. W. Chapman, and Billy Sunday that winter. When the overseers of the poor dropped 250 families from the list in November 1894 because their men refused to break stone for the city, 75 hastened to apply for reinstatement, and the council had to lease an additional lot to store the broken stone until it could be spread over the streets in the spring. With some hesitation, the overseer conserved his relief funds by eliminating the allowance of $1.35 a week for rent, but doubling up created new problems. Furthermore, despite a multitude of unemployed adults, the number of child labor violations reached a new high.

The leaders of organized labor were as disillusioned as the relief officials. Their hopes for a quick recovery had vanished in 1894. A turnout of 2,000 marchers under twenty union banners maintained a bold front in the Labor Day parade that year, but when the Knights of Labor attempted to revive the Monroe County Labor Congress in 1895 a small group of socialists seized control. When both the Knights and the trade unionists withdrew, the socialists transformed the congress in 1896 into the Labor Lyceum, which convened its Sunday afternoon forums in the city hall. Although several trade unions picked up additional members from the declining assemblies of the Knights, and the Boot and Shoe Workers acquired new strength, the United Garment Workers, despite an increase in numbers to 1,200 early in 1895, failed to halt renewed reductions in rates and practically collapsed before the end of the year.

Yet the gloom of the depression, which reached its darkest pitch in 1896, obscured many constructive forces that were working for recovery. Because of an abundant supply of labor available at depression rates, men with new ideas and limited working capital were able to launch fresh ventures. The Rochester Folding Box Company was one of three that made a start in 1895, and Jacob H. Meyers was ready a year later to produce his newly invented voting machines for first use in the Rochester election that November. George B. Selden had secured the final patent on his gas combustion engine for road carriages the year before but made little effort to raise the funds necessary for its production. George Eastman, confident that the new orders received from Edison and other pioneer producers of motion pictures assured a prosperous market for his photographic film, boldly ordered the construction of a second seven-story factory building on State Street and further developments on his Lake Avenue site. Eastman's decision to double his capitalization, boosting the total to $10 million, startled many citizens, including the editor of the *Herald,* who cautiously warned his readers not to be misled by a certain "novelty works" on State Street, lest it follow the path of Warner's Safe Liver Cure fiasco. Louis M. Antisdale, who soon replaced that inept editor, made the *Herald* a force in the community, but he never enjoyed Eastman's backing, and his predecessor's unfortunate display of skepticism probably retarded some of the civic reforms Antisdale advocated.

CIVIC AND POLITICAL REFORMS

The most dramatic response to both the depression and the city's dynamic growth occurred in municipal politics. It soon became apparent that the retraction brought by the hard·times seriously aggravated many problems created by Rochester's continued development. But instead of bewailing their fate, numerous professional and business leaders joined in a concerted movement for civic improvements. Critical appraisals of "What's the Matter with Rochester?" by Rauschenbusch and others, inspired by William Allen White's famous article on Kansas, gave rise to a new spirit, aptly expressed in the slogan coined by Sidney R. Clark for the Chamber of Commerce, "Do it for Rochester."

Such a response was undreamed of in 1894 when the early demands of the depression revealed the inadequacy of the city's finances. Cries for work relief, reverberating through an empty treasury that January, prompted Alderman James Johnston to prod his fellows with sixteen sobering questions. "Why should the cost of maintaining our public schools have increased so largely while the . . . teachers are so poorly paid?" was one of them. The teachers could have stated it more bluntly, because their monthly payments of fifty dollars or less had been held up that January because of the depleted funds. Joseph T.

Alling, troubled by the lack of jobs for the YMCA boys and for members of the Men's Bible Class, said to be the largest in the country, was shocked to discover how limited their educational preparation had been. Convinced that the schools were at fault, Alling and Johnston soon gathered a number of kindred spirits into the Citizens Political Reform Association, with the Reverend Dr. Algernon Crapsey as president. Its major objective at the start was to improve the schools, which they quickly discovered had been used for political patronage by George Aldridge and his henchmen on the large school board.

To secure a firmer grasp of the problem, Alling and two of his associates attended the second National Congress for Good City Government, which met at Cleveland in the summer of 1895, and there they learned of the need to develop grass-roots support if they wished to play an effective role. Returning to Rochester, the reformers organized good-government clubs in every ward and formed a committee of sixty-five, including two delegates from each club, plus all the men who had previously displayed an interest in school and municipal reform. Walter S. Hubbell, a Kodak attorney who also led a men's Bible class and who was a former Republican assemblyman, Theodore Bacon, a former Democratic candidate for Congress, and the Reverend Clarence A. Barbour, pastor of Lake Avenue Baptist Church, were among its more prominent members and served on a subcommittee with Alling to draft a platform and draw up a bipartisan slate of acceptable candidates. When the list appeared proposing a popular Democrat, Judge George E. Warner, for mayor and, among others, Republican Samuel B. Williams for treasurer, the Democrats endorsed the entire list, but Aldridge accepted only Williams. In the election that followed, the Republicans carried all state and local contests except the post of mayor, which fell to Warner by a plurality of 648 over Hiram H. Edgerton, the Aldridge candidate.

The "Goo Goos," as the opposition press branded the reformers, named a committee of thirteen, headed by Alling, to keep an eye on the various municipal functions. Mayor Warner, facing a Republican-controlled council, saw his numerous proposals, even when backed by Alderman Johnston, hastily tabled. Most of his vetoes of unwanted measures and expenditures, though quickly overridden, proved popular in these last years of the depression and helped build support for his reelection. Alling, now attacked as "Boss Alling" by the *Post Express*, broadened his campaign to defeat Republican aldermen and to name Johnston to the Executive Board. A victory for the joint ticket prompted Alling to make a hasty visit to several New England cities to study their municipal provisions, and Mayor Warner reaffirmed his campaign pledge for economy. Unfortunately, his continued vetoes of aldermanic appropriations, some to implement improved services desired by Alling, produced a new tension within the Democratic-Good Government alliance. A split between the Mayor and Judge Charles B. Ernst over their respective responsibilities for action against pool rooms and gambling dens created still another division. Although the *Herald* remained loyal to the mayor, and the *Union & Advertiser* backed the old-line Democrats, the *Post Express* seized the opportunity to back Alling and Johnston, and urged them to return to the Republican fold.

Again, the issues centered on the schools. A critical shortage of public school facilities had attracted state censure. The impulsive Governer Roosevelt helped Aldridge in 1899 push through a bill directing Rochester to borrow $100,000 for school expansion. Mayor Warner, however, vetoed the bill. Plans for a reconstruction of the school board under a new state law were moving ahead, and the city looked forward to the election of a new and small board at the end of the year. The new board should have charge of such expenditures, the mayor declared, but the need was so great that Alling finally persuaded him to approve some new construction that summer under the supervision of a special committee headed by Captain Henry Lomb. Unfortunately, the additional facilities left one thousand youngsters unprovided for in September and finally turned the Good Government forces and most citizens against the economy-minded Warner in the election that fall.

George Aldridge had learned his lesson, or part of it. He had decided to go along with rather than try to buck a statewide move for a reform charter for second-class cities. Drafted in 1899 by a state commission on which James G. Cutler had served as the Rochester representative, the White Charter, as it was called, provided for a small elective school board and for the abolition of the executive board and the transfer of most of its responsibilities to the mayor or to department heads of his appointment. These changes, destined to take effect in 1900, prompted Aldridge to seek an agreement with Alling and the Good Government forces. As a result, he accepted three of Alling's proposed nominees for the school board, including Mrs. Helen Barrett Montgomery, and promised to give it full independence; the Democrats named only one who later refused to run. Aldridge rejected Alling's proposed nominees for mayor but named Johnston to the new post of comptroller and nominated the quite acceptable Judge George A. Carnahan for mayor. Warner won renomination by the Democrats but lost the election to the Republicans, who captured control of the council and the school board, as well as the mayor's office.

Mayor Carnahan had the difficult task of organizing a totally new government. He chose able men as his department heads, including Edwin A. Fisher as city engineer and Cutler as commissioner of safety, and he assured Dr. Edward Mott Moore that the Park Commission would be retained, with Moore as its chairman. But when Carnahan insisted that he be kept informed of important police moves, Cutler resigned, and the mayor appointed James D. Casey, a former police superintendent who had broken with Aldridge. The disgruntled *Herald*, which had unsuccessfully backed Warner, charged Carnahan with failure to enforce the antigambling ordinances. When the mayor, assured by Casey that the laws were enforced, denied the charge, Editor Antisdale swore out a warrant and led the police in a dramatic raid of the headquarters of George McLaughlin, reputed to be Rochester's gambling king, whose quarters on the second floor of a building at Main and St. Paul had enjoyed immunity for a period of eighteen years. The sordid story dominated the headlines throughout the last days of the century, but few except the *Herald* held Carnahan responsible, and the mayor, though no doubt mortified, quickly forgot his embarrassment as other troubles mounted.

A heated struggle between Aldridge and the new Board of Education did not directly involve the mayor but made the boss more determined to maintain his power. Professor George M. Forbes, elected chairman of the new board, soon discovered that a last-minute alteration in the text of the law, inserted by an Aldridge henchman at the state printers, had prolonged the old superintendent's tenure. Frustrated by his refusal to resign, the board ordered an investigation of his accounts, which disclosed a shortage of funds that was finally traced to nonresident tuition payments the superintendent had apparently pocketed. The superintendent's resignation promptly followed this announcement, and the board secured a clear field for its reforms. However, Boss Aldridge was in a quarrelsome mood and seized the opportunity in August 1900 to discipline former assemblyman James O'Grady, who had displayed too much independence after his election to Congress. By refusing O'Grady's expected renomination, Aldridge demonstrated his control of the local party and proceeded to put it to personal use.

Deprived by Governor Black of his state canal position, Aldridge was back in Rochester and soon appeared as the general manager of a proposed Citizens Light & Power Company. His announced annual salary of $10,000 was a clear warning to the Rochester Gas & Electric Company that a politically powerful new challenger had appeared on the scene. Its request for a franchise to build a conduit subway to its proposed plant on Mill Street stirred a heated controversy in the Council. Friends of Aldridge, urging the need for competition, passed the ordinance, but Mayor Carnahan vetoed it with a warning that the new company was just trying to blackmail the RG & E and would force an increase in rates to pay it off. The council readily passed the franchise over the mayor's veto, but the public debate strengthened the resistance of the RG & E and the Citizens Company temporarily suspended its drive. Aldridge, however, had the last word, for when the nominations for 1901 were announced, Adolph J. Rodenbeck was the boss's candidate for mayor.

Alling and his Good Government associates considered running Carnahan as an independent, but they decided not to do so. The O'Grady forces and a temperance faction urged it, but most of the Good Government leaders favored compromise with Aldridge in order to insure his support for the reelection of Mrs. Montgomery on the Board of Education and of Johnston as comptroller. Rodenbeck won, defeating Warner, but only by a margin of 76 votes; Johnston and other Good Government–backed candidates received large majorities. Johnston's victory proved a bit heady, however, and transformed him into the stormy petrel of the Rodenbeck years. After engaging in several noisy controversies with fellow administrators, he broke entirely from the administration and, backed by Carnahan and O'Grady, challenged the Aldridge leadership, only to be soundly defeated in the party caucus.

Mayor Rodenbeck assembled an able staff and displayed many

strong qualities. He named J. Y. McClintoch, who had made his peace
with Aldridge, as commissioner of public works and followed his lead
in backing river and port improvements, the reforestation of the Hemlock Lake watershed, and the acquisition of Cobbs Hill for a second
reservoir. When McClintoch again crossed Aldridge and again lost his
job, Rodenbeck named Edwin A. Fisher, a less imaginative but more
efficient engineer, to his post. Rodenbeck made similar shifts in other
fields. During his first year, he backed Dr. Moore and the Park Commission in the purchase of new park lands, for example, Maple Grove
and the Warner estate, but welcomed the more modest requests of his
successor for development purposes. He supported the school board
in the construction of East High but resisted the innovations of Superintendent Charles B. Gilbert, who resigned in protest, leaving the more
practical Professor Forbes as acting superintendent. An early consolidation of the power and light companies under outside ownership
and the appointment of Aldridge to the state railroad commission
enabled the mayor to step forward as the champion of lower gas and
electric rates and trolley fares. These protests had little effect, but he
did block an effort by several Aldridge aldermen to force a dismissal of
Dr. George Goler, the chief health officer who had refused to conceal
the evidence of a smallpox epidemic that ravaged the city in 1903 and
forced the construction of a new public hospital on Waring Road.
Although the council, disregarding the crisis, limited its appropriation
to $25,000, the mayor backed Dr. Goler's desperate effort to halt the
epidemic and met the full cost of $72,000. Aldridge could not tolerate
such independence, but neither could he risk adding another leader
to the opposition. He accordingly secured a judgeship for Rodenbeck
and nominated James G. Cutler as his new candidate for mayor.

A successful businessman and former president of the chamber,
Cutler was the ideal candidate. As inventor and manufacturer of the
mail chutes, he had traveled widely throughout America and abroad,
supervising the installation of his product in new business blocks and
acquiring an unrivalled knowledge of the structure and activities of
many growing cities. His service on the charter revision committee had
awakened him to the potentialities of the strong-mayor system, and he
determined to fulfill them. A tragic fire in a Chicago theater shortly
after his election prompted Cutler to station a fireman in every Rochester theater and to upgrade the fire department. The outbreak of the

great Sibley fire two weeks later provided the incentive to push his reforms through the council and enabled Rochester to escape the drastic increases in fire insurance rates applied to many other cities that winter. With the vigor that startled many observers, Cutler rushed the completion of West High and launched construction of two new grade schools and several additions; he extended the water and sewer mains and underground conduits ahead of street improvements and pressed the trolley company to extend its services; he supplied funds to enable the park commission to develop recreational facilities, and he made an inventory of the city's municipal provisions to prove that their valuation considerably exceeded the total debt and justified further investments.

Mayor Cutler more than fulfilled the hopes of the Good Government leaders, but he could not satisfy the wishes of all reform groups and soon became embroiled in several controversies. A temperance drive led by Clinton Howard had secured a court order that all saloons be closed on the Sabbath as required by state law, and the mayor endeavored to enforce its provisions, though he protested in an address before the Ministerial Union that this law only closed the poor man's saloon and did not curb the activities of the social clubs of the more affluent. He refused to close the theaters and other public places of amusement, as some clergymen advocated, and he welcomed the readiness of others to develop recreational opportunities to supply the needs of workmen on that day and of children throughout the week. He backed the efforts of the Children's Playground League to maintain programs in park lands and he established the first public playground on Brown's Square. He followed with interest the findings of a survey conducted by Walter Rauschenbusch for the YMCA, which emphasized the need for greater social outlets in congested urban areas, and when the Board of Education, on the motion of Mrs. Montgomery, moved to open three school buildings in crowded areas for neighborhood use in evening hours, the mayor supplied funds to support the Social Center program launched in December 1907 under the direction of Edward J. Ward at No. 14 School.

Mayor Cutler, who had easily won election for a second term, missed most of the drama and escaped the controversies the program created, but only because he had boldly met several other controversial issues. He backed Dr. Goler's efforts to inspect daily milk deliveries and to enforce other sanitary regulation; he provided quarters in the municipal building for the Juvenile Court, which acquired jurisdiction over cases involving children under sixteen years; he backed the health officer's action in assigning the garbage collection function to an experienced contractor from Philadelphia; he joined in the efforts of a chamber committee headed by Charles M. Robinson to draft a city plan for Rochester; and when he discovered how limited the mayor's powers were in this and other respects, he took the lead in a campaign to revise the charter and enhance the powers of the mayor. That move brought him into open conflict with Boss Aldridge, who had again lost his job as a state commissioner and was back in Rochester in 1908 and was busy mending his fences. When the charter revision passed and Rochester became a first-class city, Aldridge decided to nominate a more faithful lieutenant as mayor, and Cutler, convinced that stable party backing was essential to good administration, declined Alling's offer to run him as an independent.

Hiram H. Edgerton, the boss's new candidate, proved a tractable representative and astonished everybody by his durability. More experienced in municipal affairs at the start than any of his predecessors, his long years as president of the council and his practical experience as a building contractor equipped him with the flexibility essential to the management of a major city. Disinterested in establishing an independent image, he retained most of Cutler's chief assistants and replaced them only as they sought release. Some of his own appointments, notably Joseph M. Quigley as chief of police, were distinguished, and the support he gave to Dr. Goler in the establishment of his innovative but controversial milk stations and to Alexander B. Lamberton for recreational developments in the parks won wide approval. In annual addresses of increasing length, Mayor Edgerton advanced proposals for a public library, a boulevard to encircle the city, a new street to parallel Main Street through the downtown district, and a tuberculosis hospital. Although none of these was accomplished in his first or second term, or in some cases for many years, Edgerton kept step with the leaders in civic development. He even played host at a dinner given to Governor Charles Evans Hughes, an outspoken critic of the boss, when he addressed a Social Center assembly in Convention Hall. He watched with some interest the reaction of various women's groups as Aldridge displaced the controversial Mrs. Montgomery on the school board with the popular and able teacher Miss Helen E. Gregory, and he remained unperturbed when the boss lost his own bid for Congress in a special election early in 1910—a rebuff that failed to shake their sure grip on the city administration.

SOCIAL AND CULTURAL EXPRESSION

The fluctuating course of the Good Government movement, which achieved its last dramatic success in the 1910 election, reflected many shifting developments in the social and cultural community. Rochester's cosmopolitan population acquired a new character with the influx of a host of newcomers from Southern and Eastern Europe. Their arrival in increasing numbers brought dramatic changes in the city's religious structure as well as in its social affairs. Visitors to Rochester were equally impressed by the bustling activity in its streets, the busy schedule of associational programs, and the increased freedom and participation of women in public affairs. Residents of all walks of life, especially the host of first-generation Americans, achieved an expressiveness that marked a new stage in the city's development.

The increased emphasis on public service in the economic field and the increased recognition of public responsibility in civic and political affairs were matched by an outburst of public activity in the social and cultural arena that made life in Rochester more of a public experience than ever before. Its cosmopolitan character was brought dramatically into the open by a profusion of ethnic parades and other public affairs. Earlier St. Patrick's Day parades and German picnics and musicals were matched, if not surpassed, by Columbus Day parades and other ethnic events that added to the pageantry of the downtown scene as well as that of the ethnic neighborhoods. Bishop McQuaid, after a visit to Rome where he was impressed by the fervor of its religious pilgrimages, returned to Rochester and organized a series of parades on balmy Sundays, with entire congregations marching from one parish church to the next for successive services that provided a demonstration of Catholic strength impressive to participants as well as to onlookers. Each Memorial Day, Fourth of July, and Labor Day brought its parade on Main Street, with thousands of marchers and crowds of spectators. Visiting circuses and occasional state and national conventions frequently staged similar public demonstrations. The most spectacular of all was the Otis Day parade on June 15, 1900, when Rochester honored its own General Ellwell S. Otis on his return from command in the Philippines.

Two aspects of Rochester's demographic growth contributed to its development as an exciting outdoor town. The new migrants from Southern and Eastern Europe were increasing most rapidly; those from Southern Italy, in particular, who grew in numbers from 1,000 to 10,000 in the first decade of the twentieth century, were characteristically an outdoor people. Although residents born in Britain and Germany still outnumbered those from the rest of Europe, they were themselves outnumbered by their American-born offspring, who by the early 1900s comprised the largest number of young adults. The eagerness of many of these first generation Americans to break loose from old-country restraints and to escape from the crowded homes of their parents propelled them in great numbers into the streets and to the public amusement centers. As one observer, quoted in the *Herald*, noticed in 1906, "The children of the foreign born . . . learn the latest comic opera tunes, shout themselves hoarse at all the ball games, imitate the prevailing fashions in dress, fill the trolley cars bound for the amusement resorts and parks, and generally disport themselves as do the American youths. Hungary, Poland, Italy, Germany, Ireland fade from the faces of these young people . . . who pride themselves on their Americanism."

Ray Stannard Baker, the muckraker, was surprised and delighted in 1910 to discover how responsive the city's social and economic leaders had become to the needs of these new citizens. He was particularly impressed by the effective work of several churchmen, notably Dr. Algernon Crapsey through his St. Andrew's Church brotherhood in the mid-nineties, Joseph T. Alling through his Bible class and the YMCA, and the Reverend Paul Moore Strayer in his People's Sunday Evening meetings conducted in a downtown theater for many years after the turn of the century. An increasing number of churches carried on their parish programs in the relaxed social pattern of the post–Civil War decades, but inspired in several instances by the social-gospel teachings of Walter Rauschenbusch, these lay programs represented a new approach. Their efforts to reach and involve "all the people" were most dramatically realized in the Social Center program launched by the Board of Education under the leadership of Edward J. Ward. And because of the ready participation of these earnest churchmen in every cause, even the weekly meetings of the Labor Lyceum stressed the educational rather than the violent aspects of socialism. Moreover, they prodded the Chamber of Commerce to cooperate in the establishment of the United Charities and in the maintenance of a free employment agency. The newly formed City Club inaugurated a happy custom when in July 1910 it held its first New Citizens' Banquet, with each member acting as host to one recently naturalized citizen.

The chamber's "Do it for Rochester" slogan, used by Baker as the title of his article in the *American Magazine*, aptly described the spirit of many citizens in these decades. Thus, the Women's Educational & Industrial Union was organized in 1893 by Susan B. Anthony and other Rochester ladies startled by the plight of a woman who, having fainted in the street, was confined overnight in the jail for want of a better shelter. Its numerous programs, under the forthright leadership of Mrs. Montgomery, helped safeguard the interests of working women and strangers in the city, which had generally been designed as a man's world. That situation, in fact, had long since disappeared with the increased number of women employed in the shoe and clothing industries, even in Kimball's tobacco factory and Eastman's camera works, and with the increased employment of girls in downtown offices and stores. Many young women of the first generation not only were eager, like their brothers, to break out of their parents' homes, but also desidered to exchange their traditional domestic jobs for the more sociable work in stores and factories. The trolley cars provided a convenient means for their transit to and from work, but many joined the unending stream of pedestrians that filled the downtown streets.

To most residents Rochester was still a walking city, but for the carriage crowd and for some of the regularly employed the times were changing. Not only were the horsecars displaced by electric trolleys, greatly increasing the range and convenience of their use as well as the number of riders, but the increasing use of the bicycle brought a new flexibility to city traffic. Its recreational function was already passing by 1894, when the number of wheels in Rochester reached 6,000, and five years later, when they exceeded 40,000, the bicycle rack had become a standard feature at every downtown shop. A hastily organized sidepath association collected one dollar each from 10,000 cyclists in 1897 to build suitable sidepaths leading to suburban resorts. Rochester pressed this movement more vigorously than any other city and had 205 miles of sidepaths by 1902. By that date, however, several of the bicycle dealers were already turning to the promotion of automobiles. As the eighty gas, electric, and steam cars of that year increased to one thousand by 1905, the sidepath association disbanded, and cyclists as well as teamsters found themselves inconvenienced. Faced with the need for a new pavement that year, East Avenue residents decided by a close vote in favor of macadam, which was safer than asphalt for the horses that still drew their carriages back and forth. Five years later, when the number of automobiles owned in the city exceeded 4,000, the decision to repave East Avenue with asphalt met no opposition.

Automobiles, of course, were the expensive toys of rich sportsmen in the early 1900s, and the bicycles that occupied the racks along Main Street during business hours often overflowed similar racks near the entrance to the ball park at Culver Field. A collapse of the grandstand there in 1906 prompted the manager of the Rochester Baseball Club to acquire a new park on Bay Street where the Rochester team, renamed the Hustlers, attracted crowds of 16,000 on several occasions as it captured the Eastern League pennant three years in succession. Even larger throngs journeyed by foot, cycle, crowded open trolleys, and packed excursion trains to Ontario beach on warm Sundays in July 1909 to witness the pioneer flights of Captain Jack Dallas of Rochester in a cigar-shaped propeller-driven airship. Other crowds had gathered at the Rochester Driving Park in the nineties to witness cycle and automobile exhibits as well as horse races, but state laws against betting diverted interest after the turn of the century to the more participatory activities at the beaches and public parks. When cold weather closed these resorts to family and group picnics, hikers, bathers, boaters, and other summer visitors, many resorted to the roller-skating rinks, bowling alleys and dance halls that accommodated thousands of eager patrons. Basketball, introduced at the new YMCA gymnasium in the early 1900s, attracted popular interest as the new East and West high schools developed rival teams after 1907, which gave birth to a new school spirit that strengthened other neighborhood ties as well.

As Rochesterians acquired a more democratic and more abundant social life around the turn of the century, many strove to popularize and broaden their participation in the arts. The two high schools made advanced instruction available to a wider enrollment of students, including many from ethnic minorities that had previously felt excluded. Although some of the high cultural institutions of earlier decades, such as the Powers art gallery and the Philharmonic Orchestra, succumbed during the depression, new and more widely based institutions arose and in several instances achieved a more spontaneous and rewarding expression of community aspirations.

Despite its pride in the Powers art gallery, Rochester was not prepared to give it public support. When hard times prompted Daniel Powers to seek a reduction in the tax assessment on the Powers block, because of its partial use as an art gallery, the city, hard pressed to meet its expenses, rejected his plea, and following his death in 1897, the embittered family closed the gallery and arranged for the sale of its paintings and other objects in New York. The Rochester Art Club, which had struggled in vain to save the Powers collection, deplored the closing of that gallery and the sale of 275 of its 1,000 items for a total of $148,800. However, the club soon acquired another hall for the annual display of the works of its members and for traveling exhibits. George L. Herdle, president of the club after 1902, brought a selection of the paintings of leading French Impressionists to Rochester for a special exhibit in 1908 that stirred considerable interest and debate. Two years later the club collaborated with the Federation of Social Centers and the Board of Education in staging the city's first public art exhibit in East High School, which attracted unprecedented crowds that exceeded 10,000 in two weeks.

In similar fashion the demise of the earlier Philharmonic Orchestra, as a result of friction between its leaders, led to the formation of several independent groups. Several men, struggling to earn their living as musicians, formed the Rochester Orchestra as a professional organization in 1900 with Herman Dossenbach as its leader. A year later a group of amateurs—aspiring youngsters and older men who played chiefly for their own pleasure—formed a symphony orchestra under the leadership of Ludwig Schenck. The Tuesday Musicals, started a few years before by a group of ladies who wished to study and promote musical performances, lent its encouragement to both orchestras and scheduled occasional concerts by visiting orchestras from other cities. It sponsored a chorus under the direction of Henrich Jacobsen, the German-born director of the Maennerchor whose songfests were now occasionally open to the public. A mandolin orchestra collaborated with the younger members of several church choirs in occasional community sings at the rink or on the beach at Charlotte, and after the turn of the century Theodore Dossenbach, Herman's younger brother, organized a park band to play on special occasions at one or another of the city parks. Several churches had installed elaborate pipe organs, and their frequent week-day recitals, together with the programs of numerous music classes and choirs, provided a rich selection for interested listeners. When, following the example of William Kimball and several other rich men, George Eastman installed a pipe organ in his new mansion on East Avenue in 1905, he launched a program of Sunday musicales that contributed a high tone to Rochester's social elite. The Music Festival staged in Convention Hall in 1909 reached a wider audience and provided a pattern for later community festivals there and in the parks.

The most excited audiences were those that crowded both the legitimate and popular theaters during these decades. Claude Bragdon recalled years later the realms of feeling and the new insights he had acquired while watching Mrs. Fiske play the lead in Ibsen's *A Doll's House*, among other dramatic events at the Lyceum, which maintained its schedule of choice performances even during the depression years. The older Opera House resorted to light opera and variety shows during the hard times and competed with the still more gusty fare of the Musée, remodeled as the Wonderland in 1894. With the return of prosperity, the new Baker Theater was opened on North Fitzhugh Street in 1899, and the National Theater on West Main Street three years later. The Shubert brothers of Syracuse soon leased the Baker Theater and made it part of their vaudeville circuit, the Lyceum came under the control of the theatrical trust organized by Charles Froman in New York, and the occasional independents found a welcome in one of the other theaters. Rochester enjoyed a continuing procession of one- or two-night and matinee visitations by the current New York plays and other touring troupes. After 1905 Rochester began to acquire the status of a tryout town, which added the thrill of viewing the premier performance of plays whose success depended, in part, on the local response.

As Rochester became more discerning in its tastes, the popularity of Joseph Jefferson's perennial hit in *Rip Van Winkle* and the oft-presented *Old Homestead* declined. The new favorites were light-opera pieces, which proved more appealing to many immigrants than the American rural melodrama and the more urban vaudeville skits. The old Corinthian Academy of Music, damaged by fire in 1899, was rebuilt and reopened as a variety theater five years later, and two additional amusement centers soon made their appearance. Among the features they presented were acrobats, "living pictures," song-and-dance bits, comedians, and even ballet, as well as the melodramas performed by stock companies and the sometimes serious plays presented by local or visiting companies that featured a dramatic star such as Lillian Russell or David Belasco, two favorites in Rochester.

The theater's remarkable growth was, in part, due to its hospitality to a new entertainment medium—the motion-picture film—which would eventually supersede its host. Edison's kinetoscopes, first seen in Rochester in the basement of the Sibley, Lindsay, & Curr store in December 1894, proved a sufficient curiosity to prompt the manager of the Wonderland to install two in his lobby. A year passed before Edison's rivals developed practical methods of projecting life-size motion pictures on a screen. Again, the Wonderland provided the setting, but soon the manager of the Lyceum was ready to display a kinematograph production as an intermission feature. Enthusiastic crowds lined up to pay the nickle charge to see short scenes of a man walking, a bather swimming, a railroad train steaming by, and other astonishing displays of the new technical use of the camera. However, few as yet suspected the impact this development would have on Rochester's leading industry. When the Wonderland was demolished to make way for Sibley's new store, the Bijou Dream—the city's first motion-picture house—made its appearance in 1906 at the corner of Main and Water streets. By the end of the decade three of the variety theaters had converted to motion pictures and, with seven new cinemas, boasted a total seating capacity of almost 8,000.

The wider expression in and enjoyment of the arts was matched by a greater diffusion of literature and learning. Although Professor Swift packed his telescope in a long box and smuggled it out of the city early one morning in April 1894, after the failure of H. H. Warner had deprived him of a backer, his departure to establish a new observatory in California was of little concern to the average citizen. Rochesterians were more directly affected by the competitive efforts of the editors and publishers of five English and one German language dailies to win and hold their patronage. When Edward S. Martin, the talented editor of the *Union & Advertiser*, left to become an associate editor of *Harper's Weekly* in 1897, his successors made it more strictly a spokesman for the Democrats, as the *Democrat & Chronicle* was for the Republicans. The latter's more vigorous promotion of popular features, cartoons, and other illustrations, and the first local introduction of a comic strip in 1899, gave it a circulation that doubled that of its nearest rival. The *Herald*, which swung to the Democratic side under the editorship of Louis M. Antisdale after 1898, devoted considerable attention to the theater and the arts and launched a Sunday edition, but it never quite matched the *Union*, let alone the *Democrat*, in circulation or the *Post Express* in the quality of its columns on the city's cultural life. The *Times*, after several bankruptcies, became the chief spokesman for Boss Aldridge, but even with a free use of blatant headlines, it failed to challenge the old leaders, though it gradually pulled ahead of the *Post Express* in circulation. All the papers increased their coverage of sports and other amusements, which helped to promote popular outdoor events and other associational activities.

An increasing number and variety of societies and clubs contributed to the enrichment of the city's social and cultural affairs. When the Reynolds Library opened its new headquarters in the spacious old Reynolds mansion on Spring Street in 1895, sixteen literary and discussion groups hastened to reserve rooms for their weekly or monthly meetings, and a total of thirty societies registered book requests with the librarian. Several of the well-established clubs kept lists and longhand copies of the papers presented at their meetings, some of which were eventually published. Thus, a paper on city planning prepared by young Charles M. Robinson for the Humdrum Club attracted so much favor that it directed his talents into that field, and Claude Bragdon found stimulus there and in the Theosophical Society for his books on architecture and the fourth dimension. Several of the papers delivered by the ladies before the Roundabout and the Wednesday clubs later appeared in print, notably those of Evangeline O'Connor and Jane Marsh Parker. Special clubs were devoted to the works of Browning, Tennyson, and Shakespeare, and others focused on the study of botany, geology and astronomy. Less formal groups with special interests gathered around such leaders as Dr. Charles Forbes, a professor at the old Free Academy, and Lafe Heidell, whose restaurant on Water Street was a favorite haunt for visiting dramatic stars and their admirers.

The University of Rochester, the Rochester Theological Seminary, St. Bernard's Seminary, established by Bishop McQuaid in 1893, and Mechanics Institute provided other centers of stimulation. Although their enrollments were still small, the public activities of their professors were widely diffused and significant. Thus, Professors George Forbes and Samuel A. Lattimore at the university, Professor Walter Rauschenbusch at the theological seminary, and Professor Edward J. Hanna at St. Bernard's were all deeply involved in the affairs of the city and made major contributions to its life. Some talented individuals remained detached from local institutions, notably Adelaide Crapsey, the poet whose sensitive verses were only discovered after her early death, and Arthur C. Smith, a reticent banker whose short stories won wide acclaim when published in two little volumes, *The Monk and the Dancer* (1900) and *The Turquoise Cup* (1903). But the trend generally was towards wider participation, and one young professor at the university presented in 1910 the first course on citizenship offered in any American college.

The university, like the city, was reaching out to recognize and serve additional groups of citizens in these years. Susan B. Anthony's earnest campaign to open the university to women achieved success in 1900, even before they attained full citizenship. Long before that date the university had graduated several young men from local German, Irish, and Jewish families, and although none of the city's approximately 400 Negroes nor any of the more recently arrived Italians had yet enrolled in college, several of both groups had graduated from the old Free Academy or the new East High School. Rochester indeed had honored Frederick Douglass at his death with a stately funeral procession from city hall to the Central Presbyterian Church and followed the service there with a solemn march to Mount Hope Cemetery. The response to this official ceremony in recognition of his distinguished services as a statesman prompted a move for a suitable monument, which was finally erected and dedicated by Governor Roosevelt in June 1899.

"ROCHESTER MADE MEANS QUALITY"

In an era characterized by the popularization of culture and the arts, Rochester's quest for quality in industry was not as anomalous as it might seem. Instead it was a recognition of the fact that the city's prosperity, indeed its future, depended on the skills and talents of all its people. Lacking local sources of raw materials and dependent on outside monopolies for their import, as well as for supplies of fuel and for access to markets, Rochester could not compete with the heavy-industry lake ports to the west, or with the Atlantic ports to the east, which enjoyed easier access to world markets. The city had long since developed the agricultural and horticultural potentials of its region, and its further growth depended on the inventive talents, managerial enterprise, and productive skills of its inhabitants. Fortunately, each wave of newcomers brought new specialties, and many of the products for which Rochester was becoming famous had made their appearance before 1908 when the Chamber of Commerce coined its new slogan: "Rochester Made Means Quality."

Rochester's limitations were clearly revealed by its problems with the railroads and with its other public utilities. The many decades during which it had relied on the lake and the state-owned canal for its shipments and on the waterfalls for power had passed, as had the briefer period in the late eighties when competing rail lines and rival gas and electric companies had encouraged new entrepreneurial efforts. By the early nineties the New York Central had acquired control over both the Buffalo, Rochester & Pittsburgh and the Rome, Watertown & Ogdensburg, and neither the old Erie Railroad nor the new Lehigh Valley, which came into the city on the east bank of the river in 1892, provided effective competition. These southern roads, with the Buffalo, Rochester & Pittsburgh and the new Western New York & Pennsylvania Railroad in the old Genesee Valley Canal, increased the coal deliveries and stimulated a new lake trade of coal shipments to Canada; they also supplied improved passenger service between Rochester and settlements in the upper valley, although many villages had more frequent and more direct ties to Buffalo.

Disillusionment even followed the construction of four new electric lines to Sodus Bay in 1900, to Canandaigua and Geneva in 1903, and to Lockport and Buffalo in the west and Syracuse and Utica in the east during the next four years. The New York Central soon acquired ownership of the Sodus Bay and Canandaigua lines and, by absorbing the Rochester [Street] Railway Company into its New York State Railways subsidiary, also secured control over the two independent electrics that had no direct entry into the heart of Rochester. The city's only hope for adequate local service lay in an appeal to the Public Service Commission, established by Governor Hughes in 1907, and Mayors Cutler and Edgerton dispatched frequent pleas for its assistance.

Rochester secured somewhat better service for a time from its gas and electric companies, at least while it remained their major market. The progressive consolidation of the gas and electric companies into the Rochester Gas & Electric in 1902 kept the rates high, but a threat by Mayor Cutler to bring electricity from Niagara for the city's street lights in 1906 was sufficient to secure a 25 percent reduction from the newly formed Rochester Railway & Light Company. All competitive possibilities disappeared, however, when the Vanderbilt-Andrews syndicate in control of the New York Central also acquired control of all electric lines and their affiliates, and Mayor Cutler had to resort the next year to the Public Service Commission to obtain a reduction in the increased gas and electric rates.

When the Bell Telephone Company, which had absorbed Rochester's early telephone companies, boosted its charges in the mid-nineties, a group of local investors launched a competitor that became the Rochester Telephone Company in 1900. An effort to form a network of independents to challenge the national dominance of the Bell System collapsed, however, when the United States Independent Telephone Company failed to secure an entry into New York City. Numerous local backers of that venture, who had brought the Stromberg-Carlson Telephone Manufacturing Company of Chicago to Rochester to supply its equipment, experienced financial losses. But the Rochester Telephone Company survived the crisis and served almost 10,000 subscribers in 1907, when the Bell System, despite its higher rates,

listed 14,000. The necessity many residents faced of installing duplicate phones prompted even the Rochester Chamber of Commerce to
endorse an extension in 1910 of the regulatory powers of the Public
Service Commission to the telephone companies.

If the incessant intrusion of monopoly control into the utility field
required the development of public regulatory safeguards there, competition still provided the necessary incentive in the private industrial
field. Although most of the old flour and lumber mills had now sold
their water rights to the power companies and disposed of their sites
for other uses, and the few that remained were content to produce
flour and lumber for local markets, the nursery and seed firms still held
first place in national production. The rate of their growth had subsided, however, and even the expansion that occurred among the fruit
processors who were centered in Rochester failed to match the growth
potential of some of its other industries.

Rochester's Genesee hinterland had in fact become more important
as a market for its products and a training field for its merchants than
as a source of raw materials or manpower. In addition to the traveling
salesmen dispatched by the nurserymen and the shoe and clothing
firms in earlier decades, a new group of traveling representatives of
wholesale distributors fanned out from the city, and the Rochester
Chamber of Commerce conducted a series of promotional tours by
local merchants and industrialists to neighboring towns seeking outlets
for their products. The city itself was becoming a rich market for
merchandise, as the growth of its department stores, which now increased to five, and the multiplication of its specialty shops demonstrated. Though proportionately much less numerous than in many
commercially oriented cities, Rochester's sales personnel and other
so-called white-collar workers numbered nearly half those employed in
industry by 1910. And when the newly formed association of clerks,
3,000 strong, launched a campaign for the Saturday half-holiday, forty
stores accepted that schedule during the summer of 1901, and many
continued it in successive summers as a demonstration of their public
spirit.

Rochester's growth depended more directly on its technical industries and on their capacity to reach a popular market. None succeeded
so dramatically as George Eastman, though his reticence, coupled with
his absorption in business, kept him out of the public eye for several

years. The modest cost and novelty of taking amateur pictures assured Eastman a market even during the depression, when more expensive amusements were curtailed, and the development of the motion-picture industry brought huge orders for his film, which necessitated the construction of additional factories both at his State Street center and at Kodak Park. Eastman's astute policy of buying up related patents that would assist or might obstruct the development of his product made Rochester the focal center of the expanding photographic industry and prompted him to organize the General Aristo Company as a subsidiary and to give long-term production contracts to Bausch & Lomb for lenses and to Wollensack for shutters, for example. Several independents, notably the Anthony & Scoville Company and the Rochester Optical & Camera Company, whose claims were rejected as unreasonable, provided a measure of competition, but with the organization in 1901 of the Eastman Kodak Company, capitalized at $35 million, its supremacy was unchallenged.

George Eastman accepted the presidency of the new company, which was chartered in New Jersey as a holding company to combine his varied interests in Rochester and in England. In the reorganization leading to this merger, he had, as treasurer, disposed of some of his personal stock options for cash and proceeded to distribute $178,000 among his employees as bonuses and to make his first sizable gift of $200,000 to Mechanics Institute for a new building. He refused to negotiate with a group of workers in the plating and polishing shop who endeavored to form a craft union, but after closing the shop to get rid of their union, he agreed to buy their products when produced cooperatively by a Union Polishing & Plating Company formed on the outside. To accommodate his workers, who now outnumbered those of any other local factory, he supplied not only dining rooms, rest rooms, and lockers, but also a library reading room and a hospital room in each factory. Although the camaraderie of the early days, when the two or three hundred "Kodakers" had enjoyed an occasional holiday at a beach picnic, had disappeared as the number employed increased tenfold, Eastman took an interest in the bowling clubs and ball teams formed by his men and invited many of his executives and their wives to attend the Sunday musicals in his new mansion on East Avenue. Although his quiet absorption in business had kept him out of the limelight, his gift of $400,000 to the City Hostpital building fund in

1909 revealed a new image, one destined for remarkable developments in the next decade.

None could rival Eastman's accomplishments, but several local industrialists made noteworthy efforts, some with happy results. Key inventions gave the start in several instances, but the search for capital and the competition for markets generally determined the outcome. Thus, two inventors of special gear devices for chainless bicycles organized competing companies in 1898, but more aggressive backers of the bicycle trust in Hartford soon acquired their patents and closed their shops. Three rival inventors of voting machines attracted Rochester capital, but soon the backers decided to merge and moved the entire enterprise to Jamestown to escape further strife. George B. Selden used some of the royalties received from the Association of Licensed Automobile Manufacturers on his basic patent to develop the Selden car, which was introduced with great ceremony in front of the Seneca Hotel in October 1908. But Selden, a patent lawyer, not a businessman, retired three years later when the United States Circuit Court relieved Henry Ford and other producers from obligations to the Selden patent. His company continued to produce a few cars, but they were not as competitive in either design or quality as the automobile chassis turned out for the luxury market by the Cunningham carriage works after 1908.

Several of the well-established firms likewise depended on the acquisition of new patents and the promotion of new markets. The Kimball Tobacco Company was absorbed by the American Tobacco Company for its patents, and the Rochester factory was closed shortly after the death of its founder in 1895. The local breweries continued under British management until closed by the prohibition laws a few years later, but the Pfaudler Company, holder of the patent on vacuum fermentation and on the construction of glass-lined tanks, expanded and acquired a subsidiary in Germany in 1907 to produce for the European market. E. G. Miner, its enterprising vice president, became president of the chamber two years later. Meanwhile, the Pneumatic Signal Company organized in 1897 to manufacture a railway signaling device invented in Rochester, soon absorbed two rival signal firms and emerged as the General Railway Signal Company in 1904, with $5 million in capital and a $2 million contract from the New York Central that forced an expansion of its work force to 500 men. After suffering two foreclosures during the depression, the Ritter Dental Company, under new management and with a more vigorous sales force, acquired a new plant in 1908 and increased its employment to 400 in two years. An improved electric elevator developed by H. B. Graves proved so safe and efficient that his company won a wide market and became the first in Rochester in 1900 to pay annual wage dividends to its workers.

Several local firms found themselves strategically located at the threshold of expanding national markets. The Gleason Company, with increasing demands from bicycle companies for its gear cutting machines, erected a new factory on University Avenue in 1905 and was soon inundated by similar orders from automobile makers. The Todds, who invented and produced the protectograph, found bankers everywhere eager to take advantage of this safeguard against forgeries. The Taylor Instruments Company, ready to supply the needs of the expanding host of weathermen, soon faced a demand for industrial thermometers and gauges. Bausch & Lomb, with a firm grip on the spectacle trade, had to expand its factories to produce lenses and shutters for camera companies; microscopes for an expanding scientific and school market; and telescopes and field glasses for naturalists, mariners, and an increasing number of militarists, all eager for the latest and most reliable equipment. To assure an adequately trained work force, Henry Lomb devoted much time and money to the promotion of the Mechanics Institute and the development of its technical instruction.

Despite the rapid growth of the photographic, optical, and other instrument companies, the two industries that supplied the city's major employment were shoes and clothing. Both depended on the enterprise of the managers and the skills of the workers, and both learned a lesson during the depression. Amidst the numerous failures that occurred in both fields, a limited number of firms survived and, almost without exception, these proved to be the quality producers. By the late nineties the demand for better shoes for women was justifying the expansion of the Utz & Dunn factory, among several others, and the demand for fine clothing for men was prompting Henry Michaels, Simon Stein, and several other manufacturers of trademark suits to hire the skilled men from the closed shops of their cheaper competitors and to build more substantial factories. Because of the high repute of the city's products, some manufacturers, such as the

Morris & Vaisley Shoe Company, moved to Rochester in order to share its labor skills and reputation. Both the shoe and clothing manufacturers exerted a larger influence in their respective national association than the relative size of their output justified. Indeed, Sol Wile of Rochester served for a time as secretary of both national associations.

In the shoe and clothing fields, the major reliance on the skills and productivity of the workers made the relations between manufacturers and employees a subject of primary concern. In the middle and late nineties, when the Boot and Shoe Workers and the United Garment Workers, who had taken over from the older Knights of Labor assemblies, were forming locals and building their strength, the workers were generally content when the unions secured a restoration of earlier cuts. But after the turn of the century, when the long decline in the cost of living in the United States gave way to a new cycle of rising prices, a new pressure for wage increases developed and brought renewed conflict in both the shoe and clothing fields. The shoe firms, by the introduction of new machinery, were able to dispense with the services of the more skillful cutters and some other skilled craftsmen, among whom unionism was strong, but their position as style setters in the industry was thereby endangered. The leading clothing firms— Hickey-Freeman, Levi Adler and Company, and Stein-Black, among others refused to substitute machine production for hand work at crucial steps in the manufacturing process and therefore retained their reputation for quality garments. The skilled workers in the clothing factories comprised only a fraction of the greater number who worked under subcontractors in scattered lofts and sweatshops or who carried bundles home to be fitted together by the entire family. The wages and especially the working conditions of the factory workers were so much better than those of the sweatshops that it was with the subcontractors that the United Garment Workers generally had to battle. In 1903, however, they lost a brief strike for an eight-hour day for the skilled cutters in the factories but only because the steady influx of skilled tailors from abroad gave the Clothiers Exchange a clear advantage.

Public sentiment was nevertheless swinging to the side of labor in an increasing number of cases. Neither the tobacco nor the liquor industries could afford to fight labor, for too many of their customers were workingmen. Rivalry between the Knights of Labor and the

AFL locals limited the power of unions in these industries, however, and delayed the growth of strong AFL unions in several other fields until after the turn of the century. Both the machinists and the metal-workers engaged in crucial struggles with various firms; they won victories in 1901 but suffered defeats in renewed strikes a few years later, after the trade associations had strengthened their ranks. The woodworkers and the carpenters, by close collaboration, won better contracts, as did the typographical workers and the pressmen. The laborers' union formed in 1899 lost its first strike, but the losses suffered by the construction contractors were so much greater that the next year they settled more quickly at one-cent-an-hour increase; a year later they granted a two-cent increase without a strike.

The Central Trades Council increased its affiliated unions to 103 in 1903, with a total membership in excess of 13,000, and although the number of unions dropped to 75 in five years, the membership climbed to approximately 15,000, and the turnout for Labor Day parades amply demonstrated their strength. Emanuel Koveleski, business agent of the brewery union, served repeatedly as president of the Central Trades Council, and with Gad Martindale of the Boot and Shoe Workers, who frequently chaired the Labor Lyceum forums, he became a familiar figure in the city. Both were well known to Joseph Alling, Mayor Cutler, Walter Rauschenbusch and, especially, Police Chief Quigley, who made it his business to attend crucial strike meetings. The Reverend Paul Moore Strayer became the Ministerial Union's representative at Central Trades meetings, marched in their Labor Day parades, and also sat on the platform at many strike meetings to demonstrate the public interest in their deliberations. With Miss Florence Cross, a trusted volunteer visitor and interpreter among the Italian laborers, young Rabbi Horace Wolf, who was able to reach the Eastern Jews, and Professor Hanna, a welcome counselor among the Poles and Italians as well as the Germans, Rochester had established channels of communication among all its varied inhabitants, and neither George Aldridge nor Joseph T. Alling, George Eastman nor James G. Cutler, Susan B. Anthony nor Helen B. Montgomery, Bishop McQuaid nor Walter Rauschenbusch could speak for all of them. It had become a complex community, more a city of the people than at any previous period.

7

George Eastman's Town, 1910–1929

FEW would have guessed in the early 1900s that the cosmopolitan community they knew would by the late teens be popularly described as "George Eastman's town." In the first place his interest in city affairs had been minimal and his participation almost nonexistent before 1905, and most citizens concerned with local problems had practically abandoned the effort to enlist his help in their endeavors. Only the managers of Mechanics Institute had found him responsive, as his gifts grew from $50 in 1887 to $10,000 in 1892, and to $200,000 in 1899 when he paid for the construction of its new building, later called the Eastman building. He made a few other modest contributions in these years and gave the University of Rochester $75,000 for a new science building in 1903, but he sought to avoid personal requests by supplying Mrs. Helen D. Arnold, secretary of the Society for Organized Charity, with an occasional $500 check to take care of worthy applicants.

Eastman's attitude began to change in mid-decade as his gifts to local hospitals and other institutions increased in number and size, reaching a high of $400,000 for new buildings for the City Hospital in 1909. Several donations of park lands to the city and of funds to clear the deficits in the Rochester orchestra's budgets disclosed his increased interest in community affairs. Moreover, the opening of his new mansion on East Avenue, with a sumptuous reception on October 8, 1905, marked the start of a more social life revolving around recitals on the pipe organ he had installed there as a special favor to his mother. Her death two years later diverted him from family to community interests and transformed the mansion from a private home into what became in time a community institution. In addition to the Sunday evening organ recitals presented there fairly regularly after 1908 to a select list of guests, Eastman staged occasional receptions, as in December 1913 when he sent out 1,200 invitations to a New Year's party that was reputedly designed to overshadow the traditional New Year's reception of Mrs. Warham Whitney, who had failed to respond to the YM and YW appeals that year.

Eastman was learning to use his mounting wealth in various ways. At the office he set aside $500,000 in 1911 as a special benefit fund for his employees and the next year announced a distribution of his first wage dividends, sending each of over 7,000 workers checks representing two percent of their wages over the previous five years. These and other benefits represented a deafening response to the socialist agitation heard in other quarters that year, and most of his charitable gifts were similarly designed to promote rather than supplant individual enterprise. Moreover, although Eastman in his early benevolences had generally defrayed the full cost of any project he endorsed, in 1912 he contributed one-half of a projected endowment fund of $1,000,000 for the University of Rochester, and three years later one-fourth of a proposed $200,000 building fund for the Rochester Friendly Home. From that date forward he usually conditioned his generous pledges on the ability of the project's promoters to reach their prescribed goal, thus spurring rather than displacing community efforts. The home-front responsibilities he assumed during the war would engender a more forthright leadership during the twenties.

DECLINING POWER OF THE BOSS

Certainly, during the prewar years, if anybody was suspected of dominating Rochester, it was not George Eastman but George Aldridge. Despite the defeat of his bid for a seat in Congress in a special election in 1910, Aldridge proved himself a good loser and not only nominated a strong candidate to recapture that post for the party in 1911 but also backed Mayor Edgerton successfully for a third term. Moreover, he managed on the latter occasion to dump Professor Forbes, his most outspoken critic, from the school board and in his absence was able finally to bring the Social Center experiment to an end. But the boss was too wise to take a solely negative position in that controversy and transferred the funds cut from the school budget (and the Social

Centers) to a new playground program, which he placed under the direction of Colonel Samuel P. Moulthrop, a popular principal who took temporary leave from No. 26 School to launch the new system.

Mounting pressures for municipal improvements had meanwhile prompted the creation of the Civic Improvement Committee. Backed by leaders of the Chamber of Commerce, it had enlisted the services of outside experts to prepare a plan for Rochester's development. Mayor Edgerton and the boss had formulated plans of their own for the opening of a north-side parallel street and for the construction of a new city hall, but the committee, headed by former Mayor Cutler, persuaded them to defer action until the new plans were received. The delay proved crucial, for when the plans submitted by Brunner and Olmsted, the outside experts, proposed a civic center on West Main Street, where the canal crossing would soon be abandoned, the disappointment of Cutler and other east-side residents was paralyzing. And when the resilient mayor directed City Engineer Fisher to calculate the cost for the acquisition of properties needed for the north-side parallel proposed in the plan, his $2,000,000 estimate aroused so much opposition that action was deferred. The counterdemand that a south-side parallel be constructed first, following the canal over the aqueduct and cutting east across Stone and Clinton streets to reach East or Park Avenues, attracted support from powerful groups advocating the construction of a subway in the old canal bed to supply direct access to the center of Rochester for the large interurban lines that were temporarily halted on its outskirts. They maintained that the south-side parallel, decking a subway in the central district, would supply two vital needs in one operation.

Other projects envisioned by Brunner and Olmsted contended for precedence, however, and threatened a general stalemate. Only in the case of the public library and the museum was action precipitated in 1911 when a move by the state to convert the abandoned buildings of the old State Industrial School into a state prison spurred Mayor Edgerton to recommend their acquisition by the city for use as a library headquarters, a municipal museum, and a winter zoo. Fortunately, in the case of the parks, earlier acquisitions by purchase and gift had supplied Rochester with a potentially great system that now invited fuller use. The extension of trolley lines into Seneca Park, the development of its zoo and of band concerts there and in Genesee

Valley Park, and the staging of annual water carnivals at that park attracted huge throngs on special occasions and enhanced their popular use throughout the summer months.

Several other developments contributed to the new emphasis on recreation. The commemoration of the centennial of the town's establishment by a parade featuring ten bands and twelve historic floats drew thousands of citizens into Main Street on September 13, 1912. When Colonel Moulthrop, having launched playground programs that attracted wide support, sought a return to his school, Mayor Edgerton moved for the consolidation of their management with that of the parks under a superintendent responsible to the mayor rather than to the park commission. Because many of its members were already overburdened by their accumulating responsibilities, few objected in 1915 when the legislature abolished the park board and consolidated its functions and those of the playgrounds under the Commissioner of Parks and Playgrounds. The appointment of the former board chairman, Alexander B. Lamberton, as the first commissioner gave assurance of continuity in these developments.

The boss had learned to back able administrators and not only supported Lamberton's more recreational uses of the parks, but after removing objectional members from the school board, gave Herbert S. Weet, the new superintendent, a free hand in developing junior high schools, among other educational advances. Indeed the boss vied with the reformers in efforts to provide special classes for the new immigrants that supplied the city's chief population gains in these years. Mayor Edgerton, who addressed separate Polish, Italian, and German gatherings during one busy evening in October 1911, was fully aware of their need to learn English and backed the efforts of Colonel Moulthrop and others to conduct evening classes for various groups of these newcomers. By October 1914, when 2,000 new applicants enrolled for such classes, the Rochester plan was gaining high praise throughout the land, and business leaders, politicians, and reformers joined in varied expressions of welcome, especially to the hundred or more newcomers who hastened to acquire citizenship each year.

Boss Aldridge had also learned to live with Dr. Goler, his health officer, and Mayor Edgerton joined Dr. Goler and the Women's Educational & Industrial Union in inviting Mrs. Caroline B. Crane of Kalamazoo to make a sanitary survey of Rochester in 1911. Many were surprised and disconcerted by the number of defects she found, including the inadequate support given the health officers. Most of her criticisms of the lack of power to make meat inspections, the poor enforcement of charges of milk infractions, and the unsanitary methods of collecting garbage could have been lifted from Dr. Goler's earlier reports. But because outside criticism was more difficult to disregard, the city health inspectors soon received additional support. However, the mayor refused to join in welcoming Dr. Anna Louise Strong, a second outside investigator brought to Rochester two years later to inspect child welfare provisions. Nevertheless, as a result of her visit, Rochester's pioneer milk stations, introduced by Dr. Goler a few years before, were converted into child welfare clinics that attracted nationwide attention.

One result of the boss's compromise with the Good Government forces was a more vigorous enforcement of the state's Sunday-closing laws and other puritanical regulations. Chief Joseph M. Quigley, named to that post in 1908, launched a drive against stall saloons and other centers of organized vice and required the city's 500 licensed saloons to keep their windows clean and unshaded so that improper activities could be detected. Although advocates of prohibition, such as Clinton N. Howard, often found fault with the enforcement, Chief Quigley was able to boast with some justification that Rochester was the "cleanest city in the world." The council responded to his request for stronger power over the regulation of dance halls and backed his appointment of a policewoman to assist in their supervision. Indeed the enforcement was so effective within the city that several entertainers congregated at Charlotte, which prompted the permanent residents of that lake-side suburb to back the movement for annexation in order to secure adequate police protection. The demands of zealous Sabbatarians that baseball and other sports be banned on that day were disregarded by the police and opposed by advocates of the social gospel, who even petitioned for the presentation of free motion pictures and conducted song and lecture programs in downtown theaters on Sunday.

Many Rochesterians believed that the proper method for the solution of community needs and urban ills was through private efforts. Although the city, which had refused to grant tax relief to Daniel

Powers on his art gallery, had staged a public art exhibit in its newly acquired Exposition Hall in 1912, it welcomed the action of Mrs. Sibley Watson in giving a permanent gallery to the university, which opened the Memorial Art Gallery on its Prince Street campus in October 1913. Rochester was ready at last to assume public responsibilities in the library field, though it started modestly with a branch system, but it relied on privately supported Mechanics Institute for the instruction of its workers in technical fields. As churchmen became more socially conscious, their traditional independence from the state strengthened the preference for volunteer action.

The Men and Religion Forward Movement, which produced an outburst of zeal and, in December 1911, conducted a new survey of the city's social needs, emphasized the goal of personal redemption as preferable to the social regulation of morals. It fostered cooperative efforts that led to the establishment of denominational homes for the aged as well as youth programs. Meanwhile, the United Charities, launched in an endeavor to draw the city's varied charitable efforts into a concerted organization, brought Dr. William Kirk to Rochester as its general secretary in 1911. It promoted the establishment of the Provident Loan Society to safeguard the poor from loan sharks, organized the Monday Club to supply a meeting place for volunteer and paid social workers, fostered the creation of two vacation camps for poor boys and of vacation homes for needy families, and established a confidential exchange at which the various agencies could register the services rendered to needy clients and check for duplicating efforts by other agencies. Harper Sibley, Edward G. Miner, and other business leaders backed this volunteer approach and in 1914 launched a drive that netted $57,231 to cover its expenses during the next two years.

The hope that efforts of the United Charities would reduce the demands of its member agencies was not realized, however, for a closer look at the community quickly revealed new needs. Not only did the legal aid program of the Women's Educational & Industrial Union merit support as an independent agency, but the dispensary opened in Baden Street Settlement required additional backing, and the Housekeeping Center conducted by Miss Florence Cross for the instruction of Italian women in American sanitary and household customs needed assistance to assure its reorganization as the Lewis Street

Settlement. The Door of Hope acquired a new dormitory on Central Avenue; the YWCA erected a new headquarters on Franklin Street, donated by Mrs. Henry A. Strong; the Rochester Orphan Asylum opened two new cottages, one for boys and one for girls; and the Industrial School on Exchange Street added a new pavilion where its young charges could play in winter months and during inclement weather. Dr. Kirk, who also taught a course in social work at the university, enlisted several of his students in volunteer work for one or another of his social agencies.

Varied groups rallied to the support of special institutions. The Boy Scouts, first introduced at the YMCA in September 1910, enlisted the cooperation of several business and professional men headed by Henry W. Morgan of the Morgan Machine Company, with Colonel Moulthrop as commissioner. As the number of local troops increased and their summer trips to Camp Iola on Canandaigua Lake became an established practice, many boys won emblems and pennants, and 350 volunteered in February 1913 to assist the Ad Club in a drive for funds for a new Infant's Summer Hospital at Charlotte. Sometimes the directors of a needy institution attracted a backer able to fill their needs single-handedly, as when George Eastman gave $45,000 for the construction of an addition to the SPCC building on Plymouth Avenue in 1914, but the new procedure was to create a committee of leading citizens and persuade them to organize a campaign for the desired sum. The astonishing success of the YMCA drive in April 1913 set the pattern for many to come. Under the direction of Charles S. Ward, a professional campaigner for the Y, several competing teams canvassed the entire city and raised a fund of $515,000 from 5,247 subscribers to clinch the $250,000 pledge of George Eastman, and thus clearly demonstrated the presence of widespread community loyalties.

Financial drives could not solve all the problems, as the directors of United Charities discovered in January 1914 when the recession that followed the outbreak of war in Europe suddenly hit Rochester. Pleas for aid were up 100 percent over the previous year. Even Dr. Kirk, who had determined to avoid any distribution of assistance, frankly recognized that temporary relief had become essential until the emergency was passed when, hopefully, the search for the causes and remedies of poverty could be resumed. To surmount the current crisis, the directors of United Charities urged the city to undertake emergency work projects. But Mayor Edgerton, pleading the city's tight budget, revived a proposal made by his opponent in the previous campaign that the city create a bureau of efficiency to find ways of improving its fiscal procedures so that it would be better able to meet its problems. When the Mayor's search for the modest sums needed for such a staff proved futile, George Eastman, attracted by the prospect of improved municipal efficiency, offered in March 1915 to pay the cost of engaging the New York Bureau of Municipal Research to make a study of the city's civic arrangements. Former Mayor Cutler and nine other leading citizens agreed to serve with Eastman as trustees of a Rochester Bureau to supervise that study and carry on a research program. Most Rochesterians applauded this effort to upgrade the city's efficiency, but James L. Brewer, a young socialist lawyer, warned that it was, in fact, a move to foist "a greater boss on a Greater Rochester."

INTERLUDE OF WAR

World War I was, of course, more than an interlude. While it interrupted some developments, it initiated others and transformed many more. By transporting thousands of Rochester's young men and some women to distant battle areas, it created a new sense of the city's involvement in historic worldwide events. It accelerated many technological developments and greatly increased the number of active participants in community affairs. For a time the heightened awareness of the personal tragedies it produced created a feeling of interdependence that silenced and submerged many old jealousies and hostilities. However, its effects were not all benign, and many of Rochester's young men returned with new experience in the exercise of violence and with many of their former restraints shattered; they would contribute in the twenties to the development of a blasé spirit that sometimes contended with the city's more traditional meliorism.

Long accustomed to watching foreign conflicts from the sidelines, Rochesterians speculated idly on the effects of the assassination of the Austrian Archduke in June 1914. When hostilities erupted in Europe, the first concern of many was for the safety of a number of parties of Rochester tourists caught in belligerent territory. As the violence mounted, members of several ethnic minorities became alarmed for their relatives at home, and twenty-seven young men of Belgian and Dutch birth hastened to return for the defense of their homelands. Some of the more numerous young Italian and Russian newcomers like-wise volunteered for service at home, and their elders established committees to raise relief funds, which multiplied in number as more countries became involved. A few Rochester boys crossed the border to enlist in the Canadian forces, but most residents endorsed President Wilson's plea for a neutral attitude. Although the City Club en-deavored to give a hearing to both sides, the invasion of Belgium stirred sympathy for its nationals and prompted Hiram W. Sibley to assume charge of its war-relief drive. Hostility towards the Germans began to mount, yet it was not until the sinking of the *Lusitania* in May 1915, with three local residents among the victims, that Roches-terians became aware of their increasing involvement.

Renewed pledges of restraint from Germany and pleas for neu-trality from the President, coupled with sufficient orders for military supplies to create full employment, lessened tension in Rochester but gave rise by the next January to an increased demand for preparedness. Judge John D. Lynn, the United States Marshall, took a census of the foreign nationals employed in local industries and found nearly 40,000, or approximately one-third of the city's labor force. Many, of course, were already naturalized, and as the survey progressed, an additional 2,300 enrolled in citizenship classes in several city school buildings. Rallies advocating preparedness and universal military training merged that fall with political rallies for former Governor Hughes for Presi-dent. And despite the popularity of the Wilson slogan, "He kept us out of war," Hughes carried Rochester and Monroe County by un-precedented majorities.

Rochester, with the rest of the country, was in the grip of larger forces as 1917 opened. The renewed U-boat campaign in January brought the reelected Wilson to the brink of war even before his second inauguration. Local demands for universal military training mounted, and Mayor Edgerton appointed a committee on national de-fense, which endeavored to secure pledges of loyalty from all adult aliens. Although several advocates of peace held a rally at Convention Hall, most citizens rejoiced when, on April 2, Wilson finally called for a declaration of war. Impatient editors applauded when a hundred young men enlisted during the next three days, and thousands gathered a week later to cheer the first unit to depart.

Most Rochesterians welcomed the passage of the Selective Service Act. The turnout for Registration Day on June 5 was unobstructed, and unofficial reports showed 22,216 citizens registered, plus 5,308 aliens, including 260 enemy aliens. After the first drawing in July, the eight local draft boards examined 5,590 selectees, over 3,600 of whom proved physically fit. Earlier enlistments, numbering over 1,300, had partially filled Rochester's quota, but 2,000 additional men were called up that month. By the close of the year Rochester and Monroe County had sent almost 6,700 men and women into the services, and although most of them were still stationed in training camps, a few had already reached the battle areas, and on January 2, 1918, William S. Ely, grandson of an early Rochester physician, was the first from the city to lose his life to enemy action.

Citizens beyond the military age seized many opportunities to display their loyalty. George Eastman, who now for the first time assumed the public role of community leadership, announced his readiness to subscribe $2.5 million to the nation's proposed Liberty Loan, even before it was authorized. Rochester promptly responded and successfully met its quota and then, with the aid of a great Liberty Day parade, surged over the top in its second and larger bond drive in October. Meanwhile, with Eastman as chairman, sparking the drive with a $250,000 pledge, Rochester had oversubscribed its first Red Cross campaign in June by 50 percent. Many citizens continued to support the Belgium and other war-relief drives and generously backed the new programs of the YMCA and other service agencies that opened canteens at the training camps and followed the troops abroad. Numerous Rochesterians left to man the Red Cross hospitals and Y canteens abroad, and none served more devotedly than the Rochester doctors and nurses who staffed the Red Cross Base Hospital No. 19 under Dr. John M. Swan at Vichy, France, from June 1918 until the close of the war.

These distant efforts and the home-front programs that endeavored to serve recruits stationed in or passing through Rochester all required increased support. To achieve better coordination, the Chamber of Commerce helped in May 1918 to establish the Rochester Patriotic and Community Fund. Patterned after war chests in other cities, it received the active leadership of George Eastman as president and Dr. Rush Rhees as chairman of the budget committee. Encouraged by earlier responses, the directors set a minimum goal of $3,750,000, three times the sum desired by the Red Cross, in order to cover not only that and other major war services but also the thirty-six local charities whose maintenance would otherwise have been threatened. In a seven-day campaign directed by Harry P. Wareham, Rochester again surged over the top, subscribing a total of $4,838,093, which was eight rather than four times Eastman's pledge—a result of the participation of 117,064 citizens.

Rochester's enthusiastic response to these special fund and successive war-bond drives reflected, in addition to the inspired leadership, the success of the city's industries in maintaining full employment. At least eighty firms received war orders for a wide variety of products ranging from buttons, belts, and caskets to cameras, range finders, and periscopes, and a host of other items including both light and heavy shells. To expedite this production, the War Department early designated Rochester as the center of an ordinance district that encompassed the entire state, except for the New York metropolitan area. As a result, Rochester industrialists were able to enlist the capacities of small as well as large firms in filling complicated orders for military supplies. None, perhaps, exceeded in importance the high-grade optical glass newly produced by Bausch & Lomb in collaboration with experts loaned by the Federal Bureau of Standards. At the same time, the new aerial cameras developed by Eastman and the new gear-cutting machines perfected by Gleason to help produce antiaircraft guns, range finders, and other tools of war, won hearty praise from military officials.

To fill these orders, the city's industrialists had to build several new factories and employ many additional workers. The demand for skilled workers in one plant often threatened vital production in other factories, and to forestall a work stoppage because of short labor skills or strikes the mayor named a community labor board. He secured the participation of Emanuel Koveleski, long-time president of the Central Trades Council, as a member of the board—labor's first association on an equal footing with leading Rochester industrialists. As a result, although major strikes were avoided, wage rates advanced sufficiently to keep pace with, if not to exceed, rising living costs. A war-garden program, endorsed by Eastman, who plowed up his front yard and parcelled out an unused tract near Kodak Park for truck gardens, helped to ward off a threatened food shortage. Careful rationing served to ease the coal crisis after a period of short work weeks, and other measures alerted the public to the gravity of the situation.

The war hastened two important political decisions, though Rochester, absorbed with other local developments, did not favor either one. Prohibition, vigorously advocated by several Rochesterians but effectively opposed by the majority of its voters, finally won national approval despite local pleas that such a decision should await the return of the nation's young men. Similarly, in the campaign for woman's suffrage, despite the long advocacy by its own Susan B. Anthony, Rochester registered its consistent opposition. When the amendment nevertheless passed, Rochester women were slow to assume their voting privileges, increasing the total votes cast by less than one-third and scarcely altering its customary results. More interest was displayed in the sudden appearance on the Rochester scene of an aggressive new daily, the *Times-Union,* which combined the moribund *Union & Advertiser* with the faltering *Times* into a crusading journal that soon placed the formerly liberal *Herald* and the elite *Post Express* on the defensive. Although the first reaction to its publisher, Frank E. Gannett, on his arrival was cool, his forthright championship of the war effort and such popular causes as urban expansion soon won him a hearing and enabled him to pose as the leader in the successful move to annex Kodak Park on the north side and Lincoln Park on the west side.

Gannett's attentive reports on the achievements of Rochester's servicemen abroad helped bring the war back into focus. A second draft had become necessary before the first was completed, and finally a third draft, which brought the total number of inductees from Rochester up to 7,627. Rochester's total contributions, including enlistments in the various branches of service, greatly exceeded that figure and reached 18,119, or nearly 7 percent of its population. This outpouring of manpower assured local support for war-bond drives and other efforts to speed victory. Local ceremonies honoring the mothers and families of the servicemen acquired a more somber character as the number of casualties mounted and finally passed 500 before the armistice was signed. The outburst of excitement that greeted the false armistice on November 7 revealed the degree of tension the war had created. Four days later everybody turned out to fill Main Street with a triumphant throng when news of peace finally arrived.

A series of seventeen banquets at the Chamber of Commerce, beginning on January 22 and ending in October, welcomed the successive groups of returning servicemen. However, the banquets did not match the popularity of the numerous homecoming parades, most notably that on April 2 when over 100,000 turned out to greet the 108th Regiment of the 27th Division, with many Rochester boys in its ranks. It proved more difficult to find jobs for these men, although the Community Labor Board and other agencies made numerous appeals in their behalf. The city responded by spending nearly $3,000,000 on new public works, and several firms developed new lines to create additional jobs, but the loss of military contracts aggravated the situation in some plants. George Eastman, by launching construction of new factories at Kodak Park, a new addition to the Chamber of Commerce, and the sumptuous quarters of the Eastman Theater, helped provide construction jobs. Moreover, his action in setting aside $12 million in stock for distribution to his employees, half the proceeds to go to the employee benefit fund and the other half to finance further expansion at the plant, gave new confidence in the city's industrial future.

While Eastman, with many business leaders, was devising plans for the city's further development, numerous other citizens were debating the nation's responsibilities for maintaining a peaceful world. At the City Club and on many other platforms, support for Wilson's Fourteen Points and the League of Nations was almost unanimous. The *Herald*, staunchly loyal to the President, urged prompt ratification without amendments, and although the *Democrat* and the *Post Express* favored the modifications proposed by Hughes, the *Times-Union* vigorously backed the league and took a poll of Chamber of Commerce members that revealed the great majority of them in favor of the proposed covenant. As the debate throughout the country progressed, however, the *Democrat* and even the *Post Express* began to swing toward the uncompromising opposition of Senator Lodge, but the issue was gradually pushed aside by the more challenging issue of Soviet communism. When the Socialist candidate for mayor received 6,246 votes in 1919, he took enough from the Democratic side to assure

Edgerton's reelection for a seventh term—the only close contest in a decade. The Socialists boosted their total in the national election a year later, when the influx of women voters brought increases to all parties; but the Republicans were the chief gainers, benefiting from the visit of Warren G. Harding, who received a rousing welcome on October 21. Despite the contrary assurance of the *Post Express*, his election, supported by 63 percent of Rochester's vote, brought the final defeat of the League of Nations and returned Rochester to firm Republican control.

CIVIC AND ECONOMIC RENEWAL

Perhaps the most striking feature of Rochester's postwar years was the emergence of George Eastman as a dominant leader in practically every aspect of the city's life. His sense of social responsibility had been developing gradually for more than a decade, and the wartime challenges had finally enabled him to overcome the reticence that had kept him aloof from the public scene. Now a combination of circumstances brought him to the fore, even in the political field. The Bureau of Municipal Research, which he had established in 1915, drew him increasingly into the mainstream of civic reform, and his commitments to the chamber involved him in many of its interests, including the new planning efforts it helped initiate. Despite his withdrawal from active direction of the company, his continued participation in its remarkable growth brought him into a position of leadership in the broader fields of community development and labor-management relations. These activities competed with but never quite matched his new interest in social and cultural affairs.

As a skilled leader, Eastman always surrounded himself with able lieutenants and relied on them for information and detailed guidance, as well as for practical action. He generally associated himself with other community leaders, as in the case of the Bureau of Municipal Research, or in that of the Community Chest, and then proceeded to employ skilled professionals to do the work—a procedure that assured both efficient and responsible action. Thus, as president for several years of the Community Chest, a successor after 1921 of the War Chest he had previously chaired, Eastman helped to establish its reputation for successfully meeting both local and national welfare quotas. Oscar W. Kuolt, brought to Rochester as secretary of the chest's services, on discovering that the United Charities had been transformed into the Family Service Organization, quickly rallied support for a new effort to integrate the local welfare programs under the Council of Social Agencies.

In similar fashion the staff of the Bureau of Municipal Research, headed by Leroy E. Snyder, soon assembled data that helped promote increased efficiency. One study introduced more scientific methods of letting city contracts; others brought improvements in the collection of garbage, the making of asphalt repairs, and the use of plows in snow removal. A bureau study of municipal finances revealed that many other cities faced Rochester's problems of mounting costs for increased responsibilities, and although this tended to relieve the local officials of charges of extravagance, it also emphasized the need for efficiency and encouraged several of the bureau's backers to look for a more businesslike form of city government.

Any move for municipal reform in the early twenties faced a serious obstacle in Boss Aldridge. The agitation of Dr. Franklin Bock and others for the commission form of government had made little headway, less in fact than Clinton Howard's unfaltering demands for the enforcement of prohibition regulations. Aldridge had agreed to replace Edgerton, who had lost favor with labor during his seventh term as mayor, with Clarence D. Van Zandt, who was similarly compliant and not yet controversial. Furthermore, he apparently responded without hostility when Eastman suggested a joint study of the merits of council-manager government, but that may have been partly due to his absorption in a new appointment as Collector of the Port of New York. Leroy Snyder, the ablest champion of municipal reform, had stepped out as director of the bureau in 1921 to press his causes more vigorously as special assistant to Frank Gannet on the *Times-Union*. James W. Routh, whose inept comment that "many officials in city hall are solid ivory from the neck up" had brought his prompt dismissal, had been succeeded by Stephen B. Story, a more disciplined engineer who, with Eastman's backing, assumed the direction of a wide-ranging study of council-manager governments in other cities.

Snyder, as president of the City Club and in a series of articles in the *Times-Union*, actively publicized the new movement, and Mrs.

Helen Probst Abbott, the president of the recently formed Women's City Club, vigorously advocated the reform. Its prospects brightened in June when the sudden deaths of both George Aldridge and Hiram Edgerton precipitated a battle for control of the dominant Republican party. James L. Hotchkiss, although elected party chairman in a primary that September, was unable to consolidate his forces. As a result the Democrats elected Meyer Jacobstein as congressman in November, their first such victory in three decades, and delivered the city's majority to Al Smith for governor. Only the earnest campaigning of Clinton Howard and a committee of twenty-five he enlisted in the battle for enforcement checked an open party retreat on the prohibition question. Police Chief Quigley redoubled his enforcement efforts, and Mayor Van Zandt, who mildly backed that action, endeavored to restore harmony between the opposing factions. With Hotchkiss he remained noncommittal on the question of charter revision and successfully won a second term in November 1923.

New charges by Howard of lax enforcement prompted the newly elected mayor to order a strict suppression of all crime, including bootlegging, and threatened a new breach in the party. Meanwhile, the campaign of the citizens' City Government Plan Committee was making progress, and to avoid an open breach, Van Zandt reluctantly backed a resolution before the Common Council that requested the bureau to draft a charter to be submitted to the voters under the home-rule law. When the bureau invited the corporation council to collaborate in the drafting of a revised charter, he indignantly refused, and the rigid opposition of Chairman Hotchkiss came into view. The mayor, however, was more conciliatory, and when George Eastman declared in a rare interview with the press that "all that I can see that [Rochester] needs now . . . is a civic center and a modern system of municipal government," Van Zandt announced his readiness to abide by the popular referendum and to cooperate in setting up the new government if it was approved. When Hotchkiss, refusing to renominate the insubordinate mayor, named a more faithful henchman for the post, Van Zandt determined to run in the primary and captured the party nomination. The Democrats, equally divided on the charter question, determined at the last moment to nominate Leroy Snyder for mayor, pinning their hopes for victory on this champion of reform. An intensive drive by a newly formed city manager league boosted the number of registered voters to an unprecedented 104,377, but when Eastman announced his willingness to stand by Van Zandt, Snyder's chances evaporated. The league, pledged at the start to nonpartisanship, carried the day for the charter but scattered its votes among the candidates, giving victory to Van Zandt and several councilmen frankly hostile to the reform.

Eastman perhaps reasoned that a Snyder victory would also have elected councilmen whose support for charter reform was equally dubious. But Eastman had another reason for supporting Van Zandt, who had accepted his gift of the old Kimball tobacco factory as a proper site for a future civic center, and he was rewarding the mayor for halting action on the construction of a new city hall on a rival site purchased by the council. Unfortunately, his sudden death the next June, the first mayor of Rochester to die in office, created a new crisis for the reformers. The council promptly elected its president, Martin B. O'Neil, a staunch Hotchkiss man, as mayor and pressed a new attack in the courts on the constitutionality of the charter amendments. When the State Court of Appeals upheld all provisions except the one prescribing nonpartisan elections, both sides claimed victory, but the real victory would go to those who controlled the strongest political party. Thus Hotchkiss had the upper hand, but his efforts to purge some backers of charter reform brought a new primary battle in which such moderates as Joseph C. Wilson, Leo MacSweeney, Harry C. Goodwin, and T. Carl Nixon, the young attorney who organized the Citizen's Republican Committee, secured Eastman's backing and captured control of the party from Hotchkiss. In order to assure victory over the Democrats, they named a slate of candidates for the small nine-man council that included Isaac Adler and Louis Foulkes, as well as Wilson and Goodwin and at least three doubtful supporters; the Democrats named four reformers and five regulars. The Republicans won all seats and chose Wilson as mayor and Adler as vice-mayor and proceeded to organize the council-manager government.

The new council promptly named Stephen B. Story as city manager, but that was almost its only unanimous action. Adler, who had pledged during the campaign to reenact the nonpartisan provision, proceeded to introduce such a bill and effectively split the council. With six votes in its favor, the nonpartisan provision passed, but its many opponents in the lower ranks of the party were not persuaded. Story retained two of former Mayor Van Zandt's department heads: Harold W. Baker as commissioner of public works and Clarence Pratt as corporation council. He appointed Clarence Higgins, a former associate on the bureau, as comptroller, and Louis Cartwright as auditor. All of these appointments attracted wide support, but when he named George J. Nier, a friend of one of the dubious councilmen, as commissioner of safety, advocates of nonpartisanship dubbed it a political concession. Because of the tension over prohibition and the recurrent outbreaks of delinquency and crime, that department was a crucial one, but with increased support both the police and fire bureaus achieved distinguished records in the first year. Much assistance in the handling of delinquency was expected from the parks and playgrounds, as a study of the city's recreational facilities conducted by the bureau suggested. When Calvin C. Laney retired as director of the parks, Story promptly appointed Charles B. Raitt, the parks-and-playground expert from California who had made the study, to fill the job. Nier, piqued at the appointment of a subordinate without his consent, and displeased by some of Raitt's comments in the report, promptly discharged him, and when Story, after a hearing, reinstated Raitt, Nier again discharged him. At this point friends of Patrick J. Slavin, long a faithful member of the staff, finally secured his appointment as park director.

With the successful passage of the council-manager amendments in November 1925, Harold Sanford, editor of the *Democrat,* started a series of thirty-three articles on the subject "City Planning: Rochester's Next Important Step." Many agreed, but many also resented the implication that nothing had been accomplished in this field. Despite the stalemate that had followed the appearance of the Brunner-Olmsted plan in 1911, a charter amendment in 1917 had authorized the creation of the Bureau of City Planning, over which Edgerton had placed Edwin A. Fisher the city engineer. When friction developed between Fisher and the Municipal Art Commission, created two years before and headed by former Mayor Cutler, Edgerton named the members of that commission as an advisory board for the planning superintendent. Fisher had been pressing for a north-side parallel at the same time that Cutler was interested in opening one on the south side, but the dispute was concluded when the completion of the new Barge Canal by the state made the route of the old Erie through the city available for the oft-proposed subway. Its construction in the mid-twenties and the completion of Broad Street, decking its tracks through the central district, provided the first segment of a south-side parallel; it also represented a real achievement for Fisher who now served as consulting engineer.

Except for the completion of Broad Street, the opening of a few dead-end streets, and the acquisition of additional land at the lake for Ontario Beach Park, most of the planning questions remained unanswered. Even the zoning ordinance, first drafted in 1919, encountered so much opposition that a satisfactory revision was not adopted for a full decade. Recurrent demands for a new city hall, a new post office, and a central library had produced numerous paper plans for civic center developments over the river on both sides of the aqueduct, at the river's edge, and elsewhere in the downtown district. Eastman's gift of the Kimball-Peabody building had helped to forestall action elsewhere, as previously noted, but the use of that structure as a city hall annex and central library branch opened in 1926 was only a temporary measure. Fisher, who was somewhat annoyed when the Bureau of Municipal Research released a report in 1918 discussing a "Reconstruction Program for Rochester," was the first to invite Harland Bartholomew to the city for advice on zoning matters. When the revived Civic Improvement Association commenced in 1928 to press for a solution of several downtown questions, City Manager Story appointed the City Planning Commission, comprised of Edward G. Miner and other leaders of the association as well as officials in the public works department, who soon engaged Bartholomew, the leading planner of the day, to prepare a master plan for Rochester. Meanwhile, the new council finally passed the controversial zoning ordinance regulating the height, use, and area of business as well as residential structures, and prescribing standards for various districts and streets as a directive for their proper development.

In the absence of such zoning regulations, the builders had made giant strides in the reconstruction of some downtown sites and in the development of new residential tracts on the outskirts. The city's continued growth, increasing 50 percent in population between 1910 and 1930, created a pressing demand for new commercial and industrial as well as housing facilities. With a trend towards smaller families, the demand for additional homes was intensified, and after the slump in construction during the war years, homebuilders enjoyed a great boom in the early twenties. As the number of building permits mounted from 1,361 in 1918 to 7,210 in 1924, Rochester began to close the gap between supply and demand. The projected outlays that year reached $29,588,762, a high for the period. As homebuilding in the city tapered off after 1925, it experienced an increase in the four suburban towns that ringed Rochester; thus, in contrast with most cities, the larger community showed a slight gain in homeownership. Despite a new resistance in the towns to annexation movements, their continued growth, almost trebling in the twenties, partly as an overspill from the city, added to its commercial and industrial vitality but presented additional demands on its services.

Many other aspects of Rochester's growth brought both pluses and minuses. The city's efforts to hold the successive outside monopolies that had taken over its transit system to the five-cent fare and other terms were complicated by the popular desire for improved and more widely extended services and by the protest of the company that the diluted traffic would not sustain such rates. When Rochester finally negotiated a service-at-cost contract, the company won a two-cent increase and further diluted its passenger load. More outlying residents resorted to automobiles, which trebled in number during the twenties, reaching a total of 110,000 registrations by 1929. The increased traffic created congestion on the major arteries and presented new parking problems to downtown merchants. But the increase brought prosperity to dealers and service stations and introduced a new flexibility and dynamics to Rochester's economy.

Although most of its other utility companies enjoyed expanding rather than contracting markets, Rochester had problems in each case. The controls afforded by the State Public Service Commission supplied some restraint on rates, though complaints multiplied at each increase, especially during the recessions of the early and late twenties. No utilities aroused so much hostility in Rochester as the telephone companies, and when the local Bell and the Rochester telephone companies merged in 1921, the general pleasure over the increased number of subscribers (over 40,000) easily available was dissipated as the company introduced meters on all business phones. When it was discovered that three local directors had authority to change the system or reduce the tolls, George Eastman offered to purchase their stock and give it to the city to be administered by trustees appointed by the mayor. When the three trustees rejected the offer as a betrayal of the outside capitalists, Eastman called for a study by the Bureau of Municipal Research. The rates it proposed were rejected, however, as inadequate, and a new appeal to the Public Service Commission secured only a moderate reduction in the charges.

The sharp conflict between public and private interests in the utility field was aggravated by fluctuations in the general price level during the early postwar years. Yet the demand for additional services helped to sustain the advanced prices, and after the mid-decade the major pressure was for increased services. All utilities except the transit company extended their facilities into the suburbs and greatly increased their subscribers. The major developments of the late twenties were the efforts to establish new transport facilities. And while the renewed agitation for the development of the port of Rochester, stimulated by the opening of the Welland Canal, saw action by the city again postponed, the announcement of Federal subsidies for airmail service spurred action in the development of an airport at Britton Field on the city's southwest border. When the hangar and runway constructed at Mayor O'Neil's order in 1927 at a cost of $30,000 proved so inadequate that an inspector for the Colonial Airways, which held the airmail contract, was caught in the mud the next April, City Manager Story requested and the council approved a $100,000 bond issue to bring the airport up to the required standard. Improvements were completed in time for the arrival of the first airmail delivery on June 2, 1928. Further criticism prompted additional outlays for the completion of a second runway and the installation of lights, assuring the continued landing of airmail and other commercial as well as private planes.

These developments, however, were overshadowed by the advances achieved in industry and commerce. The chamber pursued several cooperative programs assumed in the war years and fostered the development of new independent agencies. Among others designed to promote stability, the Better Business Bureau, established in 1920, made that its chief objective. Unfortunately the efforts of that bureau to check the intrusion of irresponsible promoters gave rise to a rumor that the chamber was opposed to a Ford factory in Rochester. The rumor sprang from the story of an agent in nearby Geneva who offered to secure it the plant the Rochester chamber had rejected, allegedly because of Eastman's fear of the Ford Company's wage rate.

The story attracted press notice and created reverberations in Rochester that the chamber could not silence. Its hasty wire to Ford executives, in which the chamber offered cooperation if a local site was desired, brought a reply denying any intention of locating a plant in the Rochester area and disclaiming any knowledge of the agent in question. Every public denial of the rumor served only to circulate it further, yet the organization in the mid-decade of the New Industries Bureau and the Rochester Industrial Corporation to locate and back new ventures and to attract new firms to the city finally refuted the charge and may have encouraged the newly formed General Motors Corporation to buy up Rochester's Northeast Electric Company and make it, in 1929, the core of its new General Motors plant in Rochester.

The chamber's emphasis on quality products was productive of, or at least consistent with, local industrial trends. Because Rochester's location presented transport drawbacks to heavy-metal firms, such firms specialized in elaborately tooled devices such as the Gleason gear cutting machines and those of the Davenport Machine Tool Company. In similar fashion the electrical companies produced specialized articles such as safety and control devices, starters, and other technical innovations; the optical and instrument firms manufactured high-quality scientific and technical devices. Even in the fields of shoes, clothing, and food supplies, quality and specialized products predominated, and the glass-lined tanks of the Pfaudler Company found a ready market in the rapidly growing chemical industry.

The Eastman Kodak Company, of course, dwarfed all other Rochester concerns in size and in the influence exerted on community affairs. Although the company, in compliance with a Federal court decision, divested itself in 1926 of the old Folmer-Graflex patents and factory, the demand for photographic supplies was mounting so rapidly that it brought a thriving trade to the newly independent Graflex Company, and to Haloid, Wollensack, Rectigraph, and Defender—Eastman's other Rochester competitors—as well as to the Kodak giant. After a moderate drop in 1920 from wartime levels, expanding operations brought a steady increase in the number of its employees to over 10,000 by the mid-decade and to 14,000 by 1927, when the number of factory buildings at the park reached 120 and the firm was preparing to add three more floors to its sixteen-story office tower. The distribution of $3,233,388 in wage dividends the next year, over two-thirds going to its workers in Rochester, and the adoption of other employee benefits set standards that few other local firms could match, though several made an effort to keep pace and most of the technological companies endeavored to follow the open-shop practices maintained at Kodak.

A startling challenge had appeared in the early postwar years when the sudden rise of Bolshevism transformed, or seemed to transform, every aggressive labor leader into a potential IWW. Several bitter strikes in the clothing, shoe, and construction fields added to the tension created by attempts to organize some of the technical industries. A drive by the Amalgamated Optical Workers, who called out 1,800 workers at the Bausch & Lomb plant, was quickly labeled IWW in origin, though the workers involved denied any such affiliation. When Chief of Police Quigley refused to become alarmed, demands for his removal mounted, but Mayor Edgerton, who issued a statement warning the strikers against violence, stood by his chief and won increased respect from labor. Bausch & Lomb announced a wage increase but took advantage of the work stoppage to reduce its work force and to make a careful screening of those reemployed. Several of the leading shoe firms made a similar attempt to take advantage of a work stoppage to weed out the troublemakers, but the strong tradition of unionism in that industry was hard to break. Even the rivalry between the United Shoe Workers, entrenched in some plants, and the younger Boot and Shoe Workers, AFL, only complicated the struggle. Although the Boot and Shoe Manufacturers Association finally assumed an open-shop posture, several of the older companies succumbed, and those that persisted lost the position of leadership Rochester had once maintained.

Fear of such an outcome had induced the Clothiers Exchange to adopt a different course. The new Amalgamated Clothing Workers, under Sidney Hillman, had gained a foothold in some factories in 1915, but the exchange had refused any recognition until the last months of the war, when the War Labor Board had successfully brought the two sides together. A display of moderation, engendered, on the one hand, by Sidney Hillman who had just achieved a settlement with a quality firm in Chicago and, on the other, by Professor Jacobstein, serving as labor manager for the companies, encouraged Samuel Weil and Jeremiah Hickey, the leaders of the exchange, to sign an agreement establishing an arbitration procedure similar to that worked out by Hillman in Chicago. However, a major Rochester firm, Michaels, Stern & Company, refused to accept this agreement, and an effort by the union to force it to comply resulted in a bitter strike and a series of suits that left the industry divided into two camps. The holdout endeavored to strengthen its position by inviting the rival United Garment Workers to organize its plant, but its advantage disappeared the next year when the other firms represented by the Clothiers Exchange secured concessions from the Amalgamated Clothing Workers, which granted a 15 percent reduction because of the hard times. By avoiding work stoppages, both the companies and the workers benefited, and the exchange not only restored the wage cut in 1923 but also granted modest increases three years later. In 1929, at a negotiation session in the Seneca Hotel ballroom, the exchange signed a contract establishing a system of unemployment insurance that gave the 10,000 union members a new sense of security unmatched by other workers in Rochester.

The wage standards of the clothing workers, of course, did not rival those in the more technical industries, most of which also enjoyed freedom from work stoppages and were able to maintain good annual wages. Construction workers, however, faced with seasonal layoffs, were constantly battling for increased wages to tide them over the slack months. In the twenties when the city's recovery brought plans for expansion and new construction, the building trades made repeated demands for increased wages and shorter hours. Construction contractors, eager to get started on new projects, were ready to make concessions if the owners would foot the bill, and industrialists who would not admit unions to their factories found themselves forced to make concessions to get the factories built. A Rochester association, formed by several leading industrialists who planned to let contracts for new buildings, demanded a 15 percent cut in wages on all projects in 1921 and pledged to stand firm against any wage increases after the contracts were signed. The announcement brought loud protests from the unions; lines of pickets soon formed at construction sites, and violence flared as some contractors endeavored to launch work with strikebreakers. When both the state and federal mediators failed to achieve a settlement, George Eastman, who had remained aloof from the association, proposed the organization of the Community Conference Board to seek a fundamental solution of the problem. He was ready, he declared, to serve as its chairman, but he would not undertake to arbitrate the present dispute.

Mayor Edgerton had meanwhile named a committee to investigate the strike, and in the wake of Eastman's proposal it secured an agreement from the unions and the contractors, backed by the association, to arbitrate all questions and to resume work under "the old contracts" until a settlement was reached. When the Common Council, which had authorized the appointment of the committee, defined "the old contracts" as those of 1920, the unions protested that this was a breach of faith because many of the construction projects had resumed without contracts after a stoppage in 1920. New picket lines successfully halted work on several projects, and finally both sides agreed to arbitrate, resuming work under the terms of "the most recent contract." Mayor Edgerton accepted the crucial place as seventh man on the panel of arbitrators who held extended hearings in the council chamber during the next two weeks. The unions submitted much evidence on the cost of living in Rochester and secured the assistance of the Labor Bureau, Incorporated, of New York in presenting their analysis, and the Rochester Association contrasted the high hourly wages of the construction workers with the lower rates of other Rochester workers. Finally, the arbiters submitted a split decision, four to three, giving the workers a 15 percent cut, as the association had demanded.

The unions were bitter over the one-sided award, as they described it, and Mayor Edgerton, who had cast the deciding vote, hastily announced his determination to retire at the end of the year, but the city rejoiced to learn that building activity that August was progressing more rapidly than in any previous month in the city's history. Many hoped that the Community Conference Board, which now proceeded to organize, would be able, as Eastman declared, to make the building industry a year-round occupation and convert its part-time jobs into full-time employment. Union leaders were invited to serve on the board and to cooperate in its efforts to promote construction work indoors throughout the winter months, but when negotiations for the next year's contracts commenced and the industrial representatives refused to restore the wage cuts, the union leaders withdrew. The board nevertheless determined to continue, because its chief job was a managerial one, and the union leaders, who had learned of the vast plans for future expansion, accepted the reduced rates that year but prepared, as construction projects mounted, to demand full restoration the next year. In April 1923, when the negotiations started, the industrialists and their contractors had so many projects to staff that the former 15 percent cuts were quickly eliminated and the stage was set for new increases a year later.

Eastman continued to preside at the monthly meetings of the Community Conference Board, and he was convinced that the increased efficiency it was promoting in the city's construction and other industries would pay off in higher productivity and in improved community standards. Having developed a statistical and analytical office under Marion Folsom in the early twenties with such success that it enabled him to turn over the active management of the company to William G. Stuber and Frank W. Lovejoy in 1925, Eastman had great confidence in the value of an informed and rational approach to problems. He loaned the services of his statistical office to the Chamber of Commerce in 1927 to enable it to launch a series of annual statistical analyses of the city's economy that upgraded the issues of *Rochester Commerce* where they appeared and gave a new boost to the city's morale. Eastman backed other chamber programs and pressed the construction of a four-story addition that made it, as described by Nicholas Murray Butler of Columbia University at its dedication in January 1927, the best-equipped headquarters in the country. Louis Foulkes, in 1923 the last president of the chamber to stress the quest for quality as Rochester's chief objective, was still promoting the beautification of industrial sites five years later when Edward A. Halbleib, head of the North East Electric was, as the new chamber president, emphasizing its new reliance on statistical analysis and industrial promotion. The publication in 1929 of a 36-page Civic and Industrial Survey of Rochester provided detailed evidence of the community's remarkable progress.

NEW DIMENSIONS OF URBAN LIFE

The social and cultural opportunities available in Rochester during the 1920s surpassed the fondest dreams of ambitious leaders a decade before. The recreational facilities supplied by the city and those proffered by commercial entertainers, the activities maintained by a multitude of associations, and the cultural provisions lavished on the city by its aging and now almost benign patron combined with the many new and exciting aspects of urban life to make Rochester, as George Eastman put it, "a good place to live and raise a family." Few were as ecstatic as Edward Hungerford who wrote at great length on the subject and found even Main Street "glorious" and "a wonderful place for parades." Yet many citizens, particularly the young adults, appropriated the new opportunities with a recklessness that seemed to many of their elders to threaten the values they promised. First-generation Americans not only outnumbered their immigrant parents but, having come of age, were rejecting ethnic customs and adopting new patterns with an unexpected freedom and excitement.

Rochester's continued population growth took a new direction in the twenties. The total of the foreign born increased slightly, but only because of a heavy influx of Italians and Poles before the new immigration laws took effect. The American-born offspring of foreign parents increased more rapidly, and among the older ethnic groups some were already raising families of their own. Gratified over the contributions these people had made during the war, the Chamber of Commerce collaborated with the art gallery in staging the Homelands Exhibit at Exposition Park in 1920. Yet despite its popular success, several attempts to repeat it met resistance, and even the efforts of the gallery to stage special ethnic exhibits encountered increased indifference. The City Club's banquets for new citizens were taken over in 1921 by the chamber's Council for Better Citizenship, which presented welcoming dinners to more than a thousand newly naturalized citizens each year throughout the twenties. Some of the older ethnic societies had difficulty maintaining their programs, however, because of the disinterest of their sons and daughters, yet several of the newer groups, such as the Ukrainian Civic Center, the Polish Falcons, and the Italian Women's Civic League, among others, enjoyed great vitality and helped to revive the Homelands Exhibit in conjunction with the Community Music Festival that continued for five successive nights at Convention Hall in 1928.

The elaborately organized programs that had attracted popular response at the hall or the parks before the war lost favor to the spectator sports, on the one hand, and to individualized amusements, on the other. The Rochester Hustlers, renamed the Red Wings, battled to the top of the International League in 1928 and captured the pennant again the next year in their new park on Norton Street. An increasing demand for ball diamonds and other athletic fields forced the park officials to require advance reservation of their facilities and to increase their staffs to supervise and maintain the picnic and play areas. As the number of automobile registrations increased from one in every thirty-five residents in 1916, to one in every six in 1920, to one in every three by 1930, the cars exceeded the number of dwelling units in the county after mid-decade and exceeded the number of families by the end of the decade. The automobiles were less evenly distributed, of course, but most families in the city had ready access to their use and, as owners or passengers, visited the parks and neighboring resorts more frequently than ever. Indeed the freedom of movement enjoyed by young adults and even teen-agers widened the natural breach between the generations, though the desire to use the family car helped to preserve that unit.

Most adults enjoyed not only the new pleasure of driving but also the excitement of other recreational experiences. Bathing at the lake became more popular as the city acquired and developed the beach at Charlotte and also opened dressing rooms there and at Durand-Eastman Park. Camping along the bay or the Finger Lakes increased in popularity among middle-class families. At this time Eastman, with a secluded lodge in North Carolina, ventured into the African and Canadian wilds on exciting big-game hunting trips. In winter months and throughout most of the year many adults, and teen-agers as well, settled for the excitement available at commercial centers of entertainment in downtown Rochester or on its periphery. There the dance halls and rinks vied with the new cinemas for patronage and overshadowed the associational activities that continued from an earlier period.

Eastman with most other Rochester leaders devoted more time and energy to the promotion of social and cultural institutions and programs than to recreational activities. There was a gratifying sense of purpose and a feeling of accomplishment that rewarded participants in these endeavors—both patrons and volunteer directors, as well as professional workers. Their organizational achievements were evident on all sides in the numerous welfare agencies, forty-nine of which were participating members of the newly formed Community Chest. When despite these efforts the number of delinquencies continued to mount, a group of youth agencies invited Dr. Henry W. Thurston of the American Child Welfare League to make a study of juvenile delinquency in Rochester. His careful check of the life experiences of sixty-four youngsters who had become involved in varied delinquencies revealed that although each had received attention from numerous agencies, most of the contacts had been fleeting and in these cases ineffective chiefly, in Thurston's view, because of the lack of coordination. His recommendation that a child welfare council be created to fulfill this need was soon expanded to provide for the organization of a council of social agencies to undertake the coordination of all welfare efforts. Its establishment in October 1924 and the appointment of Oscar Kuolt as general secretary marked a new advance in community organization.

Similar moves toward professional standards and administration had already occurred in the schools and the churches and would soon spread to other cultural fields as well. The new Board of Education and the increasingly professional administration of Superintendent Weet had brought a host of improvements in educational methods and standards. Thus, the introduction of junior high schools in these years was designed to give the increasing number of pupils who were continuing their schooling beyond the elementary grades an opportunity to begin their new programs in a more congenial setting than that of the mammoth high schools. The success of this approach won the Rochester schools a high rating among national educators and, more to the point, helped many youngsters continue their studies progressively onto higher levels.

In similar fashion the transformation of the old Ministerial Association into the Federation of Churches and the appointment of Dr. Orlo J. Price as executive secretary in September 1929 had produced several cooperative programs. Six churches collaborated in the organization of ten training classes for Sabbath school teachers, and the graduates of this interdenominational school of religious education cooperated in a daily vacation bible school program that offered classes to over 2,000 youngsters in eighteen churches the next summer. Both the Catholics and the Jews developed similar though separate community-wide programs under professional leadership and combined in their cases both welfare and religious efforts under the Columbus Civic Center projected by the Catholics in the late twenties and the Jewish Welfare Council and JYMA by the Jews. The Monday Club, renamed the Social Workers Club brought the staff members of these various agencies, together for mutual consultation and stimulus.

The professionalism and specialization that seemed so promising in the civic and welfare fields also permeated the intellectual and artistic realms. Amateur scholars, writers, artists, and performers gave place to trained professionals, many imported to the city by citizen directors or trustees. Thus the City Club, the Ad Club, and other groups that conducted public forums turned increasingly to out-of-town speakers for their lectures. The old-family publishers of local newspapers sold out to Frank Gannett who ran their papers on a more businesslike basis and staffed them with professional editors and journalists. Gannett not only acquired and merged the *Democrat & Chronicle* and the *Herald* but also expanded and improved that morning paper as a friendly rival to the evening *Times-Union,* which competed more directly with Hearst's evening *Journal & Post Express.* Gannett was one of the first to back Laurence G. Hickson, Rochester's pioneer in the radio field, but WHQ, which he helped to establish in 1922, soon acquired independent status under a new charter as WHAM, which, like WHEC, Rochester's second commercial station, developed a new group of professional specialists. In similar fashion the library, and the museum with the arrival of Dr. Arthur C. Parker in 1925, acquired professional directors.

Despite their more professional leadership, the library and the museum, dependent on public funds, had to be content with remodeled quarters in a decade when the municipal budget was strained by highway and school demands. Generous donors of new buildings would arrive in time, but meanwhile the leading patrons were focusing their interests on other institutions. Mrs. James Sibley Watson, donor of the Memorial Art Gallery, opened in 1913, supplied funds a decade later for its enlargement and made numerous gifts of choice works of art to its permanent collections. A list of gallery members helped to supplement the maintenance budget provided by the university, and the Art Club continued in these years to hold its annual show at the gallery, but the vitality of the exhibit program depended on the ability of its professional staff to bring interesting exhibits to Rochester from other cities. Mrs. Gertrude Herdle Moore, who succeeded her father as director in 1924, carried on his program of loan exhibits and transformed the annual local art show into an exhibit of regional works selected by an outside jury, thus giving it a professional character as well. Carl F. Lomb sparked a campaign that raised a sum of $2 million, of which Eastman contributed one-tenth, for Mechanics Institute.

The projects that made the most dramatic advances were those that George Eastman himself sponsored, yet each of his interests was an outgrowth or development of earlier local beginnings. The Eastman Dental Dispensary he established in 1917 attracted the hearty endorsement and backing of Dr. George Goler who had opened the first free dental dispensary in the country at No. 14 School in 1905. In 1920, when Dr. Abraham Flexner of the General Education Board proposed to Eastman and President Rhees that the board contribute $5 million, which would match a similar local sum to establish a new medical school as a branch of the University of Rochester, Eastman agreed to contribute $4 million, provided the dispensary be accepted as the fifth million for a combined School of Medicine and Dentistry. First announced in June 1920, the new school was formally opened in its newly erected buildings on Crittenden Boulevard in October 1925. Dean George H. Whipple, brought from the University of California to head it, was already assembling an able faculty, including Dr. Harvey J. Burkhart, director of the dental clinic since its opening. At the same time, construction was nearing completion on the new Strong Memorial Hospital, funded by the daughters of Eastman's original partner and first president, and on a new municipal hospital planned by Dr. Goler.

These remarkable developments were matched, if not surpassed, by the establishment of the Eastman School of Music and the Eastman Theatre. Again, Eastman was building on earlier foundations. His support of the Rochester Orchestra, headed by Herman Dossenbach, since the early 1900s and of the DKG Institute of Musical Art, directed by Alf Klingenberg, had made him the chief musical patron. He engaged Dossenbach and three of his leading artists to play as a string quartet at the Sunday evening recitals in his home in the mid-teens. In 1919 he announced plans for the erection of a joint theater and music school to be located at Main and Gibbs streets and to take over the work of the DKG Institute, which he had acquired, and develop it as the music department of the University of Rochester. President Rhees soon announced that Herman Dossenbach had accepted the directorship of a new orchestra that would provide accompaniment for the select movies to be brought to the theater, and that Alf Klingenberg would serve as director of the projected music school. In the winter of 1920–21, while work on the new buildings progressed with fits and starts because of labor difficulties, Eastman sent Klingenberg to Europe in search of new members for his faculty. Soon word arrived of the engagement of Joseph Bonnet, a noted French organist, Ernest Block, of Swiss birth, and Christian Sinding, from Norway, and of several others who with Harold Gleason, engaged by Eastman to play the organ in his mansion, and with the instructors retained from the old institute, comprised a faculty that numbered eighteen at the start in September 1921.

The opening of Kilbourn Hall in the music school on March 3, 1922, provided the first public ceremony connected with the school. Named for Eastman's mother and designed to seat 500 guests, it was dedicated by President Rhees to the musical education of the community at large, as a series of chamber concerts and other performances soon displayed. The opening of the larger Eastman Theatre on Labor Day, with a showing of *The Prisoner of Zenda* as its first film, drew a capacity audience of 3,350 and inaugurated Eastman's plan of presenting distinguished films accompanied by a full orchestra in an effort to realize the cultural value of good cinema. The regular showing of selected movies was interrupted in October by a week-long engagement with the San Carlo Opera Company, which presented *Aïda, La Boheme,* and other operas to packed audiences that included most of Rochester's leading citizens in a display of fashion and elegance never before equaled in the city.

But the establishment of the school and the theater involved personality as well as construction difficulties and produced some dramatic human episodes. Plans for the orchestra evolved through several stages in the early twenties. The aged Dossenbach had dropped out even before the theater's opening (to become director of the park band on the death of his brother Theodore in 1924) and was succeeded by Arthur Alexander, a dashing young American tenor who accepted the baton of the theater orchestra with the expectation of directing a projected new symphony orchestra as well. But the distinguished performance of Albert Coates, director of the London Symphony, as guest conductor of the New York Symphony, which visited the new Eastman Theatre in 1922, prompted Eastman on the advice of A. J. Warner, the Rochester music critic, to offer him the directorship of the projected Rochester Philharmonic Orchestra. Coates agreed to come for a half-season, to be paired with a similar engagement of Eugene Goossens, another talented English conductor. On the announcement of these appointments, the disappointed Alexander tendered his resignation, but his successor in charge of the theater orchestra soon saw that function suspended as the plan to operate the theater as an independent center for the display of choice films had to be abandoned because the development of theatrical chains with exclusive rights to the motion pictures they backed, forced Eastman to lease his theater to one of the chains and to reserve certain nights and weeks for musical events.

The Eastman school, meanwhile, was also experiencing growing pains. Several of the volatile personalities drawn to its faculty by Klingenberg in the early twenties soon found their situation disappointing in some respects and withdrew, to be replaced by other talented newcomers who added to the excitement that surrounded the school. Thus when Vladimir Rosing, a Russian singer, accepted an appointment to train opera singers in English, and Rouben Mamoulian, his youthful assistant, displayed skill as a director of dramatic work, Eastman conceived a plan to train talented students for membership in the Rochester American Opera Company. The presentation of its first performance at the Eastman Theatre in November 1924 was well received and encouraged further performances that involved close collaboration with the orchestra. In the preparation of the orchestra programs, both Coates and Goossens made eager use of several of the musical artists on the school faculty, sometimes featuring them as soloists and again supporting their separate recitals in Kilbourn Hall. The developments at the Eastman school were progressing so marvelously, as viewed from the outside, that many were astonished when, in June 1923, Klingenberg announced his resignation, which was obviously reluctant, and returned to his native home in Norway. It was several months later that Howard Hanson, destined to become his successor, paid his first visit to Rochester to conduct the first performance of his "Nordic" symphony. Brought to Rochester on that occasion by Albert Coates, Hanson quickly won Eastman's favor and in September 1924 accepted appointment as new director of the Eastman music school. A youthful American of Swedish ancestry and fresh from three years of study in Rome, Hanson combined several aspects of the cosmopolitan culture the school hoped to foster. His series of American composers concerts in the spring of 1925 proved so successful that it became an annual feature of the school's program and a unique expression of its purpose.

While Eastman was increasingly absorbed by developments at the music school, several of his industrial colleagues and President Rhees were more concerned for the future of the liberal arts college. A movement among the men of the senior class in 1920 advocating the separate establishment of a college for men attracted support among the alumni. When George W. Todd suggested the acquisition of the Oak Hill Country Club property as an admirable site for a river campus, the enthusiastic response encouraged the trustees to authorize a Greater University of Rochester campaign for $10 million to finance its development. Eastman pledged one-fourth of the total and ultimately raised his contribution to $4 million, but the city and the alumni likewise responded and carried the drive over the top. As a result President Rhees broke ground for the buildings on the new River Campus in May 1927. Excitement at the old Prince Street Campus mounted as construction progressed along the river. Additions to the faculty practically doubled its size and assured a more adequate course program for the increasing number of students enrolled. A generous bequest from former Mayor Cutler provided for the construction of a handsome new building at the old campus to serve as the social center for the women's college.

These and other developments marked the increased professional specialization of Rochester's cultural life. While the Eastman Theatre managed for a time to serve two fairly distinct publics—those interested in the cinema and those attracted by its more pretentious concerts and opera seasons—the Eastman school turned the musical education of the larger public over to the newly developed Civic Orchestra, successor to the theater orchestra and supported by the newly formed Civic Music Association. Of the city's forty theaters, only the Lyceum continued to operate as a legitimate theater, though three others offered vaudeville features and most provided music to supplement the motion pictures. The prospects of developing a Rochester-based opera company and a creative little theater were snuffed out when Eastman encouraged Vladimir Rosing to take his American Opera Company to

New York in 1927, thus removing several talented artists, including Rouben Mamoulian who had been assisting Mrs. Warham Whitney in the development of the Community Players. But if Rochester lost some of its skilled professionals and promising beginnings, it acquired other cultural contributions to replace them, as when the Rochester Theological Seminary absorbed the Colgate Baptist Seminary and with generous gifts from the Strong and Rockefeller families erected a new Colgate-Rochester Divinity School on the city's southern border.

Joseph T. Alling and at least two of his colleagues among the university's trustees could look back in the late twenties to their battle for good government and better education some three decades before with a real sense of accomplishment. They had helped to develop new professional standards in municipal administration as well as in the public schools, and they had helped to establish a cluster of cultural institutions that afforded opportunities for enjoyment and self-expression to many residents, young and old. They were perhaps less aware than in their youth of the restlessness of the new younger generation and of the limited appeal of their cultural offerings to the great majority of the city's residents. But they had extended a welcoming hand to the various groups of ethnic newcomers, recognizing their cultural as well as their productive talents, and if they failed to see the widening gap between the immigrants and their children, that was in part due to their absorption with professional and purposeful objectives. Indeed the dramatic fashion in which Eastman suddenly assumed the lead in the promotion and maintenance of professional standards had given both his volunteer associates and the new group of bureaucrats a sense of creative power and accomplishment that made them oblivious to the widening gap between leaders and followers. George Eastman's town was a more efficient and more effective embodiment of the best aspirations and provisions of his leading associates, but it was not the people's city of the turn of the century, and the thirties would reveal the weakness this division had produced.

8

The Great Depression and
World War II, 1929–1946

THE GREAT DEPRESSION of the 1930s and World War II presented challenges that tried Rochester's spirit and considerably transformed its character. Surprised as many were by the signs of economic collapse in the midst of a productive upsurge and astonished by its continued duration, George Eastman's successors at first made a bold response and only gradually discovered the limits of their self-sufficiency. The outbreak of World War II brought new calamities but also awakened fresh energies and opened broader vistas, which prompted Rochester to develop new regional and national ties that would launch it by the mid-forties onto a new surge of dynamic growth.

ONSET OF THE DEPRESSION

Most Rochesterians took the financial crash in October 1929 without serious panic. Their confidence in the productivity of local factories and in the soundness of local banks caused them to overlook the threat that more distant economic hardships posed to their markets and their income. They could not, however, overlook the swelling number of the unemployed that winter—too many unexpectedly found themselves in those ranks. Others rallied quickly and met the bleak situation with a display of community-wide responsibility that revealed the high degree of solidarity attained in the Eastman years. Yet despite their early confidence, the depression continued to deepen and revealed unsuspected limitations in the city's economy.

With pleas for jobs mounting on all sides, the Council of Social Agencies convened a special meeting at the chamber on January 22, 1930, to consider the unemployment crisis. Estimates of the number made idle by recent layoffs ranged from 10,000 to 24,000, and the council determined to seek the cooperation of the chamber and other bodies in launching constructive action. A week later, an announcement that General Motors would move its Delco-Light plant from Dayton to Rochester, with the prospect of 900 new jobs, failed to still the clamor for assistance, and City Manager Story hastily reopened the employment bureau that had been closed at the end of the war. The Community Conference Board released a reassuring statement estimating that new construction in Rochester would reach $18,000,000 that year and listed several of the larger projects to document its findings, but a throng of several thousand idle workmen who assembled on Washington Square on March 5 to demonstrate their need for jobs prompted more forthright action. Finally, ten days later, representatives of the chamber, the Council of Social Agencies, the Federation of Churches, the Catholic Charities, the Central Trades Council, and the bureau of Municipal Research convened to establish the Civic Committee on Unemployment and chose Henry H. Stebbins, Jr., the banker-son of a revered clergyman, as its chairman.

An attempt by a group of "reds" to stage a mass protest at Convention Hall a few days later fizzled as most of the unemployed displayed by their absence an eager confidence in the new committee. Stebbins soon announced the creation of seven subcommittees to tackle specific aspects of the problem. One, headed by Meyer Jacobstein, launched a series of appeals over the radio and in the churches for the creation of temporary jobs; another, headed by W. Earl Weller, sought to determine the facts concerning unemployment; still another, headed by James E. Gleason, prodded factory managers to undertake improvements when orders were slack. Marion Folsom, Kodak's representative on the committee, announced that Eastman was employing 400 additional workers. The chamber, the Community Chest, and the City Council each voted $5,000 to support the work of the committee, and Isaac Adler, as acting mayor following the death of Wilson, pledged a speedup of public works and announced preparations for the construction of the Veterans Memorial Bridge.

To demonstrate its confidence, the Community Chest took the unprecedented step of borrowing $100,000 to meet the pressing needs of some member agencies and then boldly increased the goal for its forthcoming drive to $1,623,000. Although the subscriptions did not quite reach that figure, they exceeded all previous campaigns since the great war-fund drive and assured the community that its character-building as well as its relief-giving agencies would be maintained. The JYMA &WA announced the start of construction on its $900,000 new building, and the Family Welfare Society loaned the services of its trained workers to assist the public welfare office in interviewing the many applicants for relief. Raymond N. Ball, president of the city's largest bank, wrote a series of articles for the *Times-Union* in which he reviewed the practical steps being taken by various institutions and industries. However, Mercer Brugler, when describing local conditions the next spring for the chamber, candidly admitted that "Sluggish is still the term."

The Civic Committee on Unemployment was not discouraged. It heartily endorsed the city manager's request for a work-relief budget and backed his successive pleas for additional funds. It applauded the decision of the Community Chest to launch an emergency drive in November in order to meet unexpected needs, and the $150,000 thus raised by the first emergency chest drive in the country assured the continuation of several programs threatened that winter. The Civic Committee received frequent plaudits from out-of-town, notably from Governor Franklin D. Roosevelt, and gave its support for the adoption of the first state projects for work relief. It applauded in February 1931 when Marion Folsom announced the decision of fourteen local firms, headed by Kodak, to adopt voluntary programs of unemployment insurance—the first concerted effort of this sort in the country. When these and other efforts failed to check the mounting tide of unemployment, the Civic Committee's subcommittee on temporary employment, headed now by Libanus M. Todd, launched a drive on the pattern of Community Chest campaigns and collected pledges from several thousand individuals to spend over $6,000,000 during 1931 on projects not previously planned in order to supply extra jobs. Fortunately a sixteen-inch snowstorm the next March provided temporary jobs for some 500 men, but the adequacy of such measures was beginning to appear dubious.

The gravity of the depression was finally having an effect on community morale. Many of the unemployed, who had stubbornly refused to accept charity, had now exhausted their reserves and were besieging the agencies for assistance; some were resorting to acts of desperation. Hard-pressed to maintain their families, many taxpayers were demanding new economies, and the chamber urged the county to defer building a new almshouse and infirmary. Even the Civic Improvement Association, which in 1930 had brought Carey H. Brown from Washington to press for civic improvements under the Bartholomew plan with borrowed funds, reluctantly cautioned a year later against launching large projects unless land prices were reduced. The Bureau of Municipal Research experienced a similar change of heart. Despite an optimistic report on the city's fiscal situation in 1931, in which it tabulated recent improvements and found their worth to be substantially in excess of the debt, the affluent trustees of the bureau were disturbed the next January when, in an address at the Chamber of Commerce, Daniel W. Hoan, Socialist mayor of Milwaukee, described the advantages enjoyed by a city that had steadfastly refused to go into debt.

Rochester could only dream of that propitious state in the winter of 1931–32, yet it quickly became a basic objective. Resistance to large expenditures mounted among the councilmen, but all gathered on December 27, 1931, to dedicate the newly completed Veterans Memorial Bridge. That occasion proved to be the last official appearance of City Manager Story who was replaced a few days later by C. Arthur Poole, the locally trained engineer appointed to effect a sharp reduction in expenditures. Story, who had carried on skillfully for two years with a council split four to four between his supporters and the organization Republicans, lost his backing when Charles S. Owen, the organization-backed candidate, defeated Leroy Snyder the City Manager Association's nominee for the late Mayor Wilson's post on the council in the November election that year. The council promptly elected Owen as mayor, repealed the nonpartisan provision governing elections, and slashed the budget for the coming year by $3.8 million. In the process it cut 30 percent from the library and 70 percent from the museum and effected a sharp reduction in all salaries over $3,400. When, however, the outlays for relief continued to mount, Weller of the Bureau of Municipal Research journeyed to Dayton, Cincinnati, and Cleveland to study the relief costs of these somewhat comparable cities. His report that their expenditures ranged far below those of Rochester brought an indignant protest from Oscar Kuolt who challenged the accuracy of the data. A second survey by Kuolt and Weller revealed that although some of the services of these places were less adequate than those of Rochester, the city was spending more than any of the others on relief without eliminating unemployment, and this discovery strengthened the local demand for economy.

Mayor Owen endeavored to answer the local pleas for relief by turning to the state for additional assistance. Rochester had received an allotment of $43,000 as its first work-relief payment under Roosevelt's Temporary Emergency Relief Administration the previous November, and the city now secured a promise of $734,000 in matching funds from that source for the year 1932. When an advisory board of prominent citizens appointed by the city manager found even such appropriations extravagant, Mayor Owen retorted that the bankers who criticized his budget were the same men who had pushed the city into building the subway and other costly improvements in earlier years, lending millions at high rates, which they now wished only to protect. That charge failed to endear him to the bankers, as events would prove, and meanwhile another group of critics protested the cuts in the school and library budgets and in other municipal services. "What kind of a city do we want to live in?" demanded Rabbi Philip Bernstein as the budgetary cuts were more widely applied. Apple venders, who had made their appearance on Main Street in 1930, now increased in number, and migrations from the city, dignified by County Planner J. Franklin Bonner as a back-to-the-land movement, accelerated. Only 57.6 percent of those named in the 1930 *Directory* reappeared in that of 1935—which reflected the most rapid turnover of any five-year period since the late 1860s.

It was in the dark year of 1932, perhaps the worst in the city's history, that the announcement came on March 14 of the death "by his own hand" of George Eastman. His action, of course, had no connection with the depression; he was only endeavoring to escape the debilitating pains and infirmities of advancing age, but his departure left a void in the community and weakened its morale. Thus the Community Chest, although bequeathed $100,000 by Eastman for its 1932 drive and supported by an additional gift of $50,000 from the university in his honor, cautiously trimmed its budget to $1,319,000 and then fell $200,000 short of the mark. Forced with all other agencies to curtail its expenditures, the Council of Social Agencies discharged several of Kuolt's assistants and organized the Department of Volunteers in an effort to continue most of its sorely needed services.

The New Deal

Rochester's discovery of its inability to master the depression singlehandedly had made its leaders receptive to state assistance and awakened a new interest in national politics. The aloof position of President Hoover in the face of mounting disasters had contrasted with Governor Roosevelt's responsive actions. In their contest for the presidency in November 1932, Roosevelt won a plurality of 1,100 over Hoover in the traditionally Republican city, which also gave its votes to Governor Lehman and Senator Wagner. Although it was not known whether this first clear victory for the Democrats in half a century represented votes for jobs or votes for beer, Roosevelt's success in focusing attention on Washington as the command center in the battle for recovery drew Rochester with many other cities into the mainstream of the nation's history.

Despite the throng of over 15,000 Democrats who surged up and down Main Street in a boisterous celebration on election night, Mayor Owen and City Manager Poole felt secure in their control of the city. Charles W. Stanton, the sole Democrat on the council, demanded a public hearing on some of the manager's fiscal practices, yet Poole successfully met the challenge and secured council approval for his proposed $3,600,000 bond issue to match state aid in relief measures. However, no local bank placed a bid on the bonds, and when the city manager approached the Clearing House for an offer, its Republican managers moved to adjourn without action. That was action enough, and Mayor Owen resigned. The Republican councilmen promptly elected Percival De W. Oviatt, a respected attorney, as mayor and replaced Poole by Theodore C. Briggs, president of the Lawyer's Cooperative, as city manager. Gannett's political reporter attributed leadership in this shuffle to T. Carl Nixon and Carl Hallauer, leading members of a Republican committee that had assumed direction of the party, which now secured agreement from the bankers to float the necessary bonds. Councilman Stanton branded the moves a "palace revolution" that had left the bankers in full control of the city. Nevertheless, funds were again available, and a citizens' committee, headed by Professor Dexter Perkins of the university, brought about a restoration of most of the cuts in the library budget, and the schools again received funds to match state and even federal relief-work projects.

The fact that the Rochester banks were strong enough to force the city administration to accept their fiscal leadership contrasted with the situation in some cities where such institutions were insolvent. All local banks had succesfully weathered the financial crisis of 1929, even the newest one founded early that year by Meyer Jacobstein. That former Rochester congressman now proposed the formation of a national board empowered to approve standard-price agreements to encourage industrial recovery, and when the President's Industrial Recovery Act established the NRA in 1933, Hugh Johnson, its director, secured ready collaboration from the Rochester chamber as well as from the city administration. Eastman Kodak was one of the first to announce its adoption of the photographic code. Within two months some 800 local firms had signed codes, and a survey of the results reported the re-employment of 9,126 workers. Such an accomplishment called for a celebration, and on September 26, 1933, some 175,000 Rochesterians watched from the curb as 65,000 marchers carried Blue Eagle banners for the participant firms in one of the most dramatic parades in the city's history.

Rochester was equally enthusiastic at the start about other New Deal measures. It was the first city in the state to organize a New Era Collegiate Center under New York's TERA, and it hastened to secure federal Civil Works Administration funds for white-collar as well as labor projects. It quickly enrolled 400 young men for the first regional CCC camps in May 1933, and it made hasty application for Public Works Administration funds to press ahead with the construction of a new bridge at Elmwood Avenue, a new sewage disposal plant, a new high school, and a new central library building. While all rejoiced at the announcement of these cooperative projects, however, many industrialists were critical of the recognition and safeguards Section 7a of the Industrial Recovery Act gave to labor unions. Many workers, thankful for any jobs, were slow to exercise their rights to organize, but the Amalgamated Clothing Workers, under Abraham Chatman, seized the opportunity to press their demand for recognition from all but one of the remaining clothing firms and thus strengthened their hold on that important Rochester industry.

In the midst of this early enthusiasm for the New Deal, when even Frank Gannett of the *Times-Union* was backing the Roosevelt programs, the Democrats captured control of both the city and the county for the first time in many decades. They promptly elected Stanton as mayor and called Harold W. Baker, a former director of the bureau and commissioner of public works under Story, back from a New Deal job in Washington to become city manager. The Democrats, who quickly filled many posts formerly occupied by Republicans, also had an opportunity to make many appointments to New Deal agencies, but they resisted the pressure for political favoritism in these projects by naming Arthur M. Lowenthal, a Republican businessman, as chairman of the work-relief committee. As federal funds arrived in increasing volume, City Manager Baker, relieved of the local work-relief burden, was able to retire some of the city debt and to refund another $3 million in bonds at greatly reduced interest rates, thus improving the city's credit.

These and other developments created an illusion of recovery in 1935 and prompted many who had tolerated federal intervention during the worst of the crisis to demand a release from further restraints. Many firms turned back their Blue Eagles in order to escape the control of their codes, and Frank Gannett reacted sharply when Roosevelt switched from George F. Warren, the publisher's former professor at Cornell, to John Maynard Keynes as his principal economic mentor. Despite the enthusiastic reception given Mrs. Roosevelt on her visit to Rochester as a guest of Mrs. Harper Sibley in October 1943, Harper Sibley became an outspoken critic the next year of his former schoolmate at Groton and Harvard and would help to swing the United States Chamber of Commerce, of which he became president, into open opposition to the New Deal. Even Marion Folsom, as president of the Council of Social Agencies, became critical of the "make-work" projects, which were little better than "boondoggling," as a local wit put it. Folsom believed that the real solution lay in the wide use of unemployment insurance as he had developed it at Kodak, and the emphasis he placed on that program prompted Roosevelt to invite him to serve on a new advisory committee on social security.

Roosevelt's flexibility and outspoken concern assured his triumphant reelection in 1936, with unprecedented majorities in Rochester and Monroe County. He had curtailed and finally terminated the CWA when the need seemed to disappear, but he had to replace it when the need revived with the more generously funded Works Progress Administration. He had given independent status to the National Youth Administration, which received a hearty welcome in Rochester, and had launched the Subsistence Homestead Division, which attracted immediate support from County Planner J. Franklin Bonner who hoped to develop a settlement in suburban Gates. That prospect was never realized, however, as the pressure from other areas proved stronger, and critics of the New Deal became vocal enough in the towns to enable the reorganized Republicans, under Thomas E. Broderick, to recapture control of the county in 1935. The Democrats, who had expected to control a consolidated city and county welfare department, hastily dropped that project; in their frantic preparation for the city election two years later, they fell to bickering over jobs and lost control of the city council as well.

A major issue in that campaign was economy, and because Baker had demonstrated unusual fiscal abilities, the Republicans decided to retain him as city manager. His position, however, was weakened by the creation of an independent Department of Commerce for Harold S. W. MacFarlin, one of the party's most vigorous leaders who increasingly overshadowed Baker and Mayor Lester B. Rapp, who shortly resigned. Samuel B. Dicker, an affable Jewish bachelor skilled at maintaining harmony, became Rochester's fifty-sixth mayor in 1938 and managed to steer the party through many storms as the faithful spokesman for Chairman Broderick. His secret, perhaps, was passivity, a quality displayed in abundance when MacFarlin finally moved for the ousting of Baker as city manager in 1939; but Dicker secured the appointment of Louis B. Cartwright, the former comptroller, not MacFarlin, to that post. His passivity triumphed again in the battle over public housing, when a citizens' committee he appointed prepared to recommend forthright action. To head it off, Mayor Dicker hastily named two conservative councilmen to the committee, which tipped its vote in the opposite direction and saved the Republicans from the embarrassment of endorsing the New Deal's housing program.

Yet while Rochester ended the decade in outspoken opposition to the New Deal, most of its principal accomplishments in the thirties had reflected the new partnership of the city, the state, and the nation. The Old Age Security Act, enacted at Albany in 1930, had been a first step towards the Social Security program in which Rochester had supplied a creative leader in Marion Folsom and an adviser to Congress on its 1935 program. Federal PWA funds helped to build, among many other projects, the new Rundel Library, dedicated by Mayor Stanton in 1936; federal WPA funds kept the parks and playgrounds in operation and supplied part-time staff to the schools, the museum, and even the art gallery. The NYA, under the supervision of the public library, the university, and the Gannett press, prepared an index of local newspapers from 1818, when they first appeared, to 1897, where the project was terminated at the outbreak of World War II. It proved to be the best local index of its kind in the country.

Only the University of Rochester and its appendages, richly endowed by George Eastman, managed to carry on with little dependence on the New Deal. President Rhees had the pleasant task in October 1930 of dedicating the new men's college on the River Campus. Numerous visiting scholars participated with the local faculty in academic conferences focused on the development of a new curriculum designed to promote a better orientation of specialized students to the broader fields of learning. Dr. Rhees, having greatly increased the size and stature of the faculty, tendered his resignation three years later but carried on until the appointment of young Alan Valentine as his successor in 1935. A Rhodes scholar with teaching and administrative experience at Swarthmore, President Valentine declared his purpose to be the development of a "university college," not a great university or a small college. That concept, applied at the medical school a decade before, was already bearing fruit in the excellent research work of such faculty members as Dr. John R. Murlin in diabetes.

The more tranquil and more professional developments at the Eastman School of Music under Dr. Hanson aptly reflected the spirit and objectives of its great patron, but the Eastman Theatre, which he had refused to endow because he expected it to pay its way, suffered with similar institutions from the economic breakdown. It escaped the complete collapse that overtook the old Lyceum, which was razed for a parking lot in 1936, but the Eastman's motion-picture lease was not renewed after 1933, and the theater served only the weekly performances of the Philharmonic Orchestra and occasional visits of orchestras and opera companies. The Civic Orchestra, pinched by the declining subscriptions of the depression years, nevertheless continued to supply a nucleus for the Philharmonic Orchestra, which struggled along under the direction of visiting conductors after the departure of Eugene Goossens in 1931. Fortunately, Rochester found a talented new director in José Iturbi in 1936 who was able, by arranging a series of tours to other cities, to revitalize the Philharmonic and restore some of its earlier prestige.

Despite the loss of much of its advertising, the press survived the depression because of the keen public interest in current affairs. Frank Gannett, having acquired the *Democrat & Chronicle* to balance his *Times-Union* in 1928, held undisputed control of the news media and reduced costs by spreading its coverage in an ever-widening chain of upstate newspapers. When in 1937 he finally acquired and terminated the *Journal & American* by giving Hearst a paper in Albany for it, the independent *Evening News* made its appearance in Rochester but, failing to attract sufficient support, soon expired. Only the new medium of radio presented a challenge, and Gannett retained control of WHEC, which competed vigorously with the more powerful WHAM, largely owned by the Stromberg-Carlson Company. William Fay, its manager, maintained close ties with the Eastman school, which presented frequent programs over this high-powered clear-channel station and helped win it a connection by 1938 with the National Broadcasting Company.

As both the local press and radio services acquired firmer national ties and developed regional markets, the once parochial or self-contained quality of Rochester's life was further eroded. The community made a deliberate effort to renew its local historic traditions in centennial ceremonies in 1934, and many of the important publications in this period were historical in character, notably the four-volume *Centennial History*, edited by City Historian Edward R. Foreman, and the *Fault of Angels* by Paul Horgan, which recaptured the drama of the early years of the Eastman school. However, the local outlook, although it retained a continuing appeal, was increasingly overshadowed by the community's expanding interests, and as the city developed links with the federal government and as its officials became members of national associations, so the professors at the university, with other professionals, developed broader perspectives. Rochester was better prepared than ever before to met the problems of a world war.

WORLD WAR II

In some respects Rochester's response to World War II repeated aspects of its experience twenty-five years before, but the engagement was more extensive, more protracted, and much more fundamental in character. As in World War I, Rochester began by contributing to the relief of war-stricken people abroad, which emphasized American neutrality. Again, events soon prompted demands for stronger national defense, and local industrialists competed eagerly for both defense and war orders. But the long collaboration between the city and the federal government during the depression had developed ties that made the formulation of national policy and the implementation of national programs a mutual experience. The community's response to the repeated drives and regulatory measures not only proved the degree of its loyalty to the nation but tested ingredients of its local fabric and made its citizens more consciously aware of their strength and their limitations.

An Eastern city, linked by many economic and personal ties to foreign lands, Rochester had followed the course of international affairs in the late thirties with growing concern. Many citizens could not escape a premonition of their country's ultimate involvement in the emerging crisis abroad, yet despite a pervasive desire for peace, a small band of students at the university who staged a peace demonstration in April 1936 attracted little sympathy. Some Italian-born residents resented local criticism of Mussolini's invasion of Ethiopia. The plight of the German Jews presented a more urgent challenge, and a local branch of the American Jewish Joint Distribution Committee endeavored to raise the city's share of a $5 million refugee fund voted at a conference in the Seneca Hotel. The City Club held several packed meetings at which speakers defended or attacked, on separate occasions, the Arabs as well as the Jews, the Spanish Loyalists as well as the Nationalists, or exposed the threat of an expansionist Russia as well as that of Germany, Italy, and Japan. Hitler's march into Austria prompted Mayor Rapp to request an antiaircraft unit for Rochester and spurred the United States Army to reopen its local ordinance depot.

Almost everybody rejoiced when Chamberlain announced that he had secured an agreement at Munich assuring "peace in our time," but few were surprised a year later when Germany invaded Poland. Rochester's 10,000 residents of Polish descent quickly launched a relief drive, and the Red Cross opened a depot for the collection of clothing for war refugees there and in Finland when Russia invaded that country. Gannett protested when Roosevelt proclaimed a "national emergency," but the Chamber voted overwhelmingly for a repeal of the arms embargo. When the lull in battle, following the conquest of Poland, disappeared as Hitler invaded Denmark and Norway, Holland and Belgium, the last traces of neutrality in Rochester disappeared. Professional and business leaders formed a branch of the Committee to Defend America by Aiding the Allies. Defense contracts in excess of $10 million arrived in June 1940, and many more followed in succeeding months. Mayor Dicker found many forthright citizens ready to serve on the draft boards he appointed to supervise the registration of all male citizens between the ages of twenty-one and thirty-five, and of the 39,842 registered that October, thirty-three volunteered to serve in the first unit that left the next month for Fort Dix.

The fall of France, the announcement of the three-power pact between Germany, Italy, and Japan, the attack on Greece, and the bombing of Britain brought hearty support in Rochester for Roosevelt's lend-lease program and for new war-relief drives. Although a group of conscientious objectors formed a Citizens No War Committee, other residents rallied in support of Professor Walden Moore's Stop Hitler Now Committee, and Mayor Dicker named a fifteen-man defense council to supervise the scrap-metal drives and to implement civilian defense plans. As the flood of defense contracts mounted, a surge in employment developed that created a critical housing and labor shortage. The Defense Council set up a Homes Registration Bureau and promoted job-training courses to exploit the full advantage of resident manpower. An estimated 6,000 men from Monroe County left for camp before the registration for the second draft on July 1 enrolled those who had reached age twenty-one during the preceding nine months. Most citizens still hoped that a demonstration of preparedness would ward off any hostilities, and all were astonished when the Japanese attacked Pearl Harbor on December 7.

As the gravity of the situation became apparent, Rochesterians of all stations rallied to the war effort. Action had come with startling suddenness to a score of local servicemen stationed in Hawaii and the Philippines. Four Rochesterians lost their lives in these first attacks, including three brothers from the Kramb family, which resided in Gates. These and other reports cast the war in a somber light and quickened the local response. The Navy, which had suffered the major blow, hastily organized two aviation-training units at Rochester, and Colonel Edward T. Wentworth inducted the entire staff of the 19th General Hospital, previously recruited at Rochester. Because the ninety nurses who left with that contingent were scarcely one-fourth of those sought from the Rochester region, local nursing schools re-doubled their efforts to train suitable enrollees. Recruiting for the WAACS and, later, for the WAVES attracted over one hundred girls during the first year; some two hundred physicians and thirty clergy-men also responded to the national call. In the first year Rochester had representatives in the battle of the Coral Sea, the landing on Guadal-canal, the invasion of North Africa, and many lesser engagements. On December 7, 1942, it paused in silent respect to show gratitude to thirty-four from the county who had already made the supreme sacri-fice.

With few exceptions most Rochesterians rose to the patriotic chal lenge. Of the approximately 1,600 aliens who registered in compliance with a new federal law, nearly two-thirds were women. Many of both sexes had already secured their first papers, and as soon as the ban was lifted, many others hastened to secure full citizenship. Nearly 450 of those classified as enemy aliens quickly registered with the FBI and turned in all cameras, firearms, and shortwave radio sets. The Defense Council, renamed the War Council, enrolled air-raid wardens and other volunteers and staged precautionary blackouts. It designated and equipped emergency shelters and prepared plans for mass evacuations in the event of gas attacks, and it enrolled 1,700 volunteer fire fighters to cope with all possible catastrophies of that sort. The council drama-tized these precautions in a series of events during War Week in June 1942, which was highlighted by a parade of 50,000 marchers and sixty bands.

These home-front activities not only helped to speed enlistments and to maintain the morale of inductees but also rallied support for successive scrap-metal drives and for tire, gasoline, sugar, and other rationing programs. The Community Chest took over the task of filling the needs of the various war-relief agencies; it contributed $400,000 to ten such causes in 1942, plus $250,000 to the Red Cross to supplement its separate drive. Citizen committees and women volunteers helped to enforce price ceilings and rent controls, and when the volunteer restraints proved ineffective in the latter case, a Bureau of Municipal Research survey brought the application by Washington of a rent freeze on the city's four-county area. Vigorous efforts by the university, Mechanics Institute, and public schools in conducting training programs upgraded the skills of numerous residents and, with a moderate influx of suburban workers, boosted the employment in industrial jobs from 68,000 in 1939 to approximately 120,000 by the summer of 1943. The number of women employed increased proportionately, and some like the Italians and the Negroes won admittance to jobs and factories previously closed to them. Numerous firms received special citations, and seven won the highest Army-Navy production awards, among which were Eastman Kodak for its fuses, height finders, and photographic innovations; Bausch & Lomb for its optical fire-control instruments; and Gleason for its crucially important machine tools. Several firms loaned their ablest executives for vital war-related jobs. Thus Folsom took a leave to serve the National Resources Planning Board, and Drs. Lee DuBridge and Victor Weisskopf secured releases from the university to work on highly secret research, which, as later revealed, contributed to the production of the atomic bomb.

THE URBAN RESPONSE

As the war progressed, its grim battles not only took an increasing toll of Rochester's recruits but also effected a transformation of its character. With casualties mounting, it seemed desirable to place able leaders in crucial local and congressional posts, and the elections of 1942 and after acquired new meaning. It seemed equally desirable to be prepared for responsible action at the war's end, and for the first time Rochester began to recognize the need for conscious community-wide planning. In similar fashion the wartime cooperation between dissimilar ethnic groups and between labor and management gave a new respectability to agencies working for integration and peaceful accord locally as well as nationally and internationally.

With more than 18,000 already under arms in December 1942, peace seemed far off to most Rochesterians. The second year would see the county's total surge past the 30,000 figure as eighteen-year-olds were added to the pool of draftees. A third and a fourth group of young aviation cadets completed their training at Rochester, and the university granted certificates to over 1,600 young men in a special training program for Navy and Marine Corps officers. The Rochester Red Cross dispatched over 360 nurses for active duty before the end of the second year of the war, when Monroe County's casualties had already reached 168 dead, 62 missing, and 60 listed as prisoners. Rochester maintained a sober mien throughout this trying period. New Year's celebrations in 1943 and 1944 were restrained, yet residents made a special effort to entertain all visiting servicemen at Thanksgiving and Christmas. Occasional blackout tests continued, but efforts to maintain a round-the-clock watch for enemy planes were relaxed, and officials gave more attention to the staffing of child-care centers so that mothers could be released for war work.

The War Council placed increased emphasis on constructive, as contrasted with defense, functions. Renewed scrap-metal, tin-can, and wastepaper drives, and renewed campaigns for the Red Cross, the USO, and other war-relief funds covered by the Community Chest attracted subscriptions from 144,446 in May 1942 for a total of $2,428,000, the highest in the chest's history since 1918. The USO maintained a local information booth and other services for recruits passing through the city, and the Convention and Publicity Bureau issued a four-page *Rochester Star* that it sent monthly to some 32,000 men from the Rochester area in order to provide information on home-front activities and the reports from their buddies. Rochester's response to the rationing restrictions was not as enthusiastic, but volunteer spotters and other enforcement efforts maintained a widespread compliance, and the city survived these stringencies without serious breakdowns. As gas rationing took effect, the transit company enjoyed an upsurge in its passenger loads, which reached a high of 110,477,000 in 1943, a 20 percent increase over the previous year, and the subway's payload climbed to 3,670,000 and, for the first time, pulled it out of the red.

Rochester's participation in the war effort matched that of other cities in military recruitment and in the provision of home defense. Apparently, it excelled many in the generosity of its response to wartime drives and promoted its own community morale in the process. Its most decisive and unique contributions occurred in the industrial field, where the technological competence of its firms brought a flood of orders that totaled $1,215,145,000 by November 1, 1945. Although the products were often secret in nature, the officials sometimes lifted the restrictions enough to spur increased output. Thus, a visiting general praised fourteen Rochester companies on one occasion for their part in the production of the B-29 super-fortresses. Similar praise went on other occasions to a small firm that developed a flame gun, or "atomizer," to three companies that made parts of the M-7 tank killers, and to many others. Two separate charges of defrauding the government on war contracts were dismissed after careful investigations; only one indictment brought more serious consequences. Even in the field of industrial and labor relations the tension was considerably relaxed as the cost-plus contracts enabled firms to grant wage increases in order to attract and hold skilled workers. As a result of numerous training courses, Rochester employed a larger portion of its disabled veterans and other handicapped persons than any other city in the state and increased the number of women workers to 40 percent of those engaged in ninety-two plants with war contracts. Despite the enrollment of over 7,000 of its employees in the armed services, Eastman Kodak steadily expanded its operations, opening new plants in the city to produce its many war-related products, and increased its work force to 29,000 by December 1944.

Perhaps the most striking difference between Rochester's responses to World War I and World War II was the effort exerted to make certain that the results would be satisfactory this time. The thought of returning to an isolationist position that would make a third world war probable was as distasteful as the prospect of plunging into a postwar depression. The Democrats who nominated Professor Walden Moore for Congress in 1942 did not quite succeed in ousting the isolationist incumbent, but the forthright stand he took on American responsibilities carried the city and prepared the way for one of his supporters from the towns to capture the 38th District in 1944. The Republicans, having learned their lesson, recaptured the district two years later by running Colonel Kenneth B. Keating, recently returned from active service in Southeast Asia and a staunch advocate of American participation in world affairs. In similar fashion, the Chamber of

Commerce, long hesitant to endorse the concept of planning, took the lead in 1942 in organizing the Council on Postwar Problems, which soon transformed itself, in fact, into a generator of postwar planning. Marion Folsom and Alan Valentine, as co-chairmen, appointed a series of subcommittees that tackled postwar economic, civic, educational, and welfare problems and prepared a series of forward-looking reports on the city's needs that laid down the guidelines for vigorous postwar action.

Although most improvements had to await the return of peace, some positive developments occurred during the war years. A generous gift from Edward Bausch had enabled the Museum of Arts and Sciences to erect a new building on East Avenue and to move into its spacious Bausch Hall in the early months of 1942. The same year, Nazareth College opened a new campus farther out East Avenue. Although most construction plans of other institutions were deferred many provided increasingly active programs, especially in fields of interest to servicemen. Will R. Corris, in charge of the Auditorium Theater, which had taken the place of the Lyceum as the home of legitimate drama, brought a fairly rich schedule of plays from Broadway, including *Life with Father, My Sister Eileen,* and *Porgy and Bess,* among many others, and the interest thus displayed soon prompted the park authorities to open the bandshell at Highland Park for a performance of *The Prodigal Son.* The city, however, was in a mood of self-restraint, as City Manager Cartwright seized the opportunity to concentrate on the task of paying off the city debt. His hold-the-line policy, officially launched in 1942, relieved pressure on short supplies of both building materials and manpower, reducing the debt by one-third in the early forties, but created a backlog of civic needs that would ultimately override his policy in the next decade.

In many fields the budgetary restraints were not seriously inhibiting. In the public schools, for example, a sharp drop in the number of pupils enrolled reduced the pressure for added revenues. Welfare demands were down as the wartime jobs created a demand for all but the most incompetent workers. An upsurge in juvenile delinquency offset the decline in major crimes, but shortages in the police force and social agencies, diverted by wartime needs, postponed action. A still greater deficiency appeared in the housing field, and despite the protests of Mrs. Helen Jones of the Better Housing Association, action on this front, too, was postponed until the rush of returning service men pushed it into the forefront.

Rochester's major concern throughout 1944 was the men in the battle areas. Reports of American action and of local losses in Algeria, Sicily, and Italy, as well as in the South Pacific in the last months of 1943 had brought the sober realities of the struggle home to many Rochester families. When the crescendo of battle increased after D day, the number of local casualties mounted. As the totals for the county climbed from 322 known dead on June 30 to 575 on December 7, 1944, and continued to soar to 1,177 by the next December, with 107 more still missing, the city's burden of sorrow became heavy indeed. Rochester barely paused in its production efforts to celebrate V-E Day on May 8, and even the celebration of V-J Day on August 15, 1945, lacked some of the abandon of the two armistice days at the close of World War I.

Many in the community were now fully aware that the peace had yet to be won. Rochester had had its representatives at San Francisco early in 1945 when Dexter Perkins, as official historian, and Harper Sibley, as consultant for the United States Chamber of Commerce, had participated in a modest fashion in the birth of the new United Nations. Back in Rochester Professor Perkins, young Joseph C. Wilson, soon to be elected president of the City Club, and several other concerned citizens gathered at the Sibley mansion to form the nucleus of the Rochester Association for the United Nations. Its earnest efforts to hasten the ratification and support the implementation of the UNO, as it was then designated, were intensified by the sensational news of the dropping of the first atomic bomb on Hiroshima on August 5. Rochester took a just pride in the information that four of its leading firms had played an important part in the development of the bomb and that several scholars at the university had participated in the scientific breakthrough. However, as the awesome powers the bomb had released and the appalling devastation it had created became known, the need for adequate controls commanded chief attention. The editor of the *Democrat & Chronicle* hastened to endorse a letter of Dr. Victor H. Weisskopf, written from Los Alamos, California, in which he pleaded for the hasty formation of a responsible world organization to assure the international control of the fearsome powers of the atom.

**Minister Franklin D. R. Florence, left, and Deleon McEwen,
first and second presidents of FIGHT.**

Mrs. Harper Sibley and Professor Dexter Perkins,
cofounders of RAUN, commemorating its 25th anniversary.

Dedication of the Rochester Sister-City Bridge.

Mayor Thomas P. Ryan, Jr., and County
Executive Lucien Morin leading the
march into the Masonic Temple
Auditorium for the Sesqui Gala Ball.

Town of Wheatland float in the Sesquicentennial Parade.

Official inauguration of the Sesquicentennial Year
in the atrium of the new City Hall.

Rochester's Sesquicentennial Finale, Main Street Bridge, packed with citizens
awaiting the spectacular fireworks display that ended the Sesquicentennial Year.

Ice storm, March 4, 1991. View on South Goodman Street.

New entrance wing of the Rochester Museum and Science Center.

Interior sculpture garden of the Memorial Art Gallery.

9

Metropolitan Emergence, 1946–1960

THE PROSPECTS OF PEACE, although joyfully welcomed, were much too complex and uncertain to foster complacency. New and broader commitments in the international field, both economic and political, would have to be meshed in some fashion with increasing local responsibilities, as politicians and businessmen were already discovering. New and perplexing dilemmas inherent in the city's emerging metropolitan status would have to be resolved, despite the threats they posed to old and cherished customs. New and, in some respects, more sophisticated practices, nurtured by the city's increasing diversity and broadening horizons, challenged traditional standards in social and cultural spheres. Fortunately, a host of able and aspiring leaders, both lay and professional, emerged and provided direction in their varied fields, giving the city the plural character of a dynamic metropolis.

AN INTERDEPENDENT ECONOMY

Despite the fears of a postwar recession, Rochester's economy experienced an outburst of resurgent growth in the late forties and fifties. The new energies discovered and the fresh skills developed during the long ordeal provided a basis for additional industrial enterprise, and the precautions taken against collapse facilitated the achievement of a new integration of productive and marketing efforts. Rochester retained and, in fact, intensified its industrial specialization, but fortunately, the new leaders who emerged displayed a capacity for cooperation in the chamber and other organizations on projects that helped transform the industrial city into a regional metropolis.

The managerial system, which prevailed in most companies,

brought vigorous young men to the helm in several important firms—
for example, Mercer Brugler at Pfaudler in 1945, Joseph C. Wilson at
Haloid, and Carl S. Hallauer at Bausch & Lomb—some of whom served
a term as president of the chamber. That body, already third in size
in the country, expanded its sphere of activity. A vigorous drive for
new members increased its total from 4,354 in 1945 to 5,300 three years
later. The election of Professor Perkins and Frank Gannett as new
trustees in 1946 opened fresh vistas, and Dr. Mark Ellingson, as chamber president that year, chaired a public conference on the housing
question and commended the efforts of a group of bankers headed by
Elmer B. Milliman to devise a solution. Many Rochesterians rejoiced
to see the rapid construction of the Fernwood Park project that fall,
and when one thousand applicants sought access to its 152 apartments,
priced at $48 a month for veterans' families, the reorganized Civic
Development Council hastened to promote the construction of two
additional nonprofit housing projects—Norton Village and Ramona
Park—increasing the number of apartments available for veterans to
516. Although that accomplishment only partially relieved the pressure
for housing, the chamber, under the leadership of Walter L. Todd,
turned its attention to the promotion of industrial production to supply
Marshall Plan aid to Europe.

The Rochester economy made a surprisingly quick reconversion to
civilian production. Financial transactions at the local Clearing House
soared to a new high, and the business indices in *Rochester Commerce*
reached an unprecedented level by February 1948. When renewed
orders resulting from the hostilities in Korea pushed the business index
to a new high, the chamber launched a much more sumptuous edition of
Rochester Commerce in order to provide more adequate coverage of
its many activities. These now included the work of the new Citizens
Council for a Better Rochester, launched at the suggestion of Paul
Miller, the recently arrived assistant to Frank Gannett, and headed by
Joseph C. Wilson, who, as president of the chamber, entitled his address, "Rochester's Declaration of Interdependence." He vigorously
endorsed the statement of Marion Folsom, national chairman of the
Committee for Economic Development, that Rochester's economy, like
that of the nation, was tied to the recovery of Europe and the fate of
many undeveloped countries.

Under Wilson's leadership the Citizens Council for a Better Rochester helped the city break loose from several restraints. It prompted agreement between the city and the state on the routes of the inner and outer loops, speeded construction of Hanover Houses, Rochester's first public housing project, and moved the long debated War Memorial building to the drafting stage. Ably assisted by successive chamber presidents, it endorsed a number of promotional efforts, such as a dramatic "Rochester Futurama" exhibit at the Museum of Arts and Sciences in 1953, and an elaborate "Industry on Parade" display at the newly completed War Memorial two years later. The New Industries Committee, headed by Robert E. Ginna of the Rochester Gas & Electric Company, helped launch several new enterprises, and the impending completion of the St. Lawrence Seaway prompted the chamber to reexamine the potential of the Genesee port and to reconsider the establishment of a regional market. In recognition of its broader concerns, in April 1957 the chamber renamed its monthly journal *Greater Rochester Commerce*.

The Chamber of Commerce never endeavored to represent all segments of the population. It did not exclude labor leaders from its ranks, but it failed to attract any, although some participated in the innumerable luncheon sessions of civic groups in its halls, and a few joined the Citizens Council for a Better Rochester. Most chamber members and many in its quasi-independent Industrial Management Council regarded union leaders as representatives of the opposition, and most unionists held reciprocal views. Yet they sometimes found themselves in agreement on the need for action on civic matters, such as the building of the War Memorial and the endorsement of forthright international policies. Most unionists were more concerned over the divisions within their own ranks. Efforts to bridge the gap between the CIO unions, organized along industrial rather than craft lines, and the older AFL unions produced a no-raiding pact in 1950, though it was soon broken in a few bitter contests. Nevertheless, Anthony A. Capone, as president of the Central Trades Council, and John H. Cooper of the CIO Council worked together in opposition to the Taft-Hartley Act and in support of more adequate compensation for victims of industrial accidents and unemployment, as well as for fair employment practices. Both sides rejoiced when their national bodies effected a tentative merger in 1955.

The unionists, however, were more directly concerned with their separate negotiations with specific employers. After exercising considerable restraint during the war, many unions presented urgent demands for wage increases in 1946. Nationwide strikes by the United Steel Workers and the United Electrical Workers idled several thousand in Rochester for varied periods. Pfaudler and the Kellogg division of the American Brake Shoe Company made quick settlements with the steelworkers; General Motors reached agreement, after two weeks, with its electrical workers but held out longer against the United Auto Workers and refused to recognize a struggling local at its Rochester Products plant. A protracted strike in the building trades in 1955 boosted the number of "days lost" to over 300,000 that year, but generally the services of state or federal mediators brought early settlements and helped win Rochester somewhat of a reputation for labor peace. The high-wage policy set by Eastman, followed at some distance by Gleason, Taylor Instruments, Bausch & Lomb, and Todd, enabled them to avoid unionization, but General Railway Signal and several others in strongly organized trades were more ready to negotiate in order to hold their skilled workers. Young Joseph C. Wilson, new president of Haloid, watched impassively as Chatman organized the production workers in his plant as a local under the Joint Board of Amalgamated Clothing Workers, the city's strongest union, with locals in all clothing plants and in several accessory firms as well.

Perhaps the most threatening strike of the entire period was that against the bus company in 1952. Its settlement, with the aid of a board of inquiry appointed by the governor after a three-week stoppage, demonstrated the value of mediation and promoted a spirit of moderation that helped to ease tension in the labor-management field in succeeding years. That result was particularly noticeable in the utility field where, for example, the RG&E, with 2,400 employees in 1954, not only had one of the largest work forces but also performed vitally essential services. In recognition of this fact, several leading Rochester bankers, headed by Raymond Ball, had organized an independent company in 1949 to purchase the local properties of the national trust company, which had acquired the old RG&E, and they reestablished Rochester control over that utility. In similar fashion Rochester capitalists reestablished local ownership and control over both the telephone company and the bus company and threw their weight on the side of metropolitan growth. The State Public Service

Commission, which determined the rates these utilities could charge, had control over their wage standards as well, though the achievement of new technical advances, especially in the telephone, permitted economies that enabled the management to meet wage demands independently. Only in the case of the bus company, where the mounting competition from private automobiles was reducing its payload, were frequent fare increases granted by the PSC.

As the bus fares more than doubled during the fifties, the shift to private cars accelerated, and increasing numbers of shoppers began to patronize the new commercial plazas springing up on the outskirts of Rochester. The eleven moderate-sized shopping plazas developed in the late forties, with 170 stores by 1950, doubled in number and quadrupled in size by 1956 when South Town Plaza opened on a 43-acre site able to accommodate 3,500 cars to supply customers for its twenty-four stores that included branches of leading downtown merchants. The metropolitan sprawl of Rochester's commercial functions was matched by the mushrooming of a dozen tourist courts on the city's outskirts, some with dining facilities, and by the appearance of new suburban inns and restaurants, as well as branch banks and drive-in movies. Practically all 24,000 new single-family homes erected in the county in the decade following the war were built in the suburbs, which more than doubled in population during these years, while that of the city slightly declined.

Rochester's industrial growth continued to provide the mainstay for the metropolis. Technological advances supplied the chief source of vitality, while the quality of products and the enterprise of sales promotion sustained important nontechnical industries. Thus the men's clothing and the food processing firms, although decreasing in number as consolidation progressed, retained their local importance by maintaining quality standards and by opening more distant sales outlets. Their increase was less dramatic, however, than that of such firms as the Kordite Company, built on a new technique for the manufacture of vinyl plastics, or Haloid, which acquired a new specialty when it undertook the adaption of the newly invented electrophotographic process to the production of copying machines. While its new products were effecting a revolution in office procedures, creating a flood of orders that prompted the company to erect a new plant on a spacious site in suburban Webster (as Kordite located in Macedon), many of

Rochester's older technological firms were developing new products and erecting new additions to their factories. Several, however, were establishing or acquiring new branches in distant American cities or abroad—Bausch & Lomb and Taylor Instruments, as well as Eastman and Pfaudler, which absorbed the Permutit Company of New York to become Pfaudler-Permutit. Several others were expanding their markets by merging with larger conglomerates, and their local managements sometimes suffered displacement, as in the case of Stromberg-Carlson, which became a division of General Dynamics in 1956, and of Yawman & Erbe, which passed through several mergers in the fifties but managed to maintain and, in the end, increase its local work force in the process.

Rochester continued to specialize in the field of photography. Although outside competitors managed to absorb some of the smaller local firms, such as the Defender Photo Supply Company acquired by Du Pont in 1945, and the Graflex Company, which became a division of the General Precision Corporation a few years later, the local plants generally maintained or slightly expanded their production, and the added pressure served to stimulate innovative developments at Kodak as well as at Haloid. Phenomenal as was the rise and transformation of Haloid, even more so was the growth of Eastman Kodak. After doubling its net earnings between 1942 to 1947, it doubled them again in the next ten years, despite the expenditure of from $30 to $57 million annually on plant and equipment improvements. Although the number of local employees, which fluctuated between 33,000 and 35,000 in this period, remained fairly constant, their total wage and fringe benefits increased from $132 to $257 million annually, and the number of local shareholders rose from 11,000 to 18,000, further spreading the community benefits. Eastman's emphasis on research was continued, as Dr. Cyril J. Staud succeeded Dr. Kenneth Mees in the research department, and resulted in new developments in the color, speed, safety, and quality of film; improvements in motion-picture cameras and projectors; and such new products as vitamin A capsules and other synthetics.

In sum, despite the dual impacts of automation and consolidation, Rochester maintained its character as a prosperous industrial center. Its establishments, still exceeding 1,000 in 1959, gave employment to 106,000 workers whose efforts added $1 billion to the value of the county's products for the first time that year. As the thirty-second city in size in the nation, Rochester was the twenty-first in industrial production. By a careful husbanding of their reserves, most firms avoided a resort to the banks for major loans for expansion, but their mergers, patent acquisitions, and other corporate transactions enhanced the importance of their legal advisers, as the advancement of Thomas J. Hargrave to the presidency of Eastman indicated. His law firm, headed by T. Carl Nixon, with nineteen partners, was the largest in the city, but most of the 800 practicing attorneys were associated with one of more than a dozen law firms or the more numerous partnerships. Patent law was a local specialty, and in 1954 thirty-one of its devotees formed a Patent Law Association. Most of these men as well as the thirty resident judges were also members of the Rochester Bar Association, which in 1958 became the Bar Association of Monroe County.

Civic and Political Responsibilities

Rochester's dynamic economy pumped new vitality into its civic and political affairs. Other forces contributed to the community's transformation—notably a resurgent but mobile population and more aggressive state and federal responses to urban problems. Because of its concern for local autonomy and for a balanced budget, the city resisted these latter forces for a time, but the diversified and centrifugal character of its growth and the sharp contest for political control alerted leaders of both parties to quicken their civic efforts and prepared Rochester to accept its metropolitan status.

As the returning servicemen created a baby boom and resident birth rates soared to 23.2 per 1,000 in the late forties, many observers expected a larger population increase than the census takers found in 1950. Yet if the official count proved disappointing, it served to emphasize the metropolitan character of Rochester's growth, and the Bureau of Municipal Research soon produced a table that showed the spread of the city's overflow into the suburbs. With a surplus of births over deaths of approximately 3,500 annually, Rochester's vitality was assured, but its failure to hold the increment caused some disillusionment and intensified local political contests. As the Republican hold-the-line policy deferred inner-city improvements and limited policemen and other city employees to paltry wage increases, protests mounted and, supported by labor's indignation over the passage of the Taft-Hartley Act, brought a Democratic victory in November 1948. Shocked by the unexpected Truman majority, local Republican leaders pressed the county to adopt the recently authorized business-privilege tax and prepared to launch some long-deferred public works.

After much deliberation over the flight of residents to the suburbs and over the progressive deterioration of many old districts, Broderick finally approved action on the housing front. The City Council in June 1949 assumed responsibility for the erection of a public project to be subsidized by the state. Unfortunately, the proposed location on city-owned land on the outskirts aroused the outspoken opposition of an adjoining Polish neighborhood, and the officials hastened to seek a new site on Hanover Street in Rochester's most blighted slum area. Shortly after reluctantly setting the stage for this new venture, Chairman Broderick resigned on his doctor's order and was replaced by Fred I. Parrish, former head of the Master Plumbers Association and active in Masonic circles. This effort to democratize the party enabled the Republicans to retain control of the council in a heated election that fall. The opposition, however, was vigorous, and although Peter Barry, a handsome bachelor and former naval commander as well as a member of an old Flower City family, easily led the field, and Robert B. Corris, with whom he debated the issues in the first local television forum, took fourth place, the election of two Democrats terminated the long era of one-party rule.

Public pressure for a more aggressive civic program had been mounting for several years. Robert E. Ginna, vice-president of the RG&E, had chided the city fathers in 1947 for their inaction and prompted Commerce Commissioner MacFarlin to project an extension of the subway to Kodak Park on the north. Unfortunately, as new automobiles became available, a sudden drop in the number of passengers the next spring checked that action and prompted an outside survey of the subway's usefulness. However, even when two successive studies recommended the abandonment of passenger service, numerous protests forestalled action. Attention shifted at this point to the controversy over the proposed War Memorial. The drive for $2,500,000 to finance its construction had fallen $900,000 short of the goal in 1945, but its friends now persuaded the supervisors to authorize a county-wide referendum on a $4 million bond issue designed to meet the increased cost. Unexpectedly, a slight majority of the 70,000 votes cast were negative, but since most of the city votes were favorable, Mayor Dicker appointed a new committee to recommend action. Headed by Paul Miller of the Gannett press, it proposed a modified design to be financed by the city, which hesitatingly gave approval. That decision was hastened by the final agreement of the city and state planners to bring the proposed expressway, connecting downtown Rochester with the State Thruway, into the city along the old subway route. This plan, announced in 1949, terminated former debate over use of the subway and gave assurance that the traffic bottlenecks that clogged Rochester's arterial streets every morning and night would finally be eliminated, thus restoring access to and from the central business district.

These projects absorbed so much of the city's resources that other urgent programs were threatened. The city had passed responsibility for the expansion of its airport over to the county in 1948, and Gordon A. Howe, president of the Board of Supervisors, had assumed the lead in promoting county outlays of $3.5 million to secure an additional $2.5 million in federal assistance for its proper development. A solution of the city's water problem was not so easy, but when a severe shortage during a dry spell in 1949 brought a sharp warning of increased insurance rates from the National Board of Fire Underwriters, the City Council directed Cartwright to purchase the needed water from the Kodak system and to speed the erection of a pumping and filtering plant near its Lake Ontario intake pipes. To meet the necessary outlays of $5.5 million over the next five years and to defray other mounting expenses, the Republicans, on the recommendation of a citizens' advisory committee, moved late in 1951 for the adoption of a 2 percent county sales tax that trebled returns of the business-privilege tax, which was hastily abandoned. The city's share, adding up to $17.5 million in the first three years, brought new vitality to many municipal functions.

As civic confidence revived, new plans for improvements appeared. The planning commission proposed a civic center west of the river, with the War Memorial as its first tangible expression. It further projected an urban renewal project to replace the wretched slum properties encircling Hanover Houses with moderate-rent garden apartments, a new school, and a playground. The Board of Education launched construction of a new East High School, and the City Council authorized the purchase of two additional playground sites. When the Democrats, under the leadership of Roy Bush, endeavored to obstruct these developments, an insurgent faction, headed by Richard C. Wade, a professor at the university who was chiefly disturbed by Bush's half-hearted support of Stevenson, rallied advocates of civic reform in a hotly contested primary fight in September 1954. On emerging victorious, they elected Francis J. D'Amanda as county chairman and adopted a platform calling for progressive action. The Republicans, however, had secured a sure lead in that field. When Cartwright resigned as city manager to become postmaster, Mayor Dicker brought Robert P. Aex, formerly the city comptroller, back from the city managership of Newburg to replace him, and Aex pressed the new civic program with great vigor. To finance his new projects, the Republicans increased the sales tax from 2 to 3 percent, which enabled the city not only to build its first parking ramps downtown but also to launch a program of modernization of the sewage treatment plant designed to remove the threat of pollution from the lower Genesee and the lakeshore beaches.

If, in their absorption with these long-deferred improvements, the Rochester officials tended to slight some human-relations problems, the neglect reflected their continued reliance on private volunteer efforts. The Postwar Problems Council had placed responsibility here with the Community Chest and the Council of Social Agencies, and these bodies not only had expanded their services and increased their budgets annually but also had extended their services into the suburbs where the recreational and health features proved especially popular. Thus the Rochester Hospital Council became the Council of Rochester Regional Hospitals, and both Blue Cross and the new Blue Shield extended their coverage to subscribers throughout the metropolitan district. A dozen new agencies, each focusing on a special problem, joined the council and hastened to appeal for chest support, and although the response was not always as generous as the promoters desired, the Community Chest and the Council of Social Agencies generally took the lead in fostering new approaches to the most disturbing urban problems. For example, they backed the establishment of the Montgomery Neighborhood Center in 1951 to check social deterioration in the Clarissa Street district, and five years later they supported its efforts to extend a program for juveniles into the troubled Marshall Court area across the river.

Yet the social worker's approach to the city's increasing welfare problems was but one aspect of Rochester's urbanization. As the metropolis increased in size and diversity, the need for neighborhood or special-interest groups mounted and the number of ethnic and fraternal societies multiplied. However, although these bodies gave a sense of identity to many participants, and although press notices and public programs gratified the aspirations of many of their leaders for wider recognition, the increasing diversity called for new efforts at community integration. The multiplicity of ethnic organizations presented an opportunity to the newly formed Rochester Association for the United Nations (RAUN) to draw their leaders into its educational programs. Mrs. Harper Sibley, whose parlor provided the setting for the organization of that association and for the meetings of the Cosmopolitan Club and of a number of ethnic and religious minority groups, provided a warm personal link among many discordant factions. The chamber's New Citizens Banquets, less commercial than the Welcome Wagon greetings in the suburbs, continued to offer a formal welcome to many inner-city residents, but the numbers reached in both instances were small and the contacts slight, particularly among the less-articulate and needy folk whose chief reliance was on their families.

Rochester's attitude toward minorities was tempered by gratitude for the sacrifices that young men of all races and creeds had made during World War II. The arrival in 1948 of successive shipments of caskets, brought back at the request of the mourning families of some of the war victims, called for interment ceremonies at which the diversified character, as well as the heroism, of American troops was repeatedly acclaimed. The outbreak of hostilities in Korea in 1950 reinforced these bonds. Within a month, as the names of those missing in action began to appear, Rochester was reminded of its cosmopolitan heritage. Some of its men had left as members of existing units in July, and in September the first enrollees of a new draft entrained for camp. By the end of December some 450 Rochesterians were known to be at the front in Korea, and during the next two years some 20,000 men and women from Rochester and Monroe County responded to the call of service. By October 1952 the area's casualties in this undeclared war numbered 81 killed in action, and before January 1955 a total of 176 had died in service.

It was on Memorial Day in 1957 with the dedication of the Room of Remembrance in the War Memorial that Rochester soberly expressed homage to its departed veterans in a few brief lines chiseled into the wall:

> Dedicated to all the men and women of Greater Rochester
> Who died for their country on land or sea or in the air
> Americans by birth or adoption most of all by devotion
> Rich in the joys and hopes and talents they sacrificed
> Richer still with honor and freedom so nobly maintained
> Whose courage and faith laid deep foundations for peace

Some whose faith in mankind was equally staunch endeavored to build on these foundations, The RAUN, second in size in the nation, conducted a succession of public forums and issued numerous brochures on international questions, rallying support for the UN, for UNESCO and WHO. A group of junior executives at Eastman founded Teen Age Diplomats, Incorporated, in 1952 to sponsor the exchange of students from Rochester high schools with their counterparts in foreign cities. Numerous Rochester adults served in special capacities on UNESCO and other missions, and in 1950 Professor Perkins became chairman of the board of the Seminar in American Studies, Salzburg, Austria.

These formal efforts to give expression and harmony to Rochester's emerging metropolitan elements played lesser roles than the city's public and private recreational facilities and the community's widely shared domestic customs. The public parks, the lake beaches, the ball diamonds, and other commercialized amusement resorts attracted larger and more diversified throngs and promoted a freer and more democratic interchange than the more deliberately organized relationship could produce. By inaugurating an annual series of Opera Under the Stars programs in 1953 and by upgrading the supervision of its playgrounds with the appointment three years later of Joseph M. Caverely, a trained recreation leader, the city enhanced the free use of its public facilities. By winning the International League pennant twice and the playoffs three times in these years, the Red Wings helped maintain Rochester's reputation not only for winning teams but also for enthusiastic support from local fans, a situation that contributed as well to the maintenance of community morale. When the Rochester Royals, who had captured the national basketball crown in their first franchise season and had won their divisional title five successive times in the old Edgerton Park gym, failed to fill the larger galleries at the War Memorial, they abandoned it to the Rochester Americans whose flashing skates and skilled playing cultivated a new interest in hockey. The War Memorial's big opening event had been the National Bowling Congress, which had filled its spacious floor and the encircling stands with a boisterous stream of 25,000 bowlers, including some 6,000 local contestants in a democratic tournament that lasted for 79 days.

Only the daily flood of private cars, which increased from 103,000 in 1946 to 212,000 a decade later, involved a wider participation. Despite, or perhaps because of, the increased flow of traffic, the Rochester Safety Council and other agencies were able to promote improved controls that won a high rating among the country's safest cities for successive years. To achieve this goal, Rochester steadily increased the number of traffic lights, even "walk" and "don't walk" signals for pedestrians, and adopted a policy of salting all arterial streets during the winter months. The city was encouraged to maintain its salting program, despite loud protests, chiefly because of the sharp reduction in traffic deaths (from the high thirties in the late 1920s to the low teens in the 1950s). The popularity of the family car and the widespread preference among Rochesterians for single freestanding homes, over 50 percent of them owner-occupied in these years, enhanced the status of the family and strengthened its bonds. The increased freedom enjoyed by women and their wider participation in commercial and industrial employment as well as in social activities injected fresh vitality into the social structure centered in the family.

CULTURAL AND INSTITUTIONAL ACCOMPLISHMENTS

Rochester's earlier quest for quality seemed at last to be approaching fruition in several cultural and institutional respects. Despite a number of disappointments and reverses, many professional leaders in the artistic and intellectual fields enjoyed a gratifying sense of accomplishment. The continued improvement in their material facilities had stimulated a development and expression of talents that attracted close attention both from admiring patrons and an appreciative public and from impatient critics. Most of the controversies proved stimulating and contributed to the general excitement that marked the city's cultural growth. Few of even the harshest critics commented on the limited ranks of the cultural participants, for that was an old story, though the city's metropolitan expansion was now making it a crucial issue.

The handwriting on the wall was perhaps most noticeable in the theater, formerly a vital center of entertainment in Rochester. Following in his father's footsteps, Robert B. Corris brought a succession of Broadway hits to the Auditorium each season in these years, including *The King and I*, starring Margaret Landon, but the rapid decline in the road-show business throughout the country, as the more economical and often more exciting movies closed the doors of legitimate theaters in city after city, finally brought his efforts to an end in 1956. Stock companies of summer players performed in barns and other improvised theaters in several suburban villages for successive seasons, attracting Rochesterians out for a pleasant drive and an evening's entertainment, and one headed by Miss Dorothy Chernuck established a theater-in-the-round at the Hochstein Music School for six exciting winters. Only the Community Players, relying on amateur talent and a list of perennial subscribers, continued to supply a full schedule of performances.

Even the cinema, generally blamed for the troubles of the theater, had to battle for its life after June 1949 when WHAM-TV inaugurated local television. Most of the city's thirty motion-picture houses lost part of their juvenile clientele as the 2,000 TV sets of that date multiplied sixfold in as many months, transforming the life pattern of many families. Yet, although two of the six downtown motion-picture palaces closed their doors, the number of neighborhood theaters remained constant, and seven drive-in theaters, located on the outskirts, catered to the increasing number of suburban families and car owners. Adult fans received two boons, one from the remodeling of the Cinema in 1949 as an art theater featuring foreign films, and the other from the opening two years later of the Dryden Theater in conjunction with the Eastman House, which launched a program of film revivals that brought the movies back into the city's cultural experience on a lofty, if nostalgic, plane.

Music, which had traditionally held such a plane, was beginning to face the hazards of mounting costs. The Civic Music Association, which supported the sixty-piece Civic Orchestra—the vital nucleus of the Rochester Philharmonic—and sponsored one or more artists' series at the Eastman Theatre each year, progressively increased its annual goal and boosted its subscription totals from $100,000 to $225,000 in ten years. Mounting costs, however, created a deficit that a special gift from Eastman Kodak only temporarily relieved. A special committee, appointed to study the situation, blamed the deficits on the poor attendance at some of the concerts, and the criticism may have prompted Guy Fraser Harrison, conductor of the Civic Orchestra, to accept a call to Oklahoma City in 1951 and Eric Leinsdorf, director of the Philharmonic, to leave for New York five years later to take charge of its City Opera Company. Howard Hanson and the Eastman school faculty became virtually responsible for the Philharmonic as well as the Civic Orchestra, and their academic standards created a wider gap between the symphonic performances and the newer musical programs of the jazz bands and dance orchestras that appealed to more popular tastes. Two rival opera companies competed for favor among the numerous residents of Italian origin in the late forties but soon succumbed. A Mercury Ballet group directed by Olive McCue attracted praise for its performances at the Eastman Theatre and provided dance groups for the city's Opera Under the Stars programs in the park in the late fifties.

As Hanson declared on one occasion, with respect to the Eastman Theatre programs, "the great need is for more listeners," and local promoters of other forms of artistic and intellectual expression often voiced similar views. Each of the city's cultural institutions—theaters, galleries, museums, libraries, colleges, even churches—faced a continuing search for adequate support. The increased leisure of many residents and the spreading growth of the metropolis created exciting opportunities for program expansion that threatened to dissipate their energies.

Hanson, for example, welcomed the challenge presented by the new media as an opportunity to reach a larger audience. He made

careful arrangements for new recordings at the school each year; he
eagerly exploited the advantages of radio and television and in 1957
conducted thirteen television programs on the theme, "Music as a
Language." In addition to the promotion of contemporary composers
as the annual Festival of American Music held at the school each
spring, Hanson scheduled as part of the school's tenth anniversary a
symposium for the production of Eastman school graduates. Several of
its faculty continued to direct programs at the Hochstein School where
their advanced students taught some 300 young pupils from a depressed neighborhood to play the violin, the piano, or one of several
other instruments generously made available by its sponsors.

Mrs. Gertrude Moore at the art gallery made similar efforts to reach
and involve a wider public. A drive for new members in 1946 increased
their number to 2,560 and swelled the annual attendance to over
100,000 for the first time. By a careful rationing of her resources among
part-time instructors and a limited staff, assisted by numerous volunteers, Mrs. Moore maintained an active program of creative-art classes,
periodic exhibits, and extramural services. Staff members delivered
numerous lectures each year in which they interpreted aspects of art
to diverse groups, and the gallery's practice of devoting an occasional
monthly exhibit to the native art of a local ethnic group helped draw
some of their members into its broader programs. An elaborate exhibit
prepared by a bevy of volunteers under the direction of Miss Isabel
Herdle in 1953 attracted over 40,000 visitors in nine weeks to see "The
Erie Canal—Thruway of Yesterday." The annual Finger Lakes exhibitions continued to attract an ever-widening participation of artists and
interested viewers. The contrasting works produced by the Genesee
Group, mostly representational in their treatment, and the Arena
Group, which included several abstractionists, added excitement to
successive shows, some of them hung in the sedate parlors of the
Rochester Historical Society's Woodside mansion, in the rooms of the
Art Club, or in the corridors of local theaters.

To promote more effective outreach programs and to coordinate
their efforts to involve a larger public, the directors of several cultural
institutions formed an Intermuseum Council. In addition to the art
gallery and the Historical Society, it included the Museum of Arts and
Sciences, the public library, the university library, and three historic
houses. The former Home of Susan B. Anthony, opened in her honor

in 1947, the George Eastman House, established as a museum of photography two years later, and the Campbell-Whittlesey House, headquarters since the late thirties of the Landmark Society of Western New York, performed specialized services and collaborated with the major institutions in efforts to preserve and interpret the community's cultural traditions. Under the leadership of W. Stephen Thomas as director, the Museum of Arts and Sciences, which harbored some thirty hobby clubs and scientific societies, developed, in addition to its permanent scientific exhibits, a succession of special educational displays, including a spectacular Rochester Futurama show that attracted 20,000 visitors in 1953. The public library reached out even more widely to serve the public with a bookmobile and with the establishment of an audiovisual division to supply records and educational films.The creation of a county library system, closely linked to the city system, under the direction of Harold Hacker, the new librarian, in 1954 and of a tri-county Pioneer Library System, a federation of three counties, two years later greatly increased the efficiency and extent of book services throughout the metropolitan area. The establishment of a new supporting organization, the Friends of the Rochester Public Library, resulted in the launching of several new programs, including the popular "Books Sandwiched In" series of noontime book reviews by informed and articulate citizens who for twelve successive Tuesdays each fall packed the auditorium and, frequently, the adjoining corridor with eager listeners. By accepting and pressing the circulation of paperbacks and by preparing spot announcements featuring the "Book of the Week" and "Books to Remember" for radio and television announcers, the library boosted its circulation to 1,783,000 in 1955, when a distribution of 12,900 films reached an audience of over 790,000.

Except for the mass media, only the churches could rival that coverage, but for a time some of the latter appeared to have lost their relevance to the urban scene. Several churches, responding to the outward migration of their members, built fine new edifices on the outskirts—Asbury Methodist, First Baptist, and Temple Beth El, among others—whereas a few, such as St. Luke's and First Presbyterian, rejected such moves; but a reaction against the social Christianity of an earlier era turned many of their leaders to doctrinal and other, inner concerns. A few clergymen, such as the aged Reverend David Rhys

Williams at First Unitarian, Rabbi Philip Bernstein at B'rith Kodesh, and Dr. Harold E. Nicely at Brick Presbyterian, continued to champion the needs of the poor slum dwellers and other unfortunates. However, Dr. Edwin M. Poteat at the Divinity School attacked the worldliness of the laity and the doctrinal laxity of the Protestant clergy (which, he declared, blinded them to the errors of Catholicism) with a vigor that brought an indignant response from Bishop Kearney and threatened to jettison all interfaith programs in Rochester. The aged Dr. Justin Wroe Nixon, among others, spoke in favor of moderation; and the appointment of Dr. Wilbour E. Saunders, well known locally as a champion of brotherly harmony, to succeed Poteat at the seminary, plus occasional visits by Archbishop Hanna from San Francisco and Cardinal Mooney from Detroit, both former priests in Rochester, helped quiet the furor. Neither the Reverend Dr. Hugh C. Burr of the Federation of Churches nor Mrs. Harper Sibley, in varied capacities, was able to awaken their fellow churchmen to the hazardous community ills they frequently deplored.

The schools, too, were chiefly concerned with internal rather than community problems. In contrast with other cultural institutions, the schools and colleges experienced a resurgence of enrollments, which aggravated rather than relieved their struggle for adequate support. The public schools, charged by the Council on Postwar Problems with the task of promoting "the civic, social, and personality development of the individual and the group," faced a challenge to develop new educational approaches without adequate resources. Teachers' salaries, held almost stationary during the war, proved insufficient to attract and hold able instructors. A grant of an increase of $100 for the year, starting in September 1946, stirred such indignation that local teachers supported the drive of either the State Teachers Association or the Teachers Union for a more substantial subsidy. As the teachers became absorbed in the organizational problems and successfully pressed Governor Dewey for increased state aid, Superintendent James M. Spinning became involved in a dispute with the Bureau of Municipal Research over the proper class size and the proper student-teacher ratios. Increased enrollments, resulting from the baby boom, hit the kindergarten classes in 1947 and progressed through the elementary and secondary grades, into the junior high schools by the mid-fifties. Several nearby suburbs faced even steeper increases and had to build one or two new schools almost annually. As young families from the city moved to new homes in the suburbs and were replaced in the central wards by newcomers from the South, the rapid population turnover created problems of assimilating the transients. When Dr. Howard C. Seymour, formerly the guidance director, succeeded Spinning as superintendent in 1954, his special skills promised a sensitive handling of some problems, but the immediate task of meeting the demands for increased wages, which he had previously championed, commanded first attention.

The public schools would have faced much more critical fiscal problems had it not been for the rapid expansion of the parochial school system. Several Catholic parishes erected new primary schools as their total enrollments increased from 14,000 to 24,000 in the decade. Two of the five secondary schools added new buildings and increased their total to 4,200 by the mid-fifties. Three private schools served a limited number of children, but several technical schools experienced a new burst of vitality. Rochester Business Institute responded to the growing demand for secretaries; the Eastman Dental Dispensary, inundated by pleas for trained hygienists, and the nursing schools of local hospitals, pressed to supply graduate nurses, each increased the size of its classes. But it was old Mechanics Institute, renamed the Rochester Institute of Technology in 1944, which enjoyed the most remarkable development. The dedication of its new $1,250,000 Clark building in 1947 provided workshops for printing and photographic departments. In 1950 President Mark Ellingson brought the School of American Craftsmen from Alfred to become the mainstay and catalyst of professional training at the institute. He secured authorization from the regents that year to grant Associate in Applied Science degrees and, three years later, Associate in Arts and Bachelor of Science degrees. Additional facilities and new courses attracted an increasing number of the returning veterans who were eager to improve their skills, and the 950 daytime students of 1946 grew to 2,000 a decade later, when an additional 4,800 were registered in evening classes.

The surging desire for education, assisted by veteran's benefits, boosted the enrollment of all area colleges and gave birth to two new institutions. Local Catholics, who had dedicated a new campus for Nazareth College in 1942, opened the first building of the new St. John Fisher College for men in September 1951. The major development occurred at the University of Rochester, particularly in the graduate departments. Continued support from Washington for postgraduate research programs and instruction in optics and medicine as well as in physics and chemistry threatened to transform the university into a cluster of research departments. Professor Perkins organized a program of graduate studies in history designed to prepare good teachers; President Valentine organized a Conference on the Humanities to counteract the overemphasis on science, but he could not buck the trend and resigned in 1950.

Dr. Cornelis W. de Kiewiet, who replaced Valentine, was a specialist in South African history, but administrative experience at Cornell had prepared him to accept and promote rapid developments in several scientific departments. Developments in the physics department had already acquired a momentum that carried them to new heights. Despite the resignations of Professors Lee A. Du Bridge and Victor Weisskopf shortly after their return from war-research assignments, Dr. Sidney W. Barnes, who became director of the university's new atom smasher in 1948, and Dr. Robert E. Marshak, who became chairman of the department two years later, won wide recognition as a result of an international conference on high-energy physics staged that year (provision for its repetition in subsequent years was secured). Only the medical school could rival these developments. There the research work at the Manhattan Project and in a new cancer wing, both largely financed by the government, afforded rich opportunities for postgraduate study. The establishment of a psychiatric clinic, headed by Dr. John Romano and located in a new wing dedicated in 1948, provided facilities for advanced instruction and treatment in clinical psychiatry. "Never has the world offered so many opportunities for men and women of skill and ambition," declared President de Kiewiet at his inaugural in 1951, and his announcements in the next two years of a new Chair in International Economics, endowed by the Haloid Company, and of an exchange relationship with the University of Hull in England, a gift of the R. T. French Company, gave practical expression to his emphasis on increased international understanding. De Kiewiet's chief accomplishment, however, was to bring the women's and men's colleges back together in an enlarged College of Arts and Sciences on the River Campus in 1955.

The university's continued emphasis on graduate study prompted local educators concerned over the need for increased facilities for undergraduates to launch a campaign for a community college. In December 1956 when the Board of Regents proposed the establishment of a two-year community college at Rochester, de Kiewiet, Ellingson and Murphy of St. John Fisher, and Superintendent Seymour were ready to give their tentative approval. Numerous firms endorsed the proposal, but a joint committee of city and county officials prepared to shelve the matter. However, on October 1 when news arrived of the successful launching of Sputnik, the first man-made satellite, by the Soviets, Rochester, among many other American cities, saw the need for higher education in a new light. Thus the county hastily moved to authorize the creation of a community college.

In the field of communications, no individual had played a larger role in recent decades than Frank Gannett, but his active days were now drawing to a close. Paul Miller, who joined the company in 1947 and became executive vice-president four years later, assumed full responsibility as editor and publisher shortly before Gannett's death in 1957. Gannett, a firm believer in wide travel as a safeguard against provincialism, had made a round-the-world trip himself in 1947 and sent his chief editors, Miller, Lafayette R. Blanchard, and Clifford E. Carpenter, among others, on extended journeys through the states and abroad. Each of Gannett's Rochester papers assembled able staffs, competed for local and regional preference, and increased their circulations to approximately 125,000 daily (the *Democrat & Chronicle* to 175,000 on Sunday), despite the appearance of a dozen weekly or bimonthly papers designed to serve specific suburbs. Most of these were advertising sheets distributed freely by local merchants, but Andrew D. Wolfe made his *Brighton-Pittsford Post* a model journal of suburban interests and tastes. Only the *Abendpost* of the earlier foreign language journals lived to celebrate its centennial in 1951, and its circulation of 13,000 served the entire region. Many residents received out-of-town papers, notably the *New York Times*, which shipped in 1,200 copies daily and 6,500 on Sunday.

Less concerned with the competition of regional weeklies than with the threat posed by radio and television, Gannett had taken an active part in the development of these rival media. After disposing of his early interest in WHAM, he had backed the establishment of its chief rival, WHEC, and by 1948 had acquired a controlling interest in five other radio stations scattered from Hartford, Connecticut, to Danville, Illinois. It was WHAM, however, that maintained leadership in radio and quickly established itself in television. After moving into its new home on Humbolt Street, where Stromberg-Carlson erected a modern studio known as Rochester Radio City, WHAM, with William Fay as general manager, recruited an able staff and increased its range to reach an audience estimated to number 2,000,000. By June 1949, Fay was ready to present the first telecast. Commencing with twenty-two daily programs, each locally produced, he soon acquired connections by relay cables to the emerging national networks. Four additional radio stations made their appearance locally, and WHEC joined with WVET in a successful application for a second channel in 1953. As the two television stations and the seven radio stations developed ties with national chains, their use of locally produced programs declined, prompting a resurgence of interest in local programs, especially those designed for educational uses. Several stations devoted time to local forums and church programs, but the Voluntary Educational Association, formed in 1944, which collaborated in the early fifties in preparing special programs, reorganized in 1958 as the Rochester Area Educational Television Association to press its claim to an independent television channel.

Without such a local outlet the mass communication media could not duplicate the more personal contacts supplied by City Club and other local lectures and assemblies. The annual program of the City Club, under the able leadership of such presidents as William S. Vaughn of Kodak, Joseph C. Wilson of Haloid, Donald Gaudion of Pfaudler, and Sol M. Linowitz, an able attorney, drew capacity audiences into the great hall of the Chamber of Commerce on numerous occasions. That club's collaboration with the Rochester Association for the United Nations resulted in a number of annual Institutes on Foreign Affairs, which attracted capacity crowds to Eastman Theatre to hear Mrs. Roosevelt, Ralph Bunche, J. Robert Oppenheimer, and other distinguished leaders of world movements. Thus as the city's distant contacts and commitments mounted, its horizons expanded in preparation for its new metropolitan responsibilities.

In some respects Rochester had held metropolitan status for several decades, yet the full impact of its transformation from an industrial center into a well-rounded metropolis was not evident until the late fifties. Its population had surged past the Census Bureau's standard of 200,000 for a first-class metropolis over a half century before. Its industrial initiative had earned it the requisite degree of economic autonomy, but the achievements of its specialized firms were better known in international than in regional circles. It was only as the outward migration of some of its plants as well as of numerous inhabitants swelled to major proportions, and the outward reach of its institutions created new and broader ties during the late 1950s, that Rochester began to acquire the character of a regional as well as a technological center.

Almost without realizing it, the city's population had become metropolitan in character. Except for Mayor Barry and other civic officials, few of its top leaders had a Rochester residence. Yet Paul Miller of Pittsford, Gilbert McCurdy and Joseph C. Wilson of Brighton, Donald Gaudion of East Rochester, and a host of other suburbanites who represented the city in regional and world affairs spoke as Rochesterians; and in the realm of politics Gordon Howe from Greece and William Posner from Brighton vied as Republican and Democratic chairmen, respectively, in posing as metropolitan rather than as town leaders. With their 250,000 fellow suburbanites in 1960, they proudly represented themselves as Rochesterians when they stepped beyond the town line.

Increasing numbers were in fact migrating to the suburbs. The ten most built-up towns experienced a combined growth of 100,000 in the fifties, in contrast with a drop of 16,400 in the city. Yet Rochester's stability ratio, based in the proportion of names reappearing in its directories over each five-year period, held closely to the high standard of the early fifties—65.4 percent—which was 2.5 over the average for the previous decade. Some whose names reappeared had acquired suburban addresses, however, and 27.2 percent of those who dropped out reappeared in separate suburban lists. Of course many Rochester migrants, like other mobile Americans, moved to distant places, but it was the city's industrial activity and other urban opportunities, more

than the salubrious character of its suburbs, that attracted immigrants
to replace these losses and to provide an additional 25,000 to bring
the county's total up to 586,387 in 1960.

Many of the newcomers, particularly those who were poor, settled
in the central districts, whose inhabitants were migrating to the outskirts. Some came, as in the past, from abroad, but the number of such
refugees was no longer sufficient to replace the earlier immigrants who
died or moved away. As the foreign born declined by several thousand
from the 49,127 of 1950, a new influx of blacks and Puerto Ricans developed, boosting the number of nonwhite residents from 7,845 to 24,214 in
this decade. Most of these newcomers found quarters in the blighted
housing of the Baden-Ormond and Clarissa Street districts where vacancies had already occurred. Their arrival accelerated the migration of
some former residents to the suburbs, where most of the new housing
was appearing, thus accentuating the contrast between the aging inner
city and the more spacious suburban areas where only occasional clusters
of garden apartments and shopping plazas interrupted the landscape
of free-standing houses.

Rochester's suburban expansion helped to demonstrate its metropolitan vitality, and few worried in the late fifties over the deepening
contrasts between its varied districts. Although the growth of the city,
and that of the metropolis as well, did not keep pace with the booming
growth of southern and western cities—which dropped Rochester from
thirty-second to thirty-eighth in size, and the metropolis from thirty-
seventh to fortieth place—these declines were only relative. In fact,
the rapid growth of such cities as Atlanta and Phoenix, which sped
ahead of Rochester, actually expanded the markets for its specialized
products and contributed to its economic stability. A planning study in
1960 forecast a growth of 100,000 during the decade, most of it in the
suburban towns, which would require improved contacts with and
services from the central city.

Many of the city's leaders were eager to meet these challenges. The
approaching completion of the St. Lawrence Seaway stirred renewed
interest in 1958 in foreign shipping and prompted a joint city-county
effort to improve the port's facilities. The reopening of the Genesee
Valley Regional Market that June facilitated an expansion of metropolitan marketing services. To demonstrate its confidence in the future,
the Chamber raised $600,000 to refurbish its headquarters, and two

banks as well as the leading hotel undertook to redecorate their quarters, while two other banks erected new buildings. These downtown improvements, however, were surpassed by several on the outskirts where new factories arose on Henrietta's Miracle Mile Industrial Park, on Mt. Read Boulevard in Greece, and off the Ridge Road in Webster. More seriously competitive with downtown were the new suburban shopping plazas; three prepared to accommodate 2,000 cars each, while improvements at older plazas and the opening of four new neighborhood plazas supplied space for another 4,000 cars.

None of the big downtown stores could resist this suburban trend, and each opened one or more branches. But to preserve their major investments, the McCurdy brothers and the Forman brothers joined forces in 1958 to develop a covered plaza downtown, behind their stores on Main and Clinton Streets and affording access to a score of new commercial specialties. To assure its success, Gilbert McCurdy, as spokesman for the two department stores, secured an agreement from City Manager Aex to undertake the long-contemplated extension of Broad Street east past the rear of the plaza and to construct an underground parking garage under the plaza. As this ambitious scheme developed, its promoters added a seventeen-story office and hotel tower fronting on Broad Street, and the mammoth project, tied together by Victor Gruen, a nationally famous architect, promised an investment of over $28 million by the associated firms. Despite some initial hesitation, the City Council quickly gave its consent for the necessary municipal improvements, and work on the construction of Midtown Plaza was commenced late in 1959. Suddenly the uncertainty and stagnation that had marked the central business district the year before disappeared, and to secure more adequate resources, the Lincoln Rochester Trust Company negotiated a merger with the Morgan Trust Company of New York, which was later held invalid.

The bank merger was symptomatic of Rochester's changing metropolitan position. Local autonomy no longer seemed as important as integration in the larger economy. Several industrial firms had previously entered similar mergers, and a chamber committee, under the chairmanship of Thomas Hawks, discovered that the merger movement reflected Rochester's technological vitality and concluded that as long as that vitality persisted, it posed no threat. Indeed several of the merged firms had expanded their local operations as the outside management had sought to develop their full Rochester potential. Several additional firms entered mergers in search of a broader relation to world markets, and the leading Rochester-based mergers likewise increased the number of their foreign branches. Rochester investors played a part, as did Rochester management, but it was not as dynamic a role as that of the local inventors and research men on whose talents and innovations the vitality of the metropolis finally depended.

This emphasis on research was evident in the merged firms as well as among the independents. The Stromberg-Carlson division of General Dynamics not only expanded its work force but also added thirty technological scientists to its research staff in 1960. Friden's national management was enthusiastic over the skills available for the expansion of its newly acquired Commercial Controls division in Rochester. Outside control brought new management assignments, sometimes promotions and sometimes replacements. The Rochester Chamber of Commerce generally welcomed the newcomers and endeavored to draw them into its activities, but the increased mobility of top executives presented problems as well as opportunities to community organizations. Yet despite the absorption of some companies, new enterprises continued to spring into being. Ingenious invention was the most fruitful source. Rochester had sixty independent makers of instruments, optical and photographic products—a few among its largest firms. It had twice as many printers and publishers. Several hundred enterprises in eighteen other categories helped in 1958 to boost the value added to its products to over $1 billion.

No Rochester firm made a more dramatic use of a new invention than the Haloid Company with the introduction of xerography. It was in 1948 that Joseph C. Wilson, the firm's youthful president, seized the opportunity sighted by John A. Dessauer, head of the research staff, to acquire control of a research project at the Barttelle Memorial Institute in Columbus where a new electrophotographic process invented by Chester Carlson was being perfected. After investing large sums in the project, Haloid was able in 1950 to place a commercially practical Xerox machine on the market. The phenomenal success of the new dry process revolutionized the copying process in business and professional offices and encouraged Wilson to open branches in 1954 in Canada and England and to acquire a site for a new plant in suburban Webster. A firm believer in cooperation, Wilson surrounded himself with an able team of vice presidents and endeavored to develop good relations with his 1,100 employees, the several hundred technicians as well as those represented by a union of the Amalgamated Photographic Supply Workers, an affiliate of the Amalgamated Clothing Workers. With the collaboration of Abraham Chatman, chairman of the joint board of that union, Wilson arranged a training program to be conducted by the Rochester Institute of Technology to prepare the workers in his Haloid shops for the new automated machine processes to which the company was converting. As sales soared to $20 million a year by the end of the decade, the company made increasingly generous appropriations for research and soon opened the first portion of its new plant in Webster.

As previously noted, several of Rochester's major companies had developed far-reaching industrial and commercial empires of their own, but the great value to the city was the secure markets thus afforded for its technical and labor skills. Bausch & Lomb—the oldest, with several foreign subsidiaries—and Eastman—the largest, with many American and foreign branches—each built large new plants in Rochester, as did a dozen other local firms. Although Eastman, with a high-wage policy, and several other technical firms avoided unionization, organized labor increased its representation in most plants; but, with the aid of state and national mediators, they managed to achieve wage and hour improvements with a minimal number of strikes. The chief benefit to the workers, however, came from the relatively full employment. With labor turnover at a minimum and unemployment the lowest in the state, the city regained a B classification in 1959 and saw the number gainfully employed in the city's urbanized district surge past the 250,000 mark by 1960.

Several firms had city and suburban factories, and all the larger companies drew their workers from both areas, but it was the utilities that most directly served the entire metropolitan community. The RG&E vigorously extended its electric lines to reach 200,000 separate customers by 1959, and although the gas mains served only 70,000 homes, the pressure for their extension was strong. The Rochester Telephone Company was likewise reaching into even the distant suburbs, and only the transit company buses generally stopped at the city line. Two regional bus companies helped to supplement that service and one, the Blue Valley Bus Company, carried some 3,000,000 suburban riders in 1960, when the number of auto registrations in the county had already reached 209,614.

But if it was commonplace for residents to cross boundary lines daily without noticing them, it proved exceedingly difficult to devise governmental structures adequate to cope with the emerging problems. Joint city-county committees had been active in a number of fields for several years, and one had achieved agreement for action on the new Civic Center, where work started on the construction of the underground garage in 1958. Despite protests by the Democratic minority against the projected costs for the courts building, Gordon Howe, who had become county manager in January 1960 and in that capacity served as chairman of the Civic Center Committee, achieved agreement on the construction of that building and of a public safety building as well. Meanwhile, F. Dow Hamblin, who had succeeded Aex as city manager the year before, pressed ahead with an antipollution program on which the city, state, and federal governments had in 1956 agreed to spend $18 million. But when the newly formed County Planning Council of 1958 endeavored to achieve a merger of city and county planning by naming City Planner Floyd F. Walkley as director of the country planning staff, Howard T. Cumming, recently appointed chairman of the City Planning Commission, chose Mrs. Ann Taylor, Walkley's former assistant, as chief planner for the city. Only in the fields of public health and public welfare were city and county bureaus merged into county departments, but mounting problems with juvenile delinquents prompted the creation of a new joint city-county youth board in 1960, and a shortage of funds in the city prompted park officials to turn the policing of Durand-Eastman Park and beach over to the county that summer.

Rochester's private welfare agencies, merging city and suburban volunteers, had no difficulty in surmounting civic boundaries. The Community Chest raised its funds throughout, and for service in, the entire county and brought the Red Cross and the Monroe County Cancer Society into its united drives. The YMCA created the Metropolitan Extension Committee, and the Rochester Regional Hospital Council assumed the task of planning and funding needed hospital improvements for the entire district. Even the problems of the inner city stirred the concern of some residents throughout the area, though many others hoped to escape such responsibilities. The city named two suburban representatives to its separated Housing Authority and Rehabilitation Commission in 1959, but neither was ready to propose developments beyond the city limits. Complaints of widespread discrimination against blacks looking for jobs or homes in the outer wards and the suburbs prompted the creation of the joint City-County Human Relations Commission in 1960 to seek a voluntary compliance with a newly adopted state law against discrimination, but a series of articles by Desmond Stone and Jack Germond in the *Times-Union* disclosed the increasing evidence of segregation as the influx of newcomers from the South accelerated.

Despite the ominously gray areas near its central core, Rochester had achieved a metropolitan fullness by the late 1950s that had many good characteristics. Its accomplishments in cultural fields displayed a profusion of ethnic contributions, both of tradition and spirit, that reached a stage of metropolitan diversity unmatched in other respects. Both Mrs. Moore at the art gallery and Stephen Thomas at the museum recognized and welcomed expressions of this diversity to their exhibitions and profited from the added vitality. The library, under the leadership of Harold Hacker, provided a model of metropolitan area integration, serving city branches, suburban town libraries, and bookmobile stops from a central library that also functioned as a reference and stimulating intellectual center for workers in the central business district. Music retained its favored place in Rochester, and despite mounting financial problems, the Civic Orchestra increased its performances in city and suburban high schools and in children's theater programs, and continued to give major support to the Philharmonic concerts. Several of the Eastman school faculty made public contributions, notably Dr. Frederick Fennell who had organized the Eastman Wind Ensemble in 1952 and who now directed it in the playing of a number of Civil War concerts in 1960 that directed popular interest back into native cultural traditions. Other professors, such as Bernard Rogers, taught and composed in the modern American temper as well.

The increased number of distractions in the metropolitan environment prompted Dr. Hanson, in an address opening his thirty-sixth year as director, to summon artists to a broader commitment to their creative functions. Many scientists at the university were similarly pledged to scholarship, and Dr. Marshak in 1960 welcomed to Rochester the tenth International Conference on High Energy Physics. Professors of the social sciences and the humanities were likewise engaged in the quest for truth. A conference on "Literature and the Arts in Contemporary Society," sponsored by the Department of English in 1958, and another a year later by the history department on "American Civilization" challenged students and faculty alike to avoid "imitations of imitations" and to employ their creative energies in social analysis. The university, the recently opened St. John Fisher College, the newly relocated Nazareth College, and the Rochester Institute of Technology each made determined efforts to expand and improve its facilities, but the mounting demand for college training, stimulated by the new aspirations of returned servicemen finally prompted the Board of Education to make a formal request in August 1960 for the creation of a publicly supported community college. A Bureau of Municipal Research study released in April had documented that need, pointing to the county rather than the city as the proper agency, a judgment on which County Manager Howe hastened to act.

Metropolitan Rochester's capacity to think and act as a community was abetted by its publishing and broadcasting services. Not only did the distribution regions of the daily papers and the listening and viewing areas of local radio and television stations extend throughout the county and beyond, but their news-gathering facilities also reached out for extensive coverage of a wide district. Both Gannett papers regularly printed early city editions, followed an hour or so later by main editions, which the *Democrat* first called a metropolitan edition in March 1960. They distributed these by home delivery throughout the county and sent other special editions for similar delivery in the built-up portions of six neighboring counties. Town and neighborhood weeklies served special districts, and although their coverage, except for the *Brighton-Pittsford Post*, tended to be narrowly local, the absorption of local radio and television stations by national chains gave their programs a less parochial, if not always a more sophisticated, character. Indeed the increasingly commercialized and packaged nature of the broadcasts intensified the demand for the inclusion of locally produced programs such as "Rochester, Where You Live" moderated by Professor Richard C. Wade, and "The Court of Public Opinion" moderated by Sol M. Linowitz. Advocates of educational television were not satisfied with this compromise approach, and the Rochester Area Educational Television Association, of which Harold Hacker became the new chairman in 1960, prepared to press its claim to the third television channel as soon as the FCC would make one available to Rochester.

In its cultural as in its economic and even in its civic aspects, Rochester was thus confidently preparing to assume its full metropolitan status and responsibilities.

10

Rochester—A Grass-Roots Metropolis, 1960–1980

MOST of the historic forces propelling Rochester's development as a regional metropolis were already in motion by the early 1960s. Its population had met the Census Bureau's numerical and mobility standards two decades before, and its growth and suburban surge had prompted the bureau to extend Rochester's metropolitan boundaries to encompass, in addition to its original double rings of Monroe County towns, those of three adjoining counties, Livingston, Wayne, and Orleans. The city's vibrant economy, long locally independent, was activating the development of this broader region and, as the city's origin, was serving again as the principal market center for its produce. Rochester's social and cultural institutions were likewise reaching out to participate in the life of its surrounding communities. Only a determined leadership committed to the formation of a metropolitan polity was lacking (as it was in the development of most American metropolises), but that lack could not stop the evolutionary process. Leaders were arising from several sources, grass-roots leaders, spokesmen for neighborhood and ethnic groups, organizers of occupational and professional groups—and the cacophony of their often conflicting exhortations was enlivening and would transform the Rochester community into what may best be described as a grass-roots metropolis.

A MOBILE AND CHANGING POPULATION

As during its earlier generations, the key to Rochester's development in the 1960s and 1970s was held by its inhabitants who were experiencing dramatic changes. Most of the crucial population trends were already in full swing, but their implication and consequences were only now coming to the fore. As we have previously noted, the city had reached a maximum of 332,488 inhabitants in 1950 and, chiefly because of its suburban surge, had dropped some 16,000 while Monroe's ten most thriving towns had increased by 100,000. That trend accelerated in the sixties as Rochester, now the "central city", dropped another 25,000 while its expanded metropolitan district increased by 126,000. The dichotomy would worsen in the seventies when the central city's loss of 54,492 exceeded the gains registered for Monroe's towns, which gave the county a loss of 10,401, the first in its history. Yet these declines, resulting from the shifting residential patterns of a thriving urban community that was spilling beyond the fixed city and county borders, served to highlight the centrifugal expansion of the metropolis. Not only were most of Monroe's nineteen towns experiencing a rapid development, two of them approaching capacity, but Rochester's suburban sprawl was also extending into three neighboring counties, dispelling their earlier stagnation, and boosting the population of Rochester's SMSA to 802,067 in 1970 and to 971,230 in 1980, when the Census Bureau included thriving Ontario County in Rochester's Metropolitan Statistical Areas. No comparable metropolis in the Northeast enjoyed such increases.

Yet hidden in the statistical and geographic expansion of the metropolis was a more startling and significant development, the surging growth of Rochester's black and Puerto Rican minorities. Although the nonwhites, who had tripled in number during the fifties, barely doubled during the sixties and would total only 73,639 in 1980, a simultaneous decline in the number of whites emphasized the demographic shift that was occurring. The blacks, numbering 62,332 in 1980, attained a ratio of one to every four whites and outnumbered the declining ranks of the foreign born. Some Negroes and a few Puerto Ricans were moving into the suburbs where they numbered 8,041 in 1970, but the great majority were locating in the inner-city wards, the third, fifth, seventh, eleventh and sixteenth wards, where many of the foreign born had clustered in former decades. By transforming the once cosmopolitan district north of the tracks on the east side and the old third ward on the west side (the only areas freely open to their settlement) into predominately black neighborhoods they were unwittingly providing Rochester with its first unabashed slums. In a city confident of its ability to assimilate newcomers, the resulting inner-city blight was a new experience, difficult to recognize, and because many of these newcomers were young adults of a child-bearing age, producing an upsurge in the number of children in their districts, the inner-city schools faced acute problems to be discussed later in this chapter. With an average age of 22 in 1960, a good ten years below that of white Rochesterians, and with limited education and few industrial skills, the blacks faced many disadvantages in the competition for jobs and homes.

Puerto Ricans, previously included in the nonwhite classification, along with Indians, Asians, and blacks, were first separately enumerated in 1960. The census listing of 1,990 as resident in Rochester was indignantly protested by their leaders who maintained that at least 3,000 resided in the city and that another 2,000 seasonal workers from Puerto Rico converged in Rochester from time to time. Whatever their numbers, the continued influx increased the city total to 5,456 by 1970 and to 10,345 by 1980 when the Spanish speaking total reached 13,153, most of them settling in the sixteenth ward with scattered clusters in the eighth and seventeenth wards. Unlike the Asians, whose lesser number, 600 in 1970 and 1,536 a decade later, and greater distance from homelands encouraged an earnest effort to master the language and customs of the community, the Puerto Ricans clung to their native speech and customs, which added to their problems in school and the workplace. Gradually, with the passing years, the Ibero-American Action League formed in the mid-sixties helped to bridge both gaps.

Because of the rapid influx of newcomers, especially blacks, and with the outflow of whites to the suburbs, the city lost the high degree of population stability maintained for several decades. Only twice during the previous century had the ratio of those reappearing in local directories over five-year spans fallen below 60 percent—in the depressions of the mid-1890s and the early 1930s—and now in the prosperous early and late 1960s the ratio dropped to 59.2 and 58.7 percent of the samples chosen. An increasing number of the out-migrants were moving to the outer ring of suburbs, maintaining the vitality of Rochester's SMSA, which, however, dropped from 33d to 39th place among the nation's metropolises during these decades.

A RESURGENT ECONOMY

Situated in the aged and somewhat stagnant Northeast, the Rochester area continued to grow because of the unusual vitality of its economy. Several technological breakthroughs sparked an expansion in industrial output that enabled the Rochester-Monroe County district to increase its employment from 243,000 in 1960, which was 95.6 percent of its labor force, to a peak of 317,300 six years later, when the number of unemployed fell to a low of 3,500 or barely 1.1 percent of the total. No community in the Northeast, and in fact none of the country's major metropolitan districts, could rival that accomplishment. According to George Steinlieb and James W. Hughes, only Rochester, the smallest of the nine major metropolises of the northeast, had escaped the decline all others had suffered from the interregional job shifts to the South and West.* And although several untoward factors were to produce a moderate decline in succeeding years, the city's economy displayed a resilience that contrasted sharply with reverses elsewhere.

Although nonmanufacturing workers already exceeded those in manufacturing by 10 percent in 1960, most observers now recognized that the key to the city's continued growth was held by its major fabricating industries. And, except for the processors of food products and apparel and printers and publishers, all the major firms were in the technological, electrical, and mechanical fields. Their quick adjustment to peacetime production had checked the early decline in industrial jobs and had helped to maintain relatively full employment by stimulating activity in the construction field, where the numbers employed had increased 50 percent during the fifties. Thus new capital construction by Rochester industries increased between 1954 and 1963 from $58 to $86 million for the metropolitan district, helping to boost employment by approximately 10,000. The annual announcement of new capital investments in its Rochester plants by Eastman Kodak increased from $34 million in 1961 to $48 million four years later and buttressed the confidence of nonindustrial as well as industrial workers, helping to assure Rochester's continued prosperity.

* George Steinlieb and James W. Hughes, *Post-Industrial America* (New Brunswick, N.J.: Rutgers Univ. Press, 1975), 80, 84, 94.

The formula for Kodak's success was basically related to the economy of the city and the nation. As the net earnings of the country's workers rose and their wages increased, their demand for the company's finished products assured a growing market and encouraged further technological improvements. Successive presidents and board chairmen—Thomas J. Hargrave, Albert K. Chapman, William S. Vaughn, Louis K. Eilers—not only promoted new research efforts and new technological innovations, resulting in the production, for example, of the new Instamatic camera released in 1963, but also hastened to grant wage and salary increases and generous wage dividends to assure the company's hold on the area's skilled workers and, incidentally, to promote a prosperous market. As Eastman's wage increases spurred other firms to make similar advances, its annual wage dividends, mounting steadily to $167 million in 1964, for example, gave a great boost to Rochester's retail economy and helped to push its annual sales well above the billion mark first reached in 1962.

Kodak's example not only promoted wage increases among local firms endeavoring to expand their production but also spurred the establishment of research departments to increase their technological proficiency. A state survey in 1967 listed 77 industrial research laboratories in the Rochester area and credited them with the employment of over 3,300 professional and technical workers. Some of the smaller firms pressed their research efforts so diligently that they exceeded the capacities of their production and sales departments and welcomed outside affiliations that led to their absorption by large conglomerates. Others developed the managerial talent and enterprise to promote their own innovations and to acquire new local or distant affiliates as well. Together they contributed to an increase of 50 percent in the value added to Rochester's industrial products between 1958 and 1963 and registered progressive gains in industrial employment that mounted annually from 1.1 percent in 1961 to 3.7 percent in 1964.

In the early sixties most of the industrial mergers and acquisitions, whether by expansive outside or local corporations, resulted in increased production in Rochester. The Commercial Controls Company, absorbed successively by the Friden Company and the Singer Company, was an example of the former trend and boosted its local work force above the 2,000 mark. The Stromberg-Carlson division of General Dynamics suffered fluctuations in its management, but the division continued to help that corporation retain its position as the second largest employer in Rochester in the early sixties. The much smaller Pfaudler Company, headed successively by Mercer Brugler and Donald A. Gaudion, provided a graphic demonstration of the expansive and absorptive capacities of vigorous local management. After acquiring the Permutit Company of New York in 1957, the Pfaudler Company successively added the Ritter dental and Castle hospital equipment companies and, finally, the Taylor Instruments Company, all creative local firms whose management and technical workers added to the strength and versatility of the city's most indigenous manufacturing company, which assumed the new name of the Sybron Corporation in 1968 and elected F. Ritter Shumway of the old Ritter Company as chairman of the board.

The real breakthrough had already occurred at Haloid-Xerox, as previously noted, though few, even among the insiders, fully grasped the proportion. Its first photocopying machine, released in 1950 as Xerox copier 914, had proved so successful that the company had launched the construction of a new factory in nearby Webster. Its work force there had increased to 1,000 by 1961, when the company simplified its name to the Xerox Corporation. As the annual sales and rentals soared to $268 million by 1964, the company devoted 10 percent of the gross returns to research, expanded its research and engineering division to 1,000 workers, approximately one-tenth of the total, and developed a copy printer and two additional copiers, greatly increasing the versatility and speed of their performance. As expansion in Webster progressed, the company doubled and then tripled the original 400-acre site, opened many new marketing outlets in America and abroad, and increased its total employment from 4,000 in 1961 to 11,300 in 1964. Its offices on the twelfth floor of the new Midtown Tower were already outgrown, and plans for a new 26-story building to be erected nearby were quickly discarded that year in favor of a more imposing 30-story office tower designed by Welton Becket of Los Angeles. When completed four years later, it became the dominant feature on the metropolitan skyline.

Although the phenomenal rise of the Xerox Corporation under the leadership of Joseph C. Wilson as president dwarfed many other

accomplishments in Rochester, several firms made noteworthy advances. Kodak, even without its massive new developments, still held
undisputed first place; together, the two Rochester divisions of General Dynamics held second place until surpassed by Xerox in the
mid-sixties. The two local division of General Motors—Delco and
Rochester Products—hired more workers and held a firm grasp
on fourth place, ahead of Bausch & Lomb, the Gleason Works, and
Ritter-Pfaudler until it became Sybron. Each of these firms developed
promising new innovations and enjoyed an expanding market. In contrast, several of the apparel firms and the food processors were reducing their operations partly because of their inability to attract skilled
workers in the tight labor market created by the technological firms.

The construction industry was booming, as were other nonmanufacturing enterprises. Shortly after the completion of the new Midtown Plaza—the largest enclosed shopping area in the nation—in
1961, plans for a spacious suburban shopping center, Pittsford Plaza,
were announced, with Edwards, the third largest downtown department store, a major participant. All the downtown leaders now had
their suburban branches, reflecting their recognition of the city's outward expansion. But Sibley's, now one of the twelve major stores of
the Associated Dry Goods Corporation of New York, dispatched six
buyers to Europe in 1961 to replenish the stock in its main store in
order to offset the advantage that McCurdy's, its leading competitor,
had acquired with the opening of the Midtown Plaza across Main
Street. Several of the banks, which were backing these developments
with sizeable loans, undertook to refurbish or rebuild their headquarters, and the dramatic new tower of the Security Trust, suspended on
stilts over a new street-level plaza at the corner of Main Street and
East Avenue, completed in 1964, provided a fit symbol of the city's
nonmanufacturing enterprises, which increased their employment by
14,000 during the first four years of the decade.

As the employment in contract construction increased in Monroe
County by 40 percent between 1959 and 1965, homebuilding likewise experienced a boom, but practically all of it was in the suburbs.
A planning bureau tabulation of the number of housing units demolished within the city in the early sixties for the construction of ex-
pressways and renewal projects recorded a total of 1,852 losses, which
were in part offset by the construction of 1,602 new housing units

within the city, mostly low- or middle-income rental apartments. In the towns, where the number of new housing permits mounted from 3,157 in 1961 to 5,451 four years later, the number of residential units increased 18 percent, almost matching the population growth of 19 percent as the migration from the city maintained the pressure for new housing. The pressure was even greater within the city, especially for in-migrating blacks, for the demolitions and boarding-up of many houses reduced the number of vacancies created by out-migrating whites and caused mounting densities in districts where reconversions were transforming old single-family houses into multiple dwellings.

The Gannett Press, which had alerted Rochester to the presence of racial discrimination in an excellent series on "The New Negro" by Desmond Stone and Jack Germond, published in the *Times-Union* in June 1960, featured occasional articles on local inner-city problems, but its major attention, like that of most residents, was on the city's remarkable metropolitan growth and industrial prosperity. The Gannett Press was sharing that prosperity and enjoying a remarkable expansion itself. Paul Miller, who had succeeded Frank Gannett as president, greatly increased the number of outside acquisitions in his first few years and vigorously promoted a wider metropolitan distribution of his two Rochester papers to reach an average daily circulation of 136,000 and 203,000 on Sundays, by 1965. Despite the attention they gave to current problems at home and throughout the country, notably the rising debate over civil rights, their prevailing tone was optimistic and helped to buttress the widely held confidence in Rochester's continued wellbeing.

ANTECEDENTS OF THE RIOTS

Rochester's composure was suddenly shattered in July 1964 by the outbreak of inner-city riots. Mounting tensions in other northern cities had prompted the *Democrat & Chronicle* to dispatch Earl Caldwell, a young Negro reporter who had recently joined the staff, to New York to report on the riots that had broken out in Harlem and Brooklyn. One of his articles and a related editorial by Cliff Carpenter appeared on inside pages of the July 25 issue, which carried the startling banner headline, "Negro Mob Riots Here." Little else received attention during the next two days while the rioting continued, but when it subsided following the arrival of a dozen trucks loaded with armed guardsmen, many citizens, after soberly viewing the scenes of carnage in the streets or on their TV screens, began excitedly to debate the possible causes and to piece together the records of past events that should have given warning of the unexpected riots.

Numerous Rochesterians had become aware of varied aspects of the problem, but none had gauged its full dimensions. The three leading settlement houses, each in a rapidly changing neighborhood, had been pressing for several years for additional support from the Community Chest for new programs and, with the Council of Social Agencies, had advocated the opening of a local office of the State Commission Against Discrimination. The establishment of the Human Relations Committee, soon renamed a commission, by the city and county in 1960 had led to the opening of a SCAD office to provide the indispensable legal action, and the Rochester Area Council of Churches had reactivated its Commission on Race and Religion by naming Mrs. Harper Sibley as its chair. Several black and white clergymen and choirs occasionally exchanged places in gestures of good will, and many white church members signed pledges to welcome Negroes as neighbors. The NAACP coordinated the efforts of several groups that endeavored to assist blacks in renting or buying homes in the more salubrious neighborhoods. But the increasing ratios of nonwhites to whites in the third, seventh, eleventh, and adjoining inner-city wards revealed the limited effect of these programs.

If the sponsors of most of those efforts had the middle-class Negro in mind, others were becoming concerned about unskilled workers and youths who had not yet found their place. With many other cities Rochester was suffering an upsurge of juvenile delinquency and a growing roster of unemployed teenagers. White as well as black youths were involved, and the newly created City-County Youth Board endeavored to serve both groups. William J. Bub, appointed executive director in August 1961, hastened to seek state aid for a program of counseling for dropouts designed to assure suitable jobs for idle youths or to steer them into training programs. He found the new director of the office of the State Employment Service, Edward S. Croft, eager to cooperate with this effort, especially after the passage of the federal Manpower Development and Training Act (MDTA) in 1962 provided a source of funds. Their efforts were quickened as rumblings of discontent among the unemployed, in a city of relatively full employment, focused attention on the fact that many of them were blacks. The additional fact that many lacked skills useful in a technological city supplied little comfort, and the police, often called in to quell a disturbance, bore the brunt of Negro complaints. Despite the appointment of the first black to the force in 1960, hostilities began to mount on both sides.

A series of loosely related incidents shattered the community's apathy. The trouble started in August 1962 when two policemen forcibly arrested Rufus Fairwell as he closed a service station at which he was employed. Alleging that Fairwell had refused to identify himself and had resisted arrest, the officers took him to headquarters where Fairwell claimed he was further beaten. Popular indignation mounted when the grand jury cleared both Fairwell, who had suffered two fractured vertebrae, and the two policemen of assault charges. A United Action Committee representing various portion of the black community and such mixed groups as the NAACP, the Human Relations Commission, and the Federation of Churches, appealed for an investigation by the Department of Justice and raised a Rufus Fairwell fund to finance the case. While this case was under review, a second incident, arising from a police investigation of a report that a group of Black Muslims were assembling firearms, resulted in a scuffle as the Muslims refused to permit the police to interrupt a religious meeting that Malcolm X was conducting in their headquarters. The police brought charges of riot against those who resisted their entry, but Malcolm X used the incident to advantage in gaining publicity for his cause. The situation became more tense when, two weeks later, a Negro charged with drunken driving, resisted arrest and suffered a broken arm and other injuries that sent him to the hospital. Amid the rising clamor, Chief of Police William M. Lombard suspended and then reinstated the four policemen involved in that arrest. Vigorously protesting that action, the newly formed Integrated Non-Violence Committee staged an all-day, all-night sit-in vigil at police headquarters and secured a pledge from City Manger Porter Homer to submit the matter to a citizens' review board. The City Council soon authorized the appointment of a Police

Advisory Board, similar to the pioneer body of that sort in Philadelphia, and its creation brought a welcome relaxation of tension.

The police were not the only ones placed under review because
of the increased intensity of the Negro protest. Churches, schools,
social agencies, employers, and labor unions all faced a critical reex-
amination of the adequacy and justice of their programs. Thus Executive Director Bub of the Youth Board, impatient with the inaction of
the Council of Social Agencies, invited a number of agency directors
to a special workshop on inner-city problems held at Syracuse in
September 1963. Aware of some of the experimental programs recently launched in New York and Boston, among other cities, under
the auspices of the Ford Foundation and in response to the proddings
of President Kennedy's Committee on Juvenile Delinquency, Bub,
Croft, and other directors laid plans for the development of more
extensive, but informal, counseling services at existing settlements
and for an increased provision of training facilities under the Manpower Development Training Act. On returning to Rochester, they
secured the cooperation of the Board of Education in the operation of
a job training center in the city hall annex that served some 3,000
applicants during the year. Supported by state youth funds, two settlement houses added black workers to their staffs to help the counselors
placed there by the employment service recruit idle youths for training programs.

Several additional moves occurred that year. Local leaders of the
AFL-CIO agreed to meet in a civil rights seminar at the library to
explore the possibility of increasing the opportunities of Negroes
seeking to become apprentices in various trades or requesting admittance to various unions. Troubled by the mounting clamor against
discrimination, a number of industrialists held several informal conferences with Negro leaders and agreed to reexamine the employment practices of their firms; both Kodak and Xerox strengthened
their in-plant training programs.

Perhaps the most dramatic move in the civil rights field in Rochester was that made by the Board of Education when, in September
1963, it released a tentative proposal for the reduction of de facto
segregation. The plan, submitted to the State Commissioner of Education in response to his request for local action in this field, won
praise as the most forthright of any received by that office. It an-

nounced plans for a voluntary open enrollment scheme, which would facilitate the transfer of selected pupils from schools with nonwhite enrollments in excess of 50 percent to others showing a deficiency. It outlined further steps to be taken in the years ahead to promote integration. Unfortunately, the release of these plans brought an outburst of protests from some of the parents of children in the receiving schools. Two districts in particular, dominated by an ethnic group that had only recently surmounted discriminatory practices, instituted legal suits to safeguard their schools from a black invasion. Shocked by the open display of bigotry, editors, clergymen, and educators spoke out strongly in the board's defense and disparaged the affront to the city's Negroes.

Of course that affront was only the latest of many that were not soon forgotten. Among the agencies engaged in the campaign against discrimination, those that enrolled numerous Negroes tended now to become more exclusive. The local chapter of the NAACP became more militant and relegated its white members of the back benches. Some Negroes who attracted favor from the white community, a Junior Chamber award, for example, lost stature among their fellows, who now began to insist on their identity as blacks. Only in the arts, sports, and politics, where distinction had to be won competitively, was public honor held with pride in the black community, as William Warfield, the Rochester-born baritone, Walter Dukes and Luke Easter on the playing field, and Mrs. Constance Mitchell, the Third Ward supervisor, demonstrated.

Despite the election of not one but two blacks to the Board of Supervisors in 1961, the civil rights question and other inner-city problems had played little part in the political developments of the early sixties. The reform Democrats, who had captured control of the Board of Education two years before, unexpectedly gained a majority in the City Council in 1961 and proceeded to elect Henry F. Gillette, the councilman from the northwest district, as mayor. An able attorney and the first Rochester mayor of Italian extraction, Gillette supplied strong leadership and helped draw experienced professionals into the city's service: William F. Denne from Buffalo as director of urban development, William M. Lombard from Batavia as chief of police, and Porter W. Homer from Tucson as the first professionally trained city manager. But Gillette's leadership was so meticulous and exacting that his fellow Democrats, after securing their hold on the council in the elections two years later, chose the affable Frank Lamb, council-man-at-large, to succeed him as Rochester's sixtieth mayor in January 1964. Mayor Lamb, a staff member of the YMCA and long active in the Community Chest, placed his confidence in the Human Relations Commission and associated welfare agencies and deplored the labeling of Negroes who collaborated with the commission as Uncle Toms.

Somewhat bewildered by the rejection of their well-meant overtures, few of the Negro's white friends saw it as a measure of the depths of his humiliation or comprehended the intensity of the black's reaction to all forms of patronage. But if white Rochesterians, confident of their tolerance and humanity, were unprepared for the rioting that started on a hot Friday night in July 1964, most of the city's blacks were equally astonished and unprepared.

RIOTS AND REPERCUSSIONS

Never before had Rochester experienced such a shocking ordeal as that of the riots of 1964. The great flood of 1865 and the great snowstorms of 1958 had been crippling natural calamities, as was the Sibley fire of 1905; the frightening succession of fires, in 1908 and 1909, many of them of incendiary origin, and one of which leveled the Rochester ghetto east of Gibbs Street, had human origins and stirred bitter group hostilities. Yet none had disclosed such deep feelings of resentment and frustration on the part of a large segment of the community as the riots, and none had so many or such enduring repercussions.

The incident that precipitated the rioting was a commonplace one, and the police who responded to a call to remove a drunken man from a street dance they had authorized in the Seventh Ward on a hot Friday night in July 1964 anticipated no trouble. But when a number of young blacks intervened to prevent the arrest and the police radioed for reinforcements, a crowd gathered and became increasingly restless. When two cars with police dogs arrived to assist in the arrest, the disturbance acquired a new and unexpected dimension—a confrontation with racial and civil rights overtones.

Several years before, a demonstration by some 200 young blacks headed by Lakey Ashford, a Third Ward native and Montgomery Center member, had marched to the police headquarters in Rochester in 1961, protesting the use of police dogs in making arrests particularly in Negro areas; it was an affront to their dignity and rights as men, they shouted. No promises had been made, but an assertion of rights had been expressed, and resentments festered as the practice continued to be used sporadically. The appearance of the dogs on this hot July night of 1964 ignited angry hostilities. As the disorder mounted, the sound of breaking glass transformed the crowd into a mob of rioters and looters who quickly spread throughout the ward. Chief of Police Lombard hastened to the scene and, hoping to quiet the disturbance by a conciliatory gesture, called his men back and advanced alone, urging the rioters to go home. But it was too late for reason to prevail, and as one of the police cars was overturned and set afire, the chief escaped serious injury only with the aid of some friendly Negroes. Other efforts to pacify the mob proved equally futile, and despite the arrival of additional police, the rioting extended up and down Joseph Avenue, formerly a Jewish district with many of the old merchants still in business there, and spread into North Clinton and neighboring streets. A state of emergency was declared; calls for assistance were issued to the county sheriff and dispatched to the state police. The officers were ordered to hold their fire, except when needed to prevent personal injury, and even the fire trucks that arrived to quell the numerous fires were restrained from using their hoses against the rioters, until a threatened confrontation near the station of two groups—one of whites, the other of blacks—prompted a dispersal of the advancing mobs with streams of water. Despite the arrest of hundreds of looters, the rioting continued until dawn when a ominous quiet settled over the devastated district.

While most Rochesterians first heard and discussed the shocking news of the riots in the privacy of their homes on Saturday morning, Mayor Lamb, City Manger Homer, Chief Lombard, and Sheriff Albert Skinner met with other officials to lay plans for the weekend. The first contingent of state police had begun to arrive at 4:30 that morning, and they soon established roadblocks in an attempt to prevent the influx of new troublemakers, either whites or blacks. A curfew was announced to be in effect from 8 P.M. to 7 A.M., banning all street

traffic and the congregation of crowds throughout the city, and order-
ing the closure of all bars and liquor stores for the duration. Civil
rights leaders, clergymen, and social workers held hasty conferences
and pleaded for conciliation, but as news reports of the destruction
spread, those with contacts in the Seventh or Third wards saw the
tension increase as hostile shouts greeted refuse workers who endeavored to clear the rubble from the streets.

The second night produced even more destructive rioting. While
the curfew effectively kept most whites out of the troubled areas that
night, it failed to restrain the marauding bands of blacks who again
shattered windows and looted stores not previously reached in the
Seventh Ward, and the rioting spread along South Plymouth, Clarissa,
and Jefferson streets in the Third Ward. By midnight some 550 police
officers were patrolling the streets, but shortly after each column of
deputies passed, the looters reemerged, and bottles filled with gasoline occasionally descended from an upper story of Hanover Houses
as the police approached. The officers arrested looters and curfew
violators and made frequent use of tear gas and high-pressure streams
of water to break up crowds. As the violence mounted 35 policemen
suffered riot injuries, and some 300 persons were taken to area hospitals; four deaths occurred, all apparently accidental, three of them in
an observation helicopter that crashed.

Sunday was a grim day in Rochester as 1,500 helmeted militiamen
moved in and established camp near the Culver Street armory.
Church attendance was light, but a group of clergymen meeting at
the Divinity School admonished Christians to "judge not that ye be
not judged," and the Reverend Arthur L. Whitaker of the Mt. Olivet
Baptist Church in the Third Ward warned that "while violence cannot
be condoned it must be understood." Confined to their homes for a
third night of curfew, many citizens debated the causes and character
of the riots. The argument became especially tense among the white
residents in Chatham Gardens, the integrated low-cost renewal project adjoining Hanover Houses in the Seventh Ward—should they
join the white exodus to the suburbs or continue to hold their ground?
Outside, Rochester enjoyed a night of relative quiet. A contingent to
twelve trucks loaded with armed guardsmen had moved slowly
through the former battle areas in a show of force that evening, but
otherwise these men were held in reserve, and the city and state

police patrolled the now empty streets. Citizens were able on Monday morning to move freely into town, and the central business district assumed a normal appearance. Children in the devastated districts boarded the buses that left from Montgomery and Baden Street settlements for day camps in the parks.

As tension eased on Monday, city officials lifted the curfew but held the militia in reserve for any possible outbreak. The courts quickly released with suspended sentences 659 of the 976 arrested but remanded the cases of 317 for grand jury action on riot or felony charges. A tabulation of the arrested persons revealed that 792 were blacks, 153 whites, and 31 Puerto Ricans; 85 of the total were women. The largest group, 188 were in the 25 to 29 age bracket, while 166 were teenagers, and these comprised most of the 243 who declared themselves unemployed. A closer study of those held for further action revealed that 35 percent had been residents of Rochester for ten years of more and only 18 percent had come to the city within the year. No evidence of outside instigation was detected, and Rochesterians were impelled to accept the crisis as an indigenous one and to seek local solutions.

In the weeks following the riots, Rochesterians moved on several levels to attack the newly exposed problems. The 792 blacks arrested were, of course, only a fraction of those involved, and not a representative fraction at that, but it was the best sample available. Clearly, the many unemployed youths were a major problem, overshadowing and obscuring the condition of those underemployed and frustrated adults unable to rise from years of labor into satisfying jobs. The looting and violence highlighted the criminal aspects of the riot and distinguished it from the civil rights protests in the South in which Rochesterians, blacks (including Ashford) as well as whites, had participated, but as peaceful victims, not as perpetrators of the resultant violence. Thus the problems facing Rochester were in the black community, many felt, not in society at large, as in the South.

Surely, a rich and compassionate city could solve them. The Human Relations Commission tripled its request for funds in order to open offices in the two devastated districts. The Police Advisory Board prepared to tackle a heavy schedule of hearings of cases resulting from the riots. The settlement houses intensified their efforts to recruit neighborhood youths in their programs. Several middle-class Negroes volunteered to serve as counselors in a Big Brother and Big Sister movement for fatherless teenagers. A voter-registration committee launched an effort to register 10,000 additional Negroes in Monroe County.

Desmond Stone, soon to be named editor of the *Democrat & Chronicle*, wrote a series of perceptive articles entitled "Rochester Riots—A Scar? or a Spur?" Published in the *Times-Union*, they helped to stimulate a variety of responses. The city manager appointed a task force on poverty and prepared to submit an application for assistance from the federal government. A group of business leaders launched a study of unemployment in Rochester and, meanwhile, backed a move to establish a local chapter of the Urban League. The Board of Education endeavored to upgrade its inner-city schools, extended closed circuit television to twelve elementary and two high schools, and launched a new Beacon Project under which the ethnic and racial experiences and traditions of local children were drawn into their classroom programs. But this was only a start as Superintendent Herman Goldberg prepared to draft a full schedule of reforms designed to achieve a better racial balance and a more creative program of instruction. In the Council of Churches, too, new leaders were emerging with new approaches to Rochester's problems. Indeed, if the city had in former decades sometimes seemed a bit complacent, even smug as some charged, the riots had transformed it into a community of activists abounding in leaders whose zeal and self-confidence proved inspiring, though the multiplicity of conflicting programs soon threatened to block effective action.

The first breakthrough occurred when Croft of the employment service launched Operation Outreach by sending job counselors into the streets. The State Employment Service and the Board of Education had jointly secured a grant of $1 million from the federal government for an MDTA program for high school dropouts and other youths, but few from the inner city had responded. To recruit them Croft and Harry Bray of Montgomery Center, the first Negro director of a settlement house, engaged a team of street workers early in July 1964 and placed them on the streets in August in the wake of the riots. By the end of the year they had enrolled over 600 young people from the inner city for training courses; when local funds ran short, they secured aid from the State Division of Youth. William J. Bub, who procured that grant, collaborated closely with the recruiting efforts, which soon increased the number enrolled to over one thousand.

In the meantime the city manager's antipoverty task force had successfully organized Action for a Better Community (ABC) and had secured the services of Drs. Walter M. Lifton and Walter Cooper as director and associate director, respectively, on leave from their jobs with the Board of Education and Eastman. Lifton and Cooper secured federal grants of antipoverty funds for almost a score of projects calling for an expenditure of more than $3 million in the first year. They launched the first two programs—the Lighted Schoolhouses and the Neighborhood Youth Corps summer supplement—in June and ten more in July. Otis E. Finley, Jr., former associate director of the National Urban League, arrived that month as permanent director and took over the work of implementing a half-dozen major projects.

Because most of these projects were for youths, Mayor Lamb encouraged the newly formed Urban League of Rochester to apply for federal funds to set up an On-The-Job Training Program for unemployed or underemployed adults. With the mayor's backing and the assurance of cooperation from numerous industries, the league secured a grant of $203,089 to hire an OJT director and two assistants and to reimburse cooperating employers up to $25 a week for on-the-job training given to some 400 enrolees who received regular wages for such jobs as machinist, welder, typist, and sales worker. Because of the poor communications with the poor, unexpected difficulty in recruiting and holding suitable workers prompted a linking of OJT with the Neighborhood Youth Corps of ABC in order to provide a continuing program for the youths recruited for that project and to improve their chances of securing permanent jobs.

The recruiting difficulties encountered by the out-of-town directors of these projects stemmed, in part, from, and helped to account for, a rival program launched in the spring and summer of 1965 by a group of dedicated churchmen. It was early in January, shortly after the launching of ABC, that news broke of the plans of the Board of Urban Ministry to invite Saul Alinsky of Chicago to Rochester to organize the Negroes for their own protection and improvement. Alinsky, a professional organizer of minority groups, with The Woodlawn Organization of Chicago (TWO) as his chief accomplishment,

was currently directing a program at Syracuse University that involved training blacks and other minority representatives in the techniques of organizing poor people. Backed by funds from the Office of
Economic Opportunity (OEO), Alinsky was endeavoring to train field
workers to organize the tenants of housing projects and the recipients
of welfare to supply the "maximum feasible participation" called for
in the Economic Opportunity Act. His objectives, as he approached
Rochester, was to transform the attack on the problems of the Negro
into an attack on the city's latent racism. His interpretation of the
riots as an angry blind civil rights protest, demanding a reform of the
community's attitude toward Negroes, posed a new and disturbing
challenge.

Scorning ABC and similar organizations in other cities as examples of "welfare colonialism," Alinsky won the backing of the Board
of Urban Ministry, charged by the Council of Churches to take up
the cause of the oppressed blacks. As the board's action in pledging
$100,000 to secure Alinsky's services for two years produced a bitter
controversy in many churches, the Gannett papers, a radio station,
and numerous other community leaders called for a reconsideration;
but their opposition helped to demonstrate the impact that Alinsky's
abrasive methods could produce and won him the invitation from at
least a portion of the black community on which he had insisted.
Reveling in the opposition he had aroused, Alinsky soon attracted a
number of angry blacks to his side, among them Minister Franklin D.
R. Florence of the Church of Christ, who was elected president of the
organization called FIGHT at its first convention that June. With a
turnout of approximately 1,500 delegates who carried signs identifying the participating societies and agencies, the convention overflowed the Ritter-Clark gym of the Rochester Institute of Technology
(RIT) leased for the occasion. The convention succeeded in launching the new movement pledged to "the goal of unifying the Negro
people of Rochester in order that they may assume their rightful role
in solving the problems and determining the courses of action that
affect their lives in this city."

Shunning all political alignments, an organization known as Freedom, Integration, God, Honor, and Today (FIGHT) specifically proposed to "strive for social justice in the areas of housing, education,
employment, poverty, youth, law enforcement, urban renewal and in

matters pertaining to good government." With such a comprehensive agenda, FIGHT posed a challenge not only to ABC but also to the leadership of the Council of Social Agencies, the Community Chest, the Board of Education, the Department of Urban Renewal, and other established agencies. Thus when ABC scheduled a series of open meetings conducted by its Citizens Advisory Council in poverty areas to publicize its programs, representatives of FIGHT appeared and raised questions concerning the salaries of its administrators recruited from outside. It demanded and secured representation on that board and on the boards of other community agencies and attacked the Board of Education for not moving more effectively against de facto segregation.

An umbrella organization marshalling the interests and energies of existing black societies and churches, FIGHT accepted the financial support of sympathetic white churches and the backing of Friends of FIGHT but excluded them from its meetings and deliberations. Its activities and programs would, of necessity, be participatory, but its leadership was grass-roots and sought to rally the support of blacks by an adversarial assertion of their rights and claims. Dramatic opportunities soon appeared.

The first big display of power by FIGHT was at the public hearing called by the city on its proposed urban renewal project for the redevelopment of the Third Ward. The $28 million project devised by the urban renewal planners had been rushed by the city to answer the demands of many blacks for better housing. At the hearing in Madison High School, numerous speakers protested that the plan had been prepared without the "maximum feasible participation" of the residents and was branded as "Negro removal." Shaken by the volume of protests, the City Council postponed action for eighteen months until the urban renewal department accepted a subsidiary of FIGHT as the project developer for a low-cost housing development on the old hospital site originally reserved for the Board of Education. Fight Square, as it was named, was not completed, however, for another four years because the developers encountered the many construction, labor, financing, and administrative difficulties that delayed most such projects.

FIGHT had meanwhile found a still more dramatic opportunity for a demonstration of its power in an attack on the Eastman Kodak

Company. That confrontation reflected and sprang from the opposing philosophies held by the city's dominant majority and insurgent minority. Ostensibly, both sides were endeavoring to reduce unemployment and to relieve hardships in the inner city, but as events progressed, each became more determined to maintain or establish its power, and because of popular concern over the Negro question, the contest acquired national interest.

The issue had its origin in the business community's search for the causes of the riots. Surprised at the large number unemployed or underemployed among those arrested during the riots, in a community that had the lowest ratio of unemployment in the country, Russell McCarthy of the Industrial Management Council and Loftus Carson of the Human Relations Commission, among other interested executives, secured a grant from the Wegman Foundation to launch a study by the Bureau of Municipal Research of the high incidence of unemployment in the nonwhite community in a time of general prosperity. That study, commenced early in 1965, paralleled another by the National Industrial Conference Board, which was analyzing the character and high incidence of local job vacancies in the Rochester area. Industrialists, faced early in 1966 with a tight labor market in which the number of vacancies exceeded the number of unemployed, readily collaborated with both studies, and as the results became known, emphasizing the need for additional facilities for training of the unskilled, Kodak, Xerox, Pfaudler, and several other firms increased their in-plant instruction programs and supported an expansion of the industrial training programs at RIT. Requests for job applicants ready to undertake such training programs were sent to the Urban League, the settlement houses, and FIGHT, as well as to Croft of the employment service and MDTA.

Thus, in response to such an invitation from Xerox, FIGHT undertook to supply trainees for its Project Step Up, in which the selected applicants were paid to attend ten-week courses designed to fit them for specific jobs. But other agencies were ready to provide that cooperative assistance, and to differentiate itself from the posture of those supplying workers for the jobs industrialists assigned to them, FIGHT assumed the role of labor's representative. When in September 1966 Minister Florence demanded that Kodak hire 600 hard-core unemployed to be recruited by FIGHT over the next 18 months,

William S. Vaughn, as president, affirmed the company's readiness to undertake the training and employment of additional Negroes. Vaughn welcomed FIGHT's assistance in increasing their representation among his employees, but he declared an inability to guarantee a specific number of jobs and rejected the bid for an exclusive agreement. After further discussion had proved inconclusive, FIGHT withdrew and launched a public attack on Kodak. The company at this point accepted the offer of an assistant vice-president, whose wife was a member of the Friends of Fight, to reopen the negotiations. But when Vice-president John G. Mulder signed an agreement recognizing FIGHT as the company's exclusive agent in the recruiting of blacks, with certain responsibility over their continued performance, the Kodak management promptly repudiated the contract. The company, long adamant in its refusal to share its managerial power with any union, was not about to make such a concession to FIGHT, but the national publicity Minister Florence secured, backed by the local Friends of Fight and by the church groups Alinsky had rallied to his varied causes, proved embarrassing.

The publication and circulation in the midst of this controversy of the long-awaited "Study of the Unemployed" by the Bureau of Municipal Research alerted responsible citizens to the urgent need for improved arrangement for recruiting and training of the unemployed to supply the additional workers Rochester industries needed. It was early in January that Dr. Gene Bartlett, president of the Colgate Rochester Divinity School, invited a group of clergymen and business leaders to a series of sessions at the school to seek a proper solution. Among those who attended were Vaughn of Kodak, Wilson of Xerox, Gaudion of Ritter-Pfaudler, George S. Beinetti of Rochester Telephone Company, McCarthy of the Industrial Management Council, Croft of the employment service and MDTA, Mrs. Harper Sibley, current president of the Council of Churches, and Minister Florence or a deputy from FIGHT. After several months of earnest discussion, the group reached agreement on the establishment of Rochester Jobs, Incorporated (RJI) "to mobilize the resources of the Rochester area to develop a community wide program" to insure the training and hiring of the hard-core unemployed. Although FIGHT failed to secure an assignment of quotas to each participating firm, its stand prodded the members to commit themselves as a group to undertake to train and employ 1,500 of the unemployed to be recruited by FIGHT and other agencies in the Rochester area. With the appointment of Edward S. Croft as director in June 1967, RJI got off to a good start.

Among the other agencies with which RJI cooperated was the Urban League, now under the direction of Laplois Ashford. With a long record in the civil rights movement in Rochester and New York, Ashford had resigned his position as deputy commissioner of public safety, the highest post held by a Negro in Rochester, to accept the task of revitalizing the Urban League in January 1967; and already he had infused new energies into its educational, housing, and employment divisions. He had made Project Uplift, formerly a summer program, a year-round operation, had established a housing service known as Operation Equality, and now launched a new clerical training program (ACT) to assure the advancement of workers in that field. The continued operation of the league's Neighborhood Youth Corps and on-the-job training programs and the decision of one Project Uplift team to establish a newspaper called the *Black Chronicle* demonstrated the vitality of its programs.

The Urban League's success in placing some trainees at Kodak and the active participation of the league as well as ABC and the settlement houses in referring applicants to RJI made FIGHT ready in June to respond when Vaughn brought Daniel P. Moynihan, the distinguished Harvard professor, to Rochester to negotiate a settlement of the company's controversy with FIGHT. After a week of secret negotiations the two antagonists agreed to work together to recruit and train unemployed blacks for openings at the company's plants, but they made no pledges as to the number of jobs to be filled or claims of exclusive representation.

The settlement, though not a clear victory, was welcomed by all concerned because the increasing number of inner-city riots throughout the country threatened a new outburst in Rochester. Minister Florence, when rebuffed at the company's annual meeting in April, had announced plans for a national pilgrimage of civil rights protestors to Rochester on the third anniversary of its riots to demonstrate their indignation against Kodak. That demonstration was cancelled following the agreement in June, but in the early weeks of July rumors spread of plans by disaffected Negro youths to commemorate the earlier outbreak. The police, now better trained to meet such emergencies, sent water trucks to wet streets occasionally used for drag races and quickly sealed off an area in the Seventh Ward where, on Sunday, July 24, a gang began to pelt passing cars with bottles and other missiles.

Representative of FIGHT, concerned that an outbreak of rioting would disprove its claim of being able to direct Negro protests into nonviolent confrontations, successfully quieted the disturbance that night, and city officials assembled the leaders of all interested groups for earnest conferences on Monday. Despite renewed outbreaks that evening, with several bursts of gunfire and scattered fire bombings, the police, who shot and killed one of four armed blacks who tried to break through their lines, successfully maintained control. With a show of force but under careful restraint, assisted by the entreaties of Negro leaders, they managed to avoid a serious outbreak. The press, busy with reports of the rioting at Detroit and a dozen other cities, gave the local disturbance objective coverage but waited a week before reporting its incidents in detail in an article by Peter Behr and Desmond Stone. The article contrasted the handling of the inner-city conflicts of 1964 and 1967 and congratulated the community on the greater maturity it had attained.

The task of persuading industries in need of workers to undertake the employment and training of unskilled blacks proved easier than that of opening the better housing in the city and its suburbs to Negro occupancy. FIGHT had inadvertently stalled urban renewal in the Third Ward, and repeated delays in the construction of Fight Square and of the Rush Project on outlying Floverton Street, promoted by the five settlement houses, further delayed the provision of rental housing for low-income families. A tabulation in August 1967 revealed the completion in the previous twelve years of only approximately 500 public housing units for families and another 100 for aged persons, plus approximately 1,000 low-rental units, most of them for aged couples, by Rochester Management and other limited-dividend bodies. The Rochester Housing Authority had plans for the early construction of some 500 additional units, and private groups for another 800, but the demand was increasing more rapidly than the supply. Despite the pledges churchmen received from parishioners willing to rent or sell to Negroes, few openings developed in the suburbs except for well-to-do black families. The Council of Social

Agencies, the Human Relations Commissions, and the Urban League, as well as several church groups, had agents ready to assist Negroes in the purchase or rental of decent homes, but many able to afford them objected to the subterfuges required to complete the deal.

Rochester's business leaders, long aware of the tight housing situation, had created the Metropolitan Rochester Foundation chaired by Joseph C. Wilson in March 1967 to meet it. Because of the difficulties involved in the selection of sites for low-cost housing for poor families, the foundation under the direction of Wilson and John Dale assumed the task of constructing two projects for the Rochester Housing Authority within the city and, after several rebuffs from neighboring towns, secured a 40-acre tract in Pittsford where in partnership with the state's newly established Urban Development Corporation (UDC) it constructed the 300 two-bedroom town-house Gleason Estates. To promote better housing for the underprivileged, several Rochesterians, led again by Wilson, created a Martin Luther King Memorial Housing Fund to which Wilson gave a personal check of $250,000. Its various programs for the upgrading of existing housing, the promotion of self-help projects, as well as the 53-unit project on Bronson Avenue built by the housing arm of the Southern Christian Leadership Conference, helped improve the accommodations of numerous blacks but left the major problem of housing the poor to be tackled by UDC.

The Rochester Business Opportunities Corporation (RBOC) was the third major effort of local industrialists to meet the challenge of the in-migrating blacks. Its offer of volunteer staff members to work with enterprising blacks who wished to establish new ventures—a store, a workshop, or a service station—and its assistance in procuring capital and opening up markets helped launch some eighty businesses during the next three years. And although some of them collapsed, other prospered and their managers and employees acquired valuable experience in the process. Some managers, disappointed in their hopes for quick profits, dismissed the efforts of RBOC as "tokenism," but others valued the new self-reliance they acquired. Fighton, organized in 1968 to produce special parts for Xerox, opened in December in a factory on Sullivan Street leased from RBOC with capital supplied by a Department of Labor grant; under the management of De Leon McEwen, former president of FIGHT, it quickly increased the number of employees from thirty to fifty.

The largest contribution of jobs for Negroes and Puerto Ricans was made by RJI and the affiliated local branch of the National Alliance of Business (NAB), both under the direction of Edward Croft. The task was made easier by the thriving character of Rochester's industries, especially during the mid-sixties, and by the booming activity in the construction field as the decade progressed. Large projects financed in whole or part by federal funds had to provide employment for minorities, but the tight labor market in Rochester, even after a slight slackening in production in the early seventies, helped to assure jobs to those willing to complete the necessary training programs. To make an earlier start at that task, Croft and Goldberg, who had worked so closely in the development of MDTA's training programs, jointly launched a move in 1968 to promote educational improvements and job counseling in the Sanford area of Florida from which so many of Rochester's migrants hailed. Governor Nelson A. Rockefeller of New York and Governor Claude R. Kirk, Jr., of Florida soon lent their support for this first bi-state effort to meet the needs of poor migrants.

Rochester's educators, like its industrialists, were ready and eager to tackle the problem of integration, but achievements here proved as difficult as in the housing field. The rapid influx of Negroes in the sixties had more than doubled their numbers and almost trebled the number of blacks in the school system. The volunteer busing program instituted in 1963 under the board's open enrollment plan started with some 500 pupils, most of them black children from the inner-city schools, and increased to over 1,200 as the decade advanced, but the number of schools over 50 percent nonwhite increased from seven to ten. A new effort in 1964 to correct the imbalance produced an elaborate report outlining four distinct plans for a regrouping of the schools, one paring inner- and outer-city schools to achieve racial balance through compulsory busing; another busing inner-city prima-ry-grade children out and outer-city grammar-school grades in; still another creating pie-shaped districts; and finally, one projecting new park-campus schools.

Unable to choose because of the opposition to enforced busing and to the sacrifice of the neighborhood school, as well as because of the huge costs involved, Rochester focused its attention on efforts to improve the content of inner-city school programs and to increase the opportunities for integrated education throughout the system. A plan devised at a conference headed by Superintendent Goldberg in 1964 called for the creation of a World of Inquiry school, the appointment of school advisors to parents, community teachers, and other innovations that, grouped together as Project Unique, won a grant from the United States Office of Education in 1967 and attracted nationwide praise. When Laplois Ashford was elected to the Board of Education the next year, the first Negro to win a city-wide election, and soon to become president of the board, he gave continued support to that project and to the effort to attract qualified black teachers for assignment throughout the system. When Bernard Gifford succeeded Florence as third president of FIGHT in 1969 and moved into his first house on Post Avenue, he promptly enrolled his daughter Antoinette in the World of Inquiry School to experience its integrated and innovative instruction. Moderating its adversarial origins and stance, FIGHT was becoming under Gifford an outspoken neighborhood conglomerate.

But the goal of integrated education remained, and in a move to promote it, Superintendent Goldberg appointed an Advisory Planning Council on Quality Integrated Education. After lengthy deliberations, the council submitted an elaborate plan dividing the city into eleven districts, pairing one of the largely black inner-city elementary schools with two or more largely white schools on the outskirts, and rearranging the residential areas of the elementary and secondary schools in the other districts to insure a more even racial balance. When Goldberg endorsed the plan and submitted it to the Board of Education, that body, with two new members elected on an antibusing platform, at first rejected the plan, but after an outburst of criticism from the Rochester Teachers Association, which threatened to boycott the schools, and from FIGHT's president Bernard Gifford and numerous other advocates of integration, the board adopted a modified reorganization plan. The compromise called for the reorganization of Zones A and C, neither of which would require the use of busing, and the board called for the creation of parents' advisory committees in these zones and also in Zones B and E, which should be readied for reorganization at an early date if the experiment with the first two zones proved successful. The board also directed the organization of parents' advisory councils for the east- and west-side inner-city schools to promote improvements in their programs and to encourage an extension of the voluntary busing program. Finally, the board ordered an expansion of the provision for instruction in Spanish in schools attended by the Puerto Ricans. The board's policy, however, had scarcely been implemented when politics brought a shift in its membership and a reappraisal and abandonment of its commitment to integration.

CIVIC REPERCUSSIONS

The population shifts that buffeted the School Board had a similar impact on other civic developments. Galvanized by the riots, the public response to the problems they uncovered was complicated by enduring political and economic divisions. Party rivalries intensified and acquired a geographic dimension; crime and punishment captured the headlines; bureaucrats, whether home-grown or imported, gave way to grass-roots leaders as a turbulent population made or refused to, make its decisions.

The demographic trends of the fifties, which had weakened the Republican grip on the city and gave control of the council to the Democrats late in 1961, continued with fluctuating effects into the sixties and seventies. Mayor Gillette and City Manager Homer, the first beneficiaries, made an earnest attack on several basic civic problems but failed, as we have seen, to forestall the riots. Mayor Lamb, who succeeded Gillette in January 1964, maintained a calm posture during the ordeal and subsequently moved to strengthen the police and spur the drafting of low-cost housing plans. When Homer left to become city manager of Miami and Arthur Curran succeeded him on an interim basis, Mayor Lamb helped persuade young Harper Sibley to assume charge of the public-safety department and named Laplois Ashford as his deputy. But that move to develop better communications with the inner-city blacks, which might have sufficed two years earlier, failed to please the leaders of FIGHT, for instead of joining the organization, Ashford had accepted appointment as head of its chief rival, the Urban League. The Democrats had elected Ashford to the Board of Education with black support in 1966 but, unmindful of the intensities of the rivalry, failed to rally that support three years later when he lost a bid for the council and cost the party its control in 1969. Frustrated by the local dissention, Ashford accepted an appointment as head of the Urban League in Chicago.

A major embarrassment of the Democrats in the sixties was the city's restricted budgets. The inadequacy of the real estate tax had long been recognized, and the city and county had turned for relief to the sales tax. But the county, which collected that tax, retained control over its distribution. In 1961 the Republicans who dominated the Board of Supervisors accepted the recommendation of County Manager Gordon Howe that the county's share by increased form four to ten percent at the expense of the city and towns. Howe, an advocate of metropolitan government, lost his first chance to draw the city and county together when the Democrats captured the city that fall. Rochester's mounting prosperity swelled the returns from the sales tax and enabled the city to survive despite its reduced share of the expanded totals in the early sixties. But in 1964, when the county ordered a special census over the protests of city officials, Rochester suffered a loss of more than a million dollars annually as its reduced portion of the population cut its share of the proceeds of the sales tax still further. Dr. Seymour Scher, who succeeded Curran as city manager in 1966, attempted to secure a revision of the distribution formulae by the state, which now collected the joint county and state sales tax, but his plea was rejected, as was his proposal that a separate 3 percent sales tax be collected by the city, and Rochester had reluctantly to consider possible alternatives.

County Manager Howe had presented an alternative in 1960 when he agreed on behalf of the county to assume the costs of maintaining the city as well as the county parks and to undertake full responsibility for the development of a community college. The city, which expected to provide most of the students and hoped to supply the site, was somewhat surprised to see that a location in the town of Brighton, not far from the site already chosen by Rochester Institute of Technology for its new campus, was preferred. Rochester, which suffered the loss of animated student activity near the business district as these institutions moved to the outskirts, watched with some frustration the progress of vast construction programs there in contrast to the inactivity at their former sites. But the city lacked the funds to develop the community college and could not begrudge the opportunities its facilities afforded to increasing numbers of its youths.

City Manager Scher protested when Howe used the same pressure to extend the county's jurisdiction over the central library, the Museum of Arts and Sciences, and other cultural activities. He deplored the loss of functions that had brought distinction to Rochester and he stubbornly held on to the branch libraries, the playground program, and the waterworks, despite the attempt of the county water authority to absorb that prestigious system. But he could not disregard the fact that suburban residents had an active interest in the library, among other functions, and should therefore share responsibility for its maintenance. Moreover, as the cost estimates for an adequate anti-pollution program escalated, threatening to exceed $100 million, even City Manager Scher was relieved when in 1967 the state gave the task of upgrading the sewage treatment plants of the city and the suburbs to a Pure Water Agency created by the county.

The county, which built and maintained a model jail on the new Civic Center, completed in the early sixties, faced a serious problem of congestion as the city and suburban crime rates mounted. Not only were the inner-city wards, beset by poverty and underemployment, contributing a disproportionate number of blacks to its charge, but police efforts to check an increased sale of drugs also contributed to the congestion, resulting in corridors converted into dormitories and demands for a jail annex downtown or in the suburbs. A determined effort by Sheriff Lombard and Chief of Detectives Bill Mahoney to round up the leaders of a gang of racketeers required a temporary use of some of the cells but involved the officers in questionable practices infringing on the civil rights of the suspects, as a federal jury determined in a sensational trial, finally concluded by moderate fines imposed by Judge Harold Burke.

Rochester had pressing responsibilities that neither the county nor the suburbs were willing to share. Fortunately, the federal and state governments had accepted the major costs for urban renewal, and the city under Mayor Lamb, City Manager Scher, and Denne as director of urban development pressed ahead with the crossroads project, made a start on the redevelopment of the Third Ward, and submitted successful applications for a model city project in the near northeast and for three other renewal projects. The vigor with which the local Democrats pushed their applications on the Johnson administration in Washington won Rochester thirteenth place among the larger cities in the commitment of federal funds. But so many obstacles delayed construction in Rochester, as in other cities, that City Manager Scher welcomed the creation in 1969 of the Urban Development Corporation (UDC) by the State of New York, with powers to cut local red tape and press ahead with a more vigorous construction program. The Democrats were eager to turn over several of the city's thorny developments to the UDC—for example, the Third Ward and Mt. Read-Emerson projects—but they were not ready to relinquish control over the southeast loop project or the proposed Genesee Gateway development. A contract assigning all of these to UDC was not signed until after the Republicans had regained a majority on the council in 1970.

In a hectic session on January 3, the Republicans who assumed control of the council elected Stephen May as major and chose Edward P. Curtis, Jr., as interim city manager while they conducted a nationwide search for a permanent appointment. Many voters had favored the Republicans with the hope of eliminating the friction that had obstructed cooperation between the city and the county. But the new leaders—May, Curtis, and Julian Orr, brought to Rochester from Kalamazoo, Michigan, in April as city manager—proved as reluctant as their Democratic predecessors to abandon city functions to the county. When Orr, a professional manager determined to maintain a free hand in administration, failed to retain council support and stepped out in October, Kermit Hill, who resigned his post as assistant to the county manager to become city manager, assumed an equally independent posture.

The manager's effort to maintain his administrative responsibilities were soon overshadowed by the city's need to strengthen its claims in the county, the state, and the nation. As former Mayor Gillette had discovered in the mid-sixties, only a strong and independently elected mayor could defend the city from the machinations of either Republican or Democratic county chairmen. In the early seventies Mayor May, after repeated sessions at Albany and Washington with both the New York State and the United States conferences of mayors, concluded that only such a politically secure mayor could adequately represent the city in negotiations with state and federal administrators.

While this issue, on which neither Republicans nor Democrats were in full agreement, awaited formulation by a recently created charter commission, Rochester faced a number of other somewhat related uncertainties. With the signing of an agreement between the city and UDC—Greater Rochester Incorporated, the local subsidiary of that state authority, Richard Pine, the newly appointed director, was able to move ahead with the construction of several oft-debated projects. He pressed work on the Gleason Estates in Pittsford as well as on the southeast loop project in downtown Rochester, and although most of the suburban towns continued to oppose efforts of UDC to find sites for low-rental projects beyond the city limits, the chartering of two new-town developments in the Rochester area foreshadowed a more carefully planned regional growth and kindled hope for a fresh start at community integration.

The complexity of the issues Rochester faced in these years was graphically demonstrated by the activities of another grass-roots organization—Friends of FIGHT. Formed by a group of dedicated civil rights activists, it supported FIGHT in its controversies with Eastman and the Community Chest, but it soon became impatient for independent action. A change in its name to Metro-Act in 1968 signaled its transformation into an umbrella organization drawing numerous neighborhood associations and other groups into a united attack on varied metropolitan problems. Within two years it enrolled 4000 members and 18 affiliated groups and was combatting the red-lining practices of some banks and real estate agencies and endeavoring to promote open housing in all city and suburban neighborhoods. With the outbreak of war in Vietnam, Metro-Act's civil rights devotees sprang to the defense of anti-war protestors, an issue that captured the headlines when eight protestors attempting to destroy the draft records in the Federal building were arrested. That controversy, known as the Flower City Conspiracy, prompted a sudden drop in Metro-Act membership and a withdrawal of several affiliates, but its leaders continued their critical appraisal of Rochester's housing deficiencies, the distribution of Chest funds, and the need for a fuller registration of inner-city voters and for an equitable distribution of the sales tax revenues. Some of the major neighborhood associations backed these causes but most of these groups, which now increased in number, focused on neighborhood improvements and made a sufficient impact to help characterize Rochester as a grass-roots metropolis.

An additional contribution of Metro-Act and the neighborhood associations was the training of leaders in civic affairs. Midge Costanza, Ruth Scott, Robert Mulhern, Nan Johnson, Laurence Kirwan and several other grass-roots leaders who sharpened their skills in neighborhood meetings found their way into city and county posts, displacing the old ward leaders particularly in the Democratic party. And when Kirwan became County Chairman of that party in 1973, he not only contributed to the election of Thomas P. Ryan, Jr. as mayor but also engineered the passage of a bill abolishing the ward system. But the Democrats, who held control of the City Council 8 to 1 in the early Ryan years, failed to secure a more equitable share of the sales tax funds even during the 1977–79 years when they had temporary control of the county legislature.

It was not a clear-cut party issue, for Democrats elected from the towns also had grass-roots ties. City Manager Elisha Freedman was forced to rely increasingly on state and federal funds. With the aid of UDC the Crossroads Project in the center of town was completed, opening the river to full view for the first time in a century and spurring private development downtown. The city with UDC aid constructed low rental housing projects in Model City and Block Grant programs, both involving neighborhood participation, and these with senior citizen high-rise projects helped to meet some of the needs of Rochester's mobile population, relieving but not removing its inner-city problems. Despite the recommendations of two prestigious studies, the persuasive efforts of Joseph C. Wilson, and the urgent pleas of Metro-Act leaders, the efforts to place some low-rental projects in suburban towns achieved only minimal results, for the towns were protecting their neighborhood interests.

Frustrated by the governmental dissensions and fragmented responses to the community's problems, the leaders of RIT, the Industrial Management Council, and the Center for Governmental Research sponsored an Urban Policy Conference organized by the Brookings Institution on a pattern it had followed in several other cities. The conference drew 100 selected community leaders into intensive study and discussion seminars chaired by Edward P. Curtis, Jr., over a period of ten months in 1972 considering and proposing policies on a wide range of community problems. Their recommendations, as reported in *Focus From the Future*, included a rejuvenation of the schools, open housing in all city wards, the provision of low-rental housing in the suburbs as well as the city, particularly in areas

adjacent to industrial plants, a more equitable distribution of tax resources, the preservation of open spaces on a linear pattern, a hetero-
geneous distribution of the population, and, among several other
proposals, a reorganization of the area's governmental structure on a
two-tier metropolitan pattern. That proposal, the first in its report,
called for the chartering of a metropolitan government to encompass
the major portion of 11 counties to be broken into lesser units of some
30,000 inhabitants each for more intimate neighborhood government.
Several of its recommendations endorsed and may have made more
palatable some of the earnest goals of Metro-Act and the neighborhood associations, but the two-tier metropolis was a dream which
was soon forgotten except by the chamber, which renamed itself the
Greater Rochester Chamber of Commerce in 1974, by Harold
Hacker's Pioneer Library System, which had pioneered the two-tier
system in 1956, and by the Rochester-Genesee Regional Transporta-
tion Authority organized in 1964 to absorb the Rochester Transit System and extend bus service to Monroe, Wayne, Livingston and
Genesee County towns. Further integration seemed illusory.

Both the city and the county faced more pressing organizational
and fiscal problems during the seventies. The city's vigorous efforts
in the late sixties, pressing ahead with urban renewal and other inner-
city projects, in addition to the grant of fiscal independence to the
School Board, had sharply increased its outlays, prompting the floating of large loans and increases in the real estate tax. The legislature
in Albany cooperated by passing a measure permitting the exemption
of Social Security and pension costs from the constitutional tax limits,
thus enabling Rochester and other cities to boost their tax revenues,
as the city proceeded to do until a Court of Appeals decision struck
down the law and ordered a repayment of the illegal taxes. The city
managed to defer the repayments during the late seventies, pressing
unsuccessfully for state and county assistance. Only an elected and
strong mayor would be able, many felt, to effect these ends, but
heated political debates befogged the issue, and the voters turned
down proposed strong mayor amendments to the charter in 1972 and
1973.

The strong mayor issues would not die, but meanwhile the fiscal
disputes with the county intensified, involving the distribution of
functions as well as revenues. The rapid growth of the suburbs gave

town representatives on the county legislature greater clout than the city representatives could muster and supported Howe's efforts to develop a strong county government. His take-over of the parks, the central library and museums, followed by a reduction of the city's share of the sales tax, gave no fiscal benefit to the city but spurred agitation for an elective county executive to replace the county manager.

While a settlement of these city-county controversies was postponed, the county, which had in 1967 joined five neighboring counties in organizing a Genesee and Finger Lakes Regional Planning Board, decided in 1976 to withdraw its support because the board was proving to be an ineffective agency. That action, strongly disapproved by the IMC and other advocates of metropolitan coordination, may have helped the Democrats to capture control of the county legislature that November. Their two years in control failed to produce a settlement of the city-county fiscal disputes, but the Democrats in control of the county legislature responded eagerly when the newly formed Economic Development Administration in President Jimmy Carter's Department of Commerce proposed the organization of a new Genesee/Finger Lakes Regional Planning Council charged with the drafting of a Regional Economic Development Program for Rochester's seven county area. The completion and acceptance of the first *Regional Overall Economic Development Program* in 1978–79 assured federal as well as local recognition and support for metropolitan coordination.

SOCIAL AND CULTURAL RESPONSES

The population shifts in character and location had an impact on the city's social and cultural life as well. Recreation became a dominant concern, filling the increased leisure many enjoyed. Social and cultural institutions multiplied and expanded, devised programs to attract previously untouched segments of the population, and reached out to serve distant parts of the metropolis. Scholars, educators, and the media assumed a more sophisticated approach to the city's social and institutional affairs.

The new division of responsibilities in 1961 enabled Wilbur

Wright, as director of the combined city and county park system, to secure state funds to assist in the acquisition of 1,336 additional acres for the expansion of some of the existing parks and to fund the purchase of 2,000 acres for three projected new regional parks. Joseph Caverly as director of the city playgrounds focused development on 22 of them and provided indoor facilities at another 16 recreation centers. Besides maintaining a double line of street trees throughout most of its residential districts, the city increased the number of street malls and small parks, including the Upper Falls Terrace Park overlooking the falls (on the site unsuccessfully proposed for its first park in 1834). It also built a Y-shaped foot bridge spanning the river in the Genesee Crossroads project and decorated it with the flags of its now six Sister Cities for whom the bridge was named. Hard- and softball diamonds and other playing fields at the city and county parks served a busy succession of scheduled amateur teams, while four public golf courses attracted a steady stream of senior-citizen golfers and others unattached to the numerous private courses scattered throughout the region.

An hour's drive from the city assured access to Letchworth or Hamlin Beach state parks or to any of a half-dozen county parks, all within Rochester's metropolitan area, while at least a score of its towns and most of its villages maintained small parks equipped to serve local recreational needs.

It was a sports-loving generation, and private clubs and commercial organizations supplied an abundance of leisure time activities for players and spectators. Even some of the private golf clubs, normally restricted to members, occasionally hosted regional or national tournaments that attracted crowds of interested onlookers. Lee Trevino won the championship when the Oak Hill Country Club brought the USGA to Rochester in 1968, and Jack Nicholas won the PGA championship there in 1980. The Locust Hill Country Club became a regular stop in 1977 for the Ladies Professional Golf Association (LPGA), attracting enthusiastic spectators. Baseball fans continued to flock to Silver Stadium on the city's northern border, cheering the Rochester Red Wings, now the top farm team of the Baltimore Orioles, to repeated victories—Junior World Series Championship in 1971, and the Governor's Cup winner in 1971, 1974, and 1976. Basketball at the University of Rochester and at St. John Fisher College, and the soccer games of the Rochester Lancers at Hollander Stadium in the seventies each attracted a loyal following.

Sportsmen who followed the horses motored beyond the metropolitan borders to Batavia Downs for harness racing or to the newly opened Finger Lakes tracks near Canandaigua, both of which, despite some troubled seasons, attracted large crowds eager to make a killing at the booths. Winter sportsmen, particularly skiers, likewise journeyed and in increasing numbers to distant resorts, supporting the development of the ski slopes in the Bristol Hills and many more distant winter resorts. Skaters had a choice of more convenient rinks, several maintained in the parks, and ice boats appeared on Irondequoit Bay during several frigid winters. That bay and the western Finger Lakes provided ideal water courses for thousands of motor and sailing boats while their shores became lined with summer cottages where unnumbered Rochesterians spent weekends and vacations, paying taxes that helped support the outer fringe of the city's metropolis.

Fortunately, downtown had one powerful sports magnet. The War Memorial, where the hockey games of the Rochester Americans continued to draw large crowds, attracted the largest downtown nighttime gatherings except for occasional ethnic festivals or ceremonial events. One such event was the Civil War Centennial Pageant on October 1, 1961, which drew a capacity crowd to the War Memorial and commemorated the city's participation in that most tragic and most costly war.

The Museum of Arts and Sciences was one of the first of the city's cultural institutions to extend its services into the inner city. As director, Stephen Thomas, inspired by the school board's Lighted Schoolhouse program, launched a "Museums on the Street" program in 1966 by placing exhibit cases in four inner-city neighborhood centers, enlisting volunteers who filled them with a changing succession of nature study and other artifacts supplied by the museum. That program, discontinued after two years, was later replaced by a branch museum under a black director focusing on African life. Meanwhile, the Rochester Museum and Science Center, as it was renamed, with county support was expanding its educational program and maintaining the privately endowed Strasenberg Planetarium, which attracted bus loads of visitors from regional schools and villages.

The International Museum of Photography in the George East-man House maintained the adjoining Dryden Theater to supply a continuing showing of selected early movies from the museum's col-lection, attracting a steady flow of enthusiastic, if nostalgic, viewers.

The Genesee Country Museum in suburban Mumford opened in the spring of 1976 and attracted a steady flow of fascinated visitors. Its 30 historic houses and shops were transplanted from sites through-out the region around a spacious green and simulated a country vil-lage. These major museums, together with a railroad museum in Rush, Valentown Hall in Victor, and the Cummings Nature Center in the Bristol Hills, enabled the Convention and Visitors Center to pro-mote Rochester as a tourist center and provided area residents with a wide choice of graphic displays of American life.

The Memorial Art Gallery added a modern new wing in 1969 to accommodate its expanded exhibit and educational programs. It purchased some choice new pieces for its collection of African sculp-ture, enriching its occasional exhibits of black art, and it helped sup-ply and hang exhibits at an Afro-American gallery, which opened on Portland Avenue early in 1968. The Memorial Art Gallery saluted the nation's Bicentennial with an exhibit in 1976 of paintings assembled from many public and private holdings on "The Genesee Country." Its annual Clothesline exhibits on the gallery grounds drew an in-creasing host of amateur and professional artists and craftsmen from the entire Genesee country and lent encouragement to a number of small art centers, nurturing creative ethnic as well as native talents in the graphic arts field. RIT's Bevier gallery, Nazareth College's new Art Center, and a new art center at the Harley School provided addi-tional display facilities, as did several downtown office towers by staging art exhibits in their corridors or reception centers.

The Landmark Society completed the restoration of the Stone-Tolan tavern and the Bruster-Burke mansion, which became its head-quarters, and undertook the defense and restoration of several other historic structures. It promoted the creation in 1968 of an official Pres-ervation Board to supervise developments in the East Avenue Preser-vation District and other threatened city neighborhoods. The Landmark Society, the Museum and Science Center and a private agency scheduled conducted tours in successive summers, and two architectural historians, Jean France and Betsy Brayer, produced an illustrative guide, *Of Town and the River,* highlighting the historical and architectural features of the city in 1977. The publication of the first edition of *Rochester on the Genesee* in 1973 and of *A Panoramic History of Rochester and Monroe County* in 1979 provided comprehensive reviews of the city's history.

Three troublesome issues confronted most of the public institutions in these years: civil rights, especially of blacks, the requirement of participation of afflicted individuals in federally backed projects, and the state Taylor Act's injunction in 1967 that public employers engage in collective bargaining with their workers.

Even worthy projects had to comply. Thus a move to extend the preservation program into the Third Ward was checked when FIGHT characterized it as Negro removal, and it only prevailed in a small area when the residents gave their support to a Corn Hill Preservation District. Similarly, the agreement of state and local planners on an extension of the Genesee Expressway from the Outer Loop to the Inner Loop downtown, backed by the chamber and other business groups, was successfully opposed by the South East Area Coalition of a dozen neighborhood associations supported by 15 environmental and inner-city groups. The project was halted in 1973 after some eighty homes had been destroyed in its path, and it was finally defeated two years later by a 6 to 3 vote in the City Council "supporting the community against the highway," as Councilman Christopher Lindley put it.

In similar fashion Superintendent Goldberg was frustrated in his efforts to integrate the schools as the opposition to enforced busing by the parents in neighborhood schools prevailed. Minister Raymond Scott, fourth president of FIGHT, which had shifted its emphasis from Integration to Independence, demanded that the school board devote its energies to an improvement of the inner-city schools rather than busing blacks to schools where they were not welcome. John Franco, who succeeded Goldberg as superintendent in 1971, though convinced of the merits of integration, had to comply and concentrated his efforts on the School Without Walls, the World of Inquiry School, and a junior high program to attract voluntary busing to specialized programs. The school board's fiscal problems were aggravated in these years by the demands of the newly formed teachers unions for improved salaries and smaller classes. The Rochester

Teachers Association had negotiated its first contract in 1965, and the Taylor Act strengthened its position among the teachers and encouraged union organization of other school board employees.

The higher educational institutions faced similar problems. The colleges had readily granted pleas in the late sixties for the introduction of black study courses and had made efforts to increase the enrollment of black students, and when a group of these students demanding further provisions occupied the Frederick Douglass building at the University of Rochester, W. Allen Wallis as president agreed to negotiate their demands as soon as they withdrew from the building; the confrontation ended peacefully under the benign influence of Joseph C. Wilson, chairman of the board of trustees.

The university faced a more mundane challenge as the rejuvenated labor movement tackled the organization of the service workers at its Strong Memorial Hospital. It was in a sense a three-issue attack, for many of these workers were black women struggling to keep their single-parent families above water, and it was a call from Dr. Martin Luther King, Jr., that prompted Local 1199 of the Hospital Workers Union in New York to send Lawrence Fox to organize Rochester's 10,000 hospital workers. Fox chose Strong Hospital, the largest employer, as his first objective and won a favorable vote among its 700 workers in December 1973. Strong challenged the results, and a protracted series of challenges, denials, and arbitration procedures delayed the signing of a contract until the following November. In March 1975 the maintenance workers of the university voted to join the local, but its efforts to extend its sway over Genesee Hospital's workers and into other health and nursing institutions was frustrated as several of these institutions following the Kodak strategy, raised their wages sufficiently to discourage union membership during the late seventies.

At Colgate-Rochester Divinity School, the equal rights issue had been even more dramatically posed late in 1968. Because of the important role played by clergymen in Negro communities, the seminary had made a deliberate effort since the mid-fifties to increase the number of black students and had named one Negro trustee. President Bartlett and the trustees were preparing to increase that representation and to add an additional Negro professor when in December 1968 the black caucus of nineteen students submitted a series of demands calling for the appointment of twelve black trustees and of five professors to assure them adequate participation in school management. When President Bartlett endeavored to secure agreement on a series of moves in that direction, but over a period of years, the black caucus occupied a portion of the main building and stopped classes for three weeks until the trustees were ready to pledge more speedy action. As a result the Colgate-Rochester Divinity School acquired a black studies program in the field of religion that won wide recognition for the indigenous character and quality of its contributions.

Students and faculty at the university and in several colleges in the area became deeply involved in various peace movements in the late sixties. At the university the administration maintained an objective attitude toward antiwar groups, but it was not ready to meet the demands of those who sought to exclude recruiters for munitions companies from the campus. When in 1967 a group of students staged a sit-in to obstruct the entrance to an office where Dow Chemical Company recruiters were interviewing students, the administration suspended twenty-three graduate students who participated in the demonstration. That action precipitated a much larger demonstration that closed most classes and led to protracted discussions among student leaders, faculty, and administration, which resulted, under the moderating influence of Joseph C. Wilson as chairman of the board, in the creation of a new student-faculty review board to handle disputes involving freedom of speech and assembly on the campus. When a series of protests swept the colleges in the wake of violence at Kent State early in May 1970, demonstrations erupted on all local campuses, some closing classes for a day or two. At the University of Rochester a move to collect petitions condemning the invasion of Cambodia and pleading that all troops be brought home attracted support throughout the country and assembled over 100,000 signatures in the first two weeks, making the University of Rochester the center of the National Petition Committee.

The Protestant Council of Churches, which suffered dissension in its ranks during the late sixties over the pledge of support for FIGHT, experienced a renewal of spirit and transformed itself in 1970 into the Genesee Ecumenical Ministries (GEM), welcoming Catholics and all Christian denominations to its membership. When the black churches, now preferring Independence to Integration, formed a separate United Church Ministry, it too was welcomed as a member of GEM, which meanwhile had created a committee to counsel young men protesting the draft and opposing the war in Vietnam.

Never before had the city's leaders and residents held such diverging views on the country's involvement in war, and for the first time the fact that several thousand of Rochester's young men were serving in Indo-Chinese battle areas and that 135 from Monroe County had given their lives to the cause failed to erase the uncertainty with which the community regarded the war.

That uncertainty was perhaps heightened by the lack of a community forum in which to debate and formulate local opinions. The City Club, which had served that purpose so effectively in two world wars and during the Korean conflict, was now struggling to maintain its schedule of meetings in reduced quarters. Mounting prosperity in the fifties had enabled most business firms to dispense with the Saturday morning work shift, and the number available for a Saturday noon luncheon meeting downtown had sharply declined. Although the club experimented with other meeting hours, its inability to attract many members from the suburbs, even to hear visiting statesmen, dwindled and resulted in its demise in 1965. Fortunately, Rochester had developed another institution, the Rochester Area Educational Television Association (RAETA), which had a more metropolitan potential. That potential, however, was only a promise in the early sixties, and when in 1962, under the presidency of Harold Hacker of the public library, its carefully documented bid for a joint operation (with Rochester Telecasters, Incorporated) of the new Channel 13 was rejected by the FCC, wide indignation was expressed. That decision, however, had been delayed for three years, and in the interim RAETA had developed sufficient strength to surmount its disappointment and soon undertook to operate a UHF station on Channel 21, which, when opened in September 1966, provided a community forum.

The breadth of RAETA's coverage presented a challenge to increase its viewing audience, which it endeavored to accomplish with the aid of annual auctions that did in fact develop a measure of community-wide support, enabling it to build a model station on State Street in 1975 and to maintain a dual schedule of programs: television

over WXXI and radio over AM 1370 launched that year. Indeed
RAETA's programs fitted conveniently into Rochester's new suburban life-style as families gathered around their radio and TV sets
throughout the metropolis.

By contrast, the Civic Music Association faced a declining support
as its patrons moved to the suburbs. Despite threatening budgetary
problems and wage disputes with its musicians, the Civic Orchestra
maintained a busy schedule of concerts at school auditoriums and
neighborhood plazas and parks, and the larger Philharmonic Orchestra supplemented its programs at the Eastman Theatre with visits to
suburban campuses and malls. It renewed its summer concerts at the
Highland Park Bowl and in the late seventies paid repeated visits to
the Community College of the Finger Lakes in Canandaigua where
it renewed old friendships with Rochesterians vacationing in cottages
around the lake.

Rochester's cultural institutions were reaching out to serve its scattering inhabitants in the suburbs, but in one notable case the move
was reversed, for it was suburban Brockport that discovered Garth
Fagan, recognized his talents as a dancer and brought him in 1971 to
Rochester where he soon assembled and trained a group of black
dancers, known as the Bottom of the Bucket, which quickly attracted
wide acclaims and invitations to perform in New York and other cities
in America and abroad. Their innovative and dramatic performances
each year in Rochester, in old church halls, the Eastman Theatre, and
finally, for successive reasons, in Nazareth College's new Art Center,
won Fagan and his dancers, now known as the Bucket Dancers, recognition as one of the city's prize attractions.

With several thriving colleges on its outskirts and hundreds of
research scholars in its firms and institutions, Rochester became a
productive fountain of articles and books. The annual Authors' Day at
the Public Library, hosted 22 authors in 1960, shot up to 75 in 1967,
and averaged 42 over the two decades. The two-minute limit on their
comments about their books gave an advantage to those with a sense
of humor, but left much to be gleaned later from the books. Many
merited study and two at least, *Time on the Cross: The Economics of
American Negro Slavery* by Stanley Engerman in collaboration with
Robert W. Fogel in 1974, and *Roll, Jordan, Roll: The World the Slaves
Made* by Eugene D. Genovese in 1975, received it. Both presented

controversial interpretations of the historical background of America's (and Rochester's) Negro society and stirred heated discussions among scholars at several conventions. One such session at the Holiday Inn in Rochester attracted a score of distinguished historians from as far afield as Boston, Chicago, and North Carolina vigorously debating the innovative research techniques and conceptual conclusion of *Time on the Cross.* Yet neither of these authors won one of the Literacy Awards given annually by the Friends of the Rochester Public Library, which generally favored creative rather than scholarly works.

The honored recipient in 1966, Jerre Mangione, had applied his imaginative talents to a fictional portrayal of life in the Italian neighborhood where he grew up. *Mount Allegro,* as he renamed it, had won wide acclaim and several reprintings since its first appearance in 1942, and hundreds of his fellow countrymen helped pack the chamber's grand ballroom at the award luncheon that April. It was a triumph, in a sense, for Rochester's large Italian population, and he took occasion in his response to tell of his visit that morning to the old neighborhood where he had found most of the old buildings still standing, crowded as before, but now with a new population of poor and disadvantaged people. It gave him a strange feeling, he reported, standing on the other side of the cultural fence. "Perhaps we should ponder our new responsibilities," he mused. In the pause that followed a few tentative claps started a warm applause that swept the hall—a moving occasion nine months after the riots.

Most of Rochester's numerous scientists were employed in the research and development (R&D) divisions of local industries or enterprising independent laboratories, but a number at the University of Rochester were engaged in a search for knowledge, and one notable breakthrough occurred in May 1977 when a team of nuclear physicists headed by Professor Harry E. Gove, using the university's tandem electrostatic accelerator, discovered and demonstrated that accelerator mass spectrometry could effect a revolution in the process of carbon dating that would enable geologists, archaeologists, and anthropologists to verify the character and pinpoint the age of infinitesimal deposits recovered from their exploratory digs. One of the most fascinating applications at Rochester of this new process, which quickly spread around the world, was the verification of some particles of ash found in Newfoundland as of Viking origin and dated in the late tenth century, which confirmed the viking saga of Leif Eriksson's discovery and sojourn in America some 500 years before Columbus.

After a succession of booming years, Rochester's economy suffered a moderate setback in 1970. The county's unemployment rate, which had stood at 1.9 percent in December 1969, rose to 4.4 during 1970 as a number of firms cut back or, in a few cases, closed their doors. The East Rochester car shops, the electronic division of General Dynamics, Fashion Park, and the Hickok Company were the chief casualties. The decision by Xerox in 1969 to move its headquarters to the New York metropolitan area contributed to the local despondency, but the continued expansion of its plant in Webster and the opening of a new one in Henrietta dispelled fears of its local decline. A few industrialists talked of moving to a low tax area, but their more enterprising neighbors, aware that such an area would lack Rochester's abundant services, decided to increase their local investments. Kodak expended more than $100 million in new facilities that year, including the construction of a new incinerator for the safe disposal of its industrial wastes.

The city's confidence revived as the decade progressed. The Rochester Products Division increased its output of an evaporative canister system for installation in General Motors cars to check the escape of gasoline vapors. General Railway Signal secured contracts to provide and install automatic control systems in the subways under construction in Washington and Atlanta. Although Rochester's unemployed increased slightly in slack winter months, they never approached the averages for the state or the nation, and the city's ratio generally retained its enviable advantage over other industrial cities. When in March 1972 the ratio climbed to 5.2, Kodak sales of the newly released pocket-sized Instamatic proved so great that Walter A. Fallon, its new president, hastily added a thousand new workers, almost 15 percent of them from minority groups, in an effort to keep up with the orders. This action brought the country's unemployment rate down to 4.9 percent within two months. The percentage would climb to 7.6 in 1976, but renewed enterprise would bring it down again to 4.7 in 1979. Bausch & Lomb with its new soft lense was expanding its employment at its spacious, newly acquired plant on North Goodman Street. The Gleason Company increased the range and volume of its output and, during 1977, reached $100 million in sales for the first time in its history.

Many of Monroe County's numerous smaller plants were likewise thriving, but the major employment gains were in sales, service and government jobs, which more than doubled in number during these decades. It was here too that labor unions were most active. The Amalgamated Clothing Workers, the strongest local union, opened its impressive new headquarters on East Avenue in 1967 and withstood a loss in the number of its clothing worker members, as that industry declined, only by the rapid increase from its Xerox affiliate. Local unions enjoyed their chief gains in retailing, service, and government fields most open to unskilled minorities whose members benefited perhaps more in spirit than in substance as inflation absorbed low wage gains.

The Center for Governmental Research, diligently watchful (in its annex to the restored Jonathan Child Mansion) over the city's problems, compiled statistics on trends during the seventies that revealed some of the difficulties faced by the community. As the suburban migration continued but slowed (by a non-white influx) to 18 percent in the seventies, the gap between the median family incomes of the city and the county widened, $17,161 compared to $24,276, with a reverse ratio of female householders of 36.8 percent to 27.2 percent. The number of Persons receiving family aid in the county increased from 27,300 to 31,000 during the seventies (most of them in the city), and the number of families below the poverty level stood at 6,586, 4,255 of them black.

The Community Chest had a broader field of service, as protested by FIGHT and Metro-Act, but most of the 60 participating local agencies and 29 state or national affiliates it served in 1965 had a direct relation to the welfare of the city's disadvantaged residents. It oversubscribed its goal that year, topping all previous drives, with $7,084,107 in pledges, possibly because of the inner-city challenge. But philanthropy was not the answer, declared Minister Florence and his supporters who demanded jobs and a democratic decision on further social needs. Yet, while awaiting that millennium, numerous grass-roots organizations had undertaken to supply some of the social needs and had clubbed together to raise the necessary funds, enlisting bureaucratic assistance in that effort, and the Chest, in that capacity, responded to the community's needs by increasing the size of the pie almost threefold in the next fifteen years. That expansion involved two carefully considered reorganizations and changes in name and area of responsibility as well as the inclusion after consulting with representatives of ABC, Metro-Act and neighborhood groups and settlement houses, of 23 newly devised responses to social problems. By 1980 the Greater Rochester United Way, the Chest's new name, serving Monroe and Wayne and parts of Ontario and Orleans counties, set its goal at $19,021,794, missing it by a fraction of one percent for the third time in its history.

Rochester's capitalist economy was, of course, even more defuse —"charged with dynamic enterprise" was the preferred description. No bureaucratic authority could control it, although the Greater Rochester Chamber of Commerce attempted to keep abreast of its expansive developments. Even the powerful bankers swayed with the currents of enterprise, as the shifts in the city's commercial pattern amply demonstrated.

The Lincoln First Bank, Rochester's strongest, made a bold effort to peg Rochester's commercial life downtown. When it completed the construction of its marble and glass-coated 26-story office tower on a gracious plaza, it extended a covered overpass across Clinton Avenue, linking it with the multiple commercial activities of Midtown Plaza and, by another overpass across Broad Street, with the Xerox Tower. This sheltered concourse connecting banking, industrial and commercial offices, and stores, all supported by two spacious underground garages, was further strengthened by the completion of the spectacular 7-story parking ramp at Broad Street and South Avenue with an underground connection with Lincoln First. Rochester, one of the three contenders for the unwanted title of Snow Capital of America, thus acquired a sheltered downtown core, but the opening of new and vast shopping plazas and office parks in the suburbs on all sides continued, supported of course by the leading merchants as well. Moreover, the flight of specialty stores, cinemas, and especially restaurants to neighborhood revivals, such as Park Avenue, threatened to leave downtown deserted after 5:30 P.M.

But downtown was already very much the concern of Mayor Ryan and the City Council, as well as of other alert citizens. Spurred by the alarm expressed by Dr. Robert Freeman, new director of the Eastman

School of Music, over the deterioration of Main Street in the Eastman Theatre area, the City Council gave its approval to an ambitious Cultural District project on East Main Street in 1977.

West across the river, Rochester's original 100-acre tract, still the center of governmental activity, experienced a similar rejuvenation. The old City Hall, overcrowded by multiple urban functions and antiquated by the spacious Civic Center complex across refurbished Broad Street (capping the old Erie Canal), was abandoned as the mayor and City Council moved into the marvelously restored old Federal Building on Church Street. The new City Hall and a new Federal Building on State Street, together with the refurbished Americanus Hotel, the glass-coated Crossroads Building at the Four Corners, and the towering First Federal Plaza on Main Street, marked the modernization of downtown's northwest quadrant.

When Greater Rochester Chamber of Commerce created a Downtown Development Corporation in 1978 to promote the northeast quadrant, the Landmark Society hastily secured the designation of the cast-iron-faced H. H. Warner Building and St. Joseph's Church tower as historic landmarks in order to preserve their amenities. The city's architectural interests gained new support in 1977 when the Rochester chapter of the American Institute of Architects announced its first annual list of awards to the best contemporary architectural works, giving one of the five awards to WXXI for its new station headquarters by Todd and Giroux.

Despite its massive reconstruction, downtown Rochester cherished and restored several other old landmarks. The new Liberty Pole, designed by James Johnson as a result of a nationwide competition and erected in the fall of 1965 on the site of its three predecessors, provided again an appropriate beacon for both patriotic and protest rallies by diverse grass-roots groups. The merging of three downtown Presbyterian churches, each suffering from the migrations of some of its members to the suburbs, into the revitalized Downtown United Presbyterian Church in the refurbished Brick Church and Institute, traditional stronghold of the social gospel, had left the prestigious First Presbyterian Church on South Plymouth vacant until it was acquired by Minister Florence as the new home for his Central Church of Christ in 1980, thus preserving two architecturally and culturally significant landmarks. The remounting of the statue of Mer-

cury on a fit pedestal atop the rejuvenated Co-Operative Publishing
Company building, towering over the diminutive aqueduct park and
the reopened Main Street bridge, restored Rochester's favorite skyline symbol. It gave Mercury a clear view not only of neighboring
office towers and of several new green grass plots at their bases but
also of the Genesee flowing in from the south. The Genesee itself is
a landmark in motion, reminiscent of the produce it had brought from
its fertile valley, now a major part of the city's metropolitan outreach;
the river is reminiscent also of the power generated at the city's successive waterfalls, driving the wheels of the mills, factories, and electric plants that fueled Rochester's growth. And on the river's eastern
bank stands the Rundel Building, headquarters of the Rochester Public Library and of the metropolitan wide Pioneer Library System.
This landmark structure, storehouse for the knowledge of past and
present generations, proudly symbolizes, by the splashing water
flowing through its riverside arches, that for modern Rochester, as an
inscription on one wall proclaims, "Knowledge is Power."

The Sesquicentennial Generation

ROCHESTER had grounds for confidence as it entered the eighties. The outward migration of its white residents continued but at a slower pace, and a new sense of unity with the towns was developing. The city and the schools had acute fiscal problems, but a strong mayor, many felt, could find a solution. Downtown needed a facelift and the city, having rediscovered the river, was pressing ahead with projects on both banks. A new appreciation of the merits of old landmarks quickened as the city approached the sesquicentennial of its incorporation in 1834 and prepared for its celebration. Rochesterians looked back, proudly appraising the city's accomplishments, outdid themselves in reenacting old practices, and looked forward to future improvements. The sesquicentennial spirit spread throughout the county and the metropolitan district, as towns and villages joined in Rochester's celebration and staged sesquicentennials and, finally, a few bicentennials of their own. So pervasive was the spirit that the generation—excited young leaders rubbing shoulders with old-timers —could best be described as the sesquicentennial generation.

THE COMMUNITY OF MONROE

Rochester's renewed confidence in the early eighties was one of spirit more than economy. Its industries suffered, though not as severely as many elsewhere, from the poor markets of the widespread recession. A moderate increase in unemployment appeared less threatening than the fiscal crisis facing the city, and the IMC, with many of its firms straddling city and town boundaries, created a committee to study the problem. Its chairman, Richard Turner, president of the Schlegel Company with a factory in Henrietta, had recently restored the Harper Sibley mansion on East Avenue as his headquarters and saw the need for cooperation rather than rivalry between the city and towns. He drafted a strong report with an expressive title, "The Community of Monroe," sounding a call for cooperation between the city and its suburbs. The new spirit proved effective, and Turner found a place on a financial review committee which proposed that the county assume support of the city police and other costly community services that were a benefit to the entire county. A redivision of functions and responsibilities was recommended that would give a spurt to community development.

The committee's recommendations were forthright, but their implementation proved difficult and required the earnest efforts of two additional committees comprised of industrial and civic leaders to rally community and state support sufficient to relieve Rochester of its fiscal problems.

Faced with a deferred state court order to reimburse its property owners for excess taxes collected in the mid-seventies under an illegal state law, the city was in a fiscal bind. Property taxes were already pressing the constitutional limit, and a suggested payroll tax would only prompt a more rapid flight of industry from the city, sapping the tax base. A sales tax increase proposed by one committee was voted down by the county already burdened in that field. A carefully devised plan for the creation of a county police department to absorb the police of the city and the several towns that had assumed that function, as well as the sheriff's forces, all to be supported by a county-wide tax, also failed to win voter approval in 1983. Fortunately, the state legislature, which had cancelled the loans it had made to other cities faced with reimbursements of their illegal taxes, now approved a grant of $35 million to Rochester, which had rejected a similar loan in order to safeguard its high credit rating. The state court also approved a 50 percent refund because a full payment would require heavier taxes costing property owners more than the balance due them.

The state grant did not meet the full cost of the reimbursement, which exceeded $40 million, but the same election that rejected the police amendment and the amendment for a strong mayor approved one providing for the election of a county executive. When Lucien

Morin, formerly the county manager, won that election, he promptly endorsed the Community of Monroe theme and pledged an assumption of joint services by the county, reducing the city's burden sufficiently to close a $5.8 million gap in its school budget. With their fiscal problems under control, Mayor Ryan and County Executive Morin turned their attention to the city's approaching sesquicentennial.

ROCHESTER AT 150

Plans for a proper celebration of the city's 150th birthday had in fact been under way for over a year. A group of present and former city and county officials had formed the Rochester Sesquicentennial Inc. (RSI) under the chairmanship of Edward P. Curtis, Jr., to plan, stage, and finance a year-long series of programs. A small staff headed by Rosalie C. Hanson was engaged, but the major reliance was on a 20-member citizens committee which adopted a proposed logo featuring the catchy slogan, "Our Spirit Shows," and organized a battery of program committees that recruited over a thousand participants in staging their activities. RSI officially launched its celebration with a spectacular community party on Main Street Bridge on New Year's Eve, 1983. An estimated 75,000 people packed Main Street and nearby bridges and river concourses. The boisterous crowd hushed at 11:55 P.M. as the lighted outdoor elevator on the First Federal Tower began a slow climb to the top where its final flash at midnight triggered an unprecedented fireworks display that publicly launched the sesquicentennial.

An open house at the new City Hall on January 1 initiated a series of commemorative events and exhibit openings, 150 in number, scattered three or more a week throughout the year. Each of the museums and colleges featured aspects of its history or programs, and most ethnic and cultural societies staged lectures or ceremonies commemorating their tradition; several churches joined in celebrating Frederick Douglass' birthday; several societies participated in a St. Patrick's Day parade and others in an Arbor Day at the parks. A women's week of conferences led up to the celebration of Susan B. Anthony's birthday. Mayor Ryan assumed the lead in the official commemoration of Charter Day on May 28 at which Governor Mario Cuomo delivered the principal address in the Eastman Theatre, and William Warfield delighted the packed audience with "Old Man River," followed by a Gala Ball in the Auditorium.

Three major events dramatized prominent aspects of the city's history. A Sesquicentennial Parade on June 10, aptly described as "a two and a half hour moving pageant of Rochester's history," included scores of floats depicting aspects of the city's economic and social heritage; marching bands, and dancing acrobats, intermingled with 50-odd costumed marchers impersonating leaders of earlier generations headed by City Historian Joseph Barnes as Henry O'Reilly. The waves of applause that greeted each display intensified as contingents of veterans of the First and Second World Wars, the Korean and the Vietnam engagements passed the successive blocks of onlookers that lined the East Avenue and Main Street course of the parade. A street dance that evening overshadowed the "cold water" ceremonies at the Main Falls, which marked the inauguration of Jonathan Child as Rochester's fist mayor on June 10, 1834.

From July 6 to 8, a Great Canal Caper, the second major event, focused attention on the vital importance of the Erie Canal in Rochester's early years. It rallied the participation of canal towns and villages as far east as Seneca Falls and west as Medina in the preparation of barges depicting aspects of their early history. The floating parade of 16 barges converged on the river in Genesee Valley Park where an unprecedented throng applauded replicas of Indian Allen's mill and other historic exhibits and engaged in horseshoe matches and other historic pastimes.

The rediscovery of the river was a repeated theme, with ceremonies at the Main Falls and Falls Field, but the third major event was at the mouth of the river at Charlotte where one of the Tall Ships and a host of lake vessels converged on July 12–15. That display, arranged in conjunction with Toronto, which was also celebrating its sesquicentennial, attracted a steady flood of spectators, reminding Rochesterians of the former significance of lake trade and the once popular lake beaches, which, like the river, merited rejuvenation.

As the sesquicentennial year progressed, a continuing series of events celebrated aspects of the city's social and cultural heritage. Sports events at the parks vied with programs in the theaters—Garth Fagan's Bucket Dancers, Chuck Mangione's concert, a Rochester

Philharmonic premiere of a Christopher Rouse composition, and a GeVa Theatre premiere of a prize-winning play by Thomas Babe. Perhaps the most significant among a number of historical publications, which now appeared, including "Our Spirit Shows," was the 430 page *Remaking of a City: Rochester 1964–1984* by Lou Butting and Mark Hare reviewing the history of the Rochester riots and their repercussions. A "Futures Week" explored some of the implications of contemporary technological and demographic developments on the city's future.

The sesquicentennial came to a dramatic close with another mammoth fireworks display on New Year's Eve in 1984, which established a tradition of annual New Year's Eve displays and strengthened the city's appreciation of downtown's potential. The wide participation in the year's events had brought many new leaders to the fore, especially women who, in contrast to earlier centennials, monopolized by men, now supplied over half the effective volunteer leaders and participants. The collaboration of near and distant suburbs strengthened the Community of Monroe spirit and an awareness of Rochester's metropolitan identity. In his introduction to the "1834–1984 Sesquicentennial Brochure" summarizing the year's programs, Mayor Ryan wrote: "1984 was a year of looking back, appreciating how far we have come; 1985 is the time to begin looking to the future."

Rejuvenating Downtown

Plans for the future, both public and private, were already in the works and would multiply as the decade advanced. The effective leadership Morin supplied as county executive prompted a renewed and finally successful drive for a strong mayor late in 1984, and Mayor Ryan won the city-wide election the next November. Long a promoter of central-city functions, he had collaborated with State Senator Fred Eckert in securing the promise of a $40 million state grant for a downtown convention center to help promote Rochester's economy. The opening of the Riverside Convention Center in 1985 provided the city with a spacious facility for state and national conventions and stimulated other downtown rejuvenation projects, which became a major goal of the late eighties.

The strength of the Central Business District, residing in its towering office and commercial blocks, had experienced a rebirth in the seventies and continued to enjoy a surge of growth. The enclosed concourse linking the Lincoln, now Chase-Lincoln, Tower with Midtown Plaza and the Xerox Tower, was extended in three directions: west to the new Convention Center and across Main Street to the refurbished Holiday Inn, south to the new headquarter's building of the Rochester Telephone Company and the new Washington Square garage, and north again across Main Street to the Sibley Building. The sale and closing of that prime department store cast a shadow over the city's downtown commercial life, but Wilmorite Inc. accepted the challenge of converting it to new downtown functions. Two of Rochester's leading law firms, Harris-Beach and Nixon-Hargrave, assumed the construction of modern new headquarters, the first by restoring the architectural elegance of the Granite Building and converting the interior into prime office space, the second by constructing the 14-story Clinton Square Building. Other realtors restored the Chase-Warner Building on St. Paul Street, the Ellwanger Barry Building on State Street, and finally Rochester's choice landmark, the Powers Block at the Four Corners. One towering question mark, the framework of the projected 27-story Hyatt Hotel, its construction halted by the bankruptcy of its Buffalo contractor, shadowed Main Street at South Avenue throughout the late eighties. A plastic sheathing was provided to safeguard the skeletal monolith until a concerted effort by the city, county, and ten major corporations mustered the strength needed to resume construction in January 1990 and open early in 1992.

The development of the Cultural District, projected in the late seventies to hold the Eastman School of Music downtown, made rapid progress. A new YMCA and a parking garage, straddling Main Street east of the Eastman Theatre, together with the Eastman Place Office Building and the Sibley Music Library adjoining it to the west and the Eastman Commons housing music students on the old YMCA site, provided an elegant core for the more extended Cultural District. The new Margaret Woodbury Strong Museum opened in 1982 at One Manhattan Square, and the GeVa Theatre opened in the remodeled old Convention Hall on South Clinton Avenue in 1985. A few blocks to the east lay the stunning new entrance wing of the Rochester Museum and Science Center and the new entrance and interior sculpture garden of the Memorial Art Gallery (both by Frank Grosso & Associates). Still farther east, the refurbished Eastman House with its newly constructed archives of photography and film provided a cluster of facilities that added to the architectural as well as the cultural distinction of the southeast district. The continuing schedule of lectures in the auditoriums of these institutions by the newly formed Writers and Books and numerous older societies supplied an animated intellectual fare. Generous philanthropic bequests and subscriptions largely financed these institutional developments, while the central library, more dependent on public support, had to defer its plans for expansion.

The city's major commitment was to the improvement of Main Street. Plans for a widening of the sidewalks and the resurfacing of a somewhat restricted street soon involved it in a reconstruction of the aged infrastructure, which required a protracted and costly closing of successive portions of the street for months at a time. When the project was finally completed in 1989 with improved lighting, heated bus shelters, and even historical markers, Rochester had a Main Street fit to serve the thriving daytime activity of the many thousand office and service workers in its adjoining towers. This accomplishment now challenged community leaders to provide evening attractions. Occasional ethnic and ceremonial parades and annual city-sponsored summer and New Year's festivals recaptured some of the atmosphere that had enlivened Main Street during the sesquicentennial, but it was generally fairly deserted after six o'clock.

The solution, the Rochester Downtown Development Corporation (RDDC) determined, was the development of residential neighborhoods within the Inner Loop. Encouraged by the example of the Grove Place preservation district, RDDC formed a committee comprised of representatives of area institutions and chaired by Tom Digman of Nixon-Hargrave to "address the need for additional housing in downtown Rochester." The committee's first feasibility study in 1981 designated a small redevelopment area on Water Street which, under the promotion of the Wilmorite Inc., blossomed into the "Olde Rochesterville" project and gained the support of the city and of three local foundations. The committee drafted a Downtown Rochester Residential Strategy designating three target areas in the northeastern quadrant for projected housing developments. The committee's detailed report, issued in 1985, included proposed architectural renderings of both row- and high-rise housing, landscaping, and sustaining services for the proposed neighborhoods. It stirred considerable interest and enlisted a number of buyers of projected condominiums in the Grove Place area, but the search for serious promoters of the target area faltered.

Housing and Educating a Changing Population

Rochester faced more pressing housing problems than the gentrification of the Inner Loop. The dramatic population shifts of the sixties and seventies continued at a slower pace in the eighties, but the cumulative impact on the city's housing supply was aggravated. President Johnson's urban renewal program had been terminated by President Nixon in 1973 before Rochester had reaped its full benefit. Some 5,000 household units had been demolished and replaced with 3,000 new ones, leaving a number of open spaces and forcing many poor families to double up. Fortunately, the drop in the number of housing units was not as sharp as the population decline, and the housing market enjoyed an upturn in the early eighties, with little benefit, however, to the low-income families.

The Rochester Housing Authority, the City Council's Housing and Urban Development Committee, and the Center for Governmental Research were all concerned with the problem. The Housing Authority, responsible for the maintenance of existing projects, found conditions at Hanover Houses so deteriorated in 1980 that it had to be demolished. The loss of its 392 units was partially made up by the construction of the Cena Gantt and Harriet Tubman Estates with a total of 230 town houses on and near the site in 1983 and 1984. The town-house pattern, seen in the four earlier family projects, had proved more satisfactory than the high-rise pattern, which was reserved only for senior citizens in a total of ten towers.

The Housing and Urban Development Committee, which had initiated a Home Improvement Loan program in the late seventies, granted aid to some 12,000 city householders during the eighties and inaugurated a Home Expo program in 1985 that encouraged qualified realtors to build over 100 affordable single-family houses on city-owned lots during the decade. The committee also backed a Housing Rehabilitation project in the Brown Square area, stimulating its development and promoted a greater use of the federally sponsored Home Mortgage Insurance Program. The committee prodded the authority to lease single and small multiple housing units for family use, adding 355 to the 817 family units in the ten public projects, making 1,152 available in 1985. The senior citizen towers maintained by the authority accommodated 1,320, and the leasing program another 2,786, but with 1,142 families on a waiting list for public units and 215 seniors for tower rooms, as well as 2,419 families seeking leased houses, the demand more than doubled the supply in 1985 when the authority in frustration closed the waiting list to further applicants.

The Center for Governmental Research had already in 1983 warned "that housing problems—often serious problems—persisted for significant numbers of lower income householders" in Rochester. The center assisted the Real Estate Research Corporation, engaged by the city in 1988, in conducting a housing market study. The recommendations of this study reemphasized the urgent need for more affordable housing and proposed the formation of a Housing Partnership to coordinate the efforts and energies of the city, the Housing Authority, neighborhood organizations, the Urban League, community development bodies, and industrial and financial leaders. From this spirit of cooperation emerged a campaign to preserve existing housing facilities and fill gaps in the housing market.

The complexity of the housing problem became clear at the monthly Partnership meetings. Rochester was not, as many thought, an asylum for the aged; its population included many senior citizens, but the median age was declining, especially among the blacks. Many of the city's white residents over 60 had moved to the suburbs by 1990, though some, as they became infirm, returned to find refuge in Rochester's public and private residential towers. Only 19 percent of the residents in the city's now 12 "towers" were black; since poverty could strike the aged whites, who were more numerous than the aged blacks. Black families, especially single-parent families, however, filled 92 percent of the family housing projects.

Yet these statistics, even including those on the waiting lists, represents only a small fraction of the city's total black population, which had doubled since the riots. Their increase by 1,800 in the eighties, coupled with an Hispanic increase of 7,000, gave the two minorities a third of the city's population and an increasing influence in its affairs. Many, benefiting from the numerous training programs and filling jobs recently opened to them, were renting or making down payments on homes in the outer wards where the Partnership hastened to provide monetary and other assistance to promote home ownership. They showed little desire to move to the suburbs, though industrial developments in Greece and Henrietta attracted a few thousand of each group. They were city dwellers, and in a variety of clubs, churches, and societies, they were developing a sense of community and were winning places on city councils and committees. Yet, while eager to join in general city affairs, they were not forgetting their own heritage, and like other sesquicentennial Rochesterians, they staged Afro-American and Hispanic parades and festivals and helped as staff members to prepare exhibits at local museums, and as performers, they demonstrated a richly varied musical tradition. Their role in the city's future was assured.

It was with the public schools that they were most vitally involved. They had long since gained places on the school board and in 1980 saw the appointment of a black superintendent, Lavel Wilson. While Wilson's tenure was brief, (he accepted appointment as superintendent of the Boston schools in 1983), his administration dispelled any suspicion of discrimination in the hiring of faculty and staff and focused attention on the quality of education actually delivered. During the sesquicentennial year a school report listing 1,200 high school graduates revealed that only 39 of the black students, who comprised a majority of the graduates, had attained B averages. Startled by this poor performance, William Johnson of the Urban League conferred with Peter McWalters, the newly appointed superintendent of schools, and together they formed a task force which, after lengthy deliberation, produced a 34-page "Call to Action," charting a dramatic reform program.

The report called for the maintenance of a city-wide preschool program and the development of close teacher-parent supervision of the progress of each student. New responsibilities were placed on the teachers; each teacher pledged to contact and counsel the parents of 20 students, and the board agreed to reward their efforts with a 40-percent increase in salaries over the next three years.

A Community Roundtable, composed of interested industrialists and civic leaders, promoted the reform by releasing key executives to serve in partnership programs in math and science classes. By far the most dramatic response was an offer by Wegmans to provide weekend jobs in its supermarkets for a few selected potential dropouts from each high school, who, by maintaining passing grades until graduation, would receive $5,000 scholarships to enter colleges of their choice. When 13 students of the first group successfully graduated in 1990, nine prepared to enter college, and three of the others who had become pregnant were assured aid the next year.

The reform program enjoyed wide acclaim and produced some early improvements. Unfortunately, the generous salary increases aroused resentment among some parents struggling to maintain their families, and the effort to develop cooperation, even contacts, between teachers and parents proved difficult. Some Roundtable firms lost interest as reports of the dropout rates of Rochester schools continued to fluctuate far above those of suburban districts. The Center for Governmental Research made a statistical study of minority dropout rates, delinquencies, teenage pregnancies and unemployment, and warned that Rochester, like some other cities, was in danger of developing a permanent underclass. The center noted the simultaneous emergence of a sturdy black middle class and concluded that more affordable housing, preschool child care, and job training were investments well worth accepting. A "Recall to Action," issued by a group of teachers and administrators in the spring of 1991, spurred a renewed effort by many to promote parent-teacher cooperation and a rejuvenation of the system.

Community support for school reforms had meanwhile resulted in an upsurge in educational programs for youths and adults, enabling dropouts to catch up and graduate and adults to improve latent skills while making the learning process a part of their life-style. Local museums and colleges as well as the public schools vied in the promotion of learning activities, and the local press featured examples of special interest and published lists of facilities available.

If graduation from high school was now a widely accepted mark of youthful achievement, graduation from college was becoming a prerequisite for adult participation in community affairs. With six institutions of college rank in its urbanized area, with two more within the county and another two within its metropolitan district, Rochester was well equipped to supply the needs of its residents. Each institution welcomed students from beyond these borders, but many local residents boasted degrees from distant colleges, and the number of college graduates in Monroe County in 1980 was 88,338, which was almost a third of the high school graduates and 8.35 percent of the population. Yet only 2,869 blacks had college degrees, less than a fifth of their high school graduates, and the colleges faced a recruiting problem similar to that of the public schools.

During the eighties, each of the colleges increased its enrollment of blacks, added black faculty members, and developed in-house or outreach programs to attract inner-city participation. Colgate-Rochester, with its widely acclaimed black church studies program training an increasing enrollment of ministerial candidates for work in inner cities, chose Dr. James H. Evans, Martin Luther King, Jr., Memorial Professor of Theology as its new president in 1991. Both RIT and SUNY, College at Brockport, maintained downtown day and evening work-study programs providing job training as well as academic courses in convenient proximity to inner-city residents. The establishment by Monroe Community College of a major downtown branch in the Sibley Building in 1991 further enhanced inner-city services and promised a revitalization of downtown after dark.

Collaboration between the university and RIT in technological research fields was likewise progressing. Their Joint promotion of a research park, with the backing of Kodak and Xerox, afforded facilities for other firms as well. In an effort to define the park's objectives, its collaborators, now including city officials, were determined to adopt a new nickname for Rochester, identifying it as the Imaging Center of America.

A RESILIENT ECONOMY

The Rochester economy, long firmly based on the productivity of its industries, nevertheless fluctuated in its response to shifts in national and world markets. As noted earlier, Rochester survived a moderate recession in the early eighties and rebounded in the mid- and late eighties through the creation of new businesses which often took advantage of personnel layoffs and retirements from the more established firms. The number of new firms launched in the county averaged 5,000 annually during the late eighties and, while most were small and many failed, with bankruptcies averaging over 2,000 annually, at least 21 "went public," raising some $125 million in capital. The vital spirit of enterprise was undaunted, and to bolster this initiative the city formed the Rochester Economic Development Department (REDD) to provide assistance in planning, zoning, training, and financing to new venturers. REDD collaborated with a privately backed Rochester Industrial Development Corporation with funds for strategic use. Two similar organizations were formed by the county to focus on suburban developments. Together these bodies assisted some 15 companies with projects soaring into the millions and supplying jobs to an estimated 3,600 individuals. The county also offered a 45 percent tax abatement over ten years to industries investing $1 million in improvements and meeting other stipulations relating to employment and the environment.

Rochester's traditional specialization in technological industries and quality products continued with renewed commitment. With 60 percent of the county's industrial wage earners and over 20 percent of all employees in high technology firms in 1980, the community's concerns for education was intense. Already scientists and engineers comprised approximately 4 percent of the work force, twice the national average, but the dynamics of technological production prompted an increased emphasis on research, and Rochester responded with the development of several research parks where one or more firms located laboratories in a creative atmosphere. The camaraderie among scientists engendered in these settings spurred collaboration between managements, as occurred when Kodak, the University of Rochester, and several other firms joined in the research and development of the Opticam project, initiated by Harvey Pollicope who had achieved a break through in optical manufacturing of potential economic and technological significances.*

The high quality of Rochester's products had won many of them secure markets abroad, and exports from the area, already exceeding those of any comparable metropolis, hovered in the $5 billion area during the early eighties and, benefiting from a decline in the ex-

---

* See Andrea Gaber, "Rochester Focuses: A Community's Core Competence," *Harvard Business Review* (July–Aug. 1991), 116–26.

change value of the dollar, these exports soared to $10 billion by 1991. The three major firms, Kodak, Xerox, and Bausch & Lomb, cut their export volume somewhat by their production in branch plants abroad, but several small technological firms, assisted by the industrial development departments, acquired foreign outlets that helped boost the city's exports.

The high quality of Rochester's products also made some of its firms attractive targets for the takeover operators who were ravaging the American business scene during these years. Most of the mergers in previous decades had resulted in shifts in local management, but they maintained, and sometimes increased, local production. Several mergers in the eighties followed that course, but the takeover of the conglomerate Sybron Corporation resulted in a loss of two of its major companies, as well as the headquarters division, and raised the disturbing possibility that Rochester might become a branch-office town. The loss of the top management of Xerox, Gannett, and the Lincoln Alliance Bank, as well as Sybron, pointed in that direction, but David Kearns, the locally reared chairman of Xerox, maintained his Rochester ties and served for seven years as chairman of the University of Rochester's board of trustees. And many of the top executives generously bought out in the mergers maintained their local residence and participation in community affairs.

Many junior executives and skilled workers did loose their jobs in the mergers and especially in the retrenchments of some of the major firms during the recessions. Manufacturing jobs declined in Monroe County from 38 to 27 percent of its total employment during the eighties but remained substantially higher than that of the state or the nation. Productivity per worker, based on a calculation of value added, rose from $70,805 to $95,307, well above that of the state or the nation, enabling the Rochester economy to increase the average industrial wage from $8.64 to $12.76 per hour, again well above state and national averages. Together these advances supported increased employment in trade and services, boosting the county's total employment to a new high of 354,910 in March 1989.* While the non-manu-

---

* See the excellent statistical analysis of data in the 1987 Census of Manufacturers, U.S. Department of Labor, by A. Shivish, "Manufacturing Still Matters," *Democrat & Chronicle*, Mar. 3, 1991, 1–F.

facturing jobs paid less on an average than those lost in the factories, they were in some cases more rewarding and represented for the community, as services abounded, an improvement in the quality of life.

For the unemployed, however, the recurrent recessions were bruising. Many laid-off factory workers had to accept less-paying service jobs and swelled the ranks of part-time workers and second job holders. Wives of middle-class as well as poor families were forced to join the labor force. This trend represented an increase in the total number of women workers, a boon to many women but a strain on many young families with single parents, whose number, especially among poor blacks, also increased. The total number of unemployed in Monroe County fluctuated between a high of 31,100 in March 1983 and a low of 11,900 in March 1988, and it would climb again during the recession of the early nineties.

The Community of Monroe's economy was increasingly linked with that of its four neighboring counties in the Rochester SMSA and with that of the four additional counties in the Genesee/Finger Lakes Economic Development District. As the principle Redevelopment Center for the district, Rochester provided entrepreneurial leadership in its development and shared the productive resources of its inhabitants. The annual *Overall Economic Development Program* issued by its Regional Planning Council supplied detailed information on the counties and their projects and provided a coordinating service to the evolving metropolis. But in expanding its economic team Rochester was adding weaker players, for none of the outlying counties matched Monroe in percentage of employment, wage rates, or institutional structure, and the recessions there were deeper. Yet the potential as well as the challenge was great.

PUBLIC HEALTH AND WELFARE

The plight of the unemployed did not end with their statistical tabulation. Some skilled workers, accepting early retirement with continuing benefits, had bright choices; some found lesser jobs and made economies; but many finally joined the lines at the welfare stations—2,200 a month, a new high in 1990 (although only 1,319

were accepted, as Michael Wentzel reported in the *Times-Union*).
The flood of applicants for public assistance in Monroe County, swollen by the recession of 1989–90, had reached 22,492, up 93 percent
in the city by the end of the year, and Wentzel prodded the county
department of social services for an explanation. The loss of 7,000
jobs in 1990 was a major factor but not the only one. An increased use
of drugs during the eighties, a surge in teenage pregnancies, and the
reductions in federal work programs had contributed to a doubling of
the county's caseload during the eighties. The economic revival during the mid-decade had not restored many of the good jobs, and the
number of unemployed whose insurance benefits were running out
exceeded 400 a month in 1990.

The totals would have been higher, the department reported, if
2,477 of its clients had not found jobs during 1990. Poor education
was a major handicap, and the department referred 1,079 of its applicants to basic education programs in the public schools. It successfully placed others in cooperative job training programs and worked
with public health and other social agencies in treating the needs of
its welfare clients. Unfortunately, the lack of a sufficient number of
affordable houses, even in the inner city where the need was greatest,
forced many families (unable to pay the difference between the public assistance grant of $265 for rent and the $300 plus rental charge)
to break up. The number of homeless persons seeking shelter each
winter mounted to 200, according to a Homeless Action Coalition
report in 1990, and the coalition prepared to open nine church shelters. The problem, an offshoot of the recession of the early eighties,
was not as acute as in some cities where even their local coalitions
were becoming frustrated. But a real solution seemed far off as the
recession deepened in 1991.

Rochester's charitable impulses were undaunted, as the annual
United Way drives continued to demonstrate. Even in recession years
the total was pushed up and oversubscribed, increasing from the unprecedented total of $20,550,000 in 1981 to $37,366,678 in 1991. The
United Way was not a dispenser of relief but a coordinator and sponsor of services among its participating agencies, which increased 50
percent in number during the eighties as United Way assumed full
metropolitan coverage. In response to the crucial urban problems of
the decade, the United Way added six day-care centers to the 12

already supported, and seven youth-oriented projects, including one serving teenage parents, to the dozen previously maintained. In addition, it supported five newly organized centers dealing with family problems, among them the newly highlighted plight of battered women, and eight health services including a local response to the nationwide AIDS contagion.

United Way was not the sole source of private charitable aid, for Rochester had fostered a number of corporate and foundation giving programs, and a third of the 25 programs whose grants in 1990 ranged upwards from $137,000 to $13,796,000 (by Kodak) included health and welfare agencies among their beneficiaries. One innovative grant by the Marie C. and Joseph C. Wilson Foundation spearheaded the establishment of the Wilson Commencement Park to provide housing, child care, and educational aid to single mothers with young babies. This innovative "park" with its fifty cottages and enlightened program afforded a challenging opportunity to build new lives to a small fraction of the burgeoning number of single parents who gave birth to slightly more than a fourth of the babies born in Monroe County (as reported by Planned Parenthood in 1988). Yet it was a ray of hope in a changing society. A half-dozen older, family-oriented agencies were tackling varied aspects of the problem, and a group of black mothers in the inner city banded together to study the Afro-American family heritage.

A succession of Quality of Life studies, comparing Rochester with fourteen somewhat comparable cities in the early eighties, generally gave it first place in charitable effort and participation and a fair rating in medical care. Its six major hospitals, operating near capacity, were practicing more cooperatively than those in many cities where competition was rife, and Strong Memorial Hospital developed a program of treatment for premature infants that won acclaim in 1991 for its success in saving babies. The improvement in medical services was accompanied by an upward surge in health-care employment, which mounted annually in the metropolitan district from 23,500 in 1980 to 49,000 in 1991. It was a welcomed source of jobs but it placed a heavy burden on Blue Cross, Blue Shield, HMO's, and other insurers, as well as on patients without coverage. The benefits, however, outweighed the costs, and to assure wider distribution of these benefits, the Health Association opened a Hispanic Health Center on Clinton

Avenue North to serve the 20,000 Hispanic residents chiefly concentrated in that district. The new center, publicized in connection with other Hispanic Heritage Month activities, supplied its services with bilingual attendants.

COSMOPOLITAN TRENDS

Each of the city's major ethnic and cultural groups had participated in its sesquicentennial activities, strengthening their sense of identity in the process, and each looked to the future with confidence. Annual downtown tent festivals and Main Street parades by the varied groups nurtured plans for a month-long series of Hispanic cultural programs at the Strong Museum in September 1991 and for a year-long commemoration by local Italian clubs of the 500th anniversary in 1992 of the discover of America by Columbus, with programs at the Convention Center and elsewhere. The revival of Polish traditions at three Polish Catholic churches and the Polish Civic Center supported the publication by Kathleen Shoulder of her historical account of *Polish Americans in Rochester, 1891–1991*. Similar programs by local Ukrainians, Slovaks, Germans, and Irish marked appropriate ethnic anniversaries. The city annually observed with partial holidays the birthdays of Martin Luther King, Jr., Frederick Douglass, and Susan B. Anthony, and ABC staged a series of Afro-American programs at the Convention Center and elsewhere in July 1991. Even the Chinese, whose annual celebrations of the New Year on February 14 and 15 attracted crowds to their several restaurants, maintained language and cultural programs at local colleges and museums serving some 3,000 residents of Chinese ancestry scattered throughout the metropolis.

Rochester's cosmopolitan population was still in flux, with newcomers arriving from old as well as new sources. Most of them continued to trickle in, as they had done from the beginning, attracted by job prospects or by family or friendly ties from nearby or distant states (including blacks from the south and Hispanics from Puerto Rico). Immigrants from abroad, especially those admitted as refugees, now required local sponsorship and a record of supervision for 90 days to assure proper settlement. It was a demanding but challenging assignment, but three local agencies undertook that service. The Jewish Community Federation, which had long provided a welcome to new-comers of that faith, accepted the more vigorous federal requirements when a relaxation of Soviet restrictions on migration released a flood of Jewish refugees. As 151 of these refugees headed for Rochester in 1990, local sponsors ready to provide shelter and sustenance had to be (and were) found, and preparations were made for the resettlement of another 150 in the following year. GEM, which had undertaken a moderate resettlement program in 1979 by placing three or four newcomers a month throughout the area, found itself inundated with six to eight applicants a week in 1989, as refugees from Poland, Ethiopia, Vietnam, Cuba, and Cambodia joined those from Russia on its doorstep. GEM's intensified canvass for sponsors and for church pledges of support was matched by a similar drive by the Catholic Family Center, the third local resettlement agency, which resettled some 1,300 refugees during the eighties from Vietnam and other Asian countries where American troops had been stationed.

Although still divided into divergent denominations and faiths, the churches of Rochester were engaging in increasingly tolerant co-operative efforts. GEM, an outgrowth in the seventies of an earlier Protestant Council of Churches with its emphasis on Christian educa-tion, had learned to cooperate on social reforms with Catholic churches, which were now included as full partners in GEM. Reach-ing out in the eighties to absorb the more evangelical black churches of the United Church Ministry, GEM finally reorganized in 1991 as the Community of Churches and welcomed into full membership all churches, temples, and institutions with dedicated religious goals for collaboration in joint endeavors.

GOVERNMENTAL RESPONSIBILITIES

Although animated by a host of volunteer agencies dedicated to community improvement and the solution of its problems, Rochester continued to rely in crucial matters on an unstable variety of govern-mental resources. Because Rochester's housing programs faltered when federal subsides were shut off and the plight of the unemployed increased when their entitled benefits were exhausted, County Executive Thomas Frey had to budget a tax increase to provide the welfare outlays prescribed by local and state authorities. Even in the recreational and cultural fields the support of the city and county was frequently in demand for the provision of new facilities and aid in their maintenance. In the field of public safety, governmental responsibility, though predominant, was again divided and responsive to citizen pressure groups.

Despite occasional outbreaks of crime, Rochester had won recognition as one of the least violent cities during the seventies and maintained that standing throughout the eighties. Only 7 of 70 metropolitan areas tabulated in February 1989 exceed it (by small fractions), but the situation changed dramatically as a surge of homicides hit the city during the next three years. Rochester had achieved its commendable record partly through the vigilance of its police in apprehending suspects even for minor offenses, a practice that led to a crowded county jail and forced the construction of a minimum security annex in Brighton and the addition of new cells in a civic center building adjoining the downtown jail. A study of the astonishing succession of homicides revealed that handguns had been the principal weapon (stimulating a renewed campaign for a more rigorous check on their sale), that prostitution had frequently been related to the crimes (prompting neighborhood efforts to eradicate it from two affected districts), and that drug heists or drug addiction were the most frequent causes.

Rochester had responded to President Bush's call for a war on drugs in 1989 by organizing a coalition of criminal justice and social service agencies, forming a 47-member committee under the caption, "Greater Rochester Fights Back." With funds supplied by the city, county, and United Way, the committee launched a school-oriented educational program and media campaign portraying the hazards of drugs and made a drug sweep of Fight Village and the northeast district where drug sales were notoriously abundant. A number of drug dealers were apprehended and others dislocated, but the vigor with which some of the officers questioned the suspects led to complaints of civil rights infringement from which federal indictments ensued. The simultaneous indictment and conviction early in 1992 of Police Chief Gordon Urlacher for embezzlement of funds cast a shadow over the department, a shadow which the new Chief Roy Irving and Mayor Ryan hoped to dispel by increasing the size of the force and by implementing a plan for using a drug crisis center to treat and rehabilitate drug addicts.

A widely distributed questionnaire prepared by another citizen's committee, under the caption, "Goals for a Greater Rochester," elicited responses from 39,947 householders in Rochester and Monroe County answering queries concerning the community's merits and shortcomings and endorsing goals for its improvement. Almost 60 percent of the respondents labeled drugs as the most serious problem and identified alcohol, nicotine, cocaine, and marijuana in that order as the principal hazards they had personally observed. In the search for solutions, a majority of respondents endorsed stiffer penalties for drug sellers but favored expenditures on drug treatment centers over jail cells for addicts. Two-thirds of the respondents expressed a willingness to accept tax increases for drug and alcohol control and treatment. Local as well as national action was endorsed.

A forthright effort to tackle one aspect of the problem was launched by the Rochester Housing Authority, which secured three successive grants from HUD for a program designed to ban the sale and use of drugs from the vicinity of its numerous projects. It enlisted trained police and social workers for surveillance and promoted the development of drug treatment programs at Baden Street Settlement and the Anthony S. Jordan Health Center. But the drug problem was not exclusively or even primarily an inner city concern; a state-wide survey of drug use in grades 7 through 12 in public and private schools reported a greater prevalence in the Genesee-Finger Lakes district than in New York City. This disclosure prompted a determined effort to eradicate drugs from the suburban Pittsford school district, discovered to be heavily infected by their use.

The Goals survey had found strong community support for alternative youth activities as the second best solution of the drug problem. The city and county were, in fact, already providing a host of such opportunities. They had collaborated in the celebration of the 1988 centennial of the Rochester Park System by reopening the enlarged and remodeled Lamberton Observatory with a spectacular floral and art display on March 25–26. The centennial continued throughout the year with a score of park-related activities—conducted tours, picnics, and the traditional floral festivals, band concerts, and fireworks displays.

Encouraged by the response to the parks' centennial programs,

Mayor Ryan and the City Council formulated plans for a series of development areas along the river to guide private housing and industrial as well as park and recreational improvements. They projected a waterfront revitalization of the lake shore and river below the lower falls, the development of an urban cultural park spanning the river from the lower falls to downtown, a refurbishing of the Exchange Street and Corn Hill district on the west side, and a cooperative development with the university of the south river corridor. Progress in each area was highlighted by a succession of ceremonies —a laser light and sound display at the newly opened Ponte de Rennes footbridge (formerly the Platt Street bridge) on October 25, 1990, a dedication of the Interpretive Center of the Brown's Race Historic District at the High Falls Park on July 2, 1991, and a Discover the River celebration on Columbus Discovery Day weekend in October 1991 with boat races on the South Corridor, canoe and walking tours on the lower river, and ceremonies at the High Falls. Chilly weather and a threat of showers cut attendance at the joint river and Columbus Discovery Day events, but a year later the formal opening of the Brown's Race restoration attracted crowds of enthusiastic spectators with successive laser light and sound displays at the High Falls. The event kindled hopes that the spectacular facility will not only nurture the community's appreciation of its history but provide an additional boost to Rochester's burgeoning tourist trade.

Rochester's sports and entertainment facilities had reached a point where the choices were so diverse that attendance was sometimes disappointing. A glance at the "Weekend" supplements of the two Gannett papers, or at *City's* "Newcomers" annual guides, with their extensive lists of sports clubs, music and dance clubs, and scheduled events, and with maps showing the location of motion picture and dramatic theaters, museums and galleries, as well as parks and camping areas throughout the metropolitan district, explained why some of their managers occasionally paraphrased Howard Hanson's caustic remark that "what Rochester needed most was more listeners"— more participants. Some of the 60 neighborhood associations and numerous ethnic societies active in the early eighties merged into coalitions or federations and did a fair job of enlisting participants in their activities, but they seldom recruited teenagers. The Red Wings, despite a number of happy seasons, faced a problem of declining attendance, blaming it on the defects and poor location of their park. Late in 1992, they launched a vigorous search for a suitable site downtown or at least within the metropolitan district for a proper stadium. While many of the increasing number of senior-citizen golfers frequently stood impatiently in line awaiting their turns at one or another of the 13 public golf courses in the metropolitan area, the 19 private and 28 semi-private courses readily accommodated the overflow.

Most of the area's recreational facilities were designed for leisure time use and fitted the needs of youths as well as of adults who had other purposeful activities, but dropouts as well as the unemployed were seldom engaged. Even the sports teams and other extra curricular activities in the junior and senior high schools were restricted to students with satisfactory grades. Dropouts generally found their companions in the streets of their neighborhoods, and a few neighborhood associations and suburban towns focused on the prevention of delinquency and crime. The sense of belonging to a local neighborhood was enhanced for many throughout the county and district by the practice adopted in July 1989 by the Gannett papers of including a full section on "Our Towns" in their daily issues. The practice, designed to enable local merchants to place ads to target their intended market, had the additional effect of acquainting city and suburban readers with the extent and diversity of the metropolis they inhabited.

The annual reports of the Genesee/Finger Lakes Regional Planning Council provided a similar service to city and town officials and interested business leaders. In the absence of a metropolitan authority, the council provided a coordinating leadership for the identification of regional needs and the assignments of priorities, and it offered assistance in the search for state and foundation resources. The council enhanced its influence throughout its nine-county area by creating a District Revolving Loan Fund to assist in the planning or start-up of promising new industries. Thus in 1991, after appraising the services of the newly rebuilt Greater Rochester International Airport, the council targeted funds for the planning of possible subsidiary airports at seven regional development centers. Monroe County, recognizing the inadequacy of its airport, crowded by an annual passenger load of a million travelers in the mid-eighties, had assumed the planning and reconstruction of a sumptuous new airport with the full backing of its servicing airlines. When finally completed in 1991, it provided Rochester with a spectacular threshold for its international visitors for years to come.

More visitors and infinitely more residents of the metropolis entered the city by motor car than by plane, and the completion of the Outer Loop in the early eighties channeled an increasing flow of cars through the complex eastern intersection with the Expressway, popularly known as the Can of Worms. Long protests over the intersection's hazards, combined with a need to repair some of the overpasses, persuaded the state highway department to undertake its reconstruction, a three-year task which was completed early in 1991.

Cities are frequently buffeted by external forces over which they have no control but, in their response to these forces, reveal much concerning their character. Thus the dramatic end of the Cold War in 1990 produced a local euphoria best symbolized by the action of the International Sister Cities of Rochester board in finally welcoming the privately developed Rochester-Novgorod linkage to full sister-city membership, making a family of eight. The onset of the Gulf War prompted a loyal, if not enthusiastic, mustering in of some 2,000 service men and women called up for active duty. Despite some displays of protest, including a Main Street parade of 5,000 citizens who favored a more peaceful approach to the problem, the city and towns staged joyous welcoming ceremonies for the returning units and held a Fourth of July parade in their honor in 1991.

But it was the ice storm which devastated the Rochester area on March 3–4, 1991, that produced its most characteristic response. The city's long experience with heavy snows and its reputation as one of the most effective snow fighters failed to prepare it for the freezing blast of rain and sleet that ravished its proud canopy of trees and toppled many backyard power and telephone lines. The effects of this devastation stranded some 300,000 residents in cold, dark, and silent homes and shops throughout the metropolitan district for several days and nights, and in some cases the loss of these services extended into a second and third week. While city, town, and utility crews enlisted assistance from sources as far away as Long Island, only the prompt response of the local residents, whose homes had escaped damage and who hastened to supply shelter supplementing that provided by the Red Cross and others in churches and schools, made the calamity endurable. But the crisis was also a challenge. Assured by the federal government of disaster relief, the city and towns cleared the debris, restored services, and boldly formulated plans for the planting of new trees and greening of the environment by 2000.

THE FUTURE

Many Rochesterians are looking ahead, and while historians should not make predictions, they may record the thoughts and projects of their contemporaries. Rochesterians are not only looking but also planning ahead. The university, for example, is pressing ahead with a drive for $375 million to fund a variety of improvements. RIT, having survived a bruising internal controversy over its relationship with the CIA, is preparing under its new president, Albert J. Simone, to supply the community's continuing demand for technological and scientific training. St. John Fisher is launching a program to train young adults for leadership in tackling civic problems. Local museums and galleries are vying in their efforts to develop exhibits that will portray the full range of Rochester's cultural heritage.

And in the more mundane fields, hopes and expectations that the Bush recession will end are rife. Announcements of impending layoffs at Kodak, Xerox, and other large firms are frequently paired with plans for expected breakthroughs, such as at Kodak with the Opticam project sponsored at the university, or at Xerox with its Docutech publishing system. The same issue of the *Democrat & Chronicle* that reported two sizable retrenchments printed a full page list of 100 firms that had increased their employment during the last three years. Most of them were relatively new and still small enterprises, but they were looking ahead, and two of the top five were in construction, building for the future. Several had a technological character that fitted in with Rochester's newly adopted identity alias, the World's Image Center.

Every reorganization and improvement seems to bring new problems, but instead of fretting over the possible hazards, Rochesterians are tackling those already at hand. City planners have projected the downtown redevelopment proposals for residential neighborhoods within the Inner Loop, a step forward in Vision 2000. The Goals for a Greater Rochester committee endorses that development, but it sets a shorter time schedule for its several other goals, with emphasis on the anti-drug efforts of Rochester Fights Back. Already the county, recognizing the widening spread of that problem, has projected the development of a drug treatment crisis center to coordinate with the Housing Authority's program in the city. The city schools, encouraged by a decline in the dropout rate in the high schools and spurred by a newly formed Union of Parents, are pressing ahead with parent-teacher collaboration for improved student achievement. When Peter McWalters announced his resignation to accept appointment as superintendent of the Rhode Island school system, the Rochester board promptly named as his successor Manuel Rivera, a Hispanic who had advanced in the Rochester schools in 15 years from elementary teacher, director of bilingual education, and principal of two high schools to superintendent of the northeast district. His warm relation with teachers, students, and parents assured a vigorous continuation of the reform program with additional minority support.

Stimulated by the 1990 census,* demographic projections predict Rochester will successfully check its recent declines in population chiefly by the continued increase of its black and Hispanic-American residents, who will become a majority by 2000. This nascent majority, together with women, long since a majority, already represents a major portion of the work force and is gaining acceptance into managerial and professional circles, as well as selection for responsible positions on administrative and decision-making boards of the large employers, including city and county government. Xerox, with C. Barry Rand in the top office of the loftiest tower in the city and with a fifth of his managers also recruited from minorities, is unrivaled in Rochester or in the nation—an affirmative action model in its training programs as well as in its staffing.

The women of Rochester, with a long tradition of earnest activity, highlighted by the informal civic leadership of Susan B. Anthony, Mary T. Gannett, Helen Barrett Montgomery, Helen Jones, Mildred Johnson, and Georgianna Sibley, acquired new recognition during the sesquicentennial year. The forthright participation of the League of Women Voters in civic affairs, backed by a number of socially

---

* The 1990 census gave Rochester a 4 percent drop to 231,636, Monroe County a 2 percent increase to 713,968, and the Rochester SMSA a 3.2 percent increase to 1,002,410.

influential women's clubs, found new support in the eighties through the rapid growth of the Women's Network of professional women with positions of influence in economic as well as civic and social fields. The current success of Louise Slaughter in winning a fourth term as Rochester's representative in Congress amply vindicates Susan B. Anthony's dreams.

But the city's success in attaining any of its goals depends less on the affirmative action of its executives than on the ready cooperation of all groups involved. As Barbara Henry, editor of the *Democrat & Chronicle* and the *Times-Union* put it recently in a strong statement, a sense of identity with a neighborhood, a town, an ethnic group, or a cultural heritage is desirable for individuals and families, and her papers have cultivated it with "Our Towns" and other features. But it is not sufficient to sustain and motivate a community which has acquired metropolitan proportions. A new sense of identity with and cooperation within this larger community must be cultivated.

People rather than resources have determined Rochester's history. Successive generations have had their impact, as we have seen, generally in proportion to the coordination of their efforts. One striking weakness of the sesquicentennial generation has been the low turnout of voters in local elections. The number registered in the county has increased slightly, though not as markedly as the population. The active political campaigns of the 1991 election, featured in the printed media and over the airways, has reversed, though only moderately, the traditional drop in voter participation in the third local election, producing several shifts in town and county leadership, notably the replacement of Democrat Thomas Frey by Republican Robert King as county executive. When King, encountering stringencies in the county budget, failed to secure approval in the Democratically controlled county legislature for a one-percent increase in the sales tax, he pressed for a repeal of the Morin-Ryan agreement, governing the distribution of such revenues. Alarmed by the threatened injury to the fiscal stability of the city, the core of the metropolis, officials of Kodak and the Chamber of Commerce protested, and Bausch & Lomb displayed uncertainty about its plan to erect a headquarters building downtown. The protracted controversy finally produced a compromise restoring the Morin-Ryan agreement, with a cap on the city's share as previously effected, and authorizing a current increase of 0.5

percent in the sales tax with an additional 0.5 percent increase if conditions warrant it a year later.

Voting in national elections has traditionally been much stronger than in local elections and, although it dropped a bit in the eighties from the 90.3 percent of 1972, it has surged to a new high of 90 percent of a sharply increased registration total in 1992. And if the county's tally is curiously split—Democrats winning in the presidential election and Republicans achieving control of the county legislature—it illustrates support both for Clinton's more positive governmental economy and for King's more aggressive local tax policy.

But in looking ahead, Rochesterians of the sesquicentennial generation are not forgetting or abandoning their heritage. One tradition, highlighted by Ray Stannard Baker in his laudatory comments in 1910 on Rochester in its golden age is still with us. His comments that Rochester's "preeminence over other cities of its class was not due to its material prosperity but to the earnestness with which it attacked defects today." The vigor with which the press and other local spokesmen have attacked not only local "Johns" and murderous psychopaths but also the powers-that-be when they misstep is in keeping with that tradition. And the powers-that-be are responding—Kodak in tackling its environmental contamination problems, the U of R in welcoming students of all nationalities, and RIT in reassessing its affiliation with the CIA. Some challenges are not easily met, as United Way has discovered when its decision to deny support for Planned Parenthood's projected abortion clinic threatened a cancellation of pledges by pro-Choice subscribers (or by Right to Life advocates if United Way reneged). Decisions will not be easy to make or to carry out for these or other perplexing problems, but another Rochester characteristic, a product of the Finney religious revival of 1830, remains deeply rooted. Finney's assurance that man's fate is not preordained and that salvation is attainable by all who devoutly seek it has, in 150 years, acquired a more secular interpretation—that we are free and responsible citizens. Thus the future of Rochester will be determined by its inhabitants, and if its industrialists succeed in winning recognition as the World's Imaging Center, the multi-racial, dual-gendered generation that is taking over will add a significant cosmopolitan ingredient to that moniker.

Index

Abbott, Mrs. Helen Probst, 169, 170
Academies, pioneer, 31, 53, 54, 76. *See also* Schools, private
Academy of Music, 94, 120, 144. *See also* Corinthian Hall
Academy of Music and Art, 83
Academy of Science, 118
Action for a Better Community (ABC), 257, 258
Adams, Rev. Myron, 118
Ad Club, 161, 184
Adler, Isaac, 171, 191
Adler, Levi, 153
Advertiser, established, 34. *See also* Henry O'Reilly, as editor; *Union & Advertiser*
Aex, Robert P., 218, 233
African Methodist Episcopal (A.M.E.) Zion Church, 58, 80, 123
Agassiz, Professor Louis, 68
Airport, 217, 311–12
Album, 27
Aldridge, George W.: Executive Board member, 110, 111, 116; political leadership of, 124, 131–37, passim, 154, 156–58, 169–70; serves as mayor, 128
Aldridge, George W., Sr., 90
Alexander, Arthur, 186
Alinsky, Saul, 257, 258
Allan, Ebenezer, builds mills, 3, 4
Alling, Joseph T.: as political leader, 124, 130–33, 137; social causes of, 128, 139, 154, 189
Amalgamated Clothing Workers, 177, 178, 196, 212, 235, 285
Amalgamated Optical Workers, 177

American Jewish Joint Distribution Committee, 201
Amusements: early, 33, 61, 69, 77, 92, 116, 120–21; urban, 136, 139, 141, 181–82, 220–21, 274–76
Anderson, Pres. Martin B., 69, 80, 93, 117, 118
Anderson Hall, 93
Andrews, J. Sherlock, 119
Andrews, Samuel G., 50, 75, 98
Andrews, Samuel J., 32
Andrews Street bridge, 50
Anthony, Susan B.: as abolitionist, 68, 80; demands right to vote, 91, 122; maintains women's rights, 76, 140, 146, 154, 166; memorial to, 224, 291, 306
Anthony A. Jordan Health Center, 309
Anthony & Scoville Co., 150
Anti-Catholic feelings, 44, 61, 77, 93. *See also* Know-Nothing party
Anti-Masonic Enquirer, 34
Anti-Masonry, 31, 34, 35, 41, 57
Anti-Monopoly Cheap Freight Railway League, 88
Antisdale, Louis M., 130, 133, 145
Anti-Slavery Society, 59, 68, 79
Anti-war demonstrations, 281
Appy, Henri, 119
Aqueduct: first, 25; second, 44, 45
Archer, George W., 99
Arena Group, 224
Arnold, Mrs. Helen D., 155
Art: exhibits, 78, 142, 184, 224; galleries, 61, 93, 184, 224
Ashford, Laplois, 253, 255, 262, 266, 267
Astor, John Jacob, 45
Athenaeum, 41, 55, 56, 61

317

Athenaeum and Mechanics Association, 68, 77, 83, 94
Atkinson, William, 16
Auditorium Theater, 207
Authors' Day, 282
Automobiles, 141, 174, 182, 221

Bacon, Theodore, 131
Baden Street Settlement, 160, 309
Baker, Harold W., 172, 197, 198
Baker, Ray Stannard, xiv, 139, 316
Baker Theater, 143
Balestier, Charles W., 118
Ball, Raymond N., 192, 212
Band concerts, 33, 61, 157, 186
Bank of Rochester, 20, 22–23, 38
Banks: in Depression, 89, 96, 126, 190, 194, 196; developments of, 233; early, 20, 22, 45, 65; expansion of, 74, 81, 88, 89
Baptist churches, 14, 32, 57, 60, 67
Barbour, Clarence A., 131
Barnard, Jehiel, 13
Barnes, Dr. Sidney W., 228
Barry, Patrick: business activities of, 83, 97; as nurseryman, 48, 49, 64, 104; promoter of parks, 112
Barry, Mayor Peter, 216, 231
Bartholomay, Henry, 87, 105
Bartholomew, Harland, 173, 193
Bartlett, Dr. Gene, 261, 280
Barton, D. R., 87
Baseball: early clubs, 71, 78, 92; organized teams, 120, 141, 182, 275
Basketball, 141, 275
Bausch, Edward, 207
Bausch & Lomb: develops patents, 106, 150, 152; fills war orders, 165, 204; labor struggles at, 177, 212; new plants of, 214, 235, 246, 284, 302, 315
Beckwith, Francis, 90
Beecher, Rev. George, 57
Beer gardens, 92
Beinetti, George S., 261
Bell Telephone Company, 108, 148, 174
Benedict, Nehemiah, 114
Bernstein, Rabbi Philip, 194, 226
Bersagliere La Narmora, 123
Better Business Bureau, 175
Better Housing Association, 207

Bible Society, 67, 77
Bicycles, 121, 140, 141, 151
Bijou Dream, 144
Bissel, Josiah, Jr., 10, 40
Bissel, Josiah W., 72
Black Muslims, 249
Blacks: families, 297–98, 299; influx of, 241–42, 247, 249, 251, 253, 254, 260, 264, 266, 271, 272; protests by, 280–81; See also Negroes
Blanchard, Lafayette R., 229
Blue Cross, 218, 305
Blue Shield, 218, 305
Blue Valley Bus Co., 235
Board of Education: activities of, 53, 54, 76, 83, 90; reform of, 131, 133, 134, 136, 140, 142, 183; urges new schools, 218, 238, 250; work of in inner city, 256, 258, 263
Board of Health: created, 29, 41; meets cholera epidemic, 51; programs of, 90, 111
Board of Manufacturers, 38, 46. See also Board of Trade; Chamber of Commerce
Board of Trade, 74, 87. See also Chamber of Commerce
Board of Urban Ministry, 257
Boat: lines, 44; yards, 72, 82
Bock, Dr. Franklin, 169
Bonner, J. Franklin, 194, 198
"Books Sandwiched In," 225
Bookstores, 78
Bottom of the Bucket, 282, 292
Bounties, in Civil War, 84, 85
Bowling alleys, 141
Boy Scouts, 161
Bragdon, Claude, 143, 145
Bray, Harry, 256
Brewer, James L., 162
Brewster, H. Pomeroy, 118
Brickner, Max, 125
Bridges, construction of, 23, 27, 48, 50, 70, 75, 191, 193
Briggs, Charles, 87
Briggs, Theodore C., 195
Brighton-Pittsford Post, 229, 238
B'rith Kodesh Synagogue, 58, 67
British, influx of, 47, 71, 139
Brittin, William, 25
Broad Street, 233, 287

Brockway, Zebulon, 76
Broderick, Thomas E., 198, 216
Brown, Carey H., 193
Brown, Francis, 9
Brown, Dr. Matthew, 7, 13, 21, 23, 28, 38
Brown Square, 297
Brugler, Mercer, 192, 210, 245
Brunner and Olmsted, 157, 172
Bub, William J., 248, 250, 256
Buell, George C., 125, 127
Buffalo Bill, 120
Buffalo, Rochester & Pittsburgh Railroad, 126, 147. *See also* State Line Railroad
Buffalo Street, 9, 50
Bureau of Municipal Research: advocates efficiency, 162, 168, 169, 173, 175; endorses economy, 193, 204; studies urban problems, 215, 260, 261. *See also* Center for Governmental Research
Burke, Judge Harold P., 269
Burkhart, Dr. Harvey J., 185
Burr, Dr. Hugh C., 226
Bush, Mrs. Abigail, 59
Bush, Roy, 218
Busing, enforced, 265
Butting, Lou, 293
Butts, Isaac, 84, 89, 116

Caldwell, Earl, 247
Campbell, Benjamin, 47
Campbell-Whittlesey House, 225
Canadians, influx of, 71, 122
Canandaigua: pioneer settlement, 3, 5, 11, 12, 17; railroad ties with, 44; rival to Rochester, 12, 15, 20, 22
Can of Worms, 312
Capone, Anthony A., 210
Carlson, Chester, 234
Carnahan, Mayor George A., 133, 134
Carpenter, Clifford E., 229, 248
Carroll, Maj. Charles, 6, 14, 16, 23
Carson, Loftus, 260
Carthage: early settlement at, 15, 16, 23, 24; fall of bridge at, 23; landing at, 37, 44
Cartwright, Louis, 172, 198, 207, 217, 218
Casey, James D., 133
Castle Company, 245

Catholic: churches, 23, 55, 58, 67, 68, 116, 117; Diocese of Rochester, 93, 117, 138; orphan asylum, 55; schools, 55, 114, 183–84
Caverely, Joseph M., 220, 275
Cemetery: on Buffalo St., 29; on Mount Hope, 50, 60
Centennial, 158, 200
Center for Governmental Research, 272, 285, 296, 297, 299
Central Business District, 293–94
Central Labor Union, 99
Central Trades Council, 89, 99, 126, 154, 165, 191, 211
Chamber of Commerce: establishment of, 100, 105, 125; of Greater Rochester, 273, 286, 287; promotions of, 130, 147, 149, 157, 175; social functions of, 167, 210, 211, 234; statistical work of, 180, 193, 202
Channing, William H., 67
Chapman, Albert K., 244
Charlotte: blast furnace at, 87, favors annexation, 159; as pioneer settlement, 6, 7, 9, 10, 12, 37; as resort, 70, 121
Chatham Gardens, 254
Chatman, Abraham, 196, 212, 235
Chernuck, Miss Dorothy, 222
Child, Jonathan: business affairs of, 23, 25, 40, 44, 46, 47, 64; the first mayor, 40, 43, 49; withdrawal of, 72
Children's Aid Society, 128
Children's Playground League, 136
Childs, Timothy, 21, 34
Child's Basin, 25
Chinese, 242
Cholera epidemic: of 1832, 41; of 1849, 51; of 1852, 65, 66
Christopher, John G., 11
Churches: early, 14, 32; Federation of, 307; increase of, 56, 58, 67, 77, 116; removal of, 225, 287
Churchill, L. & H., 82
Circuses, 78
Citizens Advisory Council, 259
Citizens Council for a Better Rochester, 210, 211
Citizens Light & Power Company, 134
Citizens Political Reform Association, 131

City charter: campaign for, 27, 38; revision of, 132, 137, 170–71, 269
City Club: civic programs of, 140, 181, 184; decline of, 281; holds public forum, 163, 169, 210, 230; leaders of, 208
City-County Human Relations Commission, 237
City-County Youth Board, 248
City Hall, demand for, 90; new, 287, 291
City Hospital, 83, 150, 155
City planning, 172, 173, 236
Civic Center, 171, 217, 236, 269, 287
Civic Committee on Unemployment, 191, 192
Civic Development Council, 210
Civic Improvement Association, 157, 173, 193
Civic Music Assoc., 188, 233, 274, 282
Civic Orchestra, 199, 237, 282
Civil War: casualties from, 81, 84, 85; memorial pageant, 276; Rochester's response to, 79–83
Clark, Sidney R., 130
Clarke, Freeman, 64, 72
Clarkson, George A., 91, 110
Clearing House, 97, 99, 195, 210
Clinton, Governor DeWitt, 27, 31, 32
Clinton Square Building, 294
Clothiers Exchange, 101, 126, 153, 177–78
Clothing industry: employs immigrant workers, 48, 73, 74, 101; expansion of, 87, 100, 152, 177–78; labor policy of, 196, 212
Clothing workers, 101, 178. See also Amalgamated Clothing Workers
Clubs, 69, 119, 121, 145; golf, 275
Coal: Exchange, 126; supplies of, 64, 81, 82, 88, 97, 147
Coates, Albert, 186, 187
Cobb, William, 13
Cobleigh Hall, 119
Colby, Eugene C., 114
Colgate-Rochester Divinity School, 189, 272, 279, 280, 300. See also Rochester Theological Seminary
College of the Sacred Heart, 55
Colleges: graduates of, 17, 299–300; students at, 55, 76, 114, 146, 227, 300. See also University of Rochester

Collegiate Institute, 66
Colonial Airways, 175
Columbus Civic Center, 183
Columbus Day, 138
Commercial Travelers Association, 99
Community Chest: establishment of, 168, 182; joins in relief effort, 191–92, 194, 203, 205; post-war programs of, 218, 236, 248, 252, 259, 285–86. See also United Way
Community College, 229, 238, 268
Community Conference Board, 178–80, 191
Community Music Festival, 181
Community of Monroe, 289–91, 303, 315
Community Players, 189, 222
Community Roundtable, 299
Convention and Publicity Board, 295
Cook, Frederick, 96, 98
Cooper, John H., 211
Cooper, Thomas, 4
Cooper, Dr. Walter, 257
Cooper, William, 7
Coopers, activity of, 26, 73
Corinthian Hall, 56, 61, 69, 78–84; passim, 94
Corn Hill district, 310
Cornell, Ezra, 64
Corris, Robert B., 216, 222
Corris, Will R., 207
Cosmopolitan Club, 219
Cosmopolitan influences, 116, 138, 306. See also Immigrants
Cosmos Hall, 93
Council for a Better Citizenship, 181
Council-manager government, 171
Council of Industrial Organizations (CIO), 211. See also Labor unions
Council of Social Agencies: advocates welfare reforms, 169, 190, 197, 248, 250, 259; backs relief programs, 191, 194, 218, 263
Council on Post-War Problems, 207, 226
County jail, 27, 52, 90, 269
Court House: first, 21, 27; second, 65, 128
Court Street, bridge at, 27
Cox, Patrick, 102
Craftsman, 34
Craig, Oscar, 113

Crane, Mrs. Caroline B., 158
Crapsey, Adelaide, 146
Crapsey, Dr. Algernon, 131, 139
Cribben, Henry, 87
Cricket clubs, 78
Crime in Rochester, 52, 65, 269, 308
Crittenden, DeLancey, 119
Croft, Edward S., 248, 250, 256, 260, 261, 262, 265
Cross, Miss Florence, 154, 169
Crossroads Project, 272
Cultural District, 294–95
Culver Field, 141
Cuming, Reverend Francis H., 32
Cumming, Howard T., 236
Cunningham, James, 73, 103
Cunningham carriage factory, 96, 151
Cuomo, Mario, 292
Curr, John, 92
Curran, Arthur, 267, 268
Curtice Brothers, 87
Curtis, Edward P., Jr., 270, 272, 291
Curtis, Eugene T., 125
Cutler, James G.: as business leader, 106; as civic leader, 124, 132; as mayor, 135, 136, 148, 154, 157, 162, 172, 188

Dale, John, 263
Dallas, Jack, 141
Dalzell, Robert M., 37
D'Amanda, Francis J., 218
Dancing, 55, 91
Danforth, Fanny, 93
Dansville, 8, 45
Dauby, A. G., 14, 33
Daughters of the American Revolution, 123
Davies, Captain Thomas, 2
Dean, Edwin, 61
Dean, Dr. Henry W., 92
Defender Photo Supply Co., 176, 214
Defense Council, 202, 203
de Kiewiet, Dr. Cornelis W., 228
Democrat, 81, 85
Democrat & Chronicle, 115, 116, 145
Democratic party: campaign of, 170; policies of, 195, 197, 216; reform of, 218, 251, 267, 269
Denne, William F., 251, 269
Dennis, James H., 128

Depression: of 1837, 46; of 1870s, 95–96; of 1890s, 124, 127, 129; of 1930s, 190–96
Dessauer, John A., 234
Dewey, Dr. Chester: as civic leader, 43, 56, 68–69; as educator, 54, 60, 77, 94
Dewey, D. M., 78
Dicker, Mayor Samuel B., 198, 202, 217, 218
Digman, Tom, 295
Dime Museum, 120
Directory, of 1827, 26, 31, 36
Disorderly houses, 52, 112
Divinity School, 226
DKG Institute of Musical Art, 185
Dolley, Dr. Sarah A., 122
Door of Hope, 129, 161
Dossenbach, Herman, 142, 143, 185, 186
Douglass, Frederick: editor of North Star, 59, 68; leader of anti-slavery forces, 77, 79, 84, 86; memorial to, 146, 291, 306
Douglass Union League, 123
Driving Park, 120
Drugs, 308–9
Dryden Theater, 222
DuBridge, Dr. Lee, 204, 228
Dugan, Christopher, 4
Durand-Eastman Park, 236

East Avenue, 141, 277
Easter, Luke, 251
East High School, 135, 218
Eastman, George: early career of, 106–8; industrial leadership of, 124, 128, 130, 149, 150, 167, promotes labor peace, 178–80; social interests of, 143, 154–56, 161, 165, 170, 186; urges civic reforms, 162, 168, 169, 171; war efforts of, 164–66; welfare and other bequests, 156, 173, 182, 185–89, 199; work is done, 194. See also Eastman Kodak Company
Eastman Dental Dispensary, 185, 227
Eastman House, 155, 222. See also George Eastman House
Eastman Kodak Company: in Depression, 128, 196; growth of, 150, 176, 214, 244, 274, 275; meets war-time needs, 204, 206; opposes labor organization, 150, 212, 235, 262; research programs, 300; supports community efforts, 223; works

Eastman Kodak Company (*cont.*)
training programs of, 250, 259, 260–62, 284
Eastman School of Music, 185, 200, 224, 237, 294
Eastman Theatre, 185–88, 199, 223, 230, 282, 292
Eastview Mall, 275
Edgerton, Hiram H.: as candidate, 131, 137; as mayor, 156–58, 162, 169–70, 172; as mediator, 177, 179
Edison, Thomas A., 107, 144
Eilers, Louis K., 244
Ellingson, Dr. Mark, 210, 227
Elliott, George W., 125
Ellis, Harvey, 99, 103
Ellis, Sylvannus, 114
Ellwanger, George, 48, 49, 64, 74, 104, 112
Ellwanger, George H., 119
Ellwanger and Barry, 87, 88, 89; building, 294
Elwood Building, 98
Ely, Elisha, 10, 21, 34
Ely, Hervey, 10, 37, 47
Ely, William S., 164
Ensworth, Azel, 17
Ensworth, Russel, 17
Erickson, Aaron, 82
Erie Canal: dedication of, 24–25, 27; enlargement of, 47, 63, 82, 172; plans for, 11, 43; shipments on, 47; tolls removed, 97; remembered, 292
Erie Railroad, 72, 73, 82, 88, 147
Ernst, Charles B., 132
Ethical Club, 122
Ethnic societies, 61, 95, 121. *See also* Immigrants
Eureka Club, 121, 122
Evans, Dr. James, 300
Evening News, 200
Executive Board, 110, 111, 132
Express, 81, 85, 115, 116
Expressway, 217

Fagan, Garth, 282, 292
Fairwell, Rufus, 249
Fallon, Walter A., 284
Falls Field, celebrations, 33, 292
Family Service Organization, 169

Family Welfare Society, 192
Fashion Park, 274, 284
Fay, William, 200, 230
Federation of Churches, 183, 191, 249, 281, 307. *See also* Rochester Area Council of Churches
Female Charitable Society, 83, 129
Fennell, Dr. Frederick, 237
Fernwood Park, 210
Festival of American Music, 224
Field, Joseph, 51, 72
FIGHT (Freedom, Integration, God, Honor, and Today), 258–65, passim, 267, 271, 278, 285–86
Fighton, 263
Fight Square, 258, 262, 263, 308
Fillmore, Pres. Millard, 69
Finley, Otis E., Jr., 257
Finney, Reverend Charles G., 40, 57, 77, 316
Fire: companies: 14, 29, 61, 75; engines, 28, 39, 83, 111; hazards, 39, 51, 135; insurance, 38
First Federal Tower, 291
Fish, Mayor Henry L., 91, 110
Fish, Josiah, 4, 5, 6
Fisher, Edwin A., 133, 135, 157, 172, 173
Fitch, Charles, 116
Fitzhugh, Col. William, 6
Floods, damage of, 16, 70, 85
Florence, Minister Franklin D. R., 258, 260, 261, 262, 285, 287
Flour City National Bank, 88
Flour Mills, 10, 26, 37, 45, 47
Flower City, new leaders of, 86
Flower City Conspiracy, 271
Folding Box Company, 129
Folsom, Marion: civic interests of, 197, 199, 207, 210; as treasurer of Kodak, 180, 191, 192
Football, 121
Forbes, Dr. Charles, 146, 156
Forbes, Prof. George M., 133, 135, 146, 156
Ford factory, 175
Foreign travel, 93, 119
Foreman, Edward R., 200
Forman brothers, store of, 233
Fortnightly Club, 119
Foulkes, Louis, 171

Foundations, 305
Four Corners, 9, 17, 85, 88, 99, 125
Fourth of July, celebration, 33
Fox sisters, 58
France, Jean, 277
Franco, John, 278
Franklin Institute, 31, 41
Fraternal lodges, 121
Free Academy, 83, 114. *See also* High schools
Freedman, Elisha, 272
Freeman, Robert, 286
Frey, Thomas, 308, 315
Friends of FIGHT, 259, 260, 261
Friends of the Rochester Public Library, 225, 283
Froman, Charles, 143

Gambling, 112, 133
Gannett, Frank E.: political views of, 197, 202, 210; as publisher, 166, 169, 184, 200, 229, 247
Gannett, Mrs. Mary T., 122, 314
Gannett, Rev. William C., 127
Gannett papers, 238, 247, 274, 302, 311
Garbage collectors, 50, 90, 111
Gardiner, Addison, 22, 34
Gas companies, 51, 52, 108, 125, 134, 148, 212, 235
Gaudion, Donald, 230, 231, 245, 260, 261
Gazette, 15, 33
Gem, 41
General Motors plants, 176, 191, 212, 246, 274, 284
General Railway Signal Co., 151, 284
Genesee County, 7, 12, 20, 86
Genesee County Museum, 277
Genesee falls, 2, 15, 23
Genesee/Finger Lakes Regional Planning Council, 274, 303, 309, 311
Genesee Group, 224
Genesee Hospital, 279
Genesee River, 1, 2, 8, 9, 16, 26, 43, 85, 111, 275
Genesee Valley Canal, 44, 45, 47, 50
Genesee Valley Canal Railroad, 97, 147
Genesee Valley Club, 121
Genesee Valley Park, 292
Genesee Valley Railroad, 63, 72, 73, 82
Genovese, Eugene, 282

George Eastman House, 156, 225
German-American Bank, 96
German-American Society, 61, 123, 307
German Insurance Company, 98
Germans: influx of, 47, 58, 71, 74, 122, 139; politics of, 91, 92, 154; schools for, 76, 114, 145; war services of, 80, 163
Germond, Jack, 237, 247
GeVa Theatre, 293, 294
Gifford, Bernard, 266
Gilbert, Charles B., 135
Gillette, Mayor Henry E., 251, 266, 267, 269
Gilmore, Joseph H., 118
Ginna, Robert E., 211, 216
Gleason, Harold, 186
Gleason, James E., 191
Gleason Estates, 264, 271
Gleason Works, 103, 152, 165, 176, 204, 212, 246, 284
Goldberg, Herman, 255, 264, 265, 278
Goler, Dr. George, 135, 136, 158, 159, 185
Golf, 275
Good Government forces, 131–36, passim, 159, 189
Goodwin, Harry C., 171
Goossens, Eugene, 187, 200
Gould, Jacob, 34, 48, 49, 72
Gove, Harry F., 283
Graflex Company, 176, 214
Granite Building, 125, 294
Graves, H. B., 152
Graves, L. S., 106
Greater Rochester Fights Back, 308, 314
Greentree, Myer, 48
Gregory, Helen E., 138
Grove Place, 295, 296
Gundlach, Ernst, 106
Gymnastic exercises, 114, 141

Hacker, Harold, 225, 237, 239, 273, 281
Hahnemann Hospital, 113
Halbleib, Edward A., 180
Hall, Albert D., 57
Hall, Mrs. Basil, xi
Hallauer, Carl, 195, 210
Haloid Co., 176, 213–14, 228, 234, 235, 245. *See also* Xerox Corp.
Hamblin, F. Dow, 236
Hanford brothers, 7

Hanna, Prof. Edward J., 146, 226
Hanover Houses, 211, 217, 254, 296
Hanson, Howard, 187, 188, 199, 223, 224, 237
Hanson, Rosalie C., 291
Hare, Mark, 293
Harford, Charles, 7
Hargrave, Thomas J., 215, 244
Harris-Beach, 294
Harrison, Guy Fraser, 223
Hart, Roswell, 86
Hatch, Jesse W., 48
Hawks, Thomas, 233
Hay market, 51
Hayden, Charles J., 68, 87
Heidell, Lafe, 146
Hemlock Lake, 65, 75
Henry, Barbara, 315
Herald, 116, 130, 132, 145
Herdle, George L., 142
Herdle, Miss Isabel, 224, 276
Hickey, Jeremiah, 177
Hickey-Freeman Co., 153
Hickok Co., 284
Hickson, Laurence G., 184
Higgins, Clarence, 172
High Falls Park, 310
Highland Park Bowl, 282
High schools: early, 31, 83, 90, 142. See also Board of Education
Hill, Dr. David Jayne, 118
Hill, Kermit, 269, 270
Hillman, Sidney, 177
Hincher, William, 6
Hispanics, 298, 305, 306
Hochstein Music School, 222, 224
Holiday Inn, 295
Holland Land Company, 7
Holley, Byron, 110
Holly water mains, 99, 111
Homebuilding, 174, 246, 304
Home for the Friendless, 52, 76
Homelands Exhibit, 181
Homeless Action Coalition, 304
Homeopathic Hospital, 113
Homer, Porter, 251, 253, 267
Homes Registration Bureau, 202
Hop Bitters, baseball team, 105, 120
Horgan, Paul, 200
Horse car lines, 83, 109

Horse races, 69, 78, 120, 141, 276
Horse railroad, 37, 44
Hospitals: establishment of, 82, 113, 135; organized by councils, 218, 236
Hotchkiss, James L., 170
House for Idle and Truant Children, 66
Housing: affordable housing, 304; construction of, 60, 74, 92, 213, 247; ownership of, 221; public, 207, 216, 232, 263–64, 272, 296–98, 269. See also Rochester Housing Authority
Howard, Clinton, 136, 159, 169, 170
Howe, Gordon A., 217, 236, 237, 238, 268
Hubbell, Walter S., 131
Human Relations Commission, 249, 255, 260, 263
Humane Society, 113, 128
Humdrum Club, 145
Hungarians, 242
Hungerford, Edward, 181
Hyatt Hotel, 294

Ibero-American Action League, 242
Ice storm, 312
Ignorance Club, 122
Imaging Center, 300
Immigrants: influx of, 65, 71; new immigrants, 98, 122, 138, 158, 163, 203, 241. See also Germans; Irish; Italians; Jews; Poles
Imprisonment for debt, 36
Income tax, 82
Incorporation Law, 64, 100
Indians, negotiations with, 2, 7
Industrial Management Council, 211, 260, 261, 274, 289
Industrial mergers, 302
Industrial research, 244, 301–2
Industrial School, 76, 161. See also Rochester Institute of Technology
Industries: early, 26, 38, 45; in mid-years, 63, 72–73, 87; new specialized, 100, 102–7, 149, 152, 209; productivity of, 206, 213, 243–45, 300–302
Infant's Summer Hospital, 161
Inner Loop, 295, 296
Insurance companies, 46, 96
Integrated Non-Violence Committee, 249
Intermuseum Council, 224

International Conference on High Energy Physics, 238
International League, 120, 182
Interurban electric lines, 148
Irish: immigrants, 40, 47, 58, 71, 122; political activity of, 91, 139; war service of, 80
Italians: influx of, 98, 123, 139, 146, 154, 163, 181; politics of, 201, 204, 241, 283, 306
Italian Women's Civic League, 181

Jacobsen, Henrich, 143
Jacobstein, Prof. Meyer, 170, 177, 191, 196
Jewish Welfare Council, 184, 307
Jewish Young Men's and Women's Association (JYM & WA), 184, 192
Jews: German, 58, 74, 98, 101, 117; societies of, 122, 123, 146; Russian, 154, 183
Job training, 304
Johnson, Elisha B., as developer, 15, 16, 17, 21, 32; as engineer, 20, 39, 44, 47; as mayor, 50
Johnson, James, 287
Johnson, Nan, 272
Johnson, William, 298
Johnston, James, 130–34 passim
Jones, Mrs. Helen, 207, 314
Jones, Seth C., 48
Journal & American, 200
Juvenile Court, 137
Juvenile delinquency, 65, 172, 207, 248, 250

Kane, Christopher, 89
Kearney, Bishop, 226
Kearns, David, 302
Keating, Col. Kenneth B., 206
Keeler Building, 125
Kelly, John, 102
Kelsey's Emporium of Art, 61, 78
Kempshall, Thomas, 50
Kilbourn Hall, 186, 187
Kimball, William S.: art interests of, 119, 143; factory of, 87, 95, 104, 124, 140, 151
King, Robert, 315
Kirk, Dr. William, 160, 161
Kirwan, Laurence, 272

Klingenberg, Alf, 185, 186, 187
Knights of St. Crispin, 89, 101
Know-Nothing party, 67–68, 77
Kodak Park, 150
Kordite Company, 213
Kovelski, Emanuel, 154, 165
Kuichling, Emil, 95, 111
Kuolt, Oscar W., 169, 183, 193, 194

Labor Day, 102, 103, 129, 154
Labor Lyceum, 129, 140, 154
Labor unions: early, 46, 75, 87; growth of, 88, 89, 101; negotiations by, 126, 127, 129, 153, 179; New Deal, 196; strike policies of, 154, 178, 211, 212, 235, 250
Ladies Hospital and Relief Assoc., 82
Lafayette, General, 33
Lake Ontario, 11, 48
Lake trade, 44, 147, 211
Lamb, Mayor Frank, 252, 253, 267, 269
Lamberton, Alexander B., 137, 158, 309
Landmark Society of Western New York, 225, 277, 287
Laney, Calvin C., 172
Latta, Samuel, 6, 7
Lattimore, Dr. Samuel A., 94, 117, 146
Lawyers' Cooperative, 195
League of the Iroquois, 69
League of Women Voters, 314
Lee, Rev. Henry W., 67
Lehigh Valley Railway, 127, 147
Leinsdorf, Eric, 223
Lewis Street Settlement, 160, 161
Liberal Advocate, 40, 41
Liberty Pole, 287
Libraries: circulating, 31; city, 56, 61; public, 137, 157, 184, 225, 268, 282, 288; Reynolds, 114, 145
Lifton, Dr. Walter M., 257
Lighthouse, at Charlotte, 37
Lincoln, Abraham: death mourned at Rochester, 86; receives Frederick Douglass, 84; votes for in Rochester, 79, 80
Lincoln First Bank, 286, 294
Lincoln-Rochester Bank, 233, 274, 382
Lindley, Christopher, 278
Lindsay, Alexander, 92
Linowitz, Sol M., 230, 238

Liquor licenses, 28, 49, 112, 159. *See also* Temperance
Literary awards, 283
Livingston, James K., 22
Locust Hill Country Club, 275
Lomb, Carl F., 185
Lomb, Captain Henry, 114, 132, 152
Lombard, William M., 249, 251, 253, 269
Lord, George, 90, 91
Lovejoy, Frank W., 180
Lowe, Samuel H., 118
Lowenthal, Arthur M., 197
Lutes, John, 91
Lyceum theater, 120, 143, 144, 199
Lynn, Judge John D., 163
Lyons (N.Y.), mentioned, 21

McCarthy, Russell, 260, 261
McClintock, J. Y., 125, 135
McCue, Olive, 223
McCurdy, Gilbert, 231, 233, 246
McEwen, De Leon, 264
MacFarlin, Harold S. W., 198, 216
McLaughlin, George, 133
McQuaid, Bishop Bernard, 93, 95, 114, 116, 117, 138, 146, 154
MacSweeney, Leo, 171
McWalter, Peter, 298, 314
Mack, Daniel, 13
Maennerchor, 69, 119, 143
Mahoney, Bill, 269
Mail chutes, 135
Main Street: bridge, 15, 29, 48, 50, 70, 75, 85, 288, 291; repavement of, 295
Malcolm X, 249
Mamoulian, Reubin, 187, 189
Mangione, Chuck, 292
Mangione, Jerre, 283
Mann, Rev. Newton, 93, 118
Manpower Development and Training Act (MDTA), 249, 250, 256
Mansion House, 11, 21, 31, 55
Marshak, Dr. Robert E., 228, 237
Marshall, E. F., 31
Martin, Edward S., 118, 145
Martindale, Gad, 154
Martin Luther King Memorial Housing, 264
Masonic lodges, activities of, 34, 35, 121. *See also* Anti-Masonry

Mastick, John, 32
Mathews, Robert, 118
Mathews, Selah, 53
Mathews, Vincent, 22, 28, 35
Mathies, J. S. D., 31
Maude, John, British traveler, 5
May, Mayor Stephen, 270
Mechanics Institute, 114, 150, 152, 155, 160, 185, 204, 227. *See also* Rochester Institute of Technology
Mees, Dr. Kenneth, 214
Memorial Art Gallery, 160, 184, 224, 277, 295
Men and Religion Forward Movement, 160
Mercury, statue of, 104, 288
Metro-Act, 271–72, 285–86
Methodists, 14, 32, 57, 117. *See also* Churches
Metropolitan Rochester Foundation, 264
Metropolitan Theater, 84
Meyers, Jacob H., 129
Michaels, Henry, 152
Michaels, Stern & Co., 178
Midtown Plaza, 233, 245, 246, 286, 294
Milk: inspection of, 11, 136; stations, 159. *See also* Board of Health
Miller, Paul, 210, 229, 231, 247
Miller, William, 58
Milliman, Elmer B., 210
Mills, at Rochester, 3, 10, 26, 37–38, 73, 100, 103, 149. *See also* Flour Mills
Miner, E. G., 151, 160, 173
Ministerial Union, 136, 183
Mitchell, Mrs. Constance, 251
Mixer, Albert H., 118
Monday Club, 160, 184
Monroe, Pres. James, 21
Monroe County: created, 21: Labor Congress of, 129. *See also* County jail; Court House
Monroe Community College, 300
Monroe Republican, 25, 33
Montgomery, Mrs. Helen Barrett, 124, 133, 134, 136, 140, 154, 314
Montgomery Neighborhood Center, 218, 255, 256
Moore, Dr. Edward, 11, 133, 135
Moore, Mrs. Gertrude Herdle, 184, 224, 237

Moore, Prof. Walden, 202, 206
Morey, William C., 114
Morgan, Henry W., 161
Morgan, Lewis H., 62, 69, 74, 91, 93, 95, 118
Morgan, William, activities of, 34
Morgan Machine Co., 161
Morin, Lucien, 290–91, 293
Morris, Robert, 3
Motion-picture film, 144
Motley, George, 103
Moulthrop, Samuel P., 157, 158, 161
Mount Hope Cemetery, 50, 60
Mount Morris, 45
Moynihan, Daniel P., 262
Mulder, John G., 261
Mumford, George E., 109
Municipal Art Commission, 172
Murlin, Dr. John R., 199
Musée, 143
Museum: early, 61, 94; of Arts and Sciences, 184, 207, 211, 224–25, 268, 276, 294–95
Museum and Science Center, 270
Music: at Rochester, 55, 61, 65, 78, 119; festival, 143, 237. See also Civic Music Association; Eastman School of Music

Nash, Mayor John C., 80, 83
National Alliance of Business (NAB), 265
National Association for the Advancement of Colored People (NAACP), 248, 249, 251
National Theater, 143
Nazareth College, 207, 227, 238, 277
Negroes: as early residence, 57, 146; discrimination against, 204, 232, 251, 259; riots by, 248, 262; training facilities for, 250, 252–53, 263–64, 265, 271; votes of, 267, 271. See also Blacks; FIGHT; Frederick Douglass
Neighborhood associations, 278, 286
New Citizen's Banquet, 140, 184, 219
New Era Collegiate Center, 196
New Industries Bureau, 176
Newport House, 78
Newspapers: early, 5, 14, 15, 34, 41; growth of, 62, 115, 145; in twentieth century, 166–67, 184, 199, 229, 247. See also Gannett papers

New York Central; formed, 63, 82, 88; track elevated, 97; trade area of, 147, 148
New York State Railway, 148
Nicely, Dr. Harold E., 226
Nichols, George, 89
Nier, George J., 172
Night watchmen, 14, 29, 65. See also Police
Nixon, Dr. Justin Wroe, 226
Nixon, T. Carl, 171, 195, 215
Nixon-Hargrave, 294
Nolte, Adolph, 80
Northeast Electric Co., 176, 180
North Star, 59
Norton Village, 210
Novelty Works, 63, 73
Nurserymen, 48, 64, 71, 73, 87, 100, 104, 149

Oak Hill Country Club, 188, 275
Observer, 34, 40, 41
Ocean Oyster House, 122
O'Connor, Evangeline, 146
O'Connor, Joseph, 116, 118
Odd Fellows, 121
O'Grady, James, 134
Old Rochesterville, 295
Olmsted, Frederick Law, 112
O'Neil, Martin B., 171, 175
Ontario, first steamboat, 11, 12
Ontario County, 12, 20, 21
Ontario Messenger, 9
Opera; companies, 187, 188, 199; House, 120, 143; Under the Stars, 220, 223
Optical industry, 106, 152. See also Bausch and Lomb
Opticam project, 301, 313
O'Reilly, Father Bernard, 60
O'Reilly, Henry: as civic leader, 41, 43, 53–56, 88; as editor, 34, 35, 44, 45, 47, 62, 64; honored, 292
Organ recitals, 155, 186
O'Rorke, Patrick, 84
Orphan asylums, 52, 55
Orr, Julian, 270
Osburn House, opening of, 74
Oswego, 2, 11, 37, 47
Otis, General Ellwell S., 139
Oviatt, Percival De W., 195

Owen, Mayor Charles S., 193, 194, 195
Oxford Street, 89

Paine, Nicholas E., 65
Parades: Blue Eagle, 196; Civil War, 80–
    81; early, 33, 71; labor, 102, 103, 154;
    patriotic, 128, 164, 181, 203
Park Commission, 133, 135, 158
Parker, Dr. Arthur C., 184
Parker, Mrs. Jane Marsh, 118, 122, 146
Park system, 112, 268, 275
Parrish, Fred I., 216
Parsons, Mayor Cornelius R., 95, 100, 102,
    110, 112
Patch, Sam, fatal jump of, 33
Patents, 73, 104, 106, 107, 129, 151, 215,
    234, 244
Patriotic and Community Fund, 146,
    165
Peck, Everard, 13, 15, 23, 34, 38
Peck, Myron G., 119
Peck, William F., 119
Penitentiary, 76
People's Sunday Evening meetings, 139
Perkins, Prof. Dexter, 195, 208, 210, 220,
    228
Pest house, 66
Pfaudler, Casper, 105
Pfaudler Company, 105, 151, 176, 214
Phelps, Oliver, 2, 3, 5
Philharmonic Orchestra, 199, 293. See
    also Rochester Philharmonic Orchestra
Phillips, Wendell, 68
Pine, Richard, 271
Pioneer Library System, 273, 288
Pioneer Society, 62
Pittsford, 15
Pittsford Plaza, 246
Planned Parenthood, 305
Planning Commission, 217
Playgrounds, 136, 158
Pneumatic Signal Co., 151
Poles, influx of, 98, 123, 139, 181, 202
Police: activities, 29, 83, 90, 112, 137, 157,
    170, 290; headquarters, 128; reform,
    290; training of, 249, 252, 254, 262
Police Advisory Board, 250, 255
Police dogs, use of, 252–53
Polish Civic Center, 306
Polish Falcons, 181

Politics: in city management, 170–72; in
    Depression, 193, 195, 197–98, 202, 215;
    ethnic factors in, 69, 91, 110, 116; at
    formation of city, 39–40, 49, 51: good
    government campaign, 130–37; post-
    war contests, 215, 218, 238, 267–69,
    270
Pollution, 218
Ponte de Rennes, 310
Poole, C. Arthur, 193, 195
Population: increases of, 26, 48, 110, 124,
    138, 231, 241; mobility of, 36, 47, 71,
    92, 231, 242–43
Posner, William, 231
Post Express, 132, 145
Post Office, 10, 26
Postwar Problems Council, 218
Poteat, Dr. Edwin M., 226
Powers, Daniel: as banker, 88, 89, 95, 96,
    97; cast iron block of, 88, 90, 93, 98, 125;
    death of, 124; gallery of, 95, 104, 119,
    142
Powers block, 88, 90, 98, 125, 294
Powers Hotel, 98, 122
Presbyterian churches, 14, 32, 57, 77, 287
Price, Dr. Orlan J., 183
Prior, Harris, 270
Project Uplift, 261, 262
Prostitution, 52, 112
Public markets, erected, 29, 232
Puerto Ricans, 232, 241, 242, 255, 264,
    266
Pulteney, Sir William, 3
Pundit Club, 69, 118, 119
Purcell, William, 116
Pure Water Agency, 268, 269

Quakers, 32, 58
Quality of Life studies, 305
Quigley, Joseph M., 137, 154, 159, 170,
    177
Quinby, Isaac F., 81

Raceways, 10, 16
Radio, 184, 229, 238
Railroads: early, 44–45, 47, 63; interurban
    electric, 148; trade of, 72, 88, 97, 147
Railroad stations, second, 97, 98
Raitt, Charles B., 172
Rand, C. Barry, 314

Rapp, Mayor Lester B., 198, 201
Rauschenbusch, Prof. Walter, 124, 130, 136, 146, 154
Raymond, John H., 67
Real Estate Exchange, 99
Red Cross, 113, 164, 165, 202, 204, 205, 236
Red Jacket, mentioned, 31
Red Wings, 181, 220, 275, 310. *See also* Baseball
Reichenbach, Henry M., 107
Relief funds, 75, 81, 127
Republicans, 110, 115, 130–33, 168, 193, 198, 216, 217, 218. *See also* Politics
Rescue Mission, 127, 129
Research Development Laboratories, 283, 301–2
Revivals, 40, 57, 77, 129
Reynolds, Abelard, 10, 23
Reynolds, Mortimer F., 95, 114–15
Reynolds, William A., 41, 55, 56, 68, 94
Reynolds Arcade, 10, 26, 51, 56, 81
Reynolds Library, 114, 145
Rhees, Pres. Rush, 185, 199
Riley, Col. Ashbel W., 41
Riots, inner city, 248, 252–55, 262–63
Ritter Dental Co., 152, 245
River Campus, 188
Rivers, Manuel, 314
Riverside Convention Center, 293, 306
Robinson, Charles M., 137, 145
Robinson, Dr. Ezekiel, 86
Rochester, Col. Nathaniel: at Bloomfield, 11, 13; civic leadership of, 14, 15, 16, 20, 21, 30, 32; commercial concerns of, 21–24; as founder, 6, 8, 9, 12, 17, 19; social affairs of, 33, 34, 41
Rochester, Thomas H., 50
Rochester, William B., 35
Rochester: described, xi, xii, 27, 70–71, 135; growth of, 9, 19, 20, 25, 149, 232; industries at, xiii, 35, 38, 43, 95, 190, 266; as a metropolis, 240; organization of, 49; plans for, 8, 92; rank of, 100, 209, 241, 270; war services of, 81–86, 162, 164, 166, 205, 208, 219, 273. *See also* Population
Rochester Americans, 221, 276
Rochester & Pittsburgh Railroad, 97

Rochester Area Council of Churches, 248, 255, 260, 280–81, 307. *See also* Federation of Churches
Rochester Area Educational Television Association (RAETA), 230, 238, 239, 273, 281–82, 287
Rochester Art Club, 142, 184. *See also* Art
Rochester Association for the United Nations (RAUN), 208, 219, 220, 230
Rochester Bar Association, 215
Rochester Benevolent Association, 89, 92
Rochester Business Institute, 227
Rochester Business Opportunities Corp. (RBOC), 263, 264
Rochester City and Brighton Railway, 83, 109. *See also* Rochester Railway Company
Rochester Club, 121
Rochester Collegiate Institute, 54
Rochester Commerce, 180, 210
Rochester Downtown Development Corporation, 295
Rochester Driving Park, 141
Rochester Economic Development Department, 301
Rochester Female Academy, 54
Rochester Friendly Home, 165
Rochester Gas & Electric Co., 125, 134, 148, 212, 235
Rochester Gas Light Company, 108
Rochester Historical Society, 224
Rochester Hospital Council, 218
Rochester Housing Authority, 237, 262, 263, 309
Rochester Industrial Corp., 176
Rochester Industrial Development Corp., 301
Rochester Institute of Technology, 227, 235, 238, 260, 268, 277, 300, 313, 316. *See also* Mechanics Institute
Rochester Jobs, Inc. (RJI), 261, 264–65
Rochester lamp, 106
Rochester Management, 262
Rochester Optical & Camera Co., 150
Rochester Orphan Asylum, 52, 161
Rochester Philharmonic Orchestra, 119, 142, 185, 187, 200, 223, 274
Rochester Products Division, 246, 274
Rochester Railway Company, 109, 125, 148

Rochester Regiment, 81
Rochester Regional Hospital Council, 235
Rochester Royals, 221
Rochester Savings Bank, 83, 98, 121, 122
Rochester Star, 205
Rochester Teachers Association, 266
Rochester Telephone Co., 148, 174, 235
Rochester Theological Seminary, 60, 77, 146, 189
Rochesterville, 12, 13, 27
Rodenbeck, Mayor Adolph J., 134, 135
Rogers, Bernard, 237
Roller-skating, 120
Romano, Dr. John, 228
Roosevelt, Franklin D., 192, 194, 196, 202
Rosing, Vladimir, 187, 188
Roundabout Club, 145
Routh, James W., 169
R.T. French Co., 228
Rush project, 262
Ryan, Mayor Thomas P., Jr., 272, 286, 291, 293, 315

Sabbath: observance of, 28, 40, 59, 136, 159; schools, 30–31, 32
St. Andrew's Society, 122
St. Bernard's Seminary, 146
St. Casimir Society, 123
St. John Fisher College, 227, 238, 313
St. Luke's Episcopal Church, 32, 57
St. Mary's Hospital, 82, 113
St. Patrick's Cathedral, 52, 93, 112, 116, 122
St. Patrick's Day, 138
Sales tax, 217, 218, 268–69, 290
Salvation Army, 113
Sanford, Harold, 172
Sargent, James, 103, 105
Sargent & Greenleaf, 87, 103
Saturday half-holidays, 121, 149
Saunders, Dr. Wilbour E., 226
Schenck, Ludwig, 142
Scher, Dr. Seymour, 268, 269
Schermerhorn, Abraham, 38, 47, 50
Schlegel Company, 290
School of American Craftsmen, 227
School of Medicine and Dentistry, 185
Schools: district, 30, 53; integration of, 242, 251, 264, 271; night classes, 114, 158; private, 31, 54, 55, 76, 227; public,

66, 76, 226; reform of, 132, 135, 226, 278–79, 298–300; scientists, 283, 301
Scott, Ruth, 272
Scrantom, Edwin, 33, 41, 46
Scrantom, Hamlet, pioneer, 9
Sea Breeze, 121
Second Adventists, 58, 67
Security Trust, 246
Selden, George B., 106, 129, 151
Selden, Samuel L., 64
Selye, Lewis, 48, 51, 90, 116
Seminar in American Studies, 220
Sesquicentennial, 289, 291–93
Settlement houses, 250
Seward Seminary, 54
Sewers: early, 30, 39, 49, 50, 66; system of, 75, 111, 218
Seymour, Dr. Howard C., 227
Shaw, Dr. James B., 117
Shoe industry, 48, 100–2, 126, 152
Shoe Manufacturers Assoc., 126
Shoe workers, 73, 102, 129, 153, 177
Shopping plazas, 213
Shumway, F. Ritter, 245
Shylock Association, mentioned, 36
Sibley, Harper, 160, 197, 208, 267, 290
Sibley, Mrs. Harper, 197, 219, 226, 248, 261, 314
Sibley, Hiram, 64, 74, 82, 88, 93, 94, 104, 119, 290
Sibley, Rufus, 92, 96
Sibley fire, 136, 252
Sibley, Lindsay & Curr Co., 144, 246
Sidepath Association, 141
Sidewalks, provision of, 30, 39
Silver Stadium, 275
Simone, Albert J., 313
Sister Cities, 275, 312
Sisters of St. Joseph, 114
Sherman, Sam M., 90
Skinner, Sheriff Albert, 253
Slavin, Patrick J., 172
Slovaks, 306
Smith, Arthur C., 146
Smith, E. Peshine, 60
Smith, George Hand, 73, 106
Smith, L. C., 122
Smith, Silas O., 10, 32
Snyder, Leroy E., 169, 170, 171, 193

Social Center program, 136, 137, 139, 142, 156

Society for Organized Charity, 113, 127, 155. *See also* United Charities

Soldiers Relief Committee, 81

Sons of Adam, 101

Sons of the American Revolution (SAR), 123

Soule, Asa T., 105, 120

Spencer, John C., 39

Spencer Club, 118, 119

Spinning, James M., 226

Spiritualists, 58, 67

Stage lines, 17

Stanton, Mayor Charles W., 195, 197, 199

State Commission Against Discrimination (SCAD), 248

State Industrial School, 157. *See also* Western House of Refuge

State Line Railroad, 88, 97. *See also* Buffalo, Rochester & Pittsburgh Railroad

State Teachers Association, 226

State University of New York, College at Brockport. *See* SUNY, Brockport

Staud, Dr. Cyril J., 214

Steamboats, 12, 26, 36, 44

Stebbins, Henry H., Jr., 191

Stein, Simon, 152

Stein-Black, 153

Stein Manufacturing Company, 103

Stettkeimer, Sigmund, 82, 96

Steuben County, 20

Stone, Desmond, 237, 247, 256, 263

Stone, Enos, 9, 15, 23, 32

Stone-Tolan tavern, 277

Story, Stephen B., 169, 171–75, 191, 193, 197

Strasenburgh Planetarium, 276

Strayer, Rev. Paul Moore, 139, 154

Streets: improvements of, 30, 49, 111; lighting of, 30, 52, 75, 108; planning for, 137

Stromberg-Carlson Co., 148, 200, 214, 230, 234, 245

Strong, Alvah, 40

Strong, Augustus H., 94

Strong, Elisha B., 15, 17, 21, 23, 34

Strong, Henry A., 107

Strong, Dr. Maltby, 53, 68

Strong, Margaret, Museum of, 294, 306

Strong mayor controversy, 273–74

Strong Memorial Hospital, 279, 305

Stuber, William G., 180

Suburbs, 213, 215, 233, 241, 247, 266

Subway, 217

Summerville, 121

SUNY, Brockport, 300

Superba Cravats, 274

Swabian Society, 122

Swan, Dr. John M., 164

Swift, Lewis, 94, 105, 118, 144

Sybron Corp., 245, 246, 302. *See also* Pfaudler Company

Taverns, 11

Taxpayers Association, 89

Taylor, Mrs. Ann, 236

Taylor, George, 106

Taylor Instruments Co., 152, 212, 214

Teachers Union, 226, 278–79

Teen Age Diplomats, Inc., 220

Telegraph, The, 15, 34

Telegraph lines, 60, 64, 108. *See also* Western Union

Telephone Companies, 108, 148, 174, 235

Television, 222, 229, 238, 281. *See also* Rochester Area Educational Television Association (RAETA)

Temperance: movement for, 28, 40, 91, 92, 112, 136; societies, 59, 68, 113

Theaters: licenses for, 28, 78; organized, 61, 84, 120, 135, 143, 222

Theosophical Society, 145

Thomas, W. Stephen, 225, 237, 276

Thurston, Dr. Henry W., 183

Times, 115, 145

Todd, George W., 188

Todd, Libanus, 192

Todd, Walter T., 210

Todd Company, 212

Tom Paine, society formed, 32

Tonawanda railroad, 44

Transit Company, 109, 174–75. *See also* Rochester Railway Company

Traveling salesmen, 74, 87, 149

Troup, Robert, 6

Tryon Town, 6, 8

Tuesday Musicals, 142

Turner, Orsamus, 62
Turner, Richard, 289–90
Turner Hall, 61
Turner societies, 69, 122
Tusca, Simon, 67

Ukrainian Civic Center, 181
Ukrainians, influx of, 98, 306
Unemployment: increase of, 50, 127, 190, 284, 303–4; insurance, 192, 260; rate of, 243, 275, 304. *See also* Depression
Union, 81, 84, 85, 116
Union & Advertiser, 115, 125, 132, 145
Union Course, 69, 78
Union Polishing & Plating Co., 150
Unitarians, 58, 67, 93
United Action Committee, 249
United Charities, 140, 160, 169. *See also* Council of Social Agencies; Society for Organized Charity
United Garment Workers, 129, 153
United Shoe Workers, 177
United Way, 304–5, 308
Universalists, 58
University of Rochester: established, 60, 66, 76; growth of, 118, 146, 155; on River Campus, 156, 185, 188, 199, 207, 228, 238, 279, 280, 283, 301
Upton, Charles E., 96
Urban Development Corp. (UDC), 264, 269–70, 271
Urban League, 256, 257, 260, 262, 264, 297, 298
Urban Policy Conference, 272
Urlacher, Gordon, 308
Utz & Dunn, 152

Vacuum Oil Company, 97
Valentine, Alan, 199, 207, 228
Van Zandt, Clarence D., 169, 170, 171, 172
Vaughn, William S., 230, 244, 261, 262
Veterans Memorial Bridge, 191, 193
Vick, James, 87, 104
Vietnam, 307
Village charter, 12, 27
Voluntary Educational Association, 230
Volunteer fire companies, 14, 61
Voting machines, 151

Wade, Richard C., 218, 238
Wage dividends, 156, 244
Walker, William H., 107
Walkley, Floyd F., 236
Wallis, Pres. W. Allen, 279
War Council, 203, 205
Ward, Edward J., 136, 140
Ward, Henry A., 64, 77, 93
Ward, Dr. Levi, Jr., 18, 23, 31, 41
Ward, Levi A.: business affairs of, 46, 53; as civic leader, 41, 43, 51, 54
Ward brothers, as bankers, 88
Wareham, Harry P., 165
Warfield, William, 251, 292
War Memorial, 211, 216, 217, 220, 221, 276
Warner, A. J., 99, 186
Warner, Mayor George E., 131, 133
Warner, H. H.: first president of Chamber, 100, 105; as patent medicine king, 96, 99, 119; victim of Depression, 124, 145
Warner Observatory, 105, 118
Warner's Safe Liver Cure, 105, 126
Washington Hall, 84
Water carnivals, 158
Water Street, 295
Waterworks, need for, 39, 50, 65, 75, 90, 111, 217
Watson, Mrs. James Sibley, 184
Watson, Mrs. Sibley, 160
Wednesday Club, 145, 146
Weed, Thurlow, 22–23, 34, 35, 40
Weet, Herbert S., 183
Wegmans, 299
Weil, Samuel, 177
Weisskopf, Dr. Victor, 204, 208, 228
Welcome Wagon, 219
Welfare stations, 203–4
Welland Canal, 37
Weller, W. Earl, 191, 193
Wells, provision of, 29
Wentworth, Col. Edward T., 203
Wentzel, Michael, 304
West, Jonathan B., 106
West High School, 136
Western House of Refuge, 52, 66, 76. *See also* State Industrial School
Western Inland Lock Navigation Co., 5, 10

Western Union, 64, 74, 82, 88. *See also*
    Telegraph lines
WHAM, 200, 230
WHAM-TV, 222
WHEC, 200, 230
Whipple, George H., 185
Whitaker, Arthur L., 254
White Charter, 132
Whitehouse, Henry J., 60
Whitney, George J., 87, 88, 89
Whitney, Mrs. Warham, 156, 189
Wilder, Mayor A. Carter, 90
Wilder, Samuel, 94, 98
Wilder Building, 98–99
Wile, Sol, 153
Williams, Rev. Comfort, 17, 32
Williams, Rev. David Rhys, 225, 226
Williams, Samuel B., 131
Williamsburg, mentioned, 5
Williamson, Charles, 3, 4, 5
Wilson, Mayor Joseph, 171, 191, 193
Wilson, Joseph C.: as civic leader, 272,
    279; of Haloid, 208, 210, 212, 230, 231,
    234; of Xerox, 245, 246, 261, 264
Wilson, Lavel, 298
Wolfe, Andrew D., 229
Wollensack, 150, 176
Woman's suffrage, 166. *See also* Women's
    rights
Women as workers, 59, 140, 204
Women's Christian Association, 113
Women's Christian Temperance Union
    (WCTU), 113
Women's City Club, 170

Women's Educational & Industrial
    Union, 140, 158, 160
Women's Network, 314
Women's Political Equality Club,
    122
Women's rights, 59, 91, 122, 166
Wonderland, 143, 144
Workingmen's Association, 89
Work relief, 192
World of Inquiry school, 266
Wright, Alfred, 121
Wright, Wilbur, 274–75
WVET, 230

Xerox Corp., 245, 246, 250, 259, 260, 261,
    263, 285, 300, 302, 313. *See also* Haloid
    Co.
Xerox Square, 275
Xerox Tower, 246, 286

Yates, Arthur G., 126
Yawman, Philip H., 106
Yawman & Erbe, 214
Young Men's Association, 41, 55
Young Men's Catholic Association, 113
Young Men's Christian Association
    (YMCA), 83, 113, 128, 136, 139, 164,
    236, 252
Young Women's Christian Association
    (YWCA), 161
Youth Board, 250

Zoning regulations, 173
Zornow, Gerald B., 274